Fourth **BBC** **tv**
Top of the Form Quiz Book

compiled by Boswell Taylor

Fourth BBC tv Top of the Form Quiz Book

compiled by *Boswell Taylor*

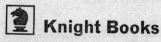 **Knight Books**

the paperback division of Brockhampton Press
by arrangement with the British Broadcasting Corporation

The publishers would like to express their gratitude for all the help in the making of this book received from the BBC Outside Broadcasts Department.

ISBN 0 340 15376 8

First published 1971 by Knight Books,
the paperback division of Brockhampton Press Ltd Leicester
Fourth impression 1974

Text copyright © 1971 Boswell Taylor
Illustrations copyright © 1965, 1967, 1968, 1969, 1970 Brockhampton Press Ltd

Printed and Bound in Great Britain by
Cox & Wyman Ltd, London, Reading and Fakenham

Contents

General knowledge 1

1 What is the largest planet in the solar system?

2 What Italian island was the home of the Roman Emperors Augustus and Tiberius?

3 What is the name of the gland which Descartes believed to be 'the seat of the soul'?

4 In what way is a Free Port 'free'?

5 What is the connection between the founder of the Scouts movement and Mafeking?

6 In a story by Jules Verne what did Phineas Fogg have to do to win a bet?

7 What is the name given to the left side of a ship when a person is facing the bow?

8 The *mistral* is a cold, dry wind; what is the *foehn*?

9 What very ordinary school object gets its name from the Latin word for 'little tail'?

10 How did the 'bikini' get its name?

11 If you wanted to know the time you might use a gnomon, and where would you look for that?

12 What kind of wood would you expect a Chippendale chair to be made from?

13 What was the result of the 'bursting' of the South Sea Bubble?

14 Name two of the three sections in Dante's *Divine Comedy*.

15 What American general in World War II was known as 'Old Blood and Guts'?

16 King Louis XIV of France was known as the 'Sun King'; how was Louis Philippe described?

17 What were the two papers that Joseph Addison edited?

18 What was the tree where the Jabberwock was slain?

19 What was the remarkable residence of Simeon Stylites for 36 years?

Nature 1

20 The plant kingdom has two main sub-divisions. Embryophyta is one, what is the other?

21 What bird has sometimes been called by the poetic name of 'Philomel'?

22 In biology many of the order names of insects end in -ptera. What does this Greek word mean?

23 The octopus has eight arms. How many arms has the squid?

24 What is the plant from which linseed oil is obtained?

25 What water insect is known as a nymph when it is young and the 'devil's darning needles' when it matures?

26 In biology how does the hydra feed itself?

27 Besides their colour, what is the difference between 'yellow' eels and 'silver' eels?

28 If an animal is not 'metazoan' what is it?

29 In botany, how many years does a biennial require to reach its full development?

30 How many wings have butterflies, moths and bees?

31 What is the name given to the short finger-like organs with which the spider spins silk?

32 What name is given to the male honeybees who do no work and have no sting?

33 Caterpillars become butterflies; but what stage of life comes in between?

34 In botany, what are stamens called if they lack anthers or if the anthers fail to produce pollen?

35 Freshwater fish that go out to sea to spawn are known as *catadromous*. What are saltwater fish said to be that go in the opposite direction?

36 Biologically and etymologically, what should all arthropods possess?

Far-away places 1

37 Vaduz is the capital of a small country which has a customs union with Switzerland. What country?

38 Which small European country pays dues bi-annually of 960 francs to the President of France and 460 pesetas to a Spanish Bishop?

39 Vietnam lies to the east of Cambodia. What two countries border Cambodia on the north?

40 Geographically, what are the 'Rockies'?

41 What is the 'Mer de Glace', and where is it?

42 On which island are there amusement parks called the Great World, the Gay World and the New World?

43 Lapland is not a separate country. The region that makes up Lapland belongs to what four countries?

44 What are the kampongs of Malay-speaking countries?

45 A French region famous for its wines has been a kingdom, a duchy, a county and a province of France. What is it?

46 If you visited the Prado to see some of El Greco's paintings in which city would you be?

47 What country has regions which are popularly known as 'Fish-hook' and 'Parrot's Beak'?

48 What is the name of the Strait that connects the Adriatic Sea with the Ionian Sea?

49 Of what country is Tiranë the capital?

50 What is the largest lake in the British Isles?

51 What artificial lake was formed by the Aswan High Dam?

52 The Shetland and Orkney Islands lie off northern Scotland. Where are South Shetland and South Orkney?

53 How many degrees south of the north pole is the Arctic Circle?

54 The grassy plains in Argentina are known as pampas; what name is given to similar grassy plains in Russia and in South Africa?

Speed quiz 1

55 What is the geometrical shape of the cells in a hive?

56 What river flows into Lake Geneva at one end and out of the other?

57 What nation came into being on May 14, 1948 under the leadership of Ben-Gurion?

58 What is the nationality of the Papal Guards at the Vatican?

59 Where are the headquarters of the Council of Europe?

60 What is the 'Silent World' explored by Jacques-Yves Cousteau?

61 What is the translation of an ancient Roman notice: *Cave Canem*?

62 Britannia and Neptune are usually pictured holding the same kind of weapon. What is it?

63 What country was once known as 'Albion'?

64 In 'Midsummer Night's Dream' what was Quince's trade when he was not producing plays for the revels?

65 Mary was Queen Elizabeth's half sister, who was her half brother?

66 The common unit for measuring electric power is equal to 1,000 watts. What is it called?

67 What name is usually given to solid carbon dioxide used in refrigeration?

68 In Shakespeare who was the fat knight who suffered at the hands of the Merry Wives of Windsor?

69 What substance has been grouped into categories that include Type A, Type B, Type AB and Type O?

70 What is 'copra' obtained from?

71 If you suffered from dermatitis what part of your body would be affected?

72 In the song what is the name of the 'one more river to cross'?

Who wrote . . . ?

73 *i* 'Two vast and trunkless legs of stone
        Stand in the desert . . .'
    ii 'I weep for Adonais . . .'
   iii 'O wild West Wind, thou breath of Autumn's being . . .'
74 *i* 'Lest we forget – lest we forget . . .'
    ii 'We're foot-slog-slog-slog-sloggin' over Africa –
        Foot-foot-foot-foot-sloggin' over Africa –
        Boots-boots-boots-boots-movin' up and down again . . .'
   iii 'You're a better man than I am, Gunga Din!'
75 *i* 'Led Eve, our credulous mother, to the Tree
        Of Prohibition, root of all our woe . . .'
    ii 'They also serve who only stand and wait . . .'
   iii 'O loss of sight, of thee I most complain . . .'
76 *i* 'Souls of Poets dead and gone,
        What Elysium have ye known . . .'
    ii 'A thing of beauty is a joy forever . . .'
   iii 'Charmed magic casements, opening on the foam
        Of perilous seas, in faery lands forlorn . . .'
77 *i* '. . . That inward eye
        Which is the bliss of solitude.'
    ii 'She dwelt among the untrodden ways
        Beside the springs of Dove . . .'
   iii 'Bliss was it in that dawn to be alive,
        But to be young was very heaven!'
78 *i* 'The Assyrian came down like the wolf on the fold . . .'
    ii 'The mountains look on Marathon –
        And Marathon looks on the sea;
        And musing there an hour alone,
        I dream'd that Greece might still be free.'
   iii 'She walks in beauty, like the night
        Of cloudless climes and starry skies . . .'
79 *i* 'Wings like bits of umbrella.
        Bats!'

ii 'I can imagine, in some otherworld
   Primeval-dumb, far back
   In that most awful stillness, that only gasped and
      hummed,
   Humming-birds raced down the avenues.'

iii 'A long, long slim cat, yellow like a lioness.
   Dead.'

80 *i* 'Long ago he was one of the singers,
   But now he is one of the dumbs.'

ii 'O my aged Uncle Arly!
   Sitting on a heap of Barley . . .'

iii 'The Owl and the Pussycat went to sea
   In a beautiful pea-green boat.'

81 *i* 'Sweet cyder is a great thing,
   A great thing to me,
   Spinning down to Weymouth town
   By Ridgeway thirstily . . .'

ii 'They throw in Drummer Hodge, to rest
   Uncoffined – just as found . . .'

iii 'And the Squire, and Lady Susan, lie in Melstock
   churchyard now!'

82 *i* 'On Linden, when the sun was low,
   All bloodless lay the untrodden snow . . .'

ii 'Of Nelson and the North
   Sing the glorious day's renown . . .'

iii 'Ye mariners of England
   That guard our native seas!'

83 *i* 'A sweet disorder in the dress
   Kindles in clothes a wantonness –'

ii 'Thou hast command of every part,
   to live and die for thee'

iii 'Fair daffodils, we weep to see
   You haste away so soon . . .'

General knowledge 2

84 What is the name of the German police force headed by Himmler in the days of the Nazis?

85 Where was the conference held that brought the War of the Spanish Succession to an end in 1712?

86 Who was the archaeologist who began a dig to discover the ancient city of Troy just about a hundred years ago?

87 What is the Roman palace that is now the official residence of the president of Italy?

88 The word 'Fascism' and the name for an ancient symbol of authority both come from the same Latin word. What was the *fasces* carried before a Roman magistrate?

89 Why is the Russian Revolution, which began on November 7th, known as the *October Revolution*?

90 What is the medicine obtained from the cinchona tree which is used to treat malaria and other diseases?

91 What is the simple description of the speed of an aircraft which is said to be travelling at 'Mach One'?

92 Which of the Canterbury pilgrims tells of three men in search of 'a secret thief men called Death'?

93 What animal did Chesterton describe as the 'devil's walking parody on all four-footed things'?

94 For what discovery was the Nobel Prize in 1945 awarded to Ernst B. Chain, Sir Howard W. Florey and Sir Alexander Fleming?

95 Who was the sergeant who was such a disturbing element in Hardy's *Far from the Madding Crowd*?

96 Christianity is founded in Christ; in whom is the Islamic religion founded?

97 What are the moraines of a glacier?

98 Members of the United Nations Security Council have power of *veto*. What is the meaning of this Latin word?

The Bible

99 Which book in the New Testament is known as the 'Apocalypse'?

100 David married Bathsheba. Who was her first husband?

101 According to the Bible, who, at the age of 969, was the champion of longevity?

102 According to the Bible, what was the magic number that brought the walls of Jericho tumbling down?

103 How did Joseph interpret Pharaoh's dream of the seven lean cows and the seven fat cows?

104 In Genesis, it is said that God first created Heaven and Earth. What was the next thing he created?

105 Who slew a lion with 'nothing in his hand'?

106 What was Jacob's dream on the road out of Beersheba?

107 What did John the Baptist eat in the wilderness?

108 What did John the Baptist wear in the wilderness of Judaea?

109 How did Jacob cheat Isaac?

110 Who said these words and on what occasion?
'Lord, now lettest thou thy servant depart in peace, according to thy word:
For mine eyes have seen thy salvation . . .'

111 What is the meaning of the word 'Messiah'?

112 What was the first miracle performed by Jesus Christ?

113 Solomon's father was King David; who was Solomon's mother?

114 What was the language in which the Old Testament was written?

115 Who was Jesus' first disciple?

116 Who was the first martyr?

117 Saul was Israel's first king; who was Israel's second king?

Science 1

118   What is the formula for the volume of a circular cylinder?

119   Propane is an aliphatic hydrocarbon. What is toluene?

120   In what three ways does heat travel?

121   What is measured in Henrys?

122   What name is given to the unit of mass that equals the mass of a cubic centimeter of water at 4 degrees centigrade?

123   Max Planck revolutionized physics with his law of radiation. What are the 'quanta' which are the basis of his theory?

124   In electronics what does a rectifier rectify?

125   What liquid is always present in any solution known as a 'tincture'?

126   Petroleum is composed of hundreds of compounds, most of which are different combinations of just two chemical elements. What are these two main elements?

127   Potash is an important plant requirement that often has to be added to the soil. Name the other two essential substances.

128   What are the chemical names of these formulas of paraffin hydrocarbons? 1. CH_4 2. C_3H_8.

129   Why does yellow phosphorus have to be kept under water?

130   What is the name of the mineral that is an important source of radium and uranium?

131   The chemical symbol for the element cobalt is Co. What is the symbol for copper?

132   What is the branch of physics known as kinetics concerned with?

133   One method of obtaining hydrochloric acid is to burn hydrogen in chlorine and dissolve the resulting gas in water, but what is the usual method chemists use to obtain hydrochloric acid in the laboratory?

Team quiz 1

134a Who was the Greek god of the Sun?

135a Who wrote the prophetic novel *War in the Air* in 1908?

136a What is the brightest star in the sky?

137a U.S.A. has had three man-in-space programmes. Project Apollo is the most recent one. Name one of the other two.

138a What is the national symbol of Holland?

139a In what sea are the Balearic Islands, and to what country do they belong?

140a What name did Rudyard Kipling give his mongoose in the Jungle Books?

141a What quality is symbolized by a blindfolded woman holding a pair of scales?

142a Supply the number that should logically follow the last one in this series: 5 10 20 8 16 32 11.

143a In the story by R. L. Stevenson what happened to Dr. Jekyll when he drank the secret potion?

144a What are the three largest Shetland Islands?

145a What are stalactite and stalagmite formations composed of?

146a What family ruled France for more than 200 years?

147a Where do alpha, beta and gamma rays originate?

148a The story of Peter Abelard and Heloise is one of the greatest love stories in history. But why isn't it a 'happy-ever-after' story?

149a A famous poem has the title taken from this quotation from Horace: 'Dulce et decorum est pro-patria mori'. What is the translation of the quotation?

134b In mythology who was the god of the sea?

135b Who wrote *Twenty Thousand Leagues Under the Sea* in 1870?

136b What is the name given to the deepest known spot in the world ocean?

137b What kind of vessel did Jacques Piccard use to descend more than 35,000 feet in the Pacific, in 1960?

138b What is the national symbol of Canada?

139b In what ocean, and near to what island, are the Grand Banks, the famous fishing grounds?

140b In *A Christmas Carol*, who was Bob Cratchit's boss?

141b What Roman goddess is symbolized by a helmet and a magic shield known as the aegis?

142b Supply the number that should logically follow the last one in this series: 50 52 56 58 62 64 68.

143b In Oscar Wilde's novel whose portrait changes in a mystical way?

144b What are the three largest islands in the Outer Hebrides?

145b Portland Stone was used by Sir Christopher Wren for St Paul's. What kind of stone is it?

146b What family ruled Russia for more than 300 years?

147b Where do 'cosmic rays' originate?

148b What is the love story behind the cryptic summary of a famous poet: 'John Donne, Ann Donne, Undone'?

149b What is the translation of this quotation from Horace: 'Indignor, quandoque bonus dormitat Homerus'?

Famous people 1

150 Who was the French actress known as the 'Divine Sarah'?

151 Who was the famous Duke of Lancaster who was the son of King Edward III and father of King Henry IV?

152 If Britain's 'Iron Duke' met Germany's 'Iron Chancellor', who would have met whom?

153 Mrs Golda Meir became Israel's Prime Minister in 1969. Where was she born?

154 What French heroine died as a witch in 1431, but was declared a saint in 1920?

155 Who was the American general in World War II who became President of the United States?

156 Joseph, John and Robert Kennedy, three brothers of one of America's most famous families, are all dead. Who is the remaining brother?

157 Von Braun directed the American team that successfully launched the first United States earth satellite. What was his job during the war?

158 Who was the German-Jewish girl who hid in an Amsterdam attic during the last war, and wrote a famous diary?

159 In the Russian Revolution who was the military genius who organized the Red Army?

160 Americans often referred to President Johnson as L.B.J. Whom did they call F.D.R.?

161 Who was said to have suffered the 'odium' of having discovered sodium?

162 George Williams was knighted by Queen Victoria for his 'distinguished service to the cause of humanity'. What was the international youth organization he founded?

163 Hudson, Frobisher and Franklin all failed to complete a voyage through the North-west Passage. Who was finally successful in 1906?

164 In optics, concave and convex are opposites; what is opposite to *real image*?

165 What literary works did Samuel Johnson imitate in his poems *London* and *The Vanity of Human Wishes*?

166 How did Hamlet discover the method of his father's death?

167 Led by William Brewster, a religious group known as the Separatists, made an historic voyage in 1620. What was the name of the ship that made the journey?

168 The composer of the hymn 'Onward, Christian Soldiers' achieved fame as the collaborator in a number of operettas; who was he?

169 Flotsam and jetsam are goods lost at sea; what name is given to goods sunk at sea but attached to buoys so that they can be recovered?

170 What kind of building was the Pharos of Alexandria?

171 In fiction what was the name of the house with the date '1500' over the principal door and the name 'Hareton Earnshaw'?

172 Who was the American folk singer who achieved Broadway success in Tennessee Williams' play *Cat on a Hot Tin Roof*?

173 Expressed more simply, what has happened to an actor who has had a trajection of hydrogen sulphide?

174 In what capacity was Trygve Lie an important 'first'?

175 Garibaldi's followers were known as 'red shirts': what were Mussolini's followers called?

176 *Libel* and *slander* are both forms of *defamation*. What is the main difference between them?

177 Who or what were the 'Mohicans' that J. Fenimore Cooper wrote about?

178 In *Alice in Wonderland* which character had the gruesome desire to decapitate anyone who offended her?

Picture quiz 1 – Inventions

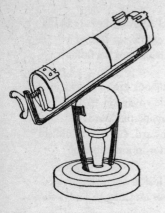

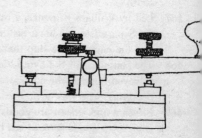

179 What is this instrument and who invented it?

180 This is a key for sending Morse Code. When was the Code invented?

181 This is one of the earliest self-propelled road vehicles. Who invented it and what was its source of power?

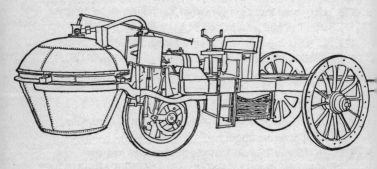

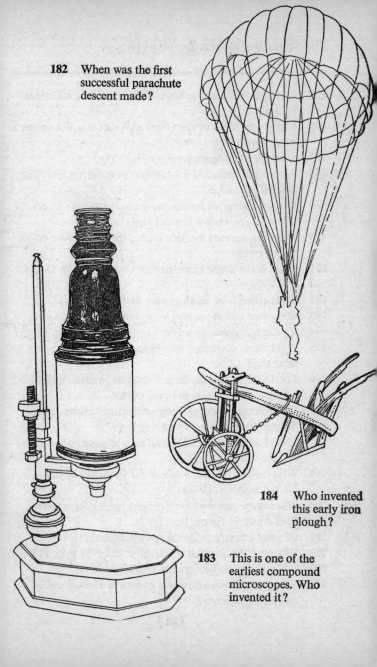

182 When was the first successful parachute descent made?

184 Who invented this early iron plough?

183 This is one of the earliest compound microscopes. Who invented it?

Speed quiz 2

185 In which year was the Great Exhibition at the Crystal Palace?

186 The fourth letter of the Greek alphabet is a geographical term; what is it?

187 Where are the headquarters of SEATO?

188 Who is the famous film-star who gave her name to the inflated life jacket?

189 Who was inspired by the gravestones in Stoke Poges graveyard to write a famous elegy?

190 Britannia appears on only one of the new British coins. Which one?

191 What is the single name now given to Vitamins G and B^2?

192 What name is given to gypsies in Hungary?

193 What bird did Picasso paint as the symbol of peace?

194 If your lachrymal glands are active what are you doing?

195 What metal combines with chlorine to form common table salt?

196 The U.S.S.R. has the largest country in area. Which country is the largest in population?

197 When Prasutagus was King of the Iceni in the days of Roman Britain, who was queen?

198 The Moslem temple is known as a mosque; what do we call the Jewish temple?

199 Who defeated Richard Nixon for President of the United States in 1960?

200 What is the name of the fictitious large village where Jane Austen's Emma lives?

201 Of what country is Damascus the capital?

202 Who was the Scottish writer often referred to as R.L.S.?

203 What flower is the national symbol of India?

204 What country was formerly known as Hellas, and its natives as Hellenes?

Nature 2

205 Squirrels and rats are rodents. What are wombats, bandicoots, koalas and kangaroos?

206 A ladybird is a beetle: what is a ladysmock?

207 Fish breathe out carbon dioxide, what gas do they breathe in?

208 What kind of creature is a marmoset?

209 How many feet has a hexapod?

210 What is the porcupine's weapon?

211 How does a swift build its nest?

212 In botany what is the 'petiole'?

213 What is meant when a horse is described as dapple-grey?

214 What is the chief difference between a tree and a shrub?

215 What creatures were almost wiped out by an epidemic of myxomatosis?

216 What is the difference between a fruit and a vegetable?

217 A man's heart has *four* chambers: how many chambers are there in a frog's heart?

218 What acid puts the sting in the stinging nettle?

219 The sundew is a carnivorous plant. How does it maintain its larder?

220 When in danger, opossums pretend to be dead; how does the bittern escape notice?

221 Is the newt an amphibian or a reptile?

222 Where does the lapwing build its nest?

Far-away places 2

223 What famous canal links the North Sea to the Baltic?

224 If a person crossed the western border of Cambodia, what country would he enter?

225 Where is the general location of the 'Lake of Dreams' and 'Lake of Death?'

226 What is the great river in Australia which is the longest tributary of the River Murray?

227 In which country do the Ashanti people live?

228 A bronze statue of Christ, known as 'Christ of the Andes', is a symbol of perpetual peace between two nations. What are the nations?

229 What country is sometimes called the 'Emerald Isle'?

230 What are the 'playas' of North America?

231 Tourists visit the Tower of Pisa to see how it leans; but what was its original function?

232 What is the name of the Associated States of which Grenada is part?

233 What are the gauchos of South America?

234 Where are the islands known as the Tierra Del Fuego – the 'Land of Fire'?

235 What is the name of the channel that separates Wales from Southern Ireland?

236 On what river is the Génissiat Dam?

237 Which of the Great Lakes is the only one that lies entirely within the United States?

238 The Uruguay river forms the boundary between Brazil and what other country?

239 The Dead Sea is famous for its salt content; what is the Sargasso Sea noted for?

240 Where do the Basques live?

General knowledge 4

241 We talk about 'flocks of birds' but a special name is given to a 'flock' of geese. What is it?

242 The characters of the ancient Egyptian's alphabet were known as hieroglyphics. What are the characters of the ancient alphabet used by Teutonic peoples called?

243 Who were the people that Gandhi called 'Harijans', the Children of God?

244 Who adopted the alias of 'Thomas Rowley' and tricked the experts?

245 In what war were the battles of Poitiers, Creçy and Agincourt fought?

246 What is the popular name of Mozart's last symphony?

247 Prison reform in the eighteenth century followed the publication of a book called *The State of the Prisons in England and Wales*. Who was the author?

248 What bi-centenary was celebrated in Australia during the Royal visit of 1970?

249 What is the equinox?

250 If you took a dose of acetylsalicylic acid you would probably give it a different name. What is the common name for this medicine?

251 In what way was Tyburn Tree more interesting historically than biologically?

252 Which of Shakespeare's heroines pretended to be Cesario, page to a duke?

253 Adolf Hitler called his government the 'Third Reich'. What was the Empire that constituted the 'First Reich'?

254 Romeo loved Juliet; in Wagner's opera, *The Ring of the Nibelungs*, whom did Siegfried love?

255 What name is given to the special breed of horses that are trained at the Spanish School of Vienna?

Picture quiz 2 — Music

Identify these tunes

a

b

c

d

Science 2

256   What are the invisible waves of light that a photographer makes use of to take pictures in almost total darkness?

257   To honour the famous French scientists a unit of measurement is known as the 'Curie'. What do scientists measure in Curies?

258   A common unit of measurement is defined by scientists as 1,650,763,73 wavelengths of the orange-red light from the spectrum of the isotope Krypton 86. What is this common unit of measurement?

259   The lightest known metallic element has the atomic number 3; what is its name?

260   What was the theory in physics which was discredited by the Michelson-Morley Experiment?

261   What whitish powder results from the action of chlorine on slaked lime?

262   What is the chemical name of that part of natural gas which is sometimes called 'marsh gas', and is the chief substance in 'firedamp'?

263   What is the alloy that is composed of mainly copper, some tin and a little phosphorus?

264   What gas is produced by the action of water on calcium carbide?

265   What is the heaviest known metal on earth?

266   How does gas chromatography help scientists in the battle against air pollution?

267   In electronics what are the two electrodes contained in a diode?

268   Among the halogens fluorine is a yellow gas; what is bromine?

269   In the flame test what colour does copper give off?

270   Chromium is never found alone. What is the metal usually found combined with it?

Myths and legends

271 In mythology if you drank the waters of Lethe what would happen to you?

272 In Norse mythology the Valkyries carried the souls of the dead to Valhalla. In Greek mythology how were the souls of the dead carried to Hades?

273 In Greek mythology what did Jason seek when he sailed to Colchis?

274 What is the legendary creature that is supposed to haunt the Himalayas?

275 What was the legendary hazard for boatmen passing the Lorelei rock on the banks of the river Rhine?

276 Two of the mythological gorgons were immortal; what happened to the third one?

277 According to legend for how many nights did Scheherazade tell her stories of the Arabian Nights?

278 The love of Venus (or Aphrodite if you prefer the Greek name) and Adonis has been the theme for many poems including one by Shakespeare. How did Venus show her grief when Adonis was killed by a wild boar?

279 A legendary magician was the chief character in a play by Marlowe, works by Goethe and an opera by Gounod. Who was he?

280 In a mythological beauty contest Hera and Athena were the losers; who was the winner?

281 In the Old Testament Eve was the first woman on earth; according to Greek mythology who was the first woman on earth?

282 Fauna and flora are scientific terms. What or who are Faun and Flora in mythology?

283 In mythology how did Ulysses manage to avoid being drawn to destruction by the singing of the Sirens?

284 The word 'tantalize' is derived from a character in Greek mythology. How was Tantalus tantalized?

General knowledge 5

285 Kirov of Leningrad is one of the two major Russian
ballet companies; what is the name of the other one?

286 What were the three living creatures sent up in
Montgolfier's balloon in September 1783?

287 By what name were the seven major Anglo-Saxon
kingdoms known?

288 Archimedes once said 'Give me a place to stand on,
and I will move the earth'. What was the simple, though
gigantic, tool he would need to do the job?

289 What are the two major political parties of the United
States of America?

290 What is St Elmo's Fire?

291 Except for the sun and its planets, what is the nearest
star to Earth?

292 What is the name of the fly that transmits African
sleeping sickness?

293 The United Nations was set up after World War II.
What is the name of the international peace organization
that was set up after World War I?

294 What was the picture that Leonardo da Vinci painted
on the monastery wall next to the Church of Santa
Maria Delle Grazie in Milan?

295 There are three main classes of food essential to the
body; fats and proteins are two, what is the third?

296 In a game, dominoes are flat pieces with dots; what are
dominoes in an Italian carnival?

297 Scientifically, what do Thule in Greenland, Clear in
Alaska and Fylingdales in Britain have in common?

298 In a book by Alexander Dumas, what was the flower
that aroused the passions of Dutch horticulturists in the
seventeenth century?

299 In the human body, what are connected by the
eustachian tube?

Picture quiz 3 – Architecture

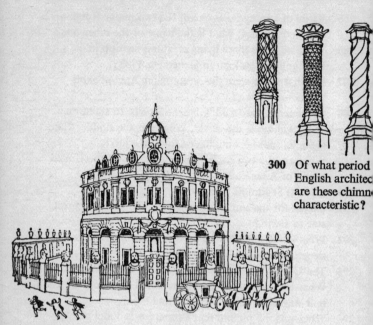

300 Of what period English architec are these chimn characteristic?

301 What and where is this building, and who designed it?

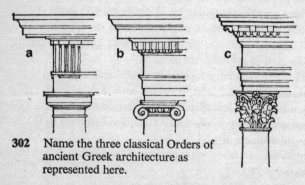

302 Name the three classical Orders of ancient Greek architecture as represented here.

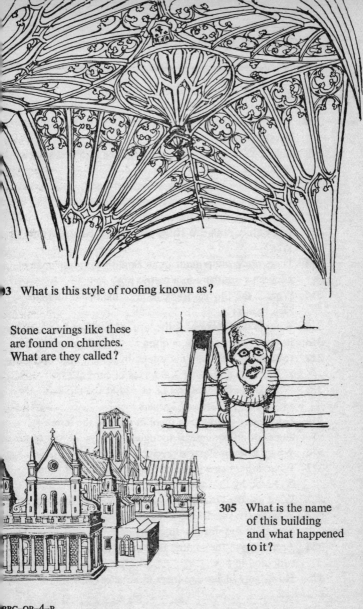

303 What is this style of roofing known as?

Stone carvings like these
are found on churches.
What are they called?

305 What is the name
of this building
and what happened
to it?

Speed quiz 3

306 How long is a surveyor's chain in yards?

307 How many Inns of Court are there?

308 What is listed on a label, inserted in a book, with the heading *errata*?

309 Long before it became a concert item who first sang a 'baccarole'?

310 What is the chemical name for iron rust?

311 In what play does George Bernard Shaw put the Salvation Army on the stage?

312 What army rank did Hitler rise to in the First World War?

313 There are 2,240 pounds in an English ton; how many kilograms are there in a metric ton?

314 What is the English translation of the opera title *Die Fledermaus*?

315 What is the function of the 'eye' of a potato?

316 In physics what name is given to the study of motion?

317 How many watts are consumed by a light bulb operating at 100 volts and using 2 amperes of current?

318 What is the fish that can be served at the table as whitebait, bloaters and kippers?

319 How many degrees are there in each of the interior angles of an equilateral triangle?

320 Where is the metatarsal arch?

321 What is the name given to the special kind of canoe first used by Eskimos?

322 What are the Orloff, the Cullinan and the Koh-i-noor?

323 What is the title of the book that Charles Dickens began but did not live to complete?

324 According to the saying, how many lives is a cat supposed to have?

325 How many inches are there in a metre?

Authors and their books

326 John Galsworthy traced the fortunes of the Forsytes; who chronicled the Herries family of the Lake District?

327 Edward Grieg composed the music for Peer Gynt: who wrote the play?

328 What Irish author has the middle names Fingal O'Flahertie Wills?

329 What is the title of George Eliot's book, which she subtitled 'A Study of Provincial Life'?

330 Harold Pinter wrote a play called *A Birthday Party*; who wrote a play called *The Cocktail Party*?

331 From which famous elegy did Thomas Hardy obtain the title for his novel *Far from the Madding Crowd*?

332 Shakespeare wrote a play about Othello, a noble Moor; in which of his plays did he introduce a Prince of Morocco?

333 Who was the poet who declared that 'Nature never did betray The heart that loved her . . .'?

334 What is the title of the book that Aldous Huxley wrote to mock all Utopias?

335 Who was the writer who named and wrote about the subtle social art of 'one-upmanship'?

336 What was the important international award made to Alexander Solzhenitsyn in 1970?

337 What single title was given to the sequence of novels written by Sartre which included *The Age of Reason*, *The Reprieve*, and *Troubled Sleep*?

338 What was the relationship between the author of *Ozymandias* and the author of *Frankenstein*?

339 Where did Kubla Khan, according to Samuel Taylor Coleridge, build his stately pleasure-dome?

340 What book did Shakespeare use as his main source for the plots of Macbeth, Richard III and Henry V?

Team quiz 2

341a Justice wields a sword in her right hand; what does she carry in her left?

342a If you sailed down the Volga river, what sea would you sail into?

343a Hever Castle in Kent was the girlhood home of a queen of England. Who was she?

344a Which of Henry VIII's wives provided him with the male heir he wanted?

345a Cider is a popular drink in Britain. What is it made from?

346a If you asked for 'sirloin' what kind of meat would you expect to get?

347a For your first course you order 'bouillabaisse', what is this?

348a Your main course is 'ragout'. What do you get?

349a What name do the French give to the English Channel?

350a What French river flows through Rouen and empties into the English Channel between Le Havre and Honfleur?

351a What is the name of the canal that connects the North Sea and the Baltic?

352a What is the river that flows through Hamburg, Germany, and empties into the North Sea at Cuxhaven?

Who were the Russian authors of these works:

353a *The Brothers Karamazov.*

354a *The Cherry Orchard.*

355a *And Quiet Flows the Don.*

356a *Anna Karenina.*

341b Liberty has a tablet in her left hand, what does she hold in her right hand?

342b If you sailed down the river Danube, what sea would you sail into?

343b A former Tudor Palace at Hatfield House, Hertfordshire, was the girlhood home of a queen of England. Who was she?

344b Who was the wife of Napoleon who provided him with the male heir he wanted?

345b In England there's a saying that we have 'chips with everything' we eat. What are chips?

346b If an Englishman asked for 'bangers and mash' what would he get?

347b From a French menu, you are served with a dessert of 'Tarte aux pommes avec fromage.' What is that in English?

348b If you asked for 'dinde aux marrons', what would you expect to get in English?

349b Which Channel Island is ruled by a Dame?

350b Operation Overlord was the codename of what military operation that took place in World War II?

351b What is the name given to the large sand bank located in the North Sea between England and Denmark?

352b What was the naval battle fought between Britain and Germany off the coast of Denmark at the end of May 1916 during the First World War?

Who were the authors of these books?

353b *Dr Zhivago.*	**355b** *Don Quixote (de la Mancha).*
354b *Mein Kampf.*	**356b** *Madame Bovary.*

General knowledge 6

357 Which knight of the Round Table was beloved by Elaine but had eyes only for the Queen?

358 The Arcadians lived in Arcadia, but where do the Orcadians live?

359 In what country did the Boxer Rebellion take place?

360 Britain has the Victoria Cross and Germany the Iron Cross. What name do the French give to their military cross?

361 What has an accused man done when he is said to have 'established an alibi'?

362 What name is given to the equivalent of our 'Cabinet' in the Soviet Union?

363 Who was the Italian composer who wrote the music for three operas based on Shakespearean themes?

364 Beethoven's 'Eroica' is a symphony. What is his 'Pathetique'?

365 Who was the author who wrote letters to women he called 'Stella' and 'Vanessa'?

366 In what way can 'floating ribs' be said to float?

367 What was the basic belief, now known to be true, which brought Galileo before the Inquisition and for which by way of penance he was told to recite once a week the seven penitential psalms?

368 Parliament passed an Act of Settlement in 1701. What did this act settle?

369 'As bald as a coot' is a common phrase. But what is the coot referred to in the phrase?

370 'Lead' pencil is a misnomer. What is the so-called 'lead'?

371 Samuel Butler wrote a book about an imaginary country which he called *Erewhon*. How did he get this title?

372 Jerusalem is a holy city to Moslems. Name one other city sacred to all Moslems.

Master brain 1

373 Hitler had a private army called the Sturm Abteilungen. What were they usually known as?

374 On April 9th, 1865, two generals met in a farmhouse at Appomatox Courthouse, Virginia, in the United States. Who were they, and why were they meeting?

375 Who assumed the pseudonymn of 'Peter Michailoff' working in the dockyards of Holland and England to get ideas for reform in his own country?

376 Perkin Warbeck was a famous 'pretender'; whom did he pretend to be?

377 Who conferred the title of 'Defender of the Faith' on Henry VIII?

378 'Civil Disobedience' is not new; what American philosopher, born in a town known as Concord, wrote a famous essay with this title in 1849?

379 In the study of cybernetics what is the human nervous system compared with?

380 Who was the German mathematician who helped to establish a branch of geometry concerned with figures that are deformed, or twisted out of shape?

381 The famous French scientist, Jean Fabre, was dismissed from his teaching post because he allowed girls to attend the classes. What was the subject matter of his book *Souvenirs Entomologiques*?

382 What is the 'Code Napoleon'?

383 Who was the French playwright who died from the strain imposed upon him through acting as a man suffering from *le Malade Imaginaire*?

384 A famous 'first' was achieved by Alfred Binet and Theodore Simon. What did Binet and Simon first develop?

385 Because of its achievements in the arts what British reign is described as the *Augustan Age*?

Games and sport

386   Name three of the events in a decathlon.

387   In badminton a ladies' single game consists of 11 points. What are the options at '9 all' and '10 all'?

388   In basketball how many free shots are awarded to the opposition team for a foul against a player on court?

389   In horse show jumping the penalty for the First Disobedience is 3 faults. What are the penalties for further disobedience?

390   Amateur golf teams from America and Great Britain compete for the Walker Cup. Who competes for the Davis Cup?

391   What sport is sometimes described as 'Catch-as-Catch-can'?

392   Which Australian swimmer introduced the crawl?

393   In the high jump two men fail at the same height. One receives the gold medal and the other the silver; why has the gold medallist won?

394   Why might a canoeist be upset to see a 'bore'?

395   In boxing what is a technical knock-out?

396   In which sport does the gold score 9, and what is the 'gold'?

397   What is taking place, in cricket, when a team 'puts the shutters up'?

398   What do we mean when we say that players are 'seeded' in a tournament?

399   What is 'long trotting' in angling?

400   With what sport is the *Doggett's Coat and Badge* connected?

401   In the 1970 America's Cup Race what was the name of the winning boat?

402   Which member of the British team won the individual gold medal in the equestrian three day event in the 1972 Olympics?

403   What is 'scuba'?

Speed quiz 4

404 How many protons are there in Oxygen?

405 The letters 'CD' are to be seen on some motorcars; what do these letters stand for?

406 Fungicides get rid of fungi; what pest is attacked with formicide?

407 In poetry, how many lines are there in a triolet?

408 Who is described by Shakespeare as 'the noblest Roman of them all'?

409 In Arthur C. Clarke's 'Space Odyssey' what was the year that mattered?

410 Which of the United States was once known as 'Seward's Icebox'?

411 According to Shakespeare's *Hamlet*, what was the question?

412 How many revolutions a minute does a 'Long Play' record make?

413 What river is linked to the city of Moscow by the Moscow canal?

414 What unit of measurement equals 0·3937 of an inch?

415 The first string of a violin is known as the E string: what are the names given to the other three strings?

416 In Irish legend, who was the old woman whose shrieks told of a coming death?

417 What is the unit of speed used by sailors for one nautical mile per hour?

418 In Shakespeare who killed Macbeth?

419 What is a madrigal?

420 What is a printer's devil?

421 How many Georges have sat on the throne of Great Britain?

422 How many lines are there in a limerick?

423 What country is the world's chief supplier of nickel?

Science 3

424 What is Bernoulli's Principle?

425 What is the chemical name for caustic soda used in the making of hard soap?

426 Light Hydrogen atom has one proton and one electron; what does a Heavy Hydrogen atom contain?

427 What is the only element that cannot be changed to a solid by cooling alone?

428 What name is given to the unit of energy needed to raise the temperature of one gram of water 1 degree Centigrade?

429 Oxides are combinations of oxygen with metals or non-metals. What are acids combinations of?

430 What is the chemical element that was first discovered by a French chemist in seaweed 170 years ago?

431 Neon in lamps is bright red. What colour does it become when a few drops of mercury are added?

432 Hydrogen has the atomic number 1; what chemical element has the atomic number 2?

433 What is the nuclear fuel produced by bombarding thorium with neutrons?

434 What is the formula for Newton's Second Law of Motion?

435 TNT is made up of four chemical elements. Hydrogen, carbon and oxygen are three of them; what is the fourth?

436 The names of the six inert gases end with '-on' with one exception; what is it?

437 What is the chemical known in its abbreviated form as LOX which is used in rockets propelled by liquid fuels?

438 In physics, what is the support called on which a lever turns or is supported in moving or lifting something?

439 What was the isotope that was adopted in 1961 as the standard for atomic weights?

General knowledge 7

440 An American state was named after her, and Edmund Spenser called her 'Gloriana'. Who was she?

441 What are the 'f-stops' on a camera?

442 What play would you expect to see performed at Kronberg Castle in Helsingør?

443 *The Beggar's Opera* was written by John Gay. What is the title of the version written by Bertolt Brecht?

444 In electric wiring, instead of the old British Standard colours, Britain is adopting the European colour code. Which colour is common to both codes?

445 In World War II, what was PLUTO?

446 Rene Laënnec (1781–1826) was a nineteenth-century physician who specialized in diseases of the lungs. He also invented a medical instrument still used by doctors today; what is it?

447 What are the Elgin Marbles?

448 What is the alternative title of the music called *Fingal's Cave* and who composed it?

449 What is the name of the Parliament of Norway?

450 Who was the Dutch scholar who prepared a Greek edition of the New Testament of the Bible and translated it into Latin?

451 What kind of horse is the 'Percheron'?

452 Who was known as the 'Great Elector' of Brandenburg?

453 The 'Oder-Neisse Line' is a disputed boundary. Which are the countries it divides?

454 Who were the 'Carbonari'?

455 What country was guaranteed perpetual neutrality at the Treaty of London in a document that was called later 'a scrap of paper'?

456 What famous book contains an account of Essex, Suffolk and Norfolk in one volume, and details about the rest of England in a second volume?

Far-away places 3

457 Once called the Gulf of Gascony, what is the bay bounded in the east by France and in the south by Spain?

458 In what city do pilgrims march seven times round the Kaaba and kiss the Black Stone?

459 What are the Walloons?

460 What is the name derived from the Latin word for *saw* which is given to the jagged ranges of mountains in Spain?

461 What is the correct name of the West Indian Island commonly called 'Saint Kitts'?

462 Rhodesia lies on one side of the Victoria Falls; what country lies on the other side?

463 In what city would you be if a guide took you to see the following: the Curia, the Column of Marcus Aurelius and the Colosseum?

464 Many geographers consider the Ural Mountains to be one of the boundaries between two continents. What are the two continents?

465 Why is the far north of the Scandinavian peninsula sometimes called the *Land of the Midnight Sun*?

466 What is the name of the narrow strait between the island of Anglesey and Caernarvonshire?

467 New Zealand is made up of a group of islands. The two largest are North Island and South Island. Although much smaller, what is the name of the third largest island?

468 What island is separated from the Italian mainland by the Strait of Messina?

469 Which one of the United States of America is separated from the rest by Canada?

470 What South American republic is named after Venice?

471 What is the Dust Bowl of America?

Master brain 2

472 How long does it take light to travel to the earth from the sun?

473 In astronomy, the word *apogee* refers to the point in the orbit of a heavenly body which is farthest from the earth. What is the opposite of apogee?

474 In Scottish history, what were the 'Casket Letters'?

475 Who was the gallant king of Sparta who died in Thermopylae?

476 What was the main subject on the agenda at the Bretton Woods Conference of 1944?

477 Bismarck obtained complete control of Schleswig-Holstein in the Seven Weeks' War. What were the pickings for Victor Emmanuel of Italy?

478 At the Congress of Vienna that met after the defeat of Napoleon, Prince von Metternich represented Austria. Who represented France?

479 In the Binary System in maths what are the only two symbols used?

480 What did Julius Caesar mean when he said, on crossing the Rubicon, 'Iacta alea est'? (or 'Alea jacta est')

481 In World War II, Churchill was prime minister when Germany surrendered; who was prime minister when Japan surrendered?

482 What are the 'Grand Trianon' and 'Petit Trianon' of Versailles?

483 What was the civil war in which the opposing armies were known as the 'Reds' and the 'Whites'?

484 What did King Henry IV of France grant in the Edict of Nantes of 1598, and to whom?

485 What was the experiment that the Russian physiologist conducted with a dog and a bell?

Team quiz 3

486a How many locks are there in the Suez Canal?

487a What was the opera commissioned to celebrate the opening of the Suez Canal?

488a Who was the American engineer who built the *Clermont*, the first commercially successful steamboat?

489a What was the achievement of the nuclear powered submarine the *Triton* in 1960?

490a Who was Olivia's steward who was taught a lesson in *Twelfth Night*?

491a Who married Petruchio in *The Taming of the Shrew*?

492a Which of Shakespeare's plays begins with the words: 'Who's there?' and the appearance of a ghost in the first scene?

493a Who was attended by Peasblossom, Cobweb, Moth and Mustardseed?

494a Who composed the *Scheherazade* ballet music?

495a Who composed the *Romeo and Juliet* ballet music?

496a What is the name of the Shakespeare play on which the musical play *Kiss Me Kate* is based?

497a For whose wedding were the Orkney Islands pledged as a dowry security, and by whom?

498a The purity of gold is measured in carats, how many carats are there in pure gold?

499a The Klondike was the scene of a famous gold rush. Where is the Klondike?

500a In the study of sound, what is the 'Doppler Effect'?

501a What is the symbol in chemistry for mercury?

486b Who was the French engineer who made a success of constructing the Suez Canal but failed with the Panama Canal?

487b What is the name of the waterway that links rivers flowing through Berlin, Bremen and Hamburg to the Rhine?

488b What is the name of the ballistic missiles that can be fired from under water?

489b What was the opera that was written about a phantom ship that never reaches port?

490b Who was Oberon's fairy attendant who helped his master to teach Titania a lesson in *Midsummer Night's Dream*?

491b Who was Miranda's father in *The Tempest*?

492b Which of Shakespeare's plays has a sonnet Prologue beginning with the words 'Two households, both alike in dignity, In fair Verona, where we lay our scene . . .'?

493b Whose daughters were Goneril, Regan and Cordelia?

494b Who composed the *Nutcracker Suite* ballet music?

495b Who composed the *Fire Bird Suite* ballet music?

496b What is the name of the Shakespeare play on which the musical play *West Side Story* is based?

497b Why is a rock that lies off the coast from Oban, between Mull and Lismore, known as Lady Rock?

498b Who was the mythological king who had the power to turn to gold everything he touched?

499b What is the name of the country that was formerly known as the Gold Coast?

500b In the study of light, what is the 'Zeeman Effect'?

501b What is the symbol in chemistry for iron?

Picture quiz 4 – Transport

502 This is the first power-driven airship. Who built it?

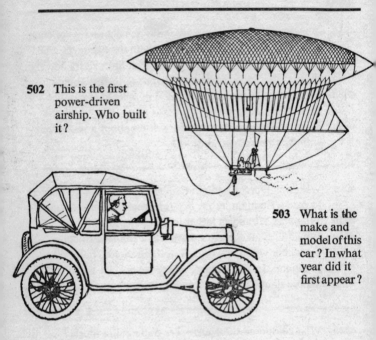

503 What is the make and model of this car? In what year did it first appear?

504 This ship was for many years the largest in the world. What was its name and who designed it?

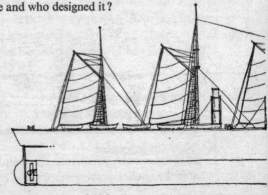

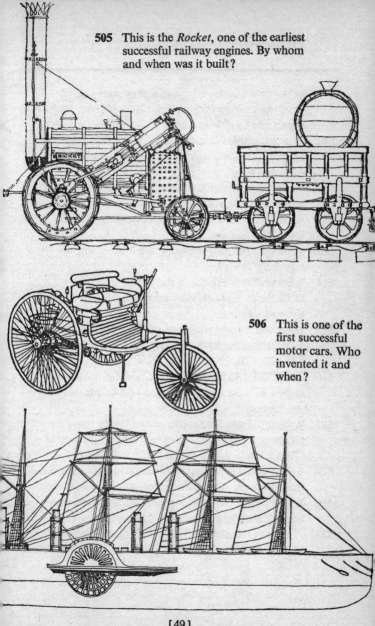

505 This is the *Rocket*, one of the earliest successful railway engines. By whom and when was it built?

506 This is one of the first successful motor cars. Who invented it and when?

History

508 In political history, who was known as 'Dizzy'?

509 What sensational excursion did Rudolf Hess, Hitler's deputy, make in May 1941?

510 One of the three countries to sign the *Triple Alliance* treaty in 1882 was Austria-Hungary. What were the other two?

511 In the bargains made at the Congress of Vienna what happened to Norway?

512 An old ship 'Great Britain' is now being restored. What is its historical significance?

513 Who were the people tried at the Nuremberg or Nurnberg Trials?

514 Who were the 'Princes in the Tower' alleged by Shakespeare and others to have been murdered by Richard III?

515 What was the historic journey of the *Victoria*, or *Vittoria* that began from Sanlucar de Barrameda on September 20, 1519?

516 In the Third Crusade King Richard I of Britain was known as 'Coeur de Lion'; who was known as 'Barbarossa'?

517 William III was Stadholder of the Dutch Republic when he came to the British throne; what was the title of George I before he came to the British throne?

518 At the Battle of Waterloo Wellington commanded the British troops, who commanded the Prussian troops?

519 Whose career was ruined when his wife, the former Sarah Jennings, quarrelled with Queen Anne?

520 What was the name of the Roman Road that ran from Lincoln and through the Cotswolds to Bath and Devon?

General knowledge 8

521 Charles Perrault was a seventeenth-century philosopher who prophesied great changes through scientific invention. For what literary works is he best known today?

522 If we accept Shakespeare's version, what was the battle in which there were ten thousand Frenchmen killed and twenty-nine Englishmen dead?

523 On one famous occasion Yehudi Menuhin had a musical session with Pablo Casals; what two musical instruments were represented?

524 Picasso's paintings between 1905 and 1906 are said to belong to his 'pink period'. What title is given to the paintings of 1901 to 1904?

525 If a man claimed to have been 'shanghaied' what would he be suggesting had happened to him?

526 What was the name that the Greeks gave to the goddess of love and beauty, known to the Romans as Venus?

527 What was it that began on the 13th December 1577 and ended successfully on 26th September 1580?

528 What city is the setting for the BBC programme *Z Cars*?

529 An abbreviation of its full name is commonly used for the Russian official news agency. What is it usually known as?

530 What is the name of the imaginary line on the map that is 23 degrees 27 minutes south of the equator?

531 When the bass clef in music is called the 'F clef', what is the treble clef called?

532 Which of the arts and what particular aspect of it is represented by Kenneth MacMillan, John Cranko and Michael Fokine?

533 Why was the Locomotives-Act that was repealed in 1896 sometimes called 'The Red Flag Act'?

534 The kilowatt is a unit of electric power; what does the kilohertz measure?

Famous people 2

535 Who was the English composer who wrote an opera
for a girls' school which he called *Dido and Aeneas*?

536 Gladstone entered Parliament as a Conservative; what
was his party when he began his fourth term as
Prime Minister?

537 In which war did Florence Nightingale first achieve fame?

538 What did Napoleon do at his coronation that shocked
the traditionalists?

539 Paderewski represented his country at the Versailles
Peace Conference; but what was his main career?

540 Who was the first Governor-General of India, who was
later impeached but acquitted on charges of corruption?

541 Mr Samuel Langhorne Clemens held a pilot's licence on
the Mississippi. By what other name and what other
work is Mr Clemens better known?

542 A famous politician was created Earl of Dwyfer in the
last year of his life; by what name is he better known?

543 When Clive of India became a peer in 1760 he took the
title Baron Clive of Plassey. Why Plassey?

544 What was the unusual way in which Martin Luther
announced his *Ninety-Five Theses* to the public?

545 What famous author had the address; Gad's Hill Place,
Higham by Rochester, Kent?

546 To whom did Jane Austen dedicate her novel *Emma*?

547 Who defeated Richard Nixon in the 1960 presidential
election?

548 The engineer responsible for the Caledonian Canal began
life as the son of a Dumfriesshire shepherd; who was he?

549 Who sacked Prince Otto Eduard Leopold von Bismarck,
Chancellor of Germany, in March 1890?

550 The composers of *Die Fledermaus* and *Der Rosenkavalier*
had the same surname but were not related. Who were
they?

Speed quiz 5

551 What is the correct name for the city we usually refer to as Hull?

552 What was the dodo?

553 Whom did Shakespeare call 'A pair of star-crossed lovers'?

554 What nursery rhyme character might be said to have extracted a drupe with his pollex?

555 By what name is the *Decalogue* better known?

556 What do we call the tides produced when the sun and moon are in opposition?

557 Monday is the 'day of the moon'; what is the 'day of war'?

558 How many sides has a snow crystal?

559 Of which country is the maple leaf recognized as a national symbol?

560 In which city is the Brandenburg Gate?

561 Where can the monument of the Little Mermaid be seen?

562 Where is the Jefferson Memorial?

563 Where is the Arch of Constantine?

564 Name the three planets closest to earth.

565 How many tides are there in 24 hours?

566 Who discovered chlorine?

567 How many pips are there in the BBC eight o'clock time signal?

568 What are Samos, Lesbos, Delos, Lemnos and Patmos?

569 What kind of race is the 'Tour de France'?

570 What is the Muslim equivalent of the organization known as the Red Cross?

571 Which planet is so much like the earth in its size and mass that it is sometimes called earth's twin?

572 In the time of the ancient Romans the aristocrats were known as patricians; what name was given to the commoners?

573 In biology, what is the common name for the saline fluid that cleanses the corneal surface?

574 In what way can William Dockwra of London be said to have anticipated Rowland Hill?

575 What was the remarkable curriculum of the class in which Charlie Bates and Jack Dawkins were star pupils, described by Charles Dickens (in *Oliver Twist*)?

576 Who sometimes used the pseudonym 'Nicholas Blake'?

577 Which country might have the initials R.F. on its postage stamps?

578 In avoirdupois weight the ounce is equal to one-sixteenth of a pound. What fraction of a pound is it in Troy weight and Apothecaries' weight?

579 An important battle of World War II was fought around the Russian city now known as Volgograd; what was the name of the city before 1961?

580 Which gland in the body secretes the hormone called 'cortisone'?

581 According to Shakespeare how did Marc Antony die?

582 What action did Peter the Great of Russia take when his son, Alexis, opposed his reform work?

583 Who were the two sisters whose romances are described by D. H. Lawrence in *Women in Love*?

584 E. M. Forster wrote a book called *Howard's End*. What was 'Howard's End'?

585 What is the meaning of the Latin phrase that is sometimes used by letter-writers to the press ... *pro bono publico*?

586 In navigation what is 'dead reckoning'?

Science 4

587 The unit used to measure the intensity of sound is named after the inventor of the telephone: what is the unit of sound?

588 What name is given to the unit of the metric system which, acting upon one gramme of matter, will give it an acceleration of one centimetre per second for every second the force acts?

589 What are the two acids that are mixed to make *Aqua Regia*, the royal water that dissolves gold?

590 What is measured in 'megatons'?

591 What is added to 'quicklime' to get 'slaked lime'?

592 Ammonia is made up of two gases. One is hydrogen; what is the other?

593 Carbon is one of the chemical elements in carbohydrates; what are the other two?

594 What are the two gases commonly used to fill scientific balloons?

595 Some metals are known scientifically as noble or base. What can happen to a metal for it to be known as 'base'?

596 What was the substance that a Nobel Prize winner obtained from a ton of uranium ore at the beginning of this century?

597 What was the 'Table' that Mendeleev devised that introduced order into inorganic chemistry?

598 The *universal gas law* combines three laws named after the scientists that discovered them. Charles and Avrogadro are two of them; who is the third scientist?

599 The chemical formula for water is H_2O; what is the formula for *heavy water*?

600 There are three kinds of radioactivity. Alpha-Rays is one kind; what are the others?

Far-away places 4

601 In which country are the cities Da Lat, Da Nang and Saigon?

602 What river rises in the springs of Mount Hermon in Syria, flows through the Sea of Galilee, and empties into the Dead Sea?

603 What sea does a ship enter if it passes from the Gulf of Suez and through the Strait of Jubal?

604 What are the Baganda of Uganda?

605 Iran lies against the southern shore of the Caspian Sea. What country surrounds it on the other three sides?

606 In which European country is the head of state a 'Grand Duke' or 'Grand Duchess'?

607 What is the name of the country completely surrounded by the Republic of South Africa?

608 In which city might you be shown the balcony where Juliet stood when Romeo wooed her?

609 The Irish Sea surrounds the Isle of Man; what surrounds the Isle of Ely?

610 What was the name of the British Colony that achieved independence in October 1970?

611 A marching song in World War I claimed that it was a long way to Tipperary? Where is Tipperary?

612 What lies in between the two 'Pillars of Hercules'?

613 What are the Norwegian skerries?

614 What is the connection between the town of Dunedin in New Zealand and the capital of Scotland?

615 Cheddar Cheese is popular throughout the world but where did it originate?

Literature

616 In Hardy's *The Mayor of Casterbridge* what was the remarkable transaction that the hero made in the 'Furmity tent' at Weydon-Priors Fair?

617 In *Treasure Island* what did John Silver's parrot cry?

618 In *Peter Pan*, Captain Hook lost his arm to a crocodile. What was the result of Captain Ahab's first encounter with his quarry in Herman Melville's story?

619 What were the 'triffids' described by John Wyndham?

620 According to Alexander Dumas what was the graveyard of the prison of Monte Cristo?

621 What was the name of the submarine that Jules Verne sent 'Twenty Thousand leagues under the sea'?

622 What race of fairy people, whose relatives are the Harpsichords, the Overmantels and the Clocks, live under the kitchen floor of an old house in Bedfordshire?

623 According to Tennyson, who was the only knight of the Round Table to survive King Arthur?

624 What novel begins with the words:
'Sir Walter Elliot, of Kellynch-hall, in Somersetshire, was a man who, for his own amusement, never took up any book but the Baronetage ...'?

625 In a poem describing an eighteenth-century 'drop-out' Wordsworth appeals

> 'As in the eye of Nature he has lived,
> So in the eye of Nature let him die!'

What is the title of the poem?

626 In the play by Sophocles who was Antigone's wicked uncle?

627 Who was Tom Sawyer's 'idle, lawless, and vulgar friend – the juvenile pariah of the village'?

628 Australia was the setting for D. H. Lawrence's novel *Kangaroo*. What country was the setting for his novel *The Plumed Serpent*?

Team quiz 4

629a Who was the pilgrim in *Pilgrim's Progress*?

630a Who was 'The Count of Monte Cristo'?

631a Who was 'Kidnapped'?

632a Who had 'Cider with Rosie'?

633a Who was the Irish poet who signed his poetry 'AE'?

634a Why did Ireland's population decline after 1845?

635a A red-haired Highland outlaw, who fought a feud against the Duke of Montrose, gave his name to one of Sir Walter Scott's novels. Who was he?

636a Which of Scott's epic poems had the sub-title *A Tale of Flodden Field*?

637a Our telephone greeting is 'Hallo'. In what countries would these greetings be: 'Pronto' and 'Shalom'?

638a Who sent this message and by what means: 'What hath God wrought'?

639a What was the nationality of these two scientists who contributed to the development of radio and television? James Clerk Maxwell and Lee de Forest.

640a Who sent the first message by radio across the Atlantic and in which county was our transmitting station?

641a The Norfolk and Suffolk type of lifeboat was first built in 1807 at the request of the Suffolk Humane Society. The inventor was a lifeboat pioneer; who was he?

642a A French earl is often said to be the founder of the British Parliament; who was he?

643a Who wrote *The Caucasian Chalk Circle*?

644a Who wrote *Waiting for Godot*?

629b Who had 'Great Expectations'?

630b Who was the 'Mayor of Casterbridge'?

631b Who, in his 'Travels into Several Remote Nations of the World', travelled to 'Lilliput'?

632b Whom was Sir Patrick Spens commanded to bring home?

633b What was the pen-name of Mary Ann Evans?

634b What is the connection between the Royal Pavilion, Brighton, The Haymarket Theatre, London and the conservatory at Shane's Castle in Ireland?

635b What was it that Burns called: 'Wee, modest, crimson-tipped flow'r . . .'?

636b What battle is commemorated by Burns in his song *The Lovely Lass o' Inverness*?

637b What is the morse code for S.O.S.?

638b Alexander Graham Bell is generally recognized as the inventor of the telephone. What was his job when he completed his university courses?

639b What contribution, made to physics in 1878 by Sir William Crookes, was eventually to benefit modern television and radar?

640b Michael Faraday's discoveries helped in the development of radio. What was his job when he first joined the Royal Institution of Great Britain?

641b What was the discovery made in 1939 at Sutton Hoo, Suffolk?

642b The royal treasurer to King Henry I founded Kenilworth Castle; who was he?

643b Who wrote *Under Milk Wood*?

644b Who wrote *The Quare Fellow*?

645 N.A.S.A. organizes civilian space missions in the United States. What do the letters N.A.S.A. stand for?

646 Who succeeded Colonel Nasser as president of Egypt?

647 Who married whom at Holyrood in August 1503 and so gave the Stuarts a claim to the English throne?

648 Great Britain buried her Unknown Soldier in Westminster Abbey. Where did France bury her Unknown Soldier?

649 For whom are the famous Swiss Guards the bodyguard?

650 The Long Parliament opened in 1640. In what year was it finally dissolved?

651 The earth's crust is made up of three major classes of rock. Sedimentary and metamorphic are the names given to two of them; what is the third class?

652 What name is given to the cartilage lid in the throat that prevents food and drink going the 'wrong way'?

653 What name is used to describe an official of the former Chinese Empire, a dialect and a citrus fruit?

654 The ancient Egyptians regarded the scarab and the apis as sacred creatures. The scarab was a beetle, what was the apis?

655 What is the name of the nation that before 1964 consisted of Tanganyika and Zanzibar?

656 Bedell Smith headed the delegation that accepted Germany's surrender on May 7th, 1945. Who signed the terms of surrender for Germany?

657 Who thought up a new religion while he meditated under the Bo Tree?

658 A 'billion' in America is one thousand millions. In Great Britain it is a million millions. What is the numerical difference between the two?

659 V–E day celebrated the end of World War II in Europe. How is the end of the War in the East identified?

Master brain 3

660 Who was the Italian count who founded the newspaper *Il Risorgimento* that prepared the way for the unification of Italy?

661 A Dutchman, named Van der Lubbe, was executed for starting a famous fire. What fire was he alleged to have started?

662 In metrication the prefixes are derived from the Greek; what number does the prefix 'myria' represent in the metric system?

663 Who was the British Prime Minister who said: 'England has saved herself by her exertions; and will, as I trust, save Europe by her example'?

664 What name is given to the instrument developed by Charles Wilson to determine the path of atomic particles?

665 Shelley's traveller saw 'two vast and trunkless legs of stone stand in the desert'. Whose statue did they belong to?

666 What is the ionosphere that plays such an important part in radio communication?

667 Monsoons are a feature of Asian weather. What causes monsoons?

668 What was the famous pamphlet written by Engels and Marx in 1847 which became the basic document of communism?

669 In the French Revolution who were the *Mountain* and the *Plain*?

670 The name of the famous Norwegian whirlpool or current has been incorporated into the English language and is generally used to mean a violent confusion. What is the word?

671 What were the two events in British history known as the 'Fifteen' and the 'Forty-Five'?

Who am I?

To be read aloud:
This is a 'Who am I?' set with facts about a person, living or dead, historical or legendary. If you know who it is after the first fact is given to you, you score 3 points; after the second fact, 2 points; after the third fact, 1 point.

672 (i) My name at birth in 1879 was Lev Davidson Bronstein. By what name am I known to history? (ii) In the Russian Revolution I was the first Soviet commissar of foreign affairs and became commissar of war. (iii) I was expelled from the Communist Party in 1927 and murdered in Mexico on August 20, 1940.

673 (i) Born on the 6th May, 1758, I became a French revolutionary. Carlyle called me the 'sea-green incorruptible'. (ii) Elected to the Committee of Public Safety I established the *Terror*. (iii) Conspirators captured me and I was executed on the guillotine on July 28, 1794.

674 (i) In 1766 I discovered the properties of hydrogen, calling it 'inflammable air'. (ii) Later I showed that water is a compound of hydrogen and oxygen. (iii) In 1798 I measured the density of the earth.

675 (i) I was born at The Hague in 1629. I invented the micrometer. (ii) I investigated and championed the wave theory of light. (iii) I was the first to use a pendulum to regulate the escapement of a clock.

676 (i) I was born in 1944 at Scunthorpe, Lincolnshire, and became a professional golfer in 1962. (ii) In 1967 I won the New Zealand P.G.A. championship and played in the British Ryder Cup Team. (iii) In 1969 I was the British Open Golf Champion; unbeaten in the Ryder Cup match in which Britain tied with the U.S.

677 (i) I was a girl who came from Ealing in London, and was coached by my father in athletics. (ii) I won the 800 metres European Athletics Championship in Athens in September 1969. (iii) I was pipped at the post by a French girl in the final of the 400 metres in the 1968 Mexico Olympics, gaining a silver medal.

678 (i) Born in 1918, I led the revolt that established Egypt as a republic. (ii) I seized control of the Suez Canal in 1956. (iii) As well as being president, I also became prime minister of Egypt in 1967.

679 (i) Born in 1892, I led the movement that abolished monarchy in Yugoslavia. (ii) In 1948 I declared Yugoslavia's independence from Russian communism. (iii) I became president of Yugoslavia in 1953.

680 (i) A hurdler I am now seeking medals for the Decathlon. (ii) I spent some years in the U.S.A. before representing Britain in the Mexico Olympic Games. (iii) I won a gold medal in the 400 metres hurdles in Mexico.

681 (i) Nobel prize winner for literature in 1923 I wrote:
'Romantic Ireland's dead and gone,
It's with O'Leary in the grave . . .'
(ii) I wrote many plays for Dublin's Abbey Theatre.
(iii) I wrote: 'I have spread my dreams under your feet:
Tread softly because you tread on my
dreams'.

682 (i) Nobel prize winner for literature in 1948 I wrote:
'Here I am, an old man in a dry month,
Being read to by a boy, waiting for rain'.
(ii) I wrote a play about Becket's murder.
(iii) I wrote: 'What images return, O my daughter . . .'

General knowledge 11

683 Who is the former film star who is governor of California?

684 G. K. Chesterton talks of going 'to Glastonbury by way of Goodwin Sands'. Where are the Goodwin Sands?

685 Somerset Maugham based his novel *The Moon and Sixpence* on the life of a famous painter. Who was he?

686 What object from top to bottom is 7,899·86 miles, and from side to side, straight through the centre, is 7,926·39 miles?

687 Who was the arch-enemy of the tenants of 221b Baker Street?

688 In embroidery what is shadow work?

689 How would you storm-set a tent?

690 What is the Gulf Stream?

691 Linus Carl Pauling won the Nobel Chemistry Prize in 1954. What was the category of his second Nobel prize which he won in 1962?

692 What process of cooking can be defined as 'to brown meat etc., quickly, and then cook long and slowly in a tightly covered pan with very little liquid'?

693 How many foot-pounds of work per second equals one horsepower?

694 On which side of its body are both eyes of the turbot?

695 What London station was the terminus of Brunel's Great Western Railway?

696 How does the fathometer work?

697 What or where was the national observatory that determined the line of the *prime meridian*?

698 Quicksilver and a planet share a name; what is it?

699 What name is given to the region of calms between the trade winds?

700 The French national flag is sometimes known as the 'tricolour'. What are the three colours?

Answers

General knowledge 1

1 Jupiter. Diameter at its equator is about 88,700 miles which is about 11 times the diameter of the earth.

2 Capri, in the Bay of Naples.

3 Pineal Gland (or Pineal *Body*). About the size of a pea situated in the upper part of the mid-brain.

4 A Free Port is a port at which goods, either imports or exports, may be loaded or unloaded without payment of customs duty.

5 Robert Baden-Powell, the founder of the Scouts, was in command of the defence of Mafeking in its historic siege in the Boer War.

6 Go round the world in 80 days. In the novel *Around the World in Eighty Days*.

7 Larboard or Port. The opposite side is starboard.

8 A warm and dry wind. The *foehn* like the *mistral* blows down from the mountains. The air loses its moisture as it rises to the mountain-top. It is heated by compression as it comes down the other side of the mountain. *Foehns* blow frequently in the Alps.

9 A pencil. Latin *penicillus* = little tail or little brush.

10 From Bikini Island in the South Pacific. (An atoll in the Marshall Islands.) May be so named from the briefness of the native dress there. Bikini Island was in the news when the fashion first began because of the atomic-bomb tests that USA was carrying out there.

11 On a sundial. It is the flat piece of metal that casts the shadow which tells the time.

12 Mahogany. Thomas Chippendale (1718–1779) worked almost exclusively in mahogany.

13 A financial crash that ruined thousands of people and shook the British Government.

14 1. Inferno (or hell); 2. Purgatorio (or Purgatory);
3. Paradiso (or Heaven). The theme is what happens to the soul after death.

15 George Smith Patton, Jnr. His toughness and rough speech earned the nickname. He commanded the Third Army in the French campaign.

16 'The Citizen King'. So called because he was elected king by the citizens of Paris (reigned 1830–1848).

17 1. *The Tatler* (1709–1711); 2. *The Spectator* (1711–1712). He founded them with Sir Richard Steele who created Sir Roger de Coverley.

18 The Tumtum Tree. Lewis Carroll in *Jabberwocky*.

19 He lived on top of a stone pillar. Born in Syria, he adopted this form of life to call attention to the evil habits of the Syrians.

Nature 1

20 Thallophyta (or Thallophytes). This sub-kingdom includes one-celled bacteria, algae (sea-weeds) and fungi.

21 Nightingale.

22 Wings.

23 Ten.

24 Flax.

25 The dragon-fly. The nymph hatches from the egg and remains in the water for 1 to 5 years.

26 The hydra has five to seven tentacles. Each tentacle has tiny cells that contain stinging threads. The hydra drives these threads into its prey, and they give off a poison that paralyses the victim. Then the tentacles draw the victim into the mouth so that the hydra can swallow it.

27 'Yellow' eels is the name given to eels in fresh water. 'Silver' eels is the name given to eels in the sea.

28 Protozoan. Metazoan are many-celled animals:
   protozoan are one-celled animals.
29 Two. In the first season the plants put forth leaves and
   roots. During the winter they remain dormant. The
   next spring or summer they bear flowers and seed, then
   die. Thus their life span is two years or two growing
   seasons.
30 Four.
31 Spinnerets. Usually 6 but can be 4 or 2. Attached to
   rear of abdomen. Tip is called the *spinning field*, and
   the surface of each spinning field is covered by as many
   as a hundred *spinning tubes*, through which liquid silk
   flows from silk glands in the spider's abdomen to the
   outside of its body. The silk then hardens into a thread.
32 Drones. Their only function is to mate with a young
   queen.
33 Pupa or chrysalis. Not *cocoon*, which is the name of
   the case.
34 Staminodes or staminodium (sing.) or staminodia
   (plural).
35 Andromous.
36 Jointed legs.

Far-away places 1

37 Leichtenstein.
38 Andorra. The country covers an area of 175 square
   miles in the Pyrenees between France and Spain. The
   official name of Andorra in Catalan is 'Valls d'Andorra'.
39 1. Thailand. 2. Laos.
40 A range of mountains that runs through the western
   part of North America. They extend, north to south, for
   over 3,000 miles, from northern New Mexico to
   northern Alaska.

41 1. A glacier. 2. Mont Blanc.
Mont Blanc is in the Alps, on the border of France
and Italy, near Switzerland.

42 Singapore.

43 1. Norway. 2. Sweden. 3. Finland. 4. Russia.

44 Villages or small hamlets.

45 Burgundy.

46 Madrid.

47 Cambodia.

48 Strait of Otranto.

49 Albania.

50 Lough Neagh, in Northern Ireland. Covers an area of
about 150 square miles.

51 Lake Nasser, after the late president of Egypt, Gomal
Abdal Nasser . . . it will be about 300 miles long.
Water from lake is to be used to irrigate.

52 They are in the British Antarctic Territory.

53 $23\frac{1}{2}$ degrees.

54 1. Steppes in Russia.   2. Veld in South Africa.

Speed quiz 1

55 Hexagon.

56 River Rhône.

57 Israel.

58 Swiss.

59 Strasbourg, in France.

60 The Undersea World. He invented the aqualung, with
Emil Gagnan in 1943, founded the French navy's
undersea research group in 1945, wrote a book *The
Silent World* in 1953. He has made many television and
feature films about his research.

61 Beware of the Dog.

62 The trident.

63 Britain.

64 Carpenter.
65 Edward VI . . . by Jane Seymour.
66 Kilowatt.
67 Dry ice . . . CO_2
68 Sir John Falstaff.
69 Blood.
70 Coconut. It is the dried meat. Copra oil is valuable for its oil used in soap etc.
71 Your skin.
72 River Jordan.

Who wrote. . .?

73 Percy Bysshe Shelley
    i Ozymandias.
    ii Adonais.
    iii Ode to the West Wind.

74 Rudyard Kipling
    i Recessional.
    ii Boots.
    iii Gunga Din.

75 John Milton
    i Paradise Lost.
    ii On His Blindness.
    iii Samson Agonistes.

76 John Keats
    i Lines on the Mermaid Tavern.
    ii Endymion.
    iii Ode to a Nightingale.

77 William Wordsworth
    i I wandered lonely as a cloud OR *The Daffodils.*
    ii Lucy: She dwelt among the untrodden ways.
    iii The Prelude. Book XI

78 Lord Byron (George Gordon Noel Byron)
    i The Destruction of Sennacherib.
    ii Don Juan.
    iii She walks in beauty.

79 D. H. Lawrence
>   *i Bat.*
>   *ii Humming-Bird.*
>   *iii Mountain Lion.*

80 Edward Lear
>   *i By way of preface.*
>   *ii Incidents in the life of my Uncle Arly.*
>   *iii The Owl and the Pussycat.*

81 Thomas Hardy
>   *i Great Things.*
>   *ii Drummer Hodge.*
>   *iii Friends Beyond.*

82 Thomas Campbell
>   *i Hohenlinden.*
>   *ii Battle of the Baltic.*
>   *iii Ye Mariners of England.*

83 Robert Herrick
>   *i A sweet disorder in the dress.*
>   *ii To Anthea who may command him everything.*
>   *iii To Daffodils.*

General knowledge 2

84 Gestapo. Short for Geheime Staatspolizei (Secret State Police) established in 1933.

85 Utrecht in Holland. The treaty was named the Peace of Utrecht. Signed in 1713, it recognized the French Duke of Anjou as King of Spain.

86 Heinrich Schliemann . . . in 1870.

87 Quirinal Palace.

88 A bundle of sticks containing an axe with the blade projecting. From the Latin *fasces* plural of *fascis* = bundle.

89 In the Russian Calendar the date was October 25th.

90   Quinine . . . which is taken from the bark of the tree mainly grown in Java, is used to reduce the fever not to cure the disease.

91   The speed of sound. Mach (pronounced mark) number is a number expressing in decimals the ratio of the speed of an object to the speed of sound in the same medium, the speed of sound being Mach One. An aircraft travelling at half the speed of sound has a Mach number of 0·5.

92   The Pardoner. In *Canterbury Tales* by Geoffrey Chaucer. The men discover a treasure, and kill each other in the vain attempt to keep it all for themselves.

93   The donkey . . . In G. K. Chesterton's *The Donkey*.

94   Discovery of penicillin. Penicillin was discovered in 1928 by Fleming. In 1940 Howard W. Florey of Australia and Ernst B. Chain of Great Britain reported how penicillin could be purified for use.

95   Sergeant Francis Troy. Bathsheba married him on a sudden impulse. He forsook her only to return on the night of the declaration of betrothal of Bathsheba to Boldwood. The infuriated farmer shot him, and was 'confined during Her Majesty's pleasure'. Bathsheba then married the man who had loved her throughout – Farmer Gabriel Oak.

96   Mohammed. Mohammed means 'Praised one'. His followers are known as *Moslems*. He was an Arab born in Mecca about A.D. 570. *Islam* is an Arabic word meaning submission.

97   The debris, consisting of rocks and soil etc., that are deposited at the side or end of the glacier or beneath the glacier as the glacier melts.

98   'I forbid'. The five permanent members of the Security Council alone have the special power to veto any decision of action of the group. These members are:

France, Great Britain, Nationalist China, Russia and the United States.

The Bible

99 The Revelation of Saint John the Divine.

100 Uriah. David sent him to his death during the siege of Rabbath-ammon by putting him in the forefront of the battle (2 Sam. 11 v. 2–17).

101 Methuselah (Genesis 5: 25–27).

102 Seven. Joshua Chapter 6: 'And ye shall compass the city, all ye men of war, and go round about the city once. Thus shalt thou do six days. And seven priests shall bear before the ark seven trumpets of rams' horns; and on the seventh day ye shall compass the city seven times . . .'

103 Joseph said that the dream meant that there would be seven years of plenty followed by seven years of famine.

104 Light.

105 Samson.

106 He saw a ladder reaching between earth and heaven, and angels ascending and descending it. The Lord was at the top of the ladder. Jacob received the prophecy of his future and the future of his race.

107 Locusts and wild honey.

108 Raiment of camel's hair and a leather girdle.

109 He took some favourite venison meat to his father pretending that he was Esau. When his father was suspicious of his voice Jacob let him feel his hands which Rebekah had covered with the skins of the kids of the goats because Esau was hairy and Jacob's skin smooth. Isaac then thought Jacob was Esau and gave him the blessing reserved for the first born.

110 Simeon at the presentation of the infant Jesus in the temple (Luke 2 v. 30).
111 The Anointed One.
112 The changing of the water into wine at a wedding in Cana of Galilee (John 2 v. 1–11).
113 Bathsheba.
114 Hebrew.
115 Andrew (John 1: 40).
116 Stephen (Acts 7).
117 David.

Science 1

118 $V = \Pi r^2 h$ (pi = r squared × height).
119 An aromatic hydrocarbon (equals methyl benzine ($C_6H_5CH_3$)).
120 1. Radiation. 2. Convection 3. Conduction.
    Radiation: The heat travels as (electro-magnetic) waves.
    Convection: The less dense warm air (or water, or any other gas or liquid medium) rises and gives place to the more dense cool air (etc.) which flows in to take its place.
    Conduction: The heat is transferred from molecule to molecule in a material.
121 Electro-magnetic inductance. Named after Joseph Henry (1797–1878), an American physicist.
122 Gram.
123 Tiny irreducible bits of energy. Planck's concept that radiant energy is composed of tiny packets or bundles of quanta disagreed completely with former ideas about the nature of radiation. Scientists had thought that radiation was a continuous stream of energy that had a wavelike motion. These theories had not explained the absorption and emission of energy by matter. Planck's

theory accounted for the red, green and ultra-violet light emitted by a glowing object. The 'quantum theory' revolutionized physics. Max Planck was awarded the Nobel Prize for Physics in 1918.

124 An alternating electric current. A rectifier is an electronic device that can change alternating current to direct current.

125 Alcohol. Usually ethyl alcohol or ethanol which is ordinary alcohol. Tincture of iodine and tincture of quinine are well-known medicines.

126 1. Hydrogen. 2. carbon. These chemical compounds are called hydrocarbons.

127 1. Nitrogen. 2. phosphorus.
Nitrogen is usually added in the form of nitrate of soda, ammonium sulphate or manure.
Phosphorus comes as bone meal or super-phosphate.
Potash is found in wood ash, and is used as potassium sulphate or potassium chloride.
A complete fertilizer contains all three elements.

128 1. Methane 2. propane.

129 Yellow phosphorus catches fire spontaneously in air. For this reason it can be stored and handled safely only under water.

130 Pitchblende. Also contained in the ore are polonium and actinium. The Curies used pitchblende in the original discovery of radium.

131 CU.

132 The effects of forces in causing or changing the motion of objects. Part of the science of dynamics deals with the properties of matter and forces. Divided into two branches – statics and kinetics. Statics deals with the conditions under which material bodies do not change motion when acted upon by various forces. Kinetics deals with the changes of motion.

133   A chloride such as sodium (common salt) is treated with hot concentrated sulphuric acid. This gives the gas, hydrogen chloride, which is dissolved in water to give hydrochloric acid.

Team quiz 1

134a   Helios.

134b   Neptune (or Neptunus) or Poseidon.

135a   H. G. Wells.

135b   Jules Verne.

136a   Sirius (Dog Star).

136b   Challenger Deep, south west of Guam in Pacific. 36,198 feet below earth's surface.

137a   Project Mercury or Project Gemini.

137b   A bathyscaphe. Designed by Auguste Piccard and his son Jacques. Jacques descended 35,800 feet with a companion. The bathyscaphe is a steel sphere.

138a   The tulip.

138b   Maple leaf.

139a   1. Mediterranean 2. Spain. The chief islands are Majorca, Minorca and Ibiza.

139b   1. Atlantic Ocean. 2. Newfoundland.
500 miles stretch of shallow water curving in an arc off the south-east coast of Newfoundland. Beginning about 100 miles from Cape Race at the south-eastern tip of Newfoundland, and extending as far as 300 miles out into the Atlantic Ocean.

140a   Rikki-Tikki-Tavi.

140b   Scrooge.

141a   Justice. As at the Old Bailey, Central Criminal Law Courts in London.

141b   Minerva. Goddess of wisdom and war, arts and crafts. Daughter of Jupiter (Zeus) and Metis (Wisdom).

Jupiter swallowed Metis before Minerva was born and Minerva (Athena) sprang fully grown and dressed in armour from the forehead of Jupiter. The magic shield had the head of Medusa in the centre of it.

142a 22. In each series of three, each number is doubled. The series beginning with 11 should continue to 22 and then 44.

142b 70. The pattern is plus 2, plus 4, and repeat. We finish with a plus 2 so we should logically follow with plus 4.

143a He turned into Mr Hyde. His worst self: a deformed maniacal sadist. He could change back again by drinking the antidote until that potion failed to act. In 'The Strange Case of Dr. Jekyll and Mr Hyde'.

143b Dorian Gray. In Wilde's only novel *The Picture of Dorian Gray* the portrait ages and grows ugly as a reflection of his moral corruption, while Dorian Gray's actual appearance remains the same.

144a 1. Mainland (378 sq. miles). 2. Yell (83 sq. miles). 3. Unst (47 sq. miles).

144b 1. Lewis (with Harris). 2. North Uist. 3. South Uist.

145a Calcite or calcium carbonate.

145b Upper Jurassic limestone (overlain with Portland Beds) or Oolitic limestone.

146a Bourbons. (1589–1792) First ruler Henry IV. Last ruler Louis XVI.

146b Romanovs. (1613–1917) First ruler was Michael. Last ruler was Nicholas II.

147a In radioactive elements, such as radium and uranium.

147b In outer space. They are extremely high-energy sub-atomic particles and many can penetrate thousands of feet of rock. Their precise origin is unknown.

148a Peter Abelard was a churchman and Heloise did not want to stand in his way in his advancement in the

Church. She denied their marriage and became a nun.
Peter Abelard became a monk. Peter Abelard
(1079–1142) lectured on philosophy in Paris. Heloise
was the niece of Canon Fulbert of Notre Dame. When
their love was discovered Heloise denied their marriage.
The Church ultimately condemned Abelard as a heretic.
The love letters of the pair are considered some of the
most moving letters ever written. When Heloise died
she was buried at Abelard's side.

148b John Donne was secretary to Sir Thomas Egerton. He
married Egerton's niece, Ann More, against her father's
will. In revenge the father had Donne imprisoned and
damaged his career.

149a 'It is a sweet and glorious thing to die for one's
country'. *Dulce et Decorum Est* by Wilfred Owen.

149b 'I think it a shame when the worthy Homer nods'.

Famous people 1

150 Sarah Bernhardt (1844–1923). She still acted after one
of her legs was amputated in 1915.

151 John of Gaunt. The Black Prince was his elder brother,
and it was his son who succeeded Edward III to become
Richard II. Bolingbroke was the Duke of Lancaster's
son and he fought against and defeated Richard II to
become the first Lancastrian king. John of Gaunt was
born at Ghent in Belgium and this is how he became
known as '. . . of Gaunt'.

152 Duke of Wellington would have met Bismarck.
Wellington, formerly Arthur Wellesley (1769–1852).
Prince Bismarck-Schonhausen, Otto Eduard Leopold
von Bismarck (1815–1898).

153 In Russia. Born Golda Mobovitz in Kiev, Russia, she
went with her family in 1906 to Milwaukee, U.S.A.

In 1921 she joined a collective farm village in Palestine.
154 Joan of Arc.
155 General Dwight D. Eisenhower
156 Edward (Ted).
1. Joseph was killed in World War II (1944).
2. John was assassinated at Dallas, Texas (1963).
3. Robert was assassinated at Los Angeles, California (1968).
157 He developed the V-2 rocket used by the Germans to bombard London.
158 Anne Frank. She died in Belsen. Her diary (The Diary of a Young Girl) was published in 1947 and was made into a play and a film.
159 Leon Trotsky. Born Lev Davidovich Bronstein in Ukraine in 1879.
160 Franklin Delano Roosevelt.
161 Sir Humphry Davy. Sir Humphry Davy (1778–1829) invented the 'Davy' lamp, a safety lamp still used by miners.
162 Y.M.C.A. or Young Men's Christian Association. Founded in London in 1844.
163 Roald Amundsen . . . in the *Gjoa*.

General knowledge 3

164 *Virtual image* – the image formed when the rays from each point of the object diverge as if from a point beyond the reflecting or refracting surface. Such images cannot be placed on a screen. *Real image* – the image formed by the actual convergence of rays. A real image can be caught on a screen, a virtual image cannot.
165 Juvenal's Satires . . . Nos. III and IX.

166 His father, King Hamlet, appeared as a ghost and described it to him.

167 Mayflower. They were later known as the Pilgrim Fathers. Puritans, they became known as Separatists because they separated from the Church of England. The Speedwell never succeeded in making the trip. The voyage lasted from September 1620 to November 21, 1620.

168 Sir Arthur Sullivan. L. Sabine Baring-Gould wrote the words for a school festival in a Yorkshire village in 1865. The pupils of Horbury Bridge School who were invited lived some distance away, so the parson wrote a hymn for the children to sing as they marched from one village to the other.

169 Lagan or lagend or ligan. From the Scandinavian *lagnir*.

170 A lighthouse. One of the Seven Wonders of the World. Built about 300 B.C. on the island of Pharos near Alexandria in Egypt. Was the world's first important lighthouse and existed for 1,000 years before it was destroyed by an earthquake.

171 *Wuthering Heights* in the book by Emily Bronte.

172 Burl Ives.

173 He has had rotten eggs thrown at him. Eggs consist of organic compounds that contain sulphur. When such compounds decompose they produce hydrogen sulphide.

174 He was the first Secretary-General of the United Nations. Elected for 5 years in 1946 and continued until 1950. He then continued in office until 1953, when he resigned because of Russia's opposition to his support of the U.N.'s action in South Korea. He was a Norwegian.

175 'Black Shirts' because they wore black shirts.

176 *Libel* is a written or printed statement. *Slander* is spoken. Defamation are false statements that will harm a person's reputation or hold him up to ridicule or contempt.

177 Red or American Indians or North American Indians. In *The Last of the Mohicans*. They were two tribes formerly living in the Upper Hudson valley and in Connecticut.

178 The White Queen who was constantly ordering 'Off with his head!'

Picture quiz 1 – Inventions

179 (*i*) Reflecting telescope. (*ii*) Isaac Newton.

180 1837, by Samuel Morse.

181 (*i*) Nicolas Joseph Cugnot. (1725–1804). (*ii*) Steam.

182 1797, by André Garnerin, who descended from a balloon over Paris.

183 John Marshall, c. 1700.

184 Jethro Tull (1647–1741).

Speed quiz 2

185 1851. The Crystal Palace was an iron and glass building designed by Joseph Paxton for the Great Exhibition in London and erected in Hyde Park. Rebuilt at Sydenham near London. Destroyed by fire in 1936.

186 Delta. Name applied to rivers which divide into branches near its mouth. So named because they take the shape of a triangle which is the Greek 'delta'.

187 Bangkok, Thailand. South-east Asia Treaty Organization.

188 Mae West. First used in World War II. Light and thin and inflated from a small bottle of compressed air built into the jacket.

189 Thomas Gray. *Elegy written in a Country Churchyard.*

190 50 (new) pence piece.

191 Riboflavin. Part of the vitamin B Complex (15 vitamins in all). Occurs in yeast, milk, liver, eggs, poultry, fish and green and leafy vegetables. For growth, healthy skin, proper functioning of eyes and body's use of oxygen.

192 Tziganes.

193 The dove.

194 Crying. The lachrymal glands lie under the outer part of the upper eyelid. They produce tears.

195 Sodium.

196 China . . . more than 742,000,000.

197 Boadicea or Boudicca.

198 A synagogue.

199 John F. Kennedy.

200 Highbury.

201 Syria.

202 Robert Louis Stevenson.

203 Lotus flower.

204 Greece.

Nature 2

205 Marsupials. Rodents are animals with front teeth especially suited to gnawing hard objects. Marsupials are animals whose young are raised in a pouch in the mother's body. Almost all marsupials live in Australia.

206 A flower. 'Cuckoo flower' is also acceptable. An alternative name for this flower is ladysmock.

207 Oxygen. Water is taken in through the mouth. Oxygen, extracted from the water, passes through the membranes, etc. of the gills to enter the blood stream.

208 A monkey.

209 Six.

210 Its spines.

211   It makes a shallow cup of bits of material glued together with saliva. Built in crevices and holes in buildings, under eaves, and sometimes in rocky cliffs.

212   The slender stalk by which the leaf is attached to the stem. The main part of the leaf is known as the 'blade'. The word comes from the Latin *petiolus* = stalk.

213   Its colour is light grey shaded or blotched with a deeper hue.

214   1. Tree has one trunk. 2. Shrub has a number of trunks or stems.

215   Rabbits.

216   1. A fruit is the seed or seeds of a plant together with parts that enclose them (Apple, tomato, etc.).
2. A vegetable is the edible stem, leaf or root of a plant (rhubarb, potato, etc.).

217   Three.

218   Formic acid.

219   A cluster of flat, rounded leaves grows at the base of the stem. Drops of sticky fluid, produced by gland-bearing hairs, appear on the leaves. Insects stick to the fluid. The hairs fold round the insect and hold it. Fluid covers the insect and finally suffocates it. The glands then produce juices that digest the victim.

220   It points its long bill upwards and stands quite still. As it lives in marshes among reeds, the camouflage is ideal. The colours merge with its surroundings and the upturned bill looks like a reed.

221   An amphibian.

222   On the ground.

Far-away places 2

223   Kiel Canal (or Nord-Ostsee Kanal or Kaiser Wilhelm Canal). Begun in 1887 and opened in 1895. In north-western Germany leading from Brunsbuttelkoog

at the mouth of the Elbe to Holtenau near Kiel.
61 miles long.

224   Thailand.

225   The Moon. On the side we see. The 'lakes' in reality
      are dry plains.

226   Darling River. About 1,700 miles long, so that the
      river system is often referred to as the Murray-Darling.
      A second tributary of some note is the 1,350 mile long
      Murrumbidgee river.

227   Ghana.

228   1. Argentina. 2. Chile. Dedicated on March 13, 1904.
      Stands on the border.

229   Ireland.

230   Plains of silt or mud, covered with water during the wet
      season.

231   It is a bell tower or campanile. Begun in 1174 and
      completed in 1350, the ground started to sink beneath
      the tower of Pisa before it was finished. Eight storeys
      altogether, each one consists of arches resting on
      columns. The top storey houses the bells.

232   West Indies Associated States. The others are:
      Antigua; Dominica; St Christopher (St Kitts);
      Nevis-Anguilla; St Lucia.

233   The cowboys on the South American pampas. Usually
      of mixed Spanish and Indian blood. Skilful riders,
      they either made their living catching wild cattle and
      selling their hides or, more legally, working as cattle
      hands on the ranches. They are a dwindling occupation
      today, their work being done by day labourers.

234   Off the southern tip of South America.

235   St George's Channel. About 100 miles long and 60 to
      100 miles wide. Channel runs from Holyhead and
      Dublin to St. David's Head.

236 River Rhône. Rises in the Rhône glacier in Switzerland. Flows through Lake Geneva and enters France. Empties into the Mediterranean.

237 Lake Michigan. The others are Lakes Superior, Huron, Erie and Ontario. These are shared by Canada and the United States.

238 Argentina. It also forms the boundary between Uruguay and Argentina.

239 Its seaweed. The Dead Sea is the saltiest body of water in the world. The Sargasso Sea has no land boundaries of any kind to mark it off from the rest of the North Atlantic Ocean. It is set apart only by the presence of seaweed which floats on the surface.

240 In the French and Spanish provinces of the Pyrenees Mountains. They live on the slopes of the Pyrenees, nearly 2 million in the Spanish provinces along the Bay of Biscay and on the French frontier. Nearly half-a-million Basques live in French provinces in the Pyrenees. They have retained their old language and customs.

General knowledge 4

241 'Gaggle'.

242 Runes. From the Gothic word meaning 'secret'. Used earlier than A.D. 1000s.

243 The 'Outcaste' of Indians known as the 'Untouchables'.

244 Thomas Chatterton, who wrote a series of poems that he claimed had been written by a monk named Thomas Rowley. The fraud was not discovered until after his death (when he was less than 18).

245 Hundred Years' War. England won the battles but did not win the war.

246 'Jupiter' Symphony.

247 John Howard. He became High Sheriff of Bedfordshire in 1773 and published his book in 1777. He was famous for his labours to secure prison reforms.

248 The landing of James Cook in Botany Bay.

249 The time of the year when the sun appears vertically overhead at noon at the Equator. All places on the earth have equal day and night – 12 hours each. The sun rises exactly in the west everywhere. There are two equinoxes: March 21 (about) which is the spring or vernal equinox: about September 20 which is the autumnal equinox.

250 Aspirin.

251 It was the popular name for the gallows in London. It occupied a site close to the present-day Marble Arch, from the 1100s to late 1700s.

252 Viola, in *Twelfth Night*. The duke is Orsino.

253 Holy Roman Empire. Ruled by German kings between 962 and 1806. 'Second Reich' was the German Empire 1871 to 1919.

254 Brünnhilde. In Wagner's opera, Siegfried rescued Brünnhilde from her mountain prison. Gunther, a half-brother of a Nibelung, gave Siegfried a magic potion that made him forget her. He was killed and Brünnhilde rode her horse into the funeral pyre.

255 Lipizzan or Lippizanners. They come from horses trained originally in Spain and Italy and imported into Austria in the sixteenth century.

Picture quiz 2 – Music

a 'The Bonny Banks of Loch Lomond' (last 2 lines).

b 'The Wraggle Taggle Gipsies, O!'

c 'The Ash Grove' (last 2 lines).

d 'The Minstrel Boy' (last 2 lines).

Science 2

256 Infra-red rays. The films used are sensitive to infra-red rays. The rays have too long a wavelength to be seen by the human eye.

257 Radioactivity.

258 A meter. 39·37 inches.

259 Lithium. Soft, silver-white metallic element, never found in the free state but always combined with other elements.

260 The ether theory: that ether was the medium in outer space through which light was transmitted. Before the experiment in 1887 many scientists believed that ether occupied the spaces between the atoms that made up matter. In the Michelson-Morley experiment their measurements of the speed of light showed that the motion of the earth in regard to the sun had no influence upon the velocity of light. Therefore light has a uniform velocity. The result of this experiment is of great importance for the theory of relativity and provided experimental verification for some aspects of Einstein's relativity theory.

261 Bleaching powder or chloride of lime. Consists mainly of calcium oxychloride $CaOCL_2$. The action of dilute acids liberates chlorine which acts as an oxydizing agent and so bleaches the material.

262 Methane.

263 Phosphor bronze. Copper (80%–95%), tin (5%–15%) and phosphorus (0·25%–2·5%).

264 Acetylene. Ethyne (C_2H_2). A colourless, poisonous, inflammable gas. Used in acetylene lamps (bicycles etc.).

265 Osmium. It has the greatest density of all known elements, and is twice as heavy as lead. Used to tip gold pen points and for weights and measures. Some electric light filaments are also made of osmium.

266 They can determine what chemical compounds are present in the air and whether they are injurious in the proportions in which they exist. Gas chromatography enables chemists to separate mixtures of gas compounds. Scientists determine what chemical compounds are present in such mixtures as petrol products, smog, cigarette smoke and coffee aromas.

267 1. Cathode. 2. Anode.
1. is a hot, or thermionic, cathode that supplies electrons by thermionic emission.
2. is a cold plate or anode that attracts and collects the electrons. Some thermionic cathodes are made of tungsten-thorium wire. Most thermionic cathodes are tiny tubes coated with a mixture of barium oxide and strontium oxide. An electric current heats a wire inside the cathode. This heat makes the coating give off electrons. The anode, usually a larger tube made of nickel, surrounds the cathode.

268 A red liquid.
Bromine: atomic number 35, atomic weight 79·909. Found only in combination with other elements. A product of salt-water processing.

269 Green. Emerald green. The Flame Test is a way of identifying a chemical element by the colour it gives off when held in the flame of a bunsen burner. The test is usually carried out by dipping a platinum wire or piece of asbestos in a compound of the element. The flame given off is always the same colour.

270 Iron. Oxygen, which of course is not a metal, is also combined with it in the mineral known as chromite.

Myths and legends

271 You would forget everything that happened before.
One of the five rivers of the Lower World (Hades).

272 They were ferried across the river Styx and the river
Acheron into the underworld. There they were judged
and were sent either to Tartarus or the Elysian Fields.
Charon, the old boatman, demanded a coin called an
obolus in payment for the trip. Souls without coins
were condemned to wander on the shores of the river.

273 The Golden Fleece. The golden wool of the sacred ram
Chrysomallus. It hung from a tree in a forest and a
fierce dragon who never slept guarded it. Jason got the
fleece.

274 Yeti or Abominable Snowman.

275 A wicked siren who lured boatmen to destruction. The
Lorelei is a high cliff towering about 430 feet above the
river Rhine between Mainz and Koblenz. The
remarkable echo was said to be the voice of a beautiful
but wicked river nymph. The myth may have been
invented by Barento in 1802.

276 She was killed by Perseus. The three gorgons were
horrible creatures with snakes instead of hair. Everyone
who looked them in the face turned to stone. Medusa
was the third gorgon (the other two were Stheno and
Euryale). Perseus was able to keep his head averted by
looking at Medusa's reflection in the mirror of his
shield. He cut off Medusa's head.

277 One thousand and one. The story goes that the Sultan
Shahriyar had his wives killed the morning after the
wedding. Scheherazade was spared her life as long as
she interested the Sultan with her story-telling. She
began a serial that always broke off at the most
exciting point, and thus kept herself alive. At last the

Sultan fell in love with her and spared her life
completely.

278 Venus (or Aphrodite) changed his blood into a flower,
which is called Anemone, or Windflower.

279 Dr Faustus. Faust was a sixteenth-century magician who
claimed to be in league with Satan.

280 Aphrodite (Greek) or Venus (Roman). Goddess of love
and beauty. Zeus, the king of the gods, arranged for
Paris to judge which of the three goddesses was the
most beautiful. The Apple of Discord, bearing the words
'To the fairest' was the prize. Aphrodite promised Paris
the most beautiful woman in the world if Paris chose
her. He did and was hated by the other two goddesses
for making this decision.

281 Pandora. Zeus became angry because Prometheus stole
fire from the gods to give to men. He ordered
Hephaestus (Vulcan) to create an evil being whom all
men would desire. He created woman from earth and
water. All the gods gave her gifts, hence the name
Pandora meaning 'all-gifts'. She brought with her a box
which the gods warned her not to open. She was too
curious and lifted the lid. All the world's vices, diseases
and sins flew out. Pandora shut the lid quickly, but only
Hope, man's last comfort, was left.

282 1. Faun was the half-human god of the woods.
2. Flora was the goddess of everything that blooms.

283 He had himself tied to the mast of his ship. His sailors'
ears were stuffed with wax. The Sirens were sea nymphs
who lived on an island. Their singing drew sailors to
their shores to forget their homes and starve to death.
Ulysses listened to the Sirens but could not go to them.
The Sirens killed themselves because they had failed.

284 He was forced to stand under the threat of an overhanging rock, up to the chin in water. When he tried to

drink, the water vanished. Fruit and grapes hung above
him. When he tried to eat them, the branches were
whirled out of reach by sudden winds. He was the son
of Zeus and was punished in this way because he
killed his son Pelops and served him to the gods as
food.

General knowledge 5

285 Bolshoi Theatre Ballet of Moscow.
286 1. Duck. 2. Cockerel. 3. Sheep.
King Louis XVI watched. The flight lasted eight minutes
and the animals landed safely. The Montgolfier brothers
Jacques Etienne and Joseph Michel sent up a man
(Pilatre de Rozier) a month later.
287 Heptarchy . . . from the Greek word meaning *rule of
seven.* They were Northumbria, Mercia, East Anglia,
Essex, Sussex, Kent and Wessex.
288 A lever. Archimedes was referring to the way a lever
can help a man move objects many times his own size.
289 Republicans and Democrats.
290 A glowing of the air around the tops of trees or ships'
masts or anything projecting into the sky. (A round
flash of light). The glow is caused by the building up
of electricity on the projections. Indicates big difference
of electric charge between earth and cloud and could
form a suitable track for a flash of lightning.
Name St Elmo from St Erasmus, patron saint of
Mediterranean sailors.
291 Alpha Centauri or Proxima Centauri. Alpha Centauri is
the third brightest star in the heavens and is about 4·3
light years from Earth. It consists of three stars
revolving around each other. The third star which
circles the others is a small red star with intermittent

brightness; this is Proxima Centauri and is the nearest star to Earth.

292 Tsetse fly. A two-winged African fly that carries the animal parasites, known as trypanosomes, that cause the disease. The insect bites an animal or person who is already infected, picks up the germs and infects the next person it bites.

293 League of Nations. Established January 1920 and dissolved in April 1946.

294 The Last Supper . . . on the refectory wall. The Church still stands and the picture can be seen, although it has faded somewhat.

295 Carbohydrates . . . provide living things with energy. They include all sugars and starches.

296 1. A loose cloak with a hood and a small mask covering the upper part of the face, worn as a disguise *OR*
2. A half mask.

297 They are all radar posts in the Ballistic Missile Early Warning System. Known as BMEWS. The system provides an early warning against surprise attack by an intercontinental ballistic missile.

298 The black tulip. In *La Tulipe Noire*. In the novel Isaac Boxtel tricks and connives in order to steal the black tulip grown by Cornelius van Baerle to win a competition.

299 1. Ear. 2. Throat.
A passage about $1\frac{1}{2}$ inches long, composed of bone and cartilage, extending from the middle-ear cavity to the throat. It allows the air to pass from the throat to the middle-ear.

Picture quiz 3 – architecture

300 Elizabethan period.

301 (*i*) Sheldonian Theatre. (*ii*) Oxford. (*iii*) Sir Christopher Wren (1632–1723).

302 (*a*) Doric. (*b*) Ionic. (*c*) Corinthian.

303 Fan-vaulting.

304 Gargoyles.

305 (*i*) Old St. Paul's cathedral. (*ii*) It was demolished after being damaged in the Great Fire of London in 1666.

Speed quiz 3

306 22 yards. A steel tape has now replaced the 'chain' but the term is still used.

307 Four. 1. Inner Temple.   2. Middle Temple.
         3. Lincoln's Inn.   4. Gray's Inn.

308 The mistakes, and corrections, in printing.

309 Gondoliers. It is a Venetian boat song. From the Latin *barca* to the Italian *barcarola*, to the French *barcarole*.

310 Iron oxide.

311 *Major Barbara*.

312 Corporal. He volunteered for service in 1914, and served mainly as a messenger on the western front. When Germany surrendered in 1918 he was in hospital recovering from a temporary blindness caused by poison gas.

313 One thousand.

314 *The Bat* . . . by Johann Strauss the younger.

315 It is the bud.

316 Kinematics.

317 200 watts. 1 watt is used when 1 volt of electricity drives 1 ampere of electric current through it.
100 volts × 2 amperes = 200 watts.

318 Herring.

319 60 degrees. An equilateral triangle has three equal
     sides, and the three interior angles are also equal.
320 In the foot. One of the two bony arches of the foot.
     Located across the ball of the foot, directly behind the
     toes.
321 Kayak.
322 Diamonds. The Orloff is a Russian crown jewel bought
     by Prince Orloff for Empress Catherine II. The
     Cullinan was the largest stone ever discovered. The
     Koh-i-noor is among the British crown jewels.
323 *The Mystery of Edwin Drood.*
324 Nine.
325 About 39 inches. 1 metre = 39 and $\frac{2}{5}$ inches.

Authors and their books

326 Sir Hugh Walpole. *Herries Chronicles* (1930–1933)
     a series of four historical novels describing life in the
     eighteenth century. They include: Rogue Herries,
     Judith Paris, The Fortress and Vanessa.
327 Henrik Ibsen . . . in 1874. Henrik Ibsen was a famous
     Norwegian playwright.
328 Oscar Wilde.
329 *Middlemarch.*
330 T. S. Eliot (Thomas Stearns Eliot in 1950).
331 *Elegy written in a Country Churchyard* . . . by Thomas
     Gray.
332 *The Merchant of Venice.* One of the suitors of Portia.
333 William Wordsworth . . . in *Lines composed a few miles
     above Tintern Abbey, on revisiting the banks of the Wye
     during a tour.*
334 *Brave New World.*
335 Stephen Potter . . . in a book he called *One-Upmanship.*
     One-upmanship = the skill of being able to gain the
     advantage over one's opponent. The word is patterned

on *gamesmanship*. Both words coined by Stephen Potter.

336 Nobel prize for Literature. Russian author of *Cancer Ward*, *The First Circle*, *One Day in the Life of Ivan Denisovich*.

337 *The Roads of Freedom*.

338 Husband and wife. Percy Bysshe Shelley wrote *Ozymandias* and Mary Shelley (Mary Wollstonecraft Shelley) wrote *Frankenstein*.

339 In Xanadu. 'In Xanadu did Kubla Khan
> A stately pleasure-dome decree:
> Where, Alph, the sacred river, ran
> Through caverns measureless to man
> Down to a sunless sea.'

340 Holinshed's *Chronicles*.

Team quiz 2

341a A pair of scales.

341b Torch.

342a Caspian Sea.

342b Black Sea.

343a Anne Boleyn.

343b Elizabeth Tudor.

344a Jane Seymour. Catherine of Aragon, his first wife, bore 5 children, but only one lived and she was Mary (I). Anne Boleyn was the mother of Elizabeth (I). Edward VI succeeded his father in 1547 and died in 1553.

344b Marie Louise. He divorced Josephine in 1810 and married Archduchess Marie Louise, daughter of Emperor Francis I, of Austria. His son received the title of King of Rome and was proclaimed Napoleon II in 1815. The French ignored him and he remained in Austria. He was given the title of Duke of Reichstadt in 1818 and died in 1832.

345a Apples.
345b Fried potatoes.
346a Beef.
346b Sausage and potato (Mashed: beaten into a pulpy mass).
347a A fish soup (also accept a fish dish).
347b Apple pie and cheese.
348a A highly seasoned stew of meat and vegetables.
348b Turkey with chestnuts.
349a La Manche.
349b Sark. The Dame of Sark, Sibyl Hathaway, is a feudal
      ruler; the island was granted as fief or estate to her
      medieval predecessors by the king, in return for military
      and other services. If the ruler is a man, he is called
      the Seigneur (French for Lord).
350a Seine.
350b The Allied Invasion of Normandy of June 6, 1944.
351a Kiel Canal (Kaiser Wilhelm Canal or North Sea–Baltic
      Canal).
351b Dogger Bank.
352a Elbe River.
352b Battle of Jutland (accept Battle of the Skagerrak).
353a (Fyodor) Dostoyevsky (1880).
353b Boris Pasternak.
354a (Anton) Chekov.
354b Adolf Hitler.
355a (Mikhail) Sholokhov (1928).
355b Miguel de Cervantes.
356a (Leo) Tolstoy (1875–1877).
356b Gustave Flaubert.

General knowledge 6

357   Sir Lancelot (Du Lac). Guinevere was King Arthur's
      wife. Elaine, the maid of Astolat.

358   In the Isle of Orkney. The ancient name for the Orkney
      Islands is Orcades.

359   China. In northern China in 1900–1. Started by secret
      society against the Manchus who ruled China. These
      people were nicknamed 'Boxers' because they practised
      gymnastics. Developed into anti-foreign revolt. Final
      settlement agreed in *The Boxer Protocol*.

360   *Croix de Guerre*. The *Order of Merit* and the *Legion of
      Honour* are for both civilians and the military.

361   Proved that he was somewhere else when the crime was
      committed.

362   Presidium (The Presidium of the U.S.S.R. Council of
      Ministers). The Communist Party executive committee
      which examines and controls policy and matters of state
      in the Soviet Union.

363   Verdi, Guiseppe (1813–1901). *Macbeth* (1847),
      Othello (1887), *Falstaff* (1893).

364   A piano sonata. The names were both given by
      Beethoven. Tchaikovsky authorized the name 'Pathetic'
      for his symphony No. 6.

365   Dean Jonathan Swift. Stella was Esther Johnson, a
      life-long friend of Swift's whom some people believe
      was married, although there is no proof of the marriage.
      His letters to Stella were published as *Journal to Stella*.
      Vanessa was Esther Vanhomrigh. She is thought to
      have loved Swift passionately.

366   They are not attached to the breast bone. The other ribs
      are. They are, of course, attached to the backbone
      (vertebral column).

367   He believed that the earth went round the sun. In 1632
      Galileo published *A Dialogue on the two Principal*

Systems of the World. The Holy Office, or Inquisition, called him to appear before it. Galileo, under the threat of torture, recanted. Apochryphally, he is supposed to have said 'Eppur si muove!' (but it does move). He was condemned to incarnation and the penance as stated (for three years).

368   The Succession to the Throne. In 1700 the Duke of Gloucester, only surviving child of Princess Anne, died. This made it necessary for Parliament to decide whom should succeed Anne, already nominated as King William's heir. Sophia, the granddaughter of James I, and her husband, the Elector of Hanover, were Protestants, and Parliament's object in nominating her and her heirs was to exclude the Catholic Stuarts at all costs. Sophia died before Anne so George succeeded in 1714 as George I.

369   A bird. A duck-like wading and swimming bird with short wings and webbed feet. A prominent feature is the bald patch on its head. This gives it the name used on occasions of 'bald coot'.

370   Graphite . . . and fine clay with certain chemicals and wax. So-called because commercial graphite was originally known as black lead.

371   'Erewhon' stands for 'nowhere', which it almost spells backwards.

372   Mecca or Medina. Mecca in Saudi Arabia is the chief holy city of the Moslems. Mohammed, the founder of the Islamic religion, was born in Mecca. Medina, also in Saudi Arabia, is regarded as a sacred city because the tomb of Mohammed lies there.

Master brain 1

373 S.A. *or* Brownshirts. The S.A. (Storm Troopers) under Ernst Roehm helped Hitler into power. In the 'Night of the long knives', the S.A. were suppressed and Roehm was murdered. (Night of the long knives: night of June 29–30, 1934).

374 1. Robert E. Lee of the South (Confederates), General Ulysses S. Grant of the North (Union).
2. Lee surrendered to Grant at the end of the American Civil War.

375 Peter I of Russia (Peter the Great) 1672–1725.

376 Richard of York, the younger of the two children in the Tower of London, alleged to have been murdered by their uncle, Richard III. Perkin Warbeck confessed he was the son of John Osbek, controller of Tournai. He made several abortive attempts to gain the throne. After escaping from the Tower after one of them, he was executed (1499).

377 Pope Leo X.

378 Henry David Thoreau. He attacked those institutions he considered immoral and had faith in the religious significance of nature. The essay greatly influenced such reformers as Tolstoi, Gandhi, and present-day American civil rights movements.

379 Machines. Cybernetics = the comparative study of calculating machines and the human nervous system in order to understand better the functioning of the human brain.

380 Mobius. The full name is August Ferdinand Mobius. He was a German astronomer and mathematician. The study is known as *Topology*. Mobius has given his name to one geometrical figure in topology: the Mobius ring. Topology ignores straightness, parallelism and distance because deformation can alter them. It studies such

problems as the number of intersections made by a
curve with itself, whether a surface is closed or has
boundaries and whether or not a surface is connected.

381 Insects (and spiders). 1823–1915. His ten-volumed
work is now regarded as a great scientific authority. He
spent his life observing insects and spiders. Entomology
is the branch of zoology concerned with insects.

382 The French Civil Laws. Napoleon Bonaparte appointed
a special commission to combine all French civil laws
into one code. This code became effective in 1804. It
became known as the Code Napoleon after he took the
title of Emperor of the French. The official name is
Code Civil, and it contains the civil, as distinguished
from the criminal, law of France.

383 Molière. Molière was the stage name of Jean Baptiste
Poquelin but the reason for this is not known. *Le
Malade Imaginaire*, written by himself, was acted for
the first time on 10th February, 1673. Molière died on
17th February, the night of the fourth performance,
after bursting a blood vessel in his body during his
performance of the 'imaginary invalid'.

384 Intelligence Tests. Binet was a French psychologist who
was asked by the government to devise a method of
discovering feeble-minded children, so that they could
be given special schooling. The Binet-Simon
Intelligence tests were the first scales for measuring
intelligence and determining mental age.

385 The reign of Queen Anne. The period when Latin
literature is traditionally held to have reached its highest
point, corresponding to the reign of Augustus,
27 B.C.–14 A.D.

Games and sport

386   From 1. 100 Metres. 2. Long Jump. 3. Shot. 4. High
      Jump. 5. 400 Metres. 6. 110 Metres Hurdles. 7. Discus.
      8. Pole Vault. 9. Javelin. 10. 1500 Metres.

387   1. The player who first reached 9 has the option of
      'setting' the game to 3.
      2. The player who first reached 10 has the option of
      'setting' the game to 2.
      When a game has been 'set' the score is called
      'Love All', and the player who first scores 3 or 2
      according to the way the game has been 'set', wins the
      game.

388   Two free shots.

389   1. Second disobedience . . . 6 faults.
      2. Third disobedience . . . Elimination.
      The faults for disobedience are cumulative, not only at
      the same fence, but throughout the same round.

390   Amateur men's tennis teams from countries all over the
      world. The Walker Cup is awarded every two years. The
      Davis Cup is awarded every year.

391   Wrestling. There are two main kinds. Greco-Roman is
      the other kind. Both are Olympic Games sports.

392   Richard Cavill.

393   As all competitors have three chances to clear every
      height, the winner in this case is the athlete with less
      failures on the way up.

394   He might be capsized. A bore is a high tidal wave
      caused by the rushing of the tide up a narrowing estuary,
      or caused by the meeting of two tides. One always
      occurs at the spring tides in the River Severn when it
      can rise as high as 9 feet.

395   A technical knock-out is scored if the referee stops the
      fight when he decides one fighter should not continue
      because of his physical condition. A technical knock-out

is also scored when a fighter fails to answer the bell, or start a new round.

396 1. Archery.
2. The bull's eye of the target.

397 The batting team change from attacking to defensive play. Often happens when a team going for the runs to win gets into trouble and then decides to play for a draw.

398 The draw is so arranged that strong players are kept away from their main rivals until the later rounds in the competition.

399 A method of fishing with a float. A boat is anchored across the current. The baited tackle is fed out so that the float travels downstream. Popular method for barbel, chub and roach. By adjusting the float it can also be used for fish feeding higher in the water. Long trotting is possible from the bank if the current sweeps close in.

400 Rowing. It is the Rowing Race award and the name of the race itself for Thames Watermen. Rowed from London Bridge to Chelsea.

401 *Intrepid.* The race took place in October 1970.

402 Richard Meade . . . on Laurieston. Britain also won the team event. Other team members were Mary Gordon-Watson, Bridget Parker and Mark Phillips.

403 Underwater breathing equipment used by skin divers. *s*(elf) *c*(ontained) *u*(nderwater) *b*(reathing) *a*(pparatus).

Speed quiz 4

404 Eight. The number of protons (positively-charged particles) in an atom's centre gives its atomic number. The atomic number for Oxygen is 8.

405 Corps diplomatique. Foreign representatives accredited to a particular country and claiming special privileges.

406 Ants.

407 Eight. Only two rhymes: lines 1, 4 and 7 and lines 2 and 8. Repeats several lines. ABaAabAB.

408 Brutus. In *Julius Caesar*. Antony, Act V Sc. 5.

409 2001. The title of the book is in fact *2001, A Space Odyssey*.

410 Alaska. Secretary of State, William H. Seward, bought Alaska from Russia in 1867 for $7,200,000 – about 2 cents an acre. At that time many Americans thought the region was a worthless waste of ice and snow. They called it 'Seward's Icebox'. It has since proved to be rich in fish, minerals, timber and potential water power and oil fields.

411 'To be, or not to be?' *Hamlet*, Act III Sc. 1.

412 $33\frac{1}{3}$.

413 Volga River.

414 A centimetre.

415 A, D and G.

416 Banshee.

417 A knot.

418 Macduff. *Macbeth*, Act V Sc. VIII.

419 A part-song for several voices. Usually has no instrumental accompaniment.

420 Printer's message boy. Formerly the boy who took the printed sheets from the tympan of the press. This made him black with ink.

421 Six. Beginning with George I in 1714 and the most recent in the person of George VI, father of Queen Elizabeth.

422 Five.

423 Canada. Sudbery District, in Ontario, supplies about half the world's nickel.

Science 3

424 The higher the speed of a flowing fluid or gas, the lower the pressure. E.g. water moves faster through a narrow portion of a pipe than in the wider portion. But, as the water speeds up, the pressure in the water decreases. This happens as long as the fluid is confined to the same level.

425 Sodium hydroxide.

426 One proton, one neutron and one electron. Light Hydrogen is sometimes known as *protium*. Heavy Hydrogen is called *deuterium*. There is a third type of Hydrogen atom known as *trium*. The latter contains one proton, two neutrons and one electron.

427 Helium. Helium has to be both cooled and compressed. Freezes at −272 degrees centigrade under pressure 26 times atmospheric pressure.

428 Calorie.

429 Hydrogen with non-metals. Chemists divide inorganic compounds into 4 major groups: 1. oxides, 2. acids, 3. bases, 4. salts. *Bases* are combinations of a metal with the hydroxyl radical (OH). They are the chemical opposites of *acids*. *Salts* are combinations of metals with non-metals.

430 Iodine. Courtois obtained heavy violet vapours by adding strong sulphuric acid to the ashes of seaweed. The vapours condensed to form black crystals. Sir Humphry Davy named the element iodine. Bernard Courtois was born in Dijon and discovered the element in 1811.

431 Brilliant blue.

432 Helium.

433 U–233 or Uranium 233.

434 $F = ma$ (when F = Force, m = mass and a = acceleration). Rate of change of momentum is

proportional to the applied force, and takes place in
the direction in which the force acts.

435   Nitrogen. TNT = trinitrotoluene (a powerful explosive
made by nitrating the chemical compound *toluene*.)
Chemical formula = $CH_3C_6H_2(NO_2)_3$.

436   Helium. Lokyer invented the name *helium* from the
Greek for sun (*helios*). The six inert gases are known as
noble or *rare*. They are argon, krypton, neon, radon and
xenon . . . and helium.

437   Liquid Oxygen. Paraffin and LOX are put in the first
stage; liquid hydrogen and LOX in the second and third
stages. LOX is a common oxidizer, made by cooling
oxygen to −297 degrees F.

438   A fulcrum.

439   Carbon 12. An assigned weight of 12.0000. Oxygen was
the previous standard with an atomic weight of 16.0000.
It then became 15.9994. Carbon 12 is the most common
isotope of carbon.

General knowledge 7

440   Queen Elizabeth I of England. Virginia was named after
the 'Virgin Queen'. Probably by Raleigh in 1584 when
the Queen gave him permission to colonize the Virginia
region. Edmund Spenser called her 'Gloriana' in *The
Faerie Queen*.

441   They are the various sizes of the lens aperture. They
appear as 'f-numbers' on a scale on the camera. The
smaller the number the larger the aperture. Common
f-numbers include 2·8, 4, 5·6, 8, 11, 16, 22 and on this
scale each aperture lets through half the amount of
light as the preceding aperture. f stands for fraction
and the f-number is defined as the ratio of the focal
length of the lens to the diameter of the aperture.

442   *Hamlet, Prince of Denmark* by William Shakespeare.

443 *The Threepenny Opera.*

444 Green ... for earth wires.

445 A cross-channel system which was laid to supply the Allied forces with oil during the Allied invasion of Europe in 1944 (World War II). PLUTO stands for Pipe Line Under The Ocean.

446 Stethoscope. He died in 1826 of tuberculosis, a disease in which he had expert knowledge.

447 They are a group of sculptures collected by Lord Elgin, mainly from the Acropolis in Athens.

448 1. *Hebrides* Overture.
2. Felix Mendelssohn or Mendelssohn-Bartholdy.

449 Storting *or* Storthing. Consists of one house with two sections: 38 members in the Lagting and 112 in the Odelsting. Bills must first be approved by the Odelsting and then by the Lagting.

450 Desiderius Erasmus. The New Testament was originally written in Greek. Erasmus merely compared the manuscripts he could find to discover the most accurate reading of the New Testament. Erasmus' edition was 'virtually the first Greek text'. Erasmus' New Testament was published in 1516.

451 The Percheron is a draft horse with heavy muscles and a grey or black coat. Lively for its size and can be used as a general purpose horse.

452 Frederick William (1620–1688).

453 1. East Germany. 2. Poland.
Following World War II the lower course of the river Oder from about Frankfurt to Stettin became the boundary. This boundary is disputed by West Germany.

454 An Italian secret society organized early in the 1800s for the purpose of liberating Italy from Austrian domination and forming a republic.

455 Belgium ... in 1839.

456 Domesday Book. Compiled by the order of William the
Conqueror from 1066 onwards and completed in 1086.
A survey for assessments of taxes. Omitted from the
enquiry were Northumberland, Durham, Cumberland
and northern Westmorland.

Far-away places 3

457 Bay of Biscay.

458 Mecca. In Saudi Arabia not far from the Red Sea.

459 People who live in Belgium. Celtic people who are
descendants of the ancient Balgae of Gaul who
adopted Roman ways of life. They live in the provinces
of southern Belgium. They speak a dialect of French
known as *Walloon*. The people north of Brussels are
Flemings and speak Flemish.

460 Sierra.

461 Saint Christopher.

462 Zambia. The Falls lie about half-way between the
source and the mouth of the Zambesi River.

463 Rome.

464 1. Europe. 2. Asia. They extend 1,500 miles through
western Russia.

465 This region has continuous daylight during the middle
summer. From mid-May to the end of July. This area
is in the Arctic Circle (north of 66° 30′ north latitude).

466 Menai Strait.

467 Stewart Island.

468 Sicily.

469 Alaska. About 500 miles of Canadian territory separate
Alaska from Washington.

470 Venezuela. Spanish explorers found an Indian village
built on wooden poles above the shallow waters of Lake
Maracaibo, which reminded them of Venice. They called
the land 'Venezuela' which is Spanish for 'Little Venice'.

471   Part of the Great Plains region of the south western United States. The soil lacked sufficient vegetative cover to resist attacks by the wind. Frequent dust storms resulted and the land became impoverished.

Master brain 2

472   8 minutes 19 seconds (499 seconds).

473   Perigee.

474   The 'Casket Letters' were a number of letters and poems which were said to have been addressed by Mary, Queen of Scots, to James Hepburn, Earl of Bothwell. There has been considerable controversy as to their authenticity. They consist of a number of letters and a sequence of irregular sonnets in French. If authentic they provide proof of Mary's complicity in the murder of her husband, Henry, Lord Darnley. They were written between January and April 1566–67.

475   Leonidas I. He commanded the Spartans and Greeks who tried to defend the pass of Thermopylae against the Persians.

476   Money and/or Trade. It was the International Monetary Conference held in U.S.A. in July 1944. Transfer of money was simplified. National currency values were stabilized and plans were drawn up for the International Monetary Fund and the International Bank for Reconstruction and Development.

477   Venetia.

478   Talleyrand. Charles Maurice de Talleyrand-Perigord, Prince of Benevent.

479   0 and 1. The system, used in computers, counts from 0 to 1, and then starts with a new place. Decimal numeral 1 = Binary numeral 1; Decimal numeral 2 = Binary numeral 10; Decimal 3 = Binary 11; Decimal

4 = Binary 100; Decimal 5 = Binary 101; Decimal
16 = Binary 10000 (16 = $2 \times 2 \times 2 \times 2$).

480 'The die is cast' or the decision has been made and
there is no going back.

481 Clement Attlee. Germany surrendered in May 1945.
Attlee became prime minister in July 1945. Japan
surrendered in August 1945.

482 They are two buildings in the grounds of the Palace of
Versailles (sometimes called 'small palaces').

483 The war in Russia between the Communists (The Reds)
and the anti-Communists (The Whites). Red has been
the colour of workers or the 'proletariat' since at least
the time of the French Revolution.

484 Limited freedom of worship to the Huguenots. The
Huguenots were French Protestants who followed the
teachings of John Calvin. Henry of Navarre was their
leader. When he became King Henry IV he changed to
the Catholic faith to achieve peace. In 1598 he signed
the Edict of Nantes.

485 Pavlov rang a bell each time he brought food to a dog.
Eventually the dog's mouth began to water when
Pavlov merely rang the bell – with no food being
present. The dog associated the ringing of the bell with
the food.

Team quiz 3

486a None . . . because there is little difference between the
water levels of the Red Sea and Mediterranean.

486b Ferdinand de Lesseps.

487a Aida.

487b The Mittelland Canal.

488a Robert Fulton.

488b Polaris.

489a It travelled round the world under water (41,500 miles in 84 days).

489b *The Flying Dutchman* . . . by Richard Wagner.

490a Malvolio.

490b Puck or Robin Goodfellow.

491a Katherina.

491b Prospero.

492a *Hamlet, Prince of Denmark.*

492b *Romeo and Juliet.*

493a Titania, Queen of the Fairies . . . In *Midsummer Night's Dream.*

493b King Lear.

494a Rimsky-Korsakov. Originally a Symphonic Suite with which a ballet has been associated since 1910, two years after the death of the composer.

494b Tchaikovsky.

495a Prokoviev.

495b Stravinsky.

496a *Taming of the Shrew.*

496b *Romeo and Juliet.*

497a 1. For the wedding of Margaret and James III of Scotland.

2. By her father, King Christian I of Denmark. From early times to about 1468 the islands had been under the kings of Norway and Denmark. The promised dowry was never paid, and Scotland took the islands in 1472.

497b In 1523 Lachlan Maclean of Duart placed his wife on the rock, which is only exposed at low water, expecting that she would be drowned by the flowing tide. She was saved by her clansfolk.

498a 24.

498b King Midas.

499a The Klondike is in the Yukon in the north-west of Canada (near the Alaskan border).

499b Ghana.

500a The apparent change in frequency of sound waves caused by motion. Also in light or radio waves.

500b The splitting of spectral lines by a magnetic field.

501a Hg.

501b Fe.

Picture quiz 4 – Transport

502 Henri Giffard, in 1852.

503 (*i*) Austin. (*ii*) Seven. (*iii*) 1922.

504 (*i*) *Great Eastern*, originally called *Leviathan* because of its great size. (*ii*) Isambard Kingdom Brunel (1806–1859).

505 (*i*) George and Robert Stephenson. (*ii*) 1829.

506 (*i*) Carl Benz. (*ii*) 1886.

History

508 Benjamin Disraeli, Earl of Beaconsfield. He was a Jew who became Prime Minister of Great Britain in 1868 and from 1874 to 1880. Entered Parliament as a Tory in 1837. Opposed repeal of Corn Laws. Also novelist and wrote *Vivian Grey* and other novels.

509 He piloted a plane to Scotland with proposals for a compromise peace with Britain during World War II. He was captured and held as prisoner until the end of the war. He was then sentenced to life imprisonment at the Nuremberg Trials in 1946.

510 1. Germany. 2. Italy.

511 Sweden received Norway from Denmark. 1814/15 after the Napoleonic Wars.

512 1. *Great Britain* was the largest ship of its kind at the date of launching, or

2. It was the first large ship in which the screw propeller was used, or

3. It was one of the three great ships built by Isambard Kingdom Brunel.

513 The surviving leaders of Nazi Germany ... who were accused of crimes against peace by the planning, preparation, initiation and waging of wars of aggression which were in violation of international treaties and agreements. They were also charged with war crimes and crimes against humanity. The trial lasted from November 1945 until October 1946.

514 1. Edward V. 2. Richard. They were Richard III's nephews. Richard's elder brother was King Edward IV. He had two sons, Edward and Richard. Edward became king on the death of his father when he was only 12 years old in 1483. Richard, Duke of Gloucester, was then Protector of the Realm. Edward and his younger brother, Richard, Duke of York, were imprisoned in the Tower. Later they were killed and Richard became King Richard III.

515 The ship was the first to sail round the world. Magellan, who commanded the ship, did not complete the journey; he was killed in the Philippines.

516 The Holy Roman Emperor Frederick I.

517 Elector of Hanover.

518 Blücher ... Gebhard von Blücher, Prince of Wahlstatt. His arrival with Prussian reinforcements helped the British defeat Napoleon's French army.

519 John Churchill, Duke of Marlborough. Sarah Jennings was the Queen's closest friend. But the political enemies of the Duke turned the queen against him and his wife, with the result that he was removed from his command, and retired from public life.

520 The Fosse Way. Built as a military frontier road but remained in use as a cross country route.

General knowledge 8

521 Mother Goose Fairy Tales . . . published in 1697.

522 Battle of Agincourt . . . *King Henry V*, Act IV Scene VIII.

523 1. Violin. 2. Cello. This occurred in January 1971.

524 'Blue period' . . . because of the predominant colours used by him in these periods. From 1907 to 1909 was his 'Negro period' followed by his move to Cubism.

525 He had been forced or tricked into doing something or being taken somewhere against his wishes.

526 Aphrodite. Born from the foam of the sea near to the island of Cythera.

527 The voyage that Francis Drake made round the world in the *Golden Hind*. After a false start, the voyage began from Plymouth, and ended at Plymouth. Several ships formed the fleet. The *Pelican* (renamed the *Golden Hind* on the voyage) was the only one to complete the journey.

528 Liverpool.

529 Tass. Full name is *Telegrafnoie Agenstvo Sovietskavo Soiuza* or the *Telegraphic Agency of the Soviet Union*. Formed in 1925 as the official government news agency. Grew from two press services: *Petrograd News Agency* and *Rosta Agency*. Directly responsible to the highest executive body: the Council of Ministers.

530 Tropic of Capricorn. Marks the southern boundary of the tropical zone. Sometimes called the *southern circle*. The vertical rays of the sun shine down on the Tropic of Capricorn at noon on the day of the winter solstice, about December 22. The northern circle is the Tropic of Cancer.

531 'G clef'. The bass clef fixes the F below middle C on the second line from the top. The G clef fixes the G above middle C on the second line from the bottom of the staff.

532   1. Ballet. 2. Choreography.

533   One of its requirements was for a man with a red flag to precede mechanical road vehicles. Introduced in 1865 it limited the speed of steam vehicles to 4 m.p.h. on country roads and 2 m.p.h. on town roads. The steam carriage had to be preceded by a signalman who carried a red flag during the daytime and a red lantern at night. The Act was made less severe in 1878, although vehicles still had to be preceded by a man carrying a red flag. Its repeal in 1896 has been celebrated ever since by the RAC London to Brighton Veteran Car Run.

534   Frequency of radio and television waves. 'Frequency' means the number of vibrations per second.
One kilohertz equals 1,000 hertz (vibrations per second).

Famous people 2

535   Henry Purcell.

536   Liberal.

537   Crimean War. 1853–56. Florence Nightingale was sent by the Secretary of War to take charge of the nursing.

538   Napoleon snatched the crown from the Pope's hands and placed it on his own head. Then he crowned Josephine empress. He demonstrated in this way that he had personally won the right to wear the crown.

539   Music – especially as a pianist and composer.

540   Warren Hastings. Began as clerk in the East India Company. In 1774 was appointed Governor-General. Improved court and tax systems and encouraged study of Indian culture. His political enemies, led by Sheridan, Burke and Charles James Fox had him

impeached. The trial ruined him and he lived for the rest of his life on a pension from the East India Company.

541 1. Mark Twain. 2. Author (of *Tom Sawyer, Huckleberry Finn*, etc.).

542 David Lloyd George (1863–1945). Born of Welsh parents in Manchester. A Liberal, he became Prime Minister in 1916 and is generally recognized as one of Britain's greatest war leaders. He was active in politics until his death.

543 This was to commemorate the Battle of Plassey which was his greatest achievement as a soldier.

544 He nailed the protest known as the *Ninety-Five Theses* to a church door. This happened in 1517 at All Saints' Church in Wittenberg. He was protesting mainly at the granting of indulgences by Johann Tetzel, a Dominican monk who was authorized by Pope Leo X to preach indulgences near Wittenberg. He gained this indulgence by giving money for the building of St Peter's Church in Rome. The Ninety-Five Theses covered more theological arguments than these, but this was the main one and the one that sparked off the violent action which began the Protestant Reformation.

545 Charles Dickens.

546 'To His Royal Highness The Prince Regent'. Prince Regent, who became King George IV and who had the nickname 'the first gentleman in Europe'.

547 John F. Kennedy.

548 Thomas Telford (1757–1834). Originally a journeyman stone mason. Became surveyor of public works in Shropshire. Also built many roads and bridges, including the Menai Suspension Bridge.

549 Emperor Wilhelm II. Wilhelm wanted to go his own way. The dismissal and disgrace of Bismarck was world-shattering news and a well-known cartoon called 'Dropping the Pilot' keyed many reactions.

550   1. Johann Strauss the Younger. 2. Richard (Georg) Strauss.

Speed quiz 5

551   Kingston-upon-Hull.

552   A bird . . . now extinct. It was a flightless bird that lived on the island of Mauritius in the Indian Ocean. Sailors killed it for food, and pigs, rats and dogs stole the eggs.

553   Romeo and Juliet.

554   Little Jack Horner.
      He put in his thumb and pulled out a plum.
      drupe = plum (botany). pollex = thumb (anatomy).

555   *The Ten Commandments.* From Greek meaning *ten words.* The Hebrews called the laws the *ten words.*

556   Neap tides. They are smaller than ordinary tides. When the sun and moon are acting together a higher tide results which is known as a *spring tide.*

557   Tuesday. From Tiu or Tiw, name of the Norse god of war. French call Tuesday Mardi, for Mars, the Roman war god.

558   Six. No two snow crystals are exactly alike, but they all have six sides.

559   Canada.

560   Berlin.

561   Copenhagen.

562   Washington (D.C., U.S.A.).

563   Rome.

564   Venus, Mars, Mercury.

565   Two. Tides rise and fall twice in the time between two rising moons, about 24 hours 50 minutes.

566   Carl W. Scheele. Swedish chemist 1742–86.

567 Six.
568 Greek Islands . . . in the Aegean Sea.
569 A bicycle race. The greatest national sporting event in France and of international interest. Every summer more than a hundred professional cyclists race round the entire country, riding daily for nearly a month, and finishing in Paris.
570 The Red Crescent.
571 Venus.

General knowledge 9

572 Plebians. Included freed slaves, peasant farmers.
573 Tears.
574 He introduced a penny post. He set it up in 1680. He had several hundred receiving houses where letters were collected every hour. He had to end his penny post in 1682 as a result of legal actions that were brought against him. In 1683 it was reopened as a government service. He died in poverty. Rowland Hill advocated a uniform penny post for the whole country in 1837 and his suggestions were adopted in 1840.
575 Pick-pocketing and stealing. Fagan, the Jew fence, was the teacher.
576 Cecil Day-Lewis, who died 22 May 1972.
577 France (République Française). Not all stamps carry the initials but most of them do.
578 One-twelfth (480 grains).
579 Stalingrad. Named *Tsaritsyn* when it was founded in the 1200s. In 1925 became Stalingrad in honour of Joseph Stalin. In 1961 Stalin was downgraded and dishonoured throughout Russia and the city was renamed Volgograd. In the Battle of Stalingrad the German VIth Army was ultimately defeated and with

its commander, von Paulus, was forced to surrender (1943).

580 The adrenal glands. By the cortex or outer cover of the glands. It can be produced synthetically from the bile of animals and from vegetables. Helps in the treatment of rheumatoid arthritis and other diseases.

581 He killed himself by falling upon his sword. In *Antony and Cleopatra*, Act IV Scene XII.

582 He had him sentenced to death.

583 Ursula and Gudrun Brangwen.

584 A country house.

585 'For the good of the public' or 'For the public welfare'.

586 Finding a ship's location on the seas without using the position of the stars. A record is kept of the direction and speed. The speed is multiplied by the length of time to get the miles. Then the ship's course is traced on a map. Dead reckoning was the only method of navigation in cloudy conditions.

Science 4

587 The *bel* or the *decibel*. A decibel is a tenth of a larger unit, the *bel*. The decibel is not a unit of loudness, which is often measured in *phons*. Alexander Graham Bell was the inventor of the telephone.

588 Dyne.

589 1. Nitric acid. 2. Hydrochloric acid.
One part concentrated nitric acid plus three parts concentrated hydrochloric acid. *Aqua Regia* means royal water, and is given this name because it dissolves the royal metal, gold. It also dissolves platinum. The chemical action between the two acids forms nitrosyl chloride (NOCL) and chlorine gas. These oxidizing

agents with excess hydrochloric acid enable aqua regia to dissolve gold.

590   The explosive force of nuclear weapons (atomic bombs and hydrogen bombs). 1 megaton = explosive force of 1,000,000 tons of TNT. The explosive force of atomic weapons may also be measured in kilotons (thousands of tons of TNT).

591   Water.

592   Nitrogen. Ammonia = NH_3 and is made by combining the two elements by the Haber process.

593   Hydrogen and oxygen.

594   Helium and hydrogen. Today helium much more than hydrogen, because it is not as inflammable. Helium has 92% of the lifting ability of hydrogen.

595   It changes when exposed to air, moisture or heat. Base metals corrode, tarnish or oxidize. *Base* in contradistinction to *noble* metals which do not corrode or tarnish in air or water, and are not easily attacked by acids.

596   Radium. Also polonium. Marie Curie won the Nobel Prize for Physics with her husband in 1903 (Becquerel also shared the prize). The ore provided only a small amount (a thimbleful) of radium. The two radio-active substances were named by the Curies.

597   Periodic Table. The Periodic Table is the table in which the chemical elements, arranged in the order of their atomic weights, are shown in related groups. Dimtri Ivanovich Mendeleev was a Russian chemist, born in Siberia in 1834. He wrote *Elements of Chemistry*.

598   Boyle. Boyle's Law states that the pressure of gas increases as the volume of gas decreases. It was discovered by the Irish chemist, Robert Boyle in 1662.

599   D_2O. The *hydrogen* in water has been replaced by *deuterium*.

600 Beta-rays (or Beta Radiation, Beta Particles or Beta Electrons). Gamma Rays (or Gamma Radiation). Named from the Greek letters alpha, beta and gamma. Alpha rays or Alpha particles consist of the nucleii of helium atoms.

Far-away places 4

601 South Vietnam.
602 River Jordan.
603 Red Sea.
604 The Baganda are members of the largest and wealthiest tribe of Uganda, a country in east-central Africa.
605 Russia (or U.S.S.R.).
606 Luxembourg.
607 Lesotho. Ruled by a king who is Paramount Chief of Lesotho and also a constitutional monarch. Most of the population are Negro Africans known as Basuto.
608 Verona ... an Italian city on the Adige River.
609 The Fenland or The Fens. The Fens are alluvial flats in south-east Lincolnshire, north Cambridgeshire and north-west Norfolk. At one time the Isle of Ely was more of an island than it is now being surrounded by swamps and only accessible by boat or causeways. But the swamps were drained.
610 Fiji or Fiji Islands. Until October 1970 British Crown Colony in the South Pacific, situated just west of the International Date Line. Consists of 322 islands altogether but only 106 are inhabited.
611 In southern Ireland. In the County of Tipperary, about 40 miles south-east of Limerick. Dairy town and marketing centre.
612 Strait of Gibraltar. The Greeks called the rocks *Calpe* (the rock on the European side) and *Abyla* (the African

pillar). Greek legend says that Hercules placed the rocks there when he visited the kingdom of Geryon.

613 Rocky islets that lie just off the Norwegian coast. They form the skerry-guard or skjargaard. They protect Norway from the North Atlantic storm and winds but can be a menace to ships that stray off the well-marked coastal passageway lying between the coast and the skerries.

614 The name, which is the old Gaelic name for Edinburgh. Scottish emigrants colonized Dunedin and gave many of its streets Edinburgh names.

615 The village of Cheddar in Somerset, England.

Literature

616 Michael Henchard sold his wife to a sailor for five guineas.

617 'Pieces of eight! Pieces of eight!' The name of a coin and part of the treasure.

618 Captain Ahab lost his leg to a whale, Moby Dick . . . and afterwards chased the white whale seeking revenge.

619 Carnivorous plants that grew to a height of seven feet or more. They stung their victims and ate them. They also walked and talked. (In *The Day of the Triffids*.)

620 The sea.

621 *Nautilus*. Captain Nemo was her commander.

622 *The Borrowers* . . . by Mary Norton.

623 Sir Bedivere . . . in *Morte D'Arthur*.

624 *Persuasion*, the posthumously-published novel by Jane Austen.

625 *The Old Cumberland Beggar*.

626 King Creon of Thebes.

627 Huckleberry Finn . . . in *The Adventures of Tom Sawyer*, by Mark Twain (Chapter VI).

628 Mexico.

Team quiz 4

629a Christian . . . (*Pilgrim's Progress* by John Bunyan).

629b Pip . . . (in *Great Expectations* by Charles Dickens).

630a Edmond Dantes . . . (in *The Count of Monte Cristo* by Alexandre Dumas).

630b Michael Henchard . . . (in *The Mayor of Casterbridge* by Thomas Hardy).

631a David Balfour . . . (in *Kidnapped* by Robert Louis Stevenson).

631b Gulliver (Lemuel Gulliver) . . . (in *Gulliver's Travels* by Jonathan Swift).

632a Laurie Lee . . . (in *Cider with Rosie* by Laurie Lee).

632b The King's Daughter of Norway.

633a George William Russell.

633b George Eliot.

634a The potato famine began that year. Many people died of starvation and disease. Hundreds of thousands left Ireland for Britain and the United States.

634b John Nash, the architect, who built all three.

635a Rob Roy.

635b A mountain daisy.

636a Marmion.

636b Culloden Moor . . . in 1746.

637a 1. Italy (meaning 'Ready'). 2. Israel (meaning 'Peace').

637b Three dots, three dashes and three dots: · · · — — — · · ·

638a 1. Samuel Finley Breese Morse. 2. Morse Code. On May 24, 1844. By telegraph line from the United States Supreme Court Room of the Capitol in Washington to Baltimore.

638b Teaching deaf children.

639a 1. Scottish (British). 2. American. James Clerk Maxwell discovered that electrical impulses travel through space at the speed of light (1864).

Lee de Forest patented the triode, or three element vacuum tube (1907).

639b   The Crookes Tube (forerunner of the cathode-ray-tube).

640a   1. Guglielmo Marconi. 2. Cornwall.

640b   Laboratory assistant . . . to Sir Humphry Davy. Before that he was a journeyman bookbinder.

641a   Lionel Lukin. Lukin, a London coach builder, was one of three men (Wouldhave and Greathead were the others) who could claim to be the inventors of the lifeboat. He originally converted a Norway yawl into an 'unimmergible boat'. In 1786 he converted a coble for use at Bamburgh for saving shipwrecked sailors. The boat he built in 1807 was the forerunner of the fine lifeboats which became known as the 'Norfolk and Suffolk type'.

641b   An Anglo-Saxon burial-ship containing a wealth of treasure. Sutton Hoo is a hill at Sutton in Suffolk. There are 11 barrows on the site, and one of these in 1939 was found to contain the frame-work of a ship or large wooden boat with grave-goods. These include: iron standard, ceremonial whetstone, sword and sword-belt, gold jewelled purse, shield and helmet, coins and weapons, bowls and drinking horns. Coins suggest date of burial between A.D. 650 and 670.

642a   Simon de Montfort. There was already some kind of Parliament before Simon de Montfort. His work was to advance and strengthen a parliamentary system already in existence. The king's Great Council before de Montfort had consisted mainly of barons and prelates. Montfort called to his famous parliament in 1265 (January) two representatives from each shire and two from each town and borough.

642b   Geoffrey de Clinton . . . about 1122.

643a   Bertolt Brecht.

643b Dylan Thomas.
644a Samuel Beckett.
644b Brendan Behan.

General knowledge 10

645 National Aeronautics and Space Administration.
646 Mr Anwar Sadat. Officially elected on 15th October, 1970.
647 King James IV of Scotland married Margaret Tudor, eldest daughter of King Henry VII of England. Their great-grandson, James VI of Scotland, became James I of England.
648 Arc de Triomphe . . . at the head of the Champs Elysees in Paris. Means *Arch of Triumph*.
649 The Pope.
650 1660. Long Parliament dissolved itself after calling a Convention. King Charles II came to the throne soon afterwards.
651 Igneous. Formed by the cooling and hardening of molten material.
652 Epiglottis. Thin, triangular plate which prevents the passage of food into the trachea and thence into the lungs. The opening of the trachea into the pharynx (throat) is termed the *glottis*, and may be closed, as during swallowing, by the epiglottis.
653 Mandarin. A movement to unify the spoken dialects of China led to the adoption of the Mandarin dialect. 'Mandarin' was the English name for high officials in China.
654 A bull. They believed that Osiris, god of the underworld, lived again in the bull. They kept the bull in a temple in Memphis and celebrated its birthday every year. When the bull died, they embalmed it and buried it with ceremony.

655   Tanzania (United Republic of Tanzania).

656   Alfred Jodl. Lt General Walter Bedell Smith was Eisenhower's Chief of Staff. Jodl was Chief of Operations Staff of the German Armed Forces High Command. The terms of unconditional surrender were signed at Reims.

657   Buddha (*or* Gotama *or* Siddhartha Gautama).

658   Nine hundred and ninety-nine thousand millions (999,000,000,000).

659   V-J Day . . . Victory over Japan (V-E = Victory in Europe) September 2, 1945. Japanese signed terms of surrender aboard the battleship U.S.S. *Missouri* in Tokyo Bay.

Master brain 3

660   Cavour. Founded in 1847. This newspaper helped to prepare the way first for the freedom of Sardinia and finally for the unification of Italy.

661   The Reichstag Fire. The Reichstag, the lower house of the German Parliament was burned down on the night of February 27, 1933. A young Dutchman was arrested and immediately confessed to having set fire to the building. Hitler and the Nazis blamed the Communists for the fire. The fire was probably started by members of the Nazi party to provide an excuse to smash the Communist Party.

662   Ten thousand . . . as in *myria* – gramme, metre and litre.

663   William Pitt (The Younger).

664   Wilson Cloud Chamber. It was perfected about 1912.

665   'Ozymandias, king of kings'.

666   A layer of the air, or atmosphere, that surrounds the earth.

667   Large differences in temperature between land and sea.

This difference occurs because land heats and cools faster than water. Cooler air always rushes in over warmer regions where the air pressure is low. Summer monsoons are usually accompanied by rain and are called wet monsoons. Winter monsoons are known as dry monsoons. In summer the monsoons travel from the cooler sea to the warmer land. In winter the monsoons go from land to sea.

668 *The Communist Manifesto* . . . published in 1848.

669 Two groups of political parties who served in the legislative assembly. The *Mountain* were in the highest part of the hall on the Speaker's left. The *Plain* were in the low central section and to the right of the Speaker.

670 Maelstrom . . . name of whirlpool among the Lofoten Islands.

671 They were the attempts of the Jacobites to restore the Stuarts by force in 1715 and 1745.

Who am I?

672 Leon Trotsky.

673 Robespierre . . . Maximilien François Marie Isadore de Robespierre.

674 Henry Cavendish . . . English physicist was born on 10th October, 1731, in Nice, France. He died in 1810.

675 Christian Huygens.

676 Tony Jacklin.

677 Lillian Board.

678 President Gamal Abdel Nasser. Nasser was officially elected president in 1956. However, following the 6-day war he resigned in 1967, but was persuaded to take up office again almost immediately.

679 Tito. Josip Broz, son of Croatian peasants, born near Zagreb, then in Austria-Hungary.

680 David Hemery.
681 William Butler Yeats.
682 Thomas Stearns Eliot (T. S. Eliot).

General knowledge 11
683 Ronald Reagan.
684 Off the east coast of Kent. They lie at a distance of about 5 to 6 miles from the coast, offshore from Deal. At the north-east end of the Strait of Dover.
685 Paul Gaugin.
686 Earth.
687 Professor Moriarty.
688 Stitches are worked on the wrong side of a transparent fabric showing to the front in shadowy effects or colours.
689 The main guys of a ridge tent are brought back alongside the tent and crossed over each other.
690 A large ocean current which has its source in the warm waters of the Gulf of Mexico and moves across the Atlantic. It runs northwards past Ireland and Scotland.
691 Peace. His Chemistry prize was for his work on the structure of molecules. In 1958 he set out his views attacking American nuclear policies in *No More War*. He was awarded the Nobel Peace Prize for his efforts to secure a ban on nuclear testing in 1962 but he did not receive the award until 1963.
692 Braising.
693 550. 33,000 foot-pounds of work a minute. The power of an engine can be measured in various ways. When one pound weight is lifted one foot, one foot-pound of work is done. Horsepower is a unit used to express the power (rate of doing work) of an engine.
694 Left side.
695 Paddington.

696 This is an instrument used on ships to measure the depth of water. A sound is sent down through the water to be echoed back from the bottom. Navigators measure the depth below the ship by measuring the time it takes the sound to return. The speed of sound in water is known.

697 Greenwich, England. Decided by geographers in 1884. The meridians are lines which go half way round the globe and measure longitude, which is the distance east or west of Greenwich. Geographers consider that everywhere in the world is covered by a meridian. When the sun shines directly down on that line, it is noon all along the meridian.

698 Mercury.

699 'The Doldrums'.

700 Red, white and blue. It has equal red, white and blue vertical sections.

These are other Knight Books

Charles M. Schulz

MEET THE PEANUTS GANG

DON'T TREAD ON CHARLIE BROWN

WHAT WERE YOU SAYING, CHARLIE BROWN?

If you haven't met the Peanuts gang before, now's your chance to get acquainted with Charlie Brown and his friends (not forgetting Snoopy the dog) who have made such a hit in this country and the United States. And if you are already a Peanuts fan, these books contain some of the earlier cartoons which you probably won't have seen before.

Ask your local bookseller, or at your public library, for details of other Knight Books, or write to the Editor-in-Chief, Knight Books, Arlen House, Salisbury Road, Leicester LE1 7QS

ONE LOVE IS ENOUGH

ONE LOVE IS ENOUGH

JULIETTE BENZONI

UNABRIDGED

Translated by
JOCASTA GOODWIN

PAN BOOKS LTD : LONDON

First published in Great Britain 1964
by Wm. Heinemann Ltd.
This edition published 1966 by Pan Books Ltd.,
33 Tothill Street, London, S.W.1

330 20148 4

2nd Printing 1968
3rd Printing 1968
4th Printing 1969
5th Printing 1970

Published in France by Editions de Trévise 1963
Translation © Opera Mundi, Paris 1964
Originally published as *Il Suffit d'un Amour* Vol. 1
Opera Mundi, Paris 1963

Printed in Great Britain by
Cox & Wyman Ltd., London, Reading, and Fakenham

Prologue

DIES IRAE
1413

CHAPTER ONE

THE PRISONER

TWENTY STRONG men shouldered the battering-ram, a huge oak beam which they had taken from a timberyard near by. They would fall back a few paces with it and then rush forward and hurl it with all their might against the iron-clad gate; it reverberated under these assaults like a gigantic drum, their own grunted exclamations providing a sort of rhythmical counter-point. Urged on by the fury of the mob, the men redoubled their efforts, and soon the palace gates were creaking and groaning under the strain. One crack was already visible, despite the heavy twisted iron bars reinforcing the doors.

The gate consisted of a high double door of solid oak surmounted by a stone ogive, guarded by two stone angels, kneeling, hands folded, on either side of the French royal arms, whose golden lilies on a field of azure gleamed softly in the June sunlight. Higher up still, beyond the crenellated walls where the archers of the royal guard took aim at the mob, the rooftops and high gables of the Palace of Saint-Pol traced their flamboyant, fantastic outlines against the sky, and great embroidered silken banners waved amid the tree-tops. Up there reigned the softness of a summer day, hot sunlight flashed from painted walls gaudy as the pages of an illuminated missal; a flight of swallows sped by ... down below blood flowed and fury mounted, while the dust, scuffled by hundreds of feet, rose in choking clouds.

An arrow whistled past. Close to where Landry and Catherine were standing a man fell heavily, his throat pierced, the hideous scream he uttered abruptly changing to a strange, gargling noise. The young girl hastily covered her face with her hands and moved closer to Landry, whose arm tightened protectively about her shoulders.

'Don't look,' Landry advised her. 'Poor little thing. I should never have brought you with me. That certainly won't be the last death you will see today.'

They were both perched on a stone bench which stood conveniently near the mouth of a dark, damp, winding alley between a tailor's booth and an apothecary's shop, now heavily padlocked. From this perch they could see everything, and they watched each charge of the battering-ram with mounting excitement. Then, quite suddenly, the palace archers began shooting in a sort of frenzy. A deadly hail of arrows and heavier arbalest shafts rained down on the mob, ploughing great gaps in their ranks which almost as quickly filled up again. Wisely, Landry made Catherine get down off her perch and the two of them mingled with the crowd in search of a spot out of range of the arrows.

Their weariness was beginning to tell on them both. They had taken advantage of their parents' absence to leave their homes on the Pont-au-Change very early that morning. Their parents themselves, caught up by the fever of excitement which had been raging throughout Paris during the past twenty-four hours, had all gone off in different directions . . . one to the House of Pillars, another to help a neighbour in childbirth, and another to report to the town militia. Neither Landry nor Catherine recognized their familiar Paris in this explosive city where a thoughtless word or stray song might provoke a blood-bath at the next corner.

Their everyday world was the Pont-au-Change, or Money-lenders' Bridge, a narrow, busy thoroughfare, lined with old houses with pointed roofs, which linked the palace with the Grand Châtelet. Gaucher Legòix, Catherine's father, was a goldsmith whose shop was known by the Sign of the Holy Tabernacle above the door. Denis Pigasse, Landry's father, was also a metalworker, and their two shops stood next door to each other opposite the booths of the Norman and Lombard moneylenders which lined the other side of the bridge.

Till now Catherine, on her expeditions with Landry, had never left the Notre-Dame district with its network of sinister alleys round the great slaughter-house. She had never ventured past the drawbridges which led to the Louvre. Landry, on the other hand, being fifteen, had been able to get to know much more about the town's less reputable neighbourhoods, and by now every corner of Paris was as familiar to him as the back of his hand. It had been his idea to take his little friend along to the Palais de St Pol this Friday morning, 27 April 1413.

'Come along with me,' he had urged her. 'Caboche has threatened to break into the palace today and arrest the Dauphin's wicked counsellors. We just follow him in and then we'll be able to look round the place at our leisure.'

Caboche, otherwise known as Simon the Skinner, was employed to skin carcases at the slaughter-house. The son of a tripe-seller in Notre-Dame market, he was the man who, single-handed, had aroused the people of Paris to revolt against the illusory power of the mad king, Charles VI, and the real and ominous strength of Isabeau of Bavaria.

The French kingdom was indeed in a sorry state. The King was mad, the Queen reckless and depraved, and the country itself, since the murder of the Duc d'Orléans six years earlier by Jean-sans-Peur, Duke of Burgundy, given over to wild anarchy. Heedless of the ever-present English threat, the supporters of those two princes, Armagnacs on one hand and Burgundians on the other, waged a pitiless campaign against each other up and down France, pillaging and devastating the countryside unopposed.

The Armagnacs had now surrounded Paris. Within the beseiged city the townspeople vociferated their undying loyalty to that dangerous demagogue John, Duke of Normandy. It was he, aided by the powerful Butchers' Guild, who had stirred up the present riots and troubles. Nominally power was in the hands of the sixteen-year-old Dauphin, Louis de Guyenne, but events had clearly got out of control. In reality, the King of Paris was Caboche the Skinner, seconded by the Rector of the turbulent University, Pierre Cauchon.

Caboche and Cauchon were both to be seen in the forefront

of the mob attacking the royal palace. Caboche stood near where
some burly butchers' apprentices, still wearing their bloodstained leather aprons, kept watch over the palace guards
whom they had taken and trussed like game birds ready for
the spit. From there he bellowed his commands, timing the
wild charges of the battering-ram.

As Landry dragged her along in search of a place where
they could observe events out of range of flying arrows,
Catherine could see Caboche's impressive bulk looming above
the press of bobbing heads. His green tunic, sewn with the
Burgundian emblem, the white cross of St Andrew, strained
across his mighty shoulders. His face, sweating and swollen
with fury, shone bright scarlet. In one hand he held the white
banner emblematic of Paris and waved it furiously.

'Harder!' he roared. 'Swing the thing harder! Smash this
maggots' nest for me; 'sdeath! . . . harder still! It is cracking
already!'

As he spoke a shattering crash from the gate indicated that it
was about to give way. The men summoned up all their strength
and fell back again, staggering farther back into the crowd so as
to work up greater speed as they hurled themselves forward
again. Landry just had time to push Catherine behind a chapel
buttress and prevent her being trampled by the crowd as it was
forced back against the wall. She ducked obediently, hypnotized
by the Skinner, whose commands had now reached such a
pitch of frenzy that they were unintelligible. She saw him
suddenly tear open his tunic, revealing bulging muscle
covered with reddish hair, then push up his sleeves, and drive
the banner-staff deep into the ground before leaping forward
and seizing the head of the battering-ram.

'Forward!' he bellowed. 'Forward, and may the blessing of
Monseigneur St Jacques go with you!'

'Hurrah for Monseigneur St Jacques! Hurrah for the
Butchers' Guild!' shouted Landry in an excess of excitement.

Catherine looked at him angrily.

'If you go on shouting hurrah for Caboche, I shall go home
and leave you!'

'But why?' Landry asked in genuine amazement. 'He is a great man.'

'He isn't. He's a brute. My father hates him. And so does my sister Joyce whom he wants to marry. He scares me to death. He's so *ugly*!'

'Ugly?' Landry's eyes widened. 'What difference does that make? You don't have to be handsome to be a great man. *I* think Caboche is a hero.'

The young girl stamped her foot angrily.

'Well, *I* don't! And if you had seen him at our house last night, shouting at my father and threatening him, you wouldn't either.'

'But why should he threaten Maître Legoix?'

Instinctively, though the din around them was tremendous and no one around was likely to pay any attention, Landry lowered his voice. Catherine did likewise. In a whisper she described how, the evening before, Caboche had paid them a visit, accompanied by Pierre Cauchon and their cousin William Legoix, a rich butcher from the rue de l'Enfer.

The three rebel leaders had crossed Gaucher's threshold with one thought in mind: to gain his support for their movement. As an officer in the Paris civil militia, with fifty men under his command, Gaucher ranked among the most respected civic leaders: one, too, whose views were sure of a respectful hearing. This may have been because he was a gentle, peaceable sort of man who abhorred violence of any description. Though far from being a physical coward, he would faint at the mere sight of blood.

This physical horror of blood explained why this butcher's son should have left the Guild, and the family home, in order to apprentice himself to Maître André d'Épernon, the celebrated goldsmith. He thus at one stroke severed his ties with the whole Legoix family, who had no patience with such squeamishness.

Little by little Gaucher's skill had brought ease and comfort to the house on the Pont-au-Change. Beautifully wrought and chased covers for the gospel books, ornamental plates, sword and dagger scabbards, massive salt-cellars and table vessels were fashioned in his modest workshop in ever-increasing numbers, destined for ever more illustrious persons. The fame of Gaucher Legoix had in fact spread throughout Paris and the three men hoped great things from his support.

They had been met by a point-blank refusal. Quietly but firmly, as was his wont, Gaucher informed them of his intention of remaining loyal to the King and to the Provost of Paris, his former master André d'Épernon.

'I hold my command from the King and the Provost, and I will not lead my men against the King's palace.'

'Your King is mad, he is surrounded by traitors,' roared Guillaume Legoix, the butcher cousin. 'The real king is Milord of Burgundy. He is our only hope. . . .'

Gaucher gazed unmoved at the master-butcher's heavy countenance, now flushed and swollen with anger.

'When Milord of Burgundy has been anointed and crowned, I will kneel before him and call him king. Till then the only king I recognize is Charles VI, to whom may it please God to restore both health and sanity.'

These quiet words were enough to throw the three visitors into a towering rage. They all began shouting like maniacs, to the alarm of Catherine, who had been waiting the outcome of the dispute with the rest of the womenfolk, tucked away in the giant chimney-place.

How fierce those three men looked crowding so tall and threatening around her father's frail form! And yet, for all his lack of inches, it was Gaucher Legoix who seemed to be in command of the situation. His face stayed composed and he did not raise his voice.

All of a sudden Caboche waved his knotty fist in Legoix's face.

'You have till tomorrow to reconsider your decision, Maître Legoix. You realize that, if you are not with us, you are automatically against us and must take the consequences. You know what happens to the people who side with the Armagnacs?'

'If by that you mean you will set fire to my house, well, I

can't stop you! But you will not persuade me to take up arms against my conscience. I am neither for Armagnac nor for Burgundy. I am simply a patriotic Frenchman who fears God and serves his King. And I will never take up arms against him!'

Leaving his companions to remonstrate with Legoix, Caboche strode over to where Loyse was sitting. Catherine felt her sister stiffen all over when the Skinner planted himself in front of her. It was common practice in the great houses to marry off young daughters, so Catherine quite understood the significance of the scene that followed.

Not that Simon the Skinner made any secret of his passion for Loyse. He lost no opportunity to pester her with his attentions on those rare occasions when they met by chance. Rare because Loyse scarcely ever left her parents' home except to hear Mass at the near-by church of St Leufroy, at the other end of the bridge, or to pay a charitable visit to the recluse of St Opportune. She was a quiet secretive girl with, at seventeen, the gravity of someone twice her age. She came and went about the house quiet as a mouse, her blue eyes modestly lowered, a linen kerchief tightly bound round her pale blonde plaits. She was already, among the family, leading the cloistered existence for which she had longed since she was a little girl.

Catherine admired her sister, but she was also a little afraid of her. And she did not understand her at all. Loyse could have been pretty and attractive if she hadn't been so fond of mortifying herself and had only allowed herself to smile sometimes. She was slim but not skinny, with a pretty, supple, lissom figure. Her features were delicate, a trifle long in the nose perhaps, but she had a pretty mouth and white, almost transparent skin. Catherine, who was always ablaze with vitality herself, who loved noise, bustle and gaiety, could not for the life of her understand what had attracted Caboche, a huge uproarious fellow with a keen relish for the more robust and earthly pleasures, to this aspiring nun. Loyse, for her part, clearly found Caboche repulsive. In fact, she all but saw him as the Devil incarnate. As he came towards her she crossed herself hurriedly. Caboche scowled.

'I am not Sir Satan, my beauty, that you should greet me thus. You would be better employed in trying to persuade your father to join forces with us.'

Without raising her eyes from her shoes, Loyse murmured:

'I could not do that. It is not a daughter's place to give her father advice. What he does is right. . . .'

Her fingers closed furtively on her rosary in her apron pocket. She turned aside to poke the logs in the hearth, thus indicating clearly that her interview with Caboche was at an end. A gleam of anger flashed in the Skinner's pale eyes.

'You may pipe a very different tune tomorrow night, my pretty, when my men take you from your bed and tumble you. But don't worry, I shall be the first among them. . . .'

Of a sudden he staggered back. Gaucher Legoix had seized him by the collar and was about to throw him out. Legoix was white with fury and his anger lent him new strength. Caboche faltered in the grip of his thin hand.

'Get out!' Gaucher cried in a voice trembling with rage and indignation. 'Get out, you filthy swine! And don't let me catch you sniffing round my daughter again!'

'Your daughter!' Caboche sneered. 'You will be sorry you ever had a daughter by the time I and a few others have finished with her . . . if you haven't come to your senses by then.'

Catherine watched with horror as Gaucher hurled himself in a fury at Caboche. He was just about to strike him when Cauchon intervened. He stepped between the two men and separated them with his long skinny arms.

'Enough,' he said coldly. 'This is not the time for such disputes. Caboche has let his tongue run away with him and Legoix is both obstinate and impulsive. I suggest we take our leave now. Night will no doubt bring wise counsel to each of you. I hope that you, Gaucher Legoix, will listen to the voice of reason.'

Landry sat on a cornerstone and listened to Catherine without interrupting.

Her story gave him food for thought. He ardently admired

Caboche, but equally he valued Gaucher's good opinion. Besides, the threats against the Legoix family disgusted him. . . .

A dry, rending, splitting sound, followed almost immediately by a loud crash, broke into his thoughts. The palace gates had given way at last and, with a triumphant yell, the crowd poured into the breach like a river bursting its banks. In a second Landry and Catherine were left standing alone in a great empty space. Empty, that is, save for the dead and wounded and the dogs which sniffed and licked at the patches of bloodstained earth. The white banner still flapped where Caboche had planted it near the gates. Everyone else had vanished into the palace gardens. Landry grabbed the terrified Catherine by the hand.

'Come on then. They have gone in. . . .'

The little girl recoiled a step. Her eyes, dark with foreboding, gazed fearfully at the splintered gates.

'I don't think I want to now,' she said in a small voice.

'Don't be silly. What are you afraid of? You will never get another chance like this. Come on!'

Landry was flushed with excitement, all agog to follow the crowd and take a share in the looting and pillaging. The irrepressible curiosity of the Parisian urchin, together with a certain innate delight in violence, was proving too much for him. If she refused to follow him, Catherine realized, he was quite capable of abandoning her there in the street. She decided to go with him.

The rue Saint-Antoine was by no means deserted. Some distance beyond the palace another crowd, packed to overflowing in the space left between the Hôtel des Tournelles, Porte Saint-Antoine, Hôtel du Petit-Musc and the crenellated mass of the Bastille, were getting ready to lay siege to the newly built fortress whose white walls rose sheer above their heads.

News had reached them that Pierre des Essarts, former Provost of Paris, accused by the people of treason, had taken refuge there with five hundred men-at-arms with the intention of keeping the townspeople at bay. A steadily growing mob, armed with every conceivable sort of weapon, was making its way there determined to capture des Essarts even if it meant taking the Bastille apart, stone by stone. People arrived running from the other end of the street, by the Palace de Grève. Some went into the palace and others ran on to help in the attack on the fortress.

One of the palace windows opened and a chest came hurtling out with a metallic crash of pots and pans. The sight helped Catherine make up her mind. Curiosity got the better of fright. Seizing Landry's hand, she ran through the gate, whose shattered doors still creaked and swung from their massive hinges. Her eyes were round with excitement at the thought of what she was about to see.

The immense gardens, as they discovered once they were through the gate, had been flattened by the mob in its rush for the palace. What had been formal beds of roses and violets edged by clipped yew borders was now no more than trampled earth, leafless stalks and crushed, muddy petals. Lilies and roses lay trodden into the mud.

Beyond, Catherine had her first glimpse of that town-within-a-town which was the Saint-Pol Palace. It consisted of a huge sprawl of buildings. There were chapels, sheds for livestock, stables and small buildings designed to house an army of servants. All around lay gardens, vineyards and small thickets, intersected by cloisters and galleries and courtyards. There were menageries of lions, hunting leopards, bears and other strange beasts, and also aviaries full of exotic birds. The Royal Residence was composed of three separate buildings: the King's Palace, which faced the gardens along the Seine, the Queen's, which fronted on the little rue Saint-Pol, and the Dauphin's, usually known as the Hôtel de Guyenne, which opened on to the rue Saint-Antoine.

It was towards this latter building that the crowd directed its fury. Men-at-arms encircled the palace with the idea of blocking any attack on the dwellings of the King or Queen. But the crowd gave them no trouble. It had other things in mind.

The courtyards and staircases of the Hôtel de Guyenne were

packed with people. The din that arose from them, intensified
by the stone-vaulted ceilings and huge size of the apartments,
was deafening. Catherine had to cover her ears with her hands.
Bodies of royal servants, in their violet silk tunics, lay abou⁺ the
floor. Costly glazed windows were being wantonly smashed.
Tapestries hung in tatters from the white stone walls of the
main staircase, and there were great holes in the painted
frescoes where they had been slashed with axes or the great
iron hammers used to stun animals in the slaughter-house.
The looters had swarmed into the dining-hall, a vast apartment
whose long central table was laid out for a banquet. They
slipped and skidded in puddles of wine, blood and greasy
sauces, fought like dogs over the pastries and roast meats and
stumbled over a litter of weapons and metal plates and vessels
which had been thrown aside because they were neither gold
nor silver. There was barely room to breathe. But Catherine
and Landry were both agile and nimble on their feet and they
managed to push their way up the stairs to the floor above
without too much difficulty. Catherine got through with no
more than a scratched cheek and a few wrenched-out hairs.
Landry even succeeded in snatching up a few little marchpane
cakes on his way past the table and he shared these with his
little friend. They were welcome. Catherine felt quite faint
with hunger.

As they were wolfing down this unexpected treat they found
themselves being pushed forward with the crowd towards a
large chamber, from which angry cries and shouts were audible.
As they went in Catherine looked about her, dazzled by the
magnificence of the scene. She had never seen anything com-
parable to the colourful tapestries, woven of silk shot with
gold thread, which adorned the walls. They showed beautiful
ladies, gorgeously dressed, walking white hounds through
meadows starred with flowers, or listening to music sitting under
a canopy hung with gold tassels. The far end of the apartment
was entirely taken up by a huge white marble chimneypiece,
carved as intricately as a piece of lace, and an immense bed
which stood on a raised dais and was curtained with purple

velvet fringed with gold. The arms of Guyenne and Burgundy were carved at the head of the bed. The walls of the room were lined with settles and dressers displaying vases and goblets of precious metals encrusted with gems and fantastically shaped Venetian goblets whose rainbow-hued glass outshone the brightest jewels. Catherine's rapt and starry-eyed survey of her surroundings did not continue for long, however. Her attention was soon drawn to the dramatic scene which was being enacted in this sumptuous setting.

In the two men standing by the chimneypiece Catherine recognized the Duke of Burgundy and his son Philippe de Charolais. The latter she had often seen passing in front of her parents' house on his way over the bridge. But she had never seen the formidable Jean-sans-Peur at such close quarters before. The Duke, planted squarely on short sturdy legs, prominent eyes taking in everything around him, seemed to dominate the room. There was something implacable about this man which struck everyone who saw him, something as implacable as fate itself.

Count Philippe de Charolais was very different from his father. He was tall for his seventeen years, thin, fair-haired, with a haughty manner, finely-cut features and the sort of humorous mouth which often curves into a smile. He stood, dressed in green and silver, a little behind his father, in a very different pose. Catherine's eyes lingered on him briefly because she found him handsome and well-dressed. Beside him stood a fat youth of sixteen or so, magnificently and richly dressed in scarlet, white and black crossed by a gold sword belt. He addressed the Duke in a voice trembling with rage and misery, emotions reflected on his rather undistinguished features. This, Landry whispered to Catherine, was the Dauphin himself, Louis de Guyenne.

Around these three principal figures in the drama a fierce struggle was raging between a group of rebels and several noblemen, most of whom were wounded but still desperately resisting capture. A body slid, stabbed to the heart, to the black and white marble floor, its life blood slowly ebbing away.

The contrast between the impassive Burgundians, the violence of the rebels and the tearful Dauphin, his hands outstretched in an imploring gesture, was striking and bizarre. Catherine caught sight of Caboche once more in the thick of the brawl, his white hood and sweat-soaked tunic thrown into sharp relief by the black robes, measured gestures and glacial calm of Pierre Cauchon. She found Cauchon, with his imperturbable calm, a terrifying figure.

The noise and confusion was at its height. The rebels had seized several nobles, ranging in age from youths to old men, and were now dragging them, securely bound, towards the street. Two of them were still struggling with a young man who could not have been more than sixteen. A young lady tried to shield him with her body despite his repeated efforts to push her aside. She was dark, and delicately pretty, still childish in appearance in spite of her elegant dress of heavy bronze damask and high, double-tiered, white muslin head-dress. She clung to the young man, sobbing and imploring his assailants to spare him. Just as the rebels were about to drag her off the Dauphin intervened in a fury. Drawing his sword, he leapt towards the two men who had had the effrontery to lay hands on his wife, and cut them down with two swift strokes. Then, pointing his bloody sword at Jean-sans-Peur, he addressed him angrily.

'What sort of coward, cousin, stands by and lets his own daughter be handled by these rough curs before his very eyes ? This riot is your doing, sire. Do not trouble to deny it. I see your men among the mob. Rest assured that I shall not forget this day. . . . Fate may not always treat you so kindly!'

Philippe de Charolais had also automatically unsheathed his sword to go to his sister's aid. Now, with its point, he gently turned aside the blade that threatened his father's heart. The Duke himself had not moved. He shrugged and said, coldly, 'There is nothing I can do at this point, Louis, contrary to what you may suppose. Things have got out of hand. I can no longer control these brutes. If it were possible I would at least have attempted to save my daughter's retainers. . . .'

As Catherine looked on, helplessly, the young man whom the Dauphin had been vainly trying to protect was at last captured. When the Dauphin had dispatched his two assailants he had run to a window and was just about to leap out into the garden when he was seized and dragged back by three skinners from the slaughter-house and a pair of terrible shrieking harpies. The young Duchess collapsed on the bed and wept bitterly.

'Save him, Father, I beg of you. Don't let them take him. . . . Not Michel. . . . He's my friend!'

The Duke's reply to this appeal was an impatient gesture which drew an indignant cry from Catherine. She was deeply impressed by Mme la Dauphine and would have liked to help her if she could. This Duke who ignored his daughter's tears must be a truly evil man! The Comte de Charolais was white to the lips. He was himself married to the Dauphin's sister, the Princess Michelle, and Marguerite's distress was painful to him. But there was nothing now he could do. Caboche himself and his acolyte Denisot de Chaumont had hold of the young prisoner. They snatched him from the men who were tying him up and propped him up between them. With a sudden bound the young man broke free, and Catherine gave a cry which passed unnoticed. For his age Michel de Montsalvy was unusually strong and powerful. Thrusting the butchers aside he ran towards the Duke of Burgundy and stopped, panting, before him. His angry voice made itself heard above the tumult.

'Jean de Bourgogne, I herewith proclaim you a craven coward, and a traitor to your King whose dwelling you allow to be desecrated thus! I proclaim you unfit to wear the spurs of a knight. . . .'

Caboche and Denisot, who had by now recovered from their surprise, once more seized hold of their prisoner. They tried to force him to kneel before the man he had insulted, but he kicked out so fiercely that he managed to break free once more, in spite of his bound hands, and again went up to Jean-sans-Peur as if intending to add something further. The Duke's face was livid with rage. He opened his mouth to speak, but before he could utter a word the onlookers saw his face pale, and one hand fly up to his cheek. Michel de Montsalvy had spat in his face. . . .

Catherine realized that the young man had just signed his own death warrant.

'Take him away!' the Duke cried hoarsely. 'Do what you like with him! Let the others be taken to my house where they will remain as my guests for the night. You have my word upon it, son-in-law!'

The Dauphin did not answer, but turned his back on the Duke and leant his face against the chimneypiece. The little Duchess still wept, refusing to allow herself to be comforted by her brother.

'I will never forgive you . . . never!' she stammered between her sobs. Caboche and Denisot meanwhile had seized the prisoner firmly and were pushing him towards the stairs.

Catherine slid a trembling hand into Landry's and whispered. 'What will they do to him?'

'Hang him, and sharp about it, I should hope! It's all he deserves, dirty Armagnac scum that he is! Did you see what he did? He spat in the Duke's face. . . .'

Landry joined vigorously in the chorus of voices now chanting bloodthirstily: 'Death to him! To the gallows with him!'

Catherine snatched her hand away. She was crimson to the roots of her hair.

'Oh! Landry Pigasse! You disgust me!'

Before Landry could recover his surprise she had whirled round and vanished into the crowd, which had parted briefly to allow the prisoner and his captors to pass. She pushed frantically after him.

Catherine would have found it difficult to explain just what was going on at this point in her childish heart. She had never laid eyes on Michel de Montsalvy before. An hour before she had not even heard his name. Yet, suddenly, he seemed as near and dear as her father, or sister, and she felt as if she had always known him. Invisible bonds had suddenly been forged between the young nobleman and the goldsmith's daughter. Bonds rooted deep in the heart, and ones which would cause great suffering.

Catherine's only conscious thought was that she must follow the prisoner and discover, at all costs, what was to become of him. She had seen him twice at close quarters, once when the skinners were tying him up and once when he had insulted the Duke. Both times the light from the window had been shining full on to his face, and the sight of him made her feel quite giddy, with red spots dancing in front of her eyes, like the time she had tried to outstare the sun for a joke. It did not seem credible that a young man could be so beautiful.

Beautiful he undoubtedly was, with fine, clear-cut features which might have seemed almost feminine in their perfection but for the firm chin and mouth and haughty blue eyes. His gleaming blond hair, which he wore short at the nape and above the ears, had the smooth casque-like look which was then fashionable, and which permitted a helmet to be worn on top without discomfort. He had an athlete's shoulders under the purple silk doublet embroidered with silver leaves and his tight grey and silver hose revealed the muscular calves and thighs of a skilled horseman. Standing there between the two butchers, his hands tied behind his back and his head arrogantly raised, eyes cold with anger and a scornful smile on his lips, he looked like some archangel fallen into evil hands. Catherine was reminded suddenly of a picture she had admired in a finely illuminated gospel for which her father had been working a cover of chased gold. It showed a golden-haired young knight, in silver armour, standing on a dragon which he had transfixed with his lance. Gaucher had explained to her that this represented Michael the Archangel and his victory over the Evil One. It was he whom the young man resembled . . . and his name was Michael too.

This thought only added to Catherine's determination to help him in some way, or at least to stay near him as long as she could.

A mass of people crowded along behind the prisoner, all screaming for his punishment by death. Catherine, jostled this way and that, had the utmost difficulty in keeping up. At length a daring idea suggested itself to her; with tremendous effort she pushed up close behind the huge bulk of Caboche the Skinner himself and clung on round his waist. Elated by his recent triumphs, the Skinner did not even notice, just as Catherine was oblivious of the blows and knocks she was receiving in the press of bodies and of the feet stepping painfully on hers. She had long ago lost her cap, and from time to time someone dragged at her loosened hair. But in some mysterious way a current of hope and encouragement seemed to flow into her from the fair-haired boy in front.

There were other prisoners besides Michel de Montsalvy: the Duc de Bar, cousin of the Dauphin, Jean de Vailly, Chancellor of Guyenne, the Dauphin's Chamberlain, Jean de la Rivière, the two Giresmes brothers, and a score or so more. They were all being dragged along, in chains, like common criminals, through a volley of spit and insults. As she went through the heavily carved oak door at the head of the stairs, Catherine caught a fleeting glimpse of the long, morose features of the Maître Pierre Cauchon. He stood in his black robes, with his back to the wall, trying to avoid being swept along by the crowd. Catherine was astonished to intercept the look he cast at the prisoner as he went by. His dim, lack-lustre eyes suddenly sparkled as if the sight of the young nobleman on his way to the scaffold gave Cauchon exquisite pleasure, and satisfied some deep need for revenge. . . . A wave of nausea passed over her. Catherine had never liked Cauchon. Now he positively sickened her.

As the crowd pushed towards the palace door the struggling and jostling grew more savage. Catherine was forced to relinquish her hold on Caboche and found herself being gradually forced back. Her protesting scream went unheeded in the din. Then the feel of warm sunshine on her face a second later told her that they were once more in the open air. The rushing torrent of humanity spread out momentarily, scattering over the sanded alleys before flowing together again for the plunge through the shattered gates. Catherine took a deep breath, like a gallant little soldier before the attack. Then she was dismayed to discover that the prisoner and his escort were at that very

moment going through the archway. She could just make out
Michel's golden head in the midst of gleaming steel helmets and
halberds. A second later he vanished from sight. Catherine gave
a cry of dismay and was just about to fling herself after him when
she felt a strong hand seize her by the shoulder, holding her
back.

'Found you again at last!' came Landry's voice. 'What a
fright you gave me! This is the last time I take you anywhere
with me, you can be sure of that! There's a devil in you!'

Landry had evidently encountered considerable resistance
on his way through the stampede in the Hôtel de Guyenne. He
had a black eye, one bare and bleeding knee, and one of his
sleeves had been torn right off. The fine green tunic with its
white Burgundian emblem, which he had flaunted so proudly
that morning, was now a sorry looking, bedraggled object. He
had lost his cap and his black hair stood stiffly up all over his
head. But Catherine was beyond noticing these sartorial details.
Wiping her eyes on a corner of her torn dress, she raised her
small tragic face to her friend's.

'Landry, help me, help me to save him, I beg you!'

Landry gazed at the little girl in stunned surprise.

'Save who? The Armagnac fellow whom Caboche plans to
hang? You must be out of your mind. Anyway, what difference
does it make to you whether they string him up or not? You
don't even know him!'

'I know, I know. But I don't want him to die. You know what
happens when they hang someone. . . . They string them up on
those dreadful rusty chains between the pillars . . .'

'Well, and why not? He is nothing to us.'

Catherine shook her head violently, throwing back her long
hair with an unconsciously graceful movement which touched
the boy. Catherine's hair and eyes were her only claims to
beauty – but how beautiful they were! Her hair was a golden
fleece such as can rarely have been seen on such a young girl.
Where the sun caught it it seemed shot through with light.
Loosened, it hung about her like a magnificent cloak of soft,
living silk, reaching almost to her knees and enveloping her

in all the radiance of a summer's day – a radiance which could sometimes be heavy to carry about.

As for Catherine's eyes, her family had not yet decided just what their colour was. In quiet moments they looked dark blue, with velvety purple shadows like Lenten violets. When she was happy they sparkled with golden rays like a honeycomb held up to the sun. And on the occasions when she flew into one of her rare, inexplicably violent rages the pupils went a stygian black from which her family had learned to expect the worst.

In other respects she was like other girls of her age, a child who had shot up too quickly. She had skinny arms, knees like a small boy's, knobbly and perpetually covered with cuts and grazes, and her movements had the clumsiness of a young fawn which has not quite discovered what to do with its legs. She had a comic little pointed face with a short little nose and wide mouth, a little like a cat's. Her skin was fair, faintly golden and generously sprinkled with freckles. The general effect, however, had a distinct charm to which Landry was far from insensible, though he would rather have died than admit it. Her whims and caprices grew daily wilder. But this latest notion was far and away the most outlandish yet. . . .

'Why does his life mean so much to you?' he whispered suspiciously.

'I don't know,' Catherine said softly. 'I just know that if he dies I shall be very, very sad. It would make me cry a lot . . . for a long time.'

She said this in a calm little voice but with such conviction that Landry simply gave up trying to understand. He just knew that he would do all he could to help, bitter as the pill might be to swallow. It was easy to say 'Save the prisoner'. But his mind reeled at the thought of what those three words represented in reality. First of all it meant snatching the prisoner from his escort of archers under the very nose of the crowd, and particularly of Caboche and Denisot, both of whom were capable of flattening him with a single blow. Then, assuming that they got that far, which was not likely, they had still to find somewhere to hide him in a town where he and his like were being hunted down like dogs. They would then have to smuggle him out of the city, through barricades, padlocked gates and battlements bristling with men-at-arms. And at every stage they would have to contend with the possibility of spies, treachery and betrayal. Landry reflected that this was asking a lot even of so exceptionally resourceful a fifteen-year-old as himself.

'They will take him to Montfaucon,' he said, thinking aloud. 'It's quite a long way, but not so far that we have time to spare. How do you expect to free him before he reaches the gallows? He has an army round him and there are only two of us.'

'We must keep close behind him,' Catherine insisted. 'We'll find a way.'

'All right then,' Landry sighed, taking her hand. 'Let's go, but you mustn't be angry with me if we don't succeed.'

'You will try? You really will try?'

'Yes,' the boy groaned. 'But this is absolutely the last time I take you out with me. Next time you might want me to take the Bastille single-handed!'

Landry and Catherine were panting and breathless by the time they reached the rue Saint-Denis, but they had the satisfaction of knowing that they had caught up with Montsalvy and his escort once more. Luckily the latter had been halted several times along the route by shouting, chanting bands of townspeople. Some of these were on their way to help in the storming of the Bastille, while others were heading towards the Hôtel d'Artois, in the rue Mauconseil, residence of the Duke of Burgundy.

The escort had just halted once more when Landry and Catherine caught up with it. Capeluche, the public executioner, had ordered the halt to enable a passing Augustine friar to shrive the condemned man and help him make his peace with God before dying. It was fear rather than piety which finally persuaded the protesting monk to agree, but when the party started off again he was there, walking along beside the prisoner and telling his beads in an undertone.

'It's lucky for us that they are taking him there on foot,' whispered Landry. 'If they had decided to drag him there, or or put him in a tumbril, we would not have had a chance.'

'Have you thought of something then?'

'I'm not sure. But it is getting dark now and if I can just lay my hands on the one thing I need we might manage it yet. But we will still have to think of somewhere to hide him. . . .'

Just then they were joined by a group of students and women of the town who had come running up to take part in the procession to the gallows. Landry fell silent, but the precaution was unnecessary. Both students and doxies were uproariously drunk, the predictable result of looting a tavern. They shouted and sang at the tops of their voices as they lurched and stumbled from one side of the street to the other.

'The best thing to do,' Catherine whispered, 'would be to hide him in the cellar at home. There is a little window there which faces the river. He couldn't stay there long, but . . .'

Landry promised that she could leave the rest to him. Catherine's suggestion had suddenly inspired him and the rest of the plan presented no problem.

'I'll steal a boat tonight and bring it alongside your house. All he has to do is slide down a rope into the boat and then go on up river as far as Corbeil where Comte Bernard d'Armagnac has his camp, dropping me off somewhere along the way. Of course, he would have to get past the chains they have stretched across the river between La Tournelle and the Île Louviaux, but that should not be too difficult at present . . . there is no moon. Anyway, we should have done all we could then and the rest would be up to him, or fate. It would be something of a triumph if we even got as far as that. . . .'

The young girl silently squeezed his hand. A new hope was making her tremble with excitement. It was getting dark rapidly, but people were lighting torches all around them, and the light flickered over the near-by houses, with their overhanging eaves, gilded and painted signs and small leaded

windows, before moving on and briefly lighting up the red
faces of the crowd.

The uproar was deafening and seemed a strangely in-
appropriate accompaniment to the last moments of a man on
his way to the gallows. Landry suddenly caught sight of the
thing he had been hoping to find and gave a broad, satisfied
grin.

'There we are!' he exclaimed. 'I was hoping that there might
be a few of them around with all this commotion. . . .'

The thing he had spotted with such satisfaction turned out
to be a fine, fat pig which came round the corner of the rue
des Prêcheurs just then, in pursuit of a juicy cabbage leaf.
Pairs of these respectable animals patrolled the streets of Paris
all day long, in charge of a friar, hunting edible refuse and
rummaging among the slops.

Like all the convent pigs this one wore a blue enamelled tau
cross, emblem of St Anthony, round its neck. It paused to
masticate its cabbage leaf at the foot of a large carved post
representing the Tree of Jesse which stood at the corner of a
house. Landry let go of Catherine's hand.

'The other pig can't be far. You go on without me. I'll meet
you farther up the street by the Filles-Dieu convent. Condemned men always stop there for a while so that the sisters
can give them a little comfort. The nuns wait by the church
porch and offer them a glass of wine, three pieces of bread
and the crucifix to kiss. The guard always slackens off then,
and that's the moment I shall try to take advantage of. You
must be ready to make a run for it any time I give the signal.'

He kept one eye on the pig as he spoke. Having finished its
meal the beast was heading for the rue des Prêcheurs, where
its companion pig and the monk in charge of them were both
presumably to be found. Catherine watched Landry start off
in pursuit. They were soon lost to sight in the darkness of the
street. She set off again herself. For the first time that day
she suddenly realized the full extent of her weariness, perhaps
because she had been temporarily deprived of Landry and
his reassuring presence. Her feet hurt and every muscle in her

legs seemed to ache. Then the torchlight flashed briefly over Michel's golden head in the distance and she felt her spirits rise again. She even forced herself to walk faster, hurrying along at the back of the procession and then, in a sudden burst of energy, thrusting her way deeper into it.

Pushing through this crowd of excited, struggling, agitated people, not one of whom relinquished his or her place without a struggle, was difficult and often painful, but the emotion which propelled Catherine forward was stronger than fear of pain or blows. Somehow she succeeded in forcing her way up close behind the guard of archers. She glimpsed the prisoner's tall figure only a few feet away between a couple of men-at-arms. He walked erect, head held high, at a slow composed pace, looking so proud that Catherine was lost in admiration. As she stumbled and pushed her way along she murmured all the prayers she knew, lamenting that she was not as well versed in these things as her sister Loyse, who knew the right prayers for any contingency as well as one for each of the Saints in Heaven.

Presently they reached the Convent of the Filles-Dieu. The sisters had been forewarned of their arrival and they were waiting to receive the condemned man. Gathered on the church steps, round the abbess who stood holding the crucifix, they looked like a group of black-and-white statues, all with modestly lowered eyes. One of them proffered the bread on a plate, another came forward with a goblet and a pitcher of wine. The escort halted, and Catherine's heart missed a beat. This was the moment – but Landry was nowhere to be seen!

Capeluche grabbed the end of the rope which bound Michel's hands and twisted it round his wrist to lead the prisoner to the church steps. Just as the escort drew back to let the pair pass a wild and hideous screeching filled the air. Two pigs, screaming shrilly, rushed at whirlwind speed out of a near-by alley and charged at the soldiers with such force that four of them were knocked flying. Each of the unfortunate animals had a bundle of blazing hemp tied to its tail, which explained the screaming and frenzy. Several torches were sent flying, burning people in the crowd, while the pigs, in a paroxysm of pain and agony, kept on rushing at the guard. There was such confusion for a few minutes that no one noticed Landry insinuate himself in the wake of the pigs, deftly cut the rope which bound Michel to the executioner and push him down a dark narrow alley opposite the convent. Everyone was far too busy inspecting their cuts and bruises and trying to collect their wits. A few of the braver souls were trying to catch the pigs. Catherine, who had been watching for it, was the only person who noticed the brilliant piece of strategy which did such credit to Landry's coolness, courage and ingenuity. She raced after them down the narrow alley, stumbling in the dark on the slimy mud which was strewn with stones and other less readily identifiable objects.

She heard Landry's muffled voice.

'Is that you, Catherine? Hurry up! There's no time to lose!'

'I'm coming!'

The darkness was so intense that she sensed rather than saw their two silhouettes, one tall, the other slightly shorter. The alley turned and twisted, as though trying to lose itself in the bowels of the earth. The weird, derelict buildings on either side seemed to spring up at her out of the blackness like evil spirits. There was no light anywhere to be seen in this labyrinth of sinister, deserted alleys. All the dilapidated doors were shut and the windows blanks, their shutters torn away. Catherine was so tired that her heart felt as if it were bursting. But the three fugitives could still hear the mob roaring in the distance and fear gave them wings.

In the dark Catherine tripped over a paving-stone and fell flat with a cry of pain. She was pulled up again by Landry, almost in tears, and they all set off again on their headlong flight.

Lanes and alleys branched off on all sides, punctuated here and there by dark stairways which seemed to plunge down into the depths of the earth. They appeared to be in a labyrinth from which escape was impossible. Dragged along by Landry, breathless, and frightened, Catherine climbed three flights of steps and turned sharply into an alley which suddenly opened out into a sort of square, surrounded on all four sides by tottering, shapeless buildings which seemed in imminent danger of collapsing on top of each other. There was an unpleasant stench. Gaps in the pointed rooftops showed here and there against the sky like missing teeth. The walls of rough stone, crudely cemented together with clay, bulged like abscesses under the weight of their roof beams, now swollen with water. A few drops of rain fell.

'Rain can only be a help to us at this stage,' said Landry, coming to a stop and signalling to the others to follow suit. They leant against the wall of a house trying to get their breath back. They had all run so far and so hard that their lungs seemed about to burst.

Suddenly the profound stillness which reigned in this eerie place impressed itself on them. Catherine whispered, awe-struck: 'I can't hear anything now. Do you think they are still after us?'

'Yes, but it's a dark night and they won't follow us here. We are safe for the moment.'

'Why? Where are we then?'

Catherine's eyes had grown used to the darkness. She was now able to make out the outline of the decrepit, ramshackle buildings all round them. Across the square a light glimmered feebly in an iron cage, half extinguished by the cutting wind. Overhead, the smoky clouds, drifting across an ink-black sky, were like a canopy stretched over the island of silence their surroundings formed amid the tumult of the town. Landry made a sweeping gesture:

'This,' he announced, 'is the Grande Cour des Miracles – the place where miracles happen. There are several of them in Paris, one between the Porte Saint-Antoine and the Palais des Tournelles, for instance. This one is the most important though. It is the personal domain of the King of Thune.'

'But there is no one here,' Catherine said nervously.

'It's too early. The beggars don't return to their hovels till the rest of the world is abed . . . or later.'

Landry was busy, as he spoke, untying Michel's bonds. The youth stood leaning against a wall, breathing in painful gasps. It is not easy to run for one's life with one's hands tied behind one's back. He seemed to be exhausted. When Landry's knife finally released his hands he sighed deeply and rubbed his aching wrists.

'Why have you done this for me?' he asked in tones of utter weariness. 'Why try to save me? And why should you risk your lives on my account? Don't you realize you could be hung for this?'

'Oh, as for that, we rescued you because you seemed a little young for gibbet meat, messire. I am Landry Pigasse. This is Catherine Legoix. We live on the Pont-au-Change where our fathers trade as goldsmiths.'

Michel reached out and gently touched the girl's head.

'The little golden-haired girl! I noticed you earlier on when they were tying me up. I have never seen hair like yours before, child,' he murmured. His voice disturbed Catherine even more than the touch of his hand as it stroked her silky mane of hair. She cried fervently:

'We *want* to rescue you! We will smuggle you out of Paris tonight. We live on the bridge, as Landry says, and you can hide in the little room under my father's house which we use as a cellar. It has a skylight, and when Landry brings a boat beneath at midnight all you have to do is to slide down a rope and then go up river as far as Corbeil where Monseigneur d'Armagnac has his camp!'

In her eagerness to win the young man's trust and confidence she delivered this speech without once pausing for breath. She was frightened by the despairing note in his voice and sensed obscurely that the black wing of the angel of death had brushed him so closely that its malefic influence must linger with him still. On top of which, the manner of his rescue must seem incomprehensible at first sight.

The young nobleman's teeth gleamed in the darkness, and she realized he was smiling.

'A bold scheme and an ingenious one! But have you thought

for a minute of the danger which you and your families run if this plan is discovered?'

'If you think too much you never do anything at all,' Landry complained. 'We have made up our minds and we are going to go through with it.'

'Wise words!' said a voice which seemed to come from the heavens. 'But it is as well to make sure that circumstances and the fates are on your side first. Now, don't be afraid! I won't give you away!'

There was nothing very reassuring, however, about the face which appeared at a window above their heads, framed in festoons of cobwebs. The flickering light of a tallow candle revealed a swarthy countenance seamed with wrinkles of which the chief ornaments were a huge nose with a wart growing on it and a pair of tiny sparkling eyes half hidden by arched brows. Long black locks escaping from beneath a grimy hood completed a picture which was irresistibly reminiscent of one of the gargoyles of Notre-Dame. It was prevented from appearing quite horrendous by an ear-splitting grin which displayed a set of dazzling white ferocious-looking teeth. Landry exclaimed in surprise:

'Is that you, Barnaby? Back already?'

'As you see, my son. I'm not in good voice today . . . a slight touch of hoarseness. So I stayed at home. Just a minute now. I am on my way down.'

The candle which he had been waving amiably about during this last sentence disappeared from view, and there was a squeak as of rusty bolts being drawn.

'Do you know him?' Catherine asked in astonishment.

'Of course. And so do you for that matter. It's Barnaby of the Cockleshells. You know, the fellow who wears an old coat sewn all over with cockleshells and stands begging at the entrance to St Opportune? He says he's a pilgrim back from Compostela and sometimes manages to sell a relic or two.'

Catherine realized now whom he was talking about. She knew the man well by sight. He always smiled at her when she and Loyse went to complin or vespers at St Opportune, or when they took food to Agnes the Recluse, with whom the Cockleshell Man often passed the time of day.

Meanwhile, Barnaby had come out of his house, closing the door behind him as carefully as might any worthy burgess. Seen at close quarters he proved to be so tall and thin that he had to stand somewhat stooped. His long legs and spidery arms were half hidden by a cloak which was much frayed but of stout woollen cloth, and on which some twenty or so cockleshells had been sewn. Having attended to the business of locking up his house, he bade Landry and Catherine good evening and then, holding the candle near to Michel's face, gazed thoughtfully at it for a moment.

'You won't get far, young sir, if you continue your stroll tricked out like that!' he observed dryly. 'The devil on't! Silver leaves and the Dauphin's colours! One step outside the boundaries of the Beggars' Kingdom and they'd nab you in a trice! It's all very well to dodge the gallows, and make your excuses to Capeluche, but you must look sharp, or it'll be so much time wasted! The plan these young things have thought up is sound enough as far as it goes, but as things are ten to one the sergeants would lay hold of you somewhere between here and the Pont-au-Change.'

Barnaby disdainfully lifted a corner of the intricately cut purple and silver tunic with his long, thin, oddly flexible fingers.

'I'll take it off,' said Michel, and started to do so. But Barnaby shrugged.

'You would have to take your head off too while you were about it. They can sniff out a nobleman fifteen paces away. I must admit, I can't help wondering whether these two are not a little mad to have involved themselves in an affair like this.'

'Mad or not,' Catherine cried tearfully, 'we are going to save him!'

'Anyway,' Landry said crossly, 'all this talk is getting us nowhere. We have better things to do than stand around talking. We have to think of getting back home. It is pitch-dark now. You will have to help us get out of this place, Barnaby!'

Landry was obviously beginning to think of the sound beating which assuredly awaited both Catherine and himself on their return. Moreover, they still had to work out a way of getting Michel into the Legoix's cellar. By way of an answer Barnaby unrolled the bundle he was carrying under one arm. It proved to be a grey cloak similar to the one he was wearing, but perhaps a shade cleaner. He threw it round Michel's shoulders.

'This is my Sunday best I'm lending you,' he grinned. 'I'd be surprised if they spot you under there. And your shoes are muddy enough now for the colour to pass unnoticed.'

With obvious repugnance the young man slid his arms into the sleeves of the cloak. And then, with a rattle of shells, he drew the hood up over his head.

'A fine pilgrim from Santiago we have here!' Barnaby said jestingly. Then, with an abrupt change of tone:

'We must be off now. Keep close behind me. I shall put the light out.'

Taking Catherine's small hand in his giant paw he led the way across the muddy square. Here and there a faint light flickered, sign that life was returning to this sinister neighbourhood. Shadowy forms slipped along beside the dripping walls. With great strides Barnaby turned into an alley apparently identical to all the others they had seen that night. All the lanes and alleys in the Beggars' Kingdom looked alike, perhaps according to plan, so that any would-be pursuers would be thrown off the scent. Sometimes their route took them under a dripping tunnel, or across a stinking open sewer. Indistinct shadowy figures, fantastic-looking in the dim light, flitted past them in ever-increasing numbers. Occasionally Barnaby exchanged a few unintelligible words with one of them, probably the password which the Beggar King had chosen for that night. It was the hour when both pseudo-cripples and pilgrims, and real beggars and thieves returned to their squalid dwellings. The crumbling battlements of Philippe-Auguste's fortress, still crowned here and there by a half-ruined watch-tower, showed black against the night sky. Barnaby stopped.

'We have reached the bounds of the Beggars' Kingdom now,' he whispered. 'We must be on our guard. Can you run a bit farther?'

Landry and Michel nodded. But Catherine felt as if all her strength had drained out of her. Her eyelids kept drooping and her limbs seemed to be made of lead. Her hands trembled in Barnaby's grasp and a tear rolled down her cheek.

'She is worn out,' Michel said pityingly. 'I'll carry her. She doesn't look very heavy.'

He picked her up in his arms.

'Put your arms round my neck and hold on tight,' he said, smiling.

With a contented sigh Catherine slipped her arms round his neck and let her head droop against his shoulder. Her weariness gave place to deep contentment and a delicious lassitude overcame her. She could see Michel's profile close up now, and she was conscious of the warm scented smell of his skin, a pleasant smell which suggested that he must be a fastidious young man who made great use of soap and water. Not even the layers of filth and grime on his cloak could quite disguise it. Catherine did not know anyone else who smelt so nice. Landry scorned the use of soap and water and tended to give off a somewhat pungent odour. Caboche smelt simply of blood and sweat, Cauchon of acrid dust, fat Marion – the Legoix's servant girl, smelt of smoke and cooking, while Loyse's smell reminded her of cold wax and holy water. Not even Gaucher and his wife smelt so nice as Michel. But then he came from a different world, one which was closed to people like her. Everything was soft, easy and pleasant there. She sometimes day-dreamed about what this world was like when she saw the Court ladies, resplendent in priceless silks and jewels, being carried past in their silk-hung litters.

The three men's flying feet carried them rapidly along streets and across open squares. No one paid any attention to them. The town was still in a state of upheaval. Everyone seemed, if

anything, in a greater state of excitement than ever. The sack
of the Bastille, the successful attack on the Hôtel Saint-Pol,
and the seizure of the Dauphin's counsellors had all combined
to throw the citizens of Paris into transports of joy and excitement which found their expression in turbulent processions
and jubilant singing and dancing round fountains and at
street-corners. With all this going on it was scarcely surprising
that no one paid much attention to this particular group, who
were not, when all was said and done, running that much faster
than anyone else. But things looked quite different once they
had passed the Grand Châtelet, via the rue Pierre-à-Poisson,
and found themselves in sight of the Pont-au-Change. Torches
flamed along the wall nearest the moat, and by their flickering
light it was possible to make out the shapes of two men-at-arms
posted at the end of the bridge. One of them was on the point
of making fast the massive chain which was drawn across the
bridge at night, thus creating a barrier between the City and
the rest of Paris. It had not occurred to the fugitives that the
bridge might be under military guard during the night. The
two men in question wore the Provost's uniform, which meant
that they supported the revolt.

Michel set Catherine down and looked inquiringly at his
companions. Barnaby grimaced.

'I'm afraid I can't help you any further, my young friends. It
would be dangerous for me to have anything to do with the
likes of those two characters over there. The best thing would
be for me to turn back now. You will be better off without me.
And you, take good care of my cloak now!' he added with a
comic look at Michel.

The four of them had crossed the Châtelet's moat and stood
in the shadow of one of the pillars of the church of Saint-
Leufroy, which stood at right angles to the house on the bridge.
The stormy sky was streaked with red here and there where
fires raged below, fanned by the high wind. Huge clouds were
gathering, as black as lead. Rain began falling. Barnaby shook
himself like a skinny mongrel.

'This time it looks as if we shall have to swim for it! I'm

going back now. Good evening to you, my three young friends . . . and good luck!'

Before any of them could utter a word he had vanished into the darkness as silently as a ghost and, peer as they might, they could not make out which way he had gone.

Catherine collapsed on a cornerstone while waiting for the others to decide what to do next. Michel spoke first.

'You have both risked quite enough for me already! I want you to go home. Now that we have reached the Seine all I have to do is to go down by the water's edge and steal a boat. I will get away quite safely, don't worry. . . .'

But here Landry cut in: 'No. You would never make it. For one thing, it is much too early, and for another you have to know where you can steal a boat without running too much risk of being caught.'

'You seem to know your way about,' Michel smiled.

'Of course I do. I know the river and the river-banks like the back of my hand. I spend a lot of time wandering around these parts. You wouldn't even get as far as the water's edge. There are still too many people around.'

As if to reinforce his words, shouts and cries sounded from somewhere behind the Châtelet and parties of men brandishing torches came running towards them along the river-bank. A second later a mighty voice thundered upon the night air, dominating the noise and agitation so effortlessly that soon there was complete silence.

'Listen,' said Catherine, 'it's Caboche speaking to the people! If he comes this way and sees us we shall be lost!'

Michel de Montsalvy hesitated. Compared with this menacing voice, the precise import of which he could not catch but which clearly spelt danger, the dark bridge, guarded by only two men, seemed reassuring. Hardly any lights showed in the houses along the bridge, either because the inhabitants had gone out to swell the mob, or because they had gone to bed early in sheer fright. Landry took the young man's hand.

'Come, don't let's waste any more time. We must take the risk – it is our only chance. But you must leave all the talking to me. I know how to deal with these soldiers. Remember, not a word! They could spot you a mile off by the way you speak.'

There seemed to be no alternative. A crowd was gathering behind the Châtelet. People were flocking along the river-banks towards it. With a last regretful glance at the dark river water Michel agreed. The three young people hurriedly crossed themselves. Michel took Catherine's hand, pulled his hood down over his face and followed Landry, who was boldly advancing towards the guards.

'I shall pray hard to Our Blessed Lady while Landry talks to them,' Catherine whispered. 'She is sure to listen.' Something seemed to have happened to her all of a sudden. Now that they found themselves in real danger she found she cared about nothing except Michel's safety.

As they approached the chain across the bridge the heavens opened, unleashing a sudden torrential downpour of rain. In a second the dust underfoot had turned to squelching mud. The two guards ran for shelter under the porch of a near-by house.

'Hey, you two!' shouted Landry. 'We want to get across!'

One of the two men came suspiciously towards them, furious at being summoned out into the rain again. He trailed his weapon behind him.

'Who are you? What do you want?'

'We want to cross the bridge. We live here. I am Landry Pigasse and my friend here is the daughter of Maître Legoix, the goldsmith. Do hurry up! We are getting wet, and we shall be beaten if we get home too late!'

'What about him? Who is he?' the guard asked, pointing at Michel, who stood motionless, his hands tucked into wide sleeves and his head modestly bent under his hood. Landry was unruffled. He answered without a second's hesitation:

'That's a cousin of mine, Pierrinet Pigasse. He has just come back from Galicia in Spain, where he went to ask St James to intercede for his sins. He is coming home with me.'

'Why can't he speak for himself? He isn't dumb, is he?'

'Almost. You see he made a vow when he was travelling

through Navarre and almost fell into the hands of bandits. He swore not to speak a word for a whole year if he were allowed to return safely to his own country.'

This sort of vow was quite common and the soldier found nothing odd in it. Also, he had had enough of standing chatting under a downpour which seemed to get worse every minute. He raised the heavy chain.

'Very well. You may pass.'

In spite of the rain streaming down their necks Landry and Catherine could have danced for joy when they felt the rough, familiar surface of the bridge underfoot again. They escorted Michel to the Legoix's house.

In the kitchen, which also did duty as a communal room and opened into Gaucher Legoix's workshop, Loyse was busy at the hearth stirring a delicious-smelling stew in a cast-iron pot which was suspended over the fire. Beads of sweat stood out on her forehead along the roots of her pale blonde hair. She turned and stared at Catherine as if she were a visitor from another planet. Dripping wet, her dress torn and splashed with mud, Catherine certainly did look as if she had been splashing through a sewer. She gave a relieved sigh on finding her sister alone, and smiled sunnily at her as though her sudden appearance were the most natural thing in the world.

'Where are Maman and Papa? Are you alone?'

'Do you mind telling me where you have been, in that state?' Loyse asked when she had finally got over her surprise. 'I have been looking for you for hours!'

Catherine wanted to find out how the land lay and how severe a punishment she was likely to get. Also she had to keep talking in order to drown the trap-door's faint creak as Landry let Michel down into the cellar. So she answered by asking another question, raising her voice a little:

'Who is looking for me? Maman or Papa?'

'Neither. Marion. I sent her out to see if she could get any news of you. Papa is still at the House of Pillars, and may not get back tonight. Maman had gone to sit with Dame Pigasse, who is not well. Marion told her you went to visit your god-father so as not to alarm her.'

Catherine was relieved to find that the situation was better than she had supposed. She went up to the fire and stretched her wet hands out to it. She shivered in her wet clothes. Loyse started bustling about.

'Don't just stand there shivering! Take your clothes off. Just look at the mess you are in! Your dress is ruined and you look as though you had paddled in half the gutters in the town.'

'I did fall into one. But it is pouring with rain as well! I wanted to know what was happening, so I thought I would go for a walk and look around. . . .' Without quite knowing why, Catherine started to laugh. She was not afraid of Loyse, who was a good soul and would not talk about her escapade. And it felt good to laugh. It eased her taut nerves. She felt as if she had not laughed for years, the sensation seemed so strange and delightful. She had seen so many terrible things that day.

She began unfastening her dress while Loyse, still grumbling, opened a chest which stood near the hearth and took out a clean chemise and green linen dress which she handed to her sister.

'As you know very well, I shan't mention this to anyone so as not to get you into trouble, but you mustn't do it again, Catherine. You gave me such a fright! Dreadful things have been happening today!'

The girl's distress was genuine. Catherine suddenly felt ashamed. Loyse was paler than usual this evening and there were great dark circles round her blue eyes. A sad little line showed at the corner of her mouth. She must have been tormenting herself all day thinking of Caboche's remarks to her the night before. Impulsively, Catherine flung her arms round her neck and kissed her.

'I'm so sorry! I won't do it again. . . .'

Loyse smiled forgivingly at her, then, taking up a thick shawl, she arranged it round her shoulders.

'I am going round to the Pigasse's house now to see how Dame Pigasse is. She didn't seem too well a little while back.

I'll tell Maman you are back at the same time . . . from your visit to your godfather! Eat something and go to bed.'

Catherine would have liked to detain Loyse a moment longer, but her sharp ears could not detect any suspicious sounds coming from the direction of the workshop. Landry had had plenty of time by now to instal Michel safely in the cellar, close the trapdoor and return home. It only remained for Loyse to depart and she would be alone with Michel.

As soon as she had gone Catherine ran over to the press where bread was stored and cut off a generous hunk of bread. She filled a bowl with the bubbling stew of saffron-spiced mutton. Then she hunted about for a pot of honey and filled a pitcher with fresh water. She would have to make the most of this unexpected solitude to give Michel something to eat. He would need all his strength during the coming night.

The thought of him so close, only a few feet below where she stood, gave Catherine a feeling of indescribable happiness. It made her feel as though the house were a sort of guardian spirit under whose broad wings she and Michel had found refuge and shelter. Nothing bad could happen to Michel so long as he remained under the protection of the Sign of the Holy Tabernacle.

She paused in front of a mirror hanging on the kitchen wall and studied her little face closely. Tonight, for the first time in her life, she wished she looked really pretty – pretty like the girls whom the students whistled after and followed in the streets. With a sigh Catherine patted her barely rounded bodice. Her chances of bewitching Michel seemed pretty small. She picked up the provisions she had collected together and went into the workshop.

Gaucher's workshop was silent and empty. Stools and work tables were ranged along one wall while the tools hung tidily from nails. The big, heavily reinforced cabinets which stood open by day to display the gold and silver ware to prospective clients were now shut and padlocked. The only thing left out seemed to be the little pair of scales Gaucher used to weigh precious stones. The solid oak shutters were all in place, but the door by which Loyse would enter presently was only pushed to.

A trap-door with a heavy iron ring was let into the floor. Catherine lit her candle with a hot cinder. Then she placed the food on a large platter and lifted up the trap-door with some difficulty. Taking care not to miss her footing on the ladder, she went down into the cellar.

She didn't see Michel at first because the small room, which had been hollowed out of one of the piers of the bridge, was full of a medley of things piled high as the roof. It was there the Legoix household stored their wood, water, extra vegetables, the salt press which held a whole pig, and the household tools and ladders. The room was long, narrow and low-ceilinged, lit by a small window just large enough to admit a rather skinny youth.

'It's me, Catherine,' she whispered so as not to frighten him. Something moved in the far corner.

'I'm over here behind the logs.'

Just then her candle flame flickered up and she saw him leaning back against the pile of logs, with the pseudo-pilgrim's cloak spread under him. The silver embroideries on his tunic shone softly in the gloom, and where the candle caught them they gleamed gold. He tried to get up, but Catherine signalled to him to stay where he was. She knelt beside him and put the heavy platter, with its appetizing burden, down on the ground.

'You must be hungry,' she said gently. 'You will need all your strength tonight, so I took advantage of my sister's going out to bring you some food. The house is empty at the moment. Papa has gone to the House of Pillars. Maman is at Landry's house because Landry's mother is having a baby and heaven knows where Marion, the servant girl, has got to. If things go on like this you should be able to get out of Paris tonight without any trouble. Landry is coming back at midnight. It's ten o'clock now.'

'That smells good,' he said with a smile which seemed to melt the marrow in her bones. 'I'm really quite hungry'.

He began devouring the stew, speaking between mouthfuls.

'I still can't believe my luck, Catherine. When they were taking me to the gallows this evening I was so convinced my last hour had come that I felt quite resigned. I had made my farewells to everything I loved. And then out of the blue you come along and give me back my life! It feels quite strange!'

All of a sudden he looked very remote. Fatigue and anguish emphasized the fine-drawn look of his features. In the dancing candlelight his golden hair shone like a halo round his handsome face. He forced a smile to his lips. But Catherine noticed a look of despair in his eyes which left her suddenly afraid.

'But . . . aren't you pleased you have been rescued?'

He glanced up at her and noticed her face cloud over. She looked so frail standing there, cloaked in the shining hair which, now that it had dried, had recovered its usual brilliance. In her green dress she looked disarmingly like some little sylvan nymph. And those enormous eyes of hers, with their liquid depths, reminded him of the young does he used to chase as a child.

'I would be truly ungrateful if I were not,' he said softly.

'Well then . . . eat some honey. And then tell me what you were thinking of just then. Your eyes looked so sad.'

'I was just thinking of my own countryside. I was thinking about it on the way to Montfaucon as well. I realized that I would never see it again and I think it was that which distressed me most.'

'But you will see it again . . . now you are free.'

Michel smiled and took a piece of bread, which he dipped into the honey and then chewed absently.

'I know. But then this feeling I have gets the better of me. . . . Something tells me I shall never return to Montsalvy.'

'You mustn't let yourself think that!' Catherine said severely. 'You are only thinking these morbid thoughts because you are tired and weak. Once you have got your strength back and feel safe again you will find you think quite differently.'

The passing reference to his native region of France had kindled Catherine's curiosity. Her need to learn more about this young man who had so bewitched her was irresistible.

She slid closer to him and watched him thirstily drain the pitcher to its dregs.

'What is the countryside you come from like? Would you tell me about it?'

'Of course.'

Michel closed his eyes for a moment, possibly to evoke the beloved images of his childhood more clearly. He had imagined them so vividly and passionately during that long gallows walk of his that now they were easily conjured up against the dark screen of his closed eyelids.

He described for Catherine the high windy plateau where he had been born. It was a granite country, pierced with little valleys padded with green chestnuts. Around Auvergne the land was pitted with extinct craters, and it was from volcanic rock that the high-piled houses of the village of Montsalvy, crowded round the abbey, were all built – as was the family castle itself, and its little chapel of the Sacred Spring, built on the side of a peak.

His words were so eloquent, though simple, that Catherine seemed to see the fields of barley, the lilac twilight skies when the mountain peaks fade imperceptibly till they resemble a line of blue ghosts, the springs bubbling up crystal clear among smooth stones and then darkening suddenly before plunging into the heart of great lakes, set about with mossy granite boulders like dark carbuncles. She seemed to hear the midday wind singing between the crags and the winter storms moaning round the castle battlements. Michel talked of the flocks of sheep which grazed the countryside, the woods haunted by wolves and wild boar, and the tumbling streams where pink and silver salmon leaped and played. Catherine listened open-mouthed, oblivious of everything in her concentration on this youth and his tale.

'And your parents?' she asked when he fell silent. 'Are they still alive?'

'My father died ten years ago and I hardly remember him. He was an old soldier, and rather grim and forbidding. He spent his youth harrying the British at the side of the Great

Constable of France. After the battle of Châteauneuf-de-Randon, where Bertrand de Guesclin met his death, he hung up his sword and announced that henceforth no leader would again command his unquestioning loyalty. My mother looked after our estates and raised me to manhood. She sent me into the household of Monseigneur de Berry, our feudal lord, and I remained a year in his service before moving to that of Prince Louis de Guyenne. My mother runs our estates as efficiently as a man and brings up my younger brother too.'

These glimpses of a life so much more exalted than her own filled Catherine with respect, though it also made her a little sad.

'You have a brother?'

'Yes. He is two years younger than me and he can't wait to show how much more skilled he is at jousting and feats of arms! There is no doubt,' said Michel with a fond smile, 'that he will make a splendid soldier. You have only to see him leap up on one of those huge farm horses and lead all the village bumpkins in a charge. He is as strong as a Turk and thinks of nothing but glorious wounds and bruises. I am very fond of Arnaud. He starts his military career soon and then my mother will be left quite alone. It will be sad for her, but I know she will never complain. She is too good, and too proud to do that.'

As he talked about his family Michel's face shone so radiantly that Catherine could not resist asking him:

'Is he as handsome as you?'

Michel laughed and patted her head.

'Much handsomer! There is no comparison. And there is a loving heart under his fierce manner. He is proud, generous and passionate. I think he is very fond of me.'

Catherine trembled under his caressing hand, not daring to move. Suddenly Michel leant forward and touched her forehead with his lips.

'Unfortunately,' he said, 'I have no little sister to love.'

'She would have adored you if you had,' Catherine said warmly. Then she stopped horror-struck as footsteps sounded overhead. She had lost track of time and Loyse must have returned. She would have to go back up. Michel had heard the sounds too and raised his head, listening. Hurriedly Catherine snatched some logs up to give herself an excuse for being in the cellar and started up the ladder, putting her finger to her lips to warn Michel to keep quiet. When the trap-door closed he found himself in total darkness once more. When Catherine reached the kitchen with her candle precariously balanced on the bundle of logs she found not Loyse, but Marion. Marion looked at her with a mixture of surprise and anger.

'Where have you sprung from?'

'From the cellar, as you see,' Catherine said smoothly. 'I went to get some logs.'

Fat Marion cut a ludicrous figure. Her red-veined face gleamed scarlet as if it had been varnished. Her cap was askew. And she was evidently having trouble articulating clearly. Her eyes roamed vaguely about as if she found it hard to focus. None of this however prevented her from grabbing Catherine by the arm and giving her a good shake.

'Lucky for you your parents were out the whole blessed day, you little fool! Or you wouldn't be able to sit down now, I'll warrant! Traipsing about like that all day, and with a boy too. . . .'

She leant close enough to Catherine for her to get a whiff of her wine-laden breath. With an impatient gesture Catherine shook herself free. Then she set her candle down on a stool and picked up a couple of logs she had dropped.

'What about people who spend all day in the tavern drinking with the other gossips? Do you think that's a better way to carry on? I may be lucky, Marion, but so are you! If I were you I should go up to bed before Maman gets back.'

Marion knew she was in the wrong. She was not a bad woman at heart but she had had the misfortune to be born in the heart of the wine-producing Beaune country and she was a little too fond of wine for her own good. She didn't often get a chance to indulge because Jacquette Legoix, whose foster-sister she was, had kept a close watch over her since bringing her to Paris. Marion had been caught two or three times in an advanced state of intoxication and Jacquette had finally threatened to pack her off back to Burgundy if it should ever happen again. Marion wept, pleaded and vowed by the holy statue of Notre-Dame never to touch another drop. This relapse had no doubt been sparked off by the mood of hysteria prevailing in the town that day.

Through a fog of drunkenness Marion was dimly aware of all this and did not insist. Muttering unintelligibly she stumbled over towards the stairs and the steps soon creaked under her weight. Then Catherine heard the attic door slam behind her and sighed with relief. Loyse had not returned yet and Catherine hesitated for a moment as to what to do next. She was neither hungry nor sleepy. The one thing she wanted to do above all else was to join Michel down there in the dark once more. Listening to him talk while she knelt beside him on the dusty floor had been the happiest moment of her whole life. And that gentle kiss he had given her still made her heart beat faster. Vaguely Catherine sensed that such moments were rarely come by and she was sensible enough to realize that in a few hours Michel would be a free man again, back in his own world. The weary fugitive would become the young nobleman once more and thereby put himself far out of reach of a humble artisan's daughter. The charming companion of a moment would soon be no more than a distant stranger who would rapidly forget the little girl he had so easily dazzled. Michel was still hers. But he would soon have gone. . . .

Feeling suddenly desolate Catherine ran to the street door and opened the upper half. The rain had stopped, leaving shining puddles. Water from the roof gushed down the gutters. The bridge, deserted a little earlier, was unexpectedly astir with activity. The chain had been removed and the two guards had disappeared. Groups of people, most of them lurching dangerously, were crossing the bridge, arm-in-arm, singing at the tops of their voices. Marion was clearly not the only person who had been celebrating a victory for the people. She heard sounds of singing and shouting from the direction of the Trois

Maillets tavern at the other end of the bridge. The curfew bell of Notre-Dame had not sounded yet. It was unlikely that it would induce anyone to go home when it did. This was clearly a night for celebrating.

Catherine wondered anxiously what Landry could be doing and whether he would have thought of bringing a rope for Michel. Over in the Pigasse house lights passed to and fro behind the panes of oiled paper. Then her eyes fell on a band of soldiers, swaying arm-in-arm across the whole width of the bridge and singing:

> 'Oh, the Duke of Burgundy,
> God give him health and strength! . . .'

She hastily replaced the door in position and returned to the workshop. She paused a moment as she passed the trap-door. She really ought to see whether Landry had thought of bringing a rope. She raised the trap-door and stooped down, calling softly:

'Messire, it is I, Catherine! I wanted to know whether Landry remembered the rope.'

She heard Michel's voice, somewhat muffled:

'Don't worry, I've got it. In any case there was one here already. Landry says he will come back some time between midnight and one o'clock. He will whistle three times to show that he is waiting with a boat under the bridge. All goes well.'

'Try and sleep a little then. I am going to bed now. I will come down again when I hear Landry whistle. My room faces the river.'

A faint creak from the floor above made her drop the trap-door hurriedly, her heart thumping. Just then the great palace clock struck ten. Two more hours to wait. Catherine went back into the kitchen and covered the fire with a thick layer of ashes. Then she placed a lighted candle on the stairs for Loyse when she returned and headed for the stairs. She had got as far as the bottom step when Loyse appeared. The girl looked grave.

'Landry's mother is not at all well,' she said. 'She is fast

using up her strength. I wanted to stay but Maman sent me
back to look after you. Are you going to bed?'

'Yes. But if you want something to eat . . .'

'It's all right. I'm not really hungry. Let's go to bed. You
must be tired after your day in the sewers.'

The two sisters went up to their little room and silently undressed. Loyse, after a sleepy 'good night', fell asleep the
moment her head touched the pillow. Catherine, however,
lay down with the firm resolve that she would not even close
her eyes. It was proving very difficult. Once in bed all the
weariness which had been accumulating during this un-
forgettable day seemed to descend on her all at once. Her
heavy coverlets smelt so sweetly of bleach and bay leaves. The
desire for sleep, so powerful in the very young, seemed to be
weighting her eyelids with lead. But she must not give in. It
was essential that she stay awake to help Landry if anything
went wrong.

To help ward off sleep she began telling herself stories. Then
she went over all the things Michel had told her. And there
was that kiss he had given her. She shivered as she remembered
it. Loyse's even breathing next to her was beginning to send
her to sleep. She was on the point of dropping off when an
unexpected noise had her sitting bolt upright, wide awake.

A door squeaked softly on the floor above, as if it were being
stealthily opened. Soft footsteps shuffled along cautiously
overhead as far as the stairs, then there was the creak of a step
being trodden on. Her head raised and both ears pricked,
Catherine mentally accompanied the person, who could only
be Marion, on her way down. Where could she be going at
this time of night?

Now the footsteps were coming nearer. They stopped outside the door of their room and there was a glimmer of candlelight under the door. Marion, obviously, was listening to make
sure both girls were sound asleep. Catherine took care not to
let the bed squeak as she moved. After a moment the steps
started downstairs again, as stealthily as before. Catherine
could not help smiling to herself. After indulging so freely

Marion was doubtless in need of fresh water to clear the wine fumes from her head. She might even be hungry. She would be back as soon as she had found what she wanted in the kitchen.

Reassured, Catherine was just about to lie down again when a new sound brought her out of bed with a bound, her heart beating so wildly she felt it might burst. There was no mistaking that particular creak. Marion wasn't looking for water. She must have gone to get a further supply of wine from the barrel in the cellar.

Made clumsy by terror, the young girl dragged on her chemise and crept down the stairs after quickly ascertaining that Loyse was still sound asleep. In her hurry she forgot to look where she was going and slithered down rather than descended the last remaining stairs, almost breaking her neck. The trap-door was wide open and she could see a light through it. A second later the quiet house shook to a howl of terror.

'Help! Help!' Marion bellowed. Her voice sounded to Catherine like the last trump. 'An Armagnac! Help!'

Half dead with fright, Catherine slid down the ladder and found fat Marion in her petticoat clinging with all her might to Michel's tunic and screaming like a maniac. Michel, ashen-faced, was struggling unsuccessfully to free himself. A combination of fear and liquor seemed to have made Marion twice as strong as usual. Catherine leapt on her like a wildcat, kicking and scratching, and managed to force her to loosen her grip on Michel.

'Be quiet, you stupid old woman!' she shouted angrily. 'Be quiet, will you! . . . Make her stop, messire! Hit her! She'll have all the neighbours in!'

Marion only fell to screaming with redoubled vigour. With a violent jerk Michel shook himself free and Catherine nodded towards the skylight while hanging on to Marion as best she could.

'The skylight, quick! You will have to jump through it! It's your only chance. Can you swim?'

He was halfway through the aperture when Marion, half

beside herself by now, bit Catherine viciously on the arm to make her let go and then rushed at him and seized him by one leg, still screaming at the top of her voice. In response to her screams heavy blows sounded on the wooden shutters outside the house. Catherine reeled back against the log pile at first, dazed with pain, but a second later she was up again, hunting frantically for something with which to free Michel. Stuck half in and half out of the window, with Marion clinging to his leg he only had his free leg to defend himself with. An axe blade gleamed on the floor. Catherine seized it and rushed at Marion. But, alas, just then the street door gave way with a crash of splintering wood and a horde of people swarmed down the stairs and into the cellar. With their faces gleaming scarlet in the candlelight, they looked to Catherine like so many fiends disgorged from hell. The axe was snatched from her hands by one of the men.

'He's an Armagnac,' Marion shouted hoarsely.

That was enough. In a second Michel, despite his frantic struggles, was captured. During which time Marion, patches of fat thigh criss-crossed by rope-like varicose veins showing through the tears in her chemise, had slumped into a corner with a satisfied sigh. Then she crawled towards the barrel of wine and stretched out underneath the spigot to drink at her leisure.

Horror-stricken, Catherine only just managed to keep herself from falling in a swoon by clinging to the log-pile. The cellar was full of men, all hitting Michel. As each blow fell it seemed to strike agonizingly at Catherine's heart. In that low, vaulted room, smoky from the oil-lamps one or two people had brought down, the struggling mass of ragged, wine-bespattered figures showering vicious blows on their captive composed a scene of revolting brutality. Michel's purple and silver tunic had been ripped half off his shoulders. Someone cried.

'Why, if it isn't the pretty fellow who gave us the slip earlier tonight on the way to Montfaucon! The one who spat in the Duke's face. . . .'

The rest of his sentence was drowned in a wild outcry:
'Kill him! Kill him! . . . Hand him over to us!'

Tightly bound, Michel was half pushed, half dragged up
the ladder and out into the street, where his appearance
created an uproar. There was hatred in those voices, and a
certain wild excitement. Catherine threw herself blindly after
him. She scrambled up the ladder and was just about to rush
out into the street when Loyse, white as a sheet, tried to stop
her. The house was suddenly full of people. The workshop
was overrun by men who rummaged in the cupboards and
fought each other for possession of the valuable bowls and
pitchers. Leaving the petrified Loyse flattened against a wall
Catherine rushed out into the street.

She saw Michel struggling helplessly in the middle of a ring
of howling monsters. The crowd had blocked all access to
either the Legoix's house or the bridge itself. Lights flared at all
the windows and the narrow street was bright as day. Catherine
stared in horror at all these distorted faces, their mouths ugly
with hate, and at the waving fists and flashing weapons, their
blades glinting ominously. At the centre of all this frenzy and
violence was the prisoner. His feet were chained together. He
kept his head down to protect it from the cruel blows which
rained down on him. Blood streamed from his torn cheek
and lip. Some terrible women, brandishing spindles, were
trying to put out his eyes.

Escaping from Loyse, who was still trying to shelter her in
her arms, Catherine plunged into the midst of the tumult.
She ran the risk of being cut to pieces herself, but no human
force could have stopped her now. She screamed, sobbed,
implored and struck out with her nails and teeth, trying to
carve a way through the crowd towards her friend. Something
hot trickled down her cheek, followed by a sharp stab of pain.
The something was blood, but she ignored it. She might have
been in some sort of hell, a frail childish figure thrown to the
wild beasts.

'Michel,' she cried, 'Michel . . . wait! I am coming!'

She did actually seem to be gaining ground, inch by inch.

It was a hopeless unequal struggle, as unequal as the struggle between the migrant bird and the encircling vultures. But somehow she kept going, miraculously sustained by courage and love. If these monsters killed Michel they would have to kill her too, and then they could go to see Madame the Virgin and Milord Jesus together.

Michel suddenly crumpled under the relentless battering. He staggered forward kept upright only by an astonishingly tenacious will to survive. Then he fell on his knees, deafened and blinded by the blood streaming over his face. His whole body was one bloody wound. Catherine heard him groan:

'God . . . have mercy on me!'

A coarse insult was the only reply. He collapsed on the ground, at the limit of his endurance. The end was approaching. Catherine sensed this in the way the crowd pressed round eagerly as if to divide up the carcase. Then a voice rang out suddenly:

'Make way . . . make way . . . here comes Caboche!'

Catherine had covered her bleeding face with her hands so as not to see any more, but on hearing this she lifted her head. It was indeed Caboche the Skinner, ploughing his way through the crowd with his massive shoulders rather like a great ship in a stormy sea. She could see her cousin Legoix and Pierre Cauchon's long, pale face behind him. To make room for Caboche the crowd fell back, revealing the pathetic, crumpled heap which was Michel's body. With a sob Catherine ran towards him through the gap in the crowd. She fell on her knees and gently lifted the blond head stained with blood. His face was unrecognizable, a bloody pulp; the nose broken, the mouth torn and one eye gouged out. He moaned feebly, already half dead.

'So you found him again, eh?' said Caboche's voice from somewhere above her head. 'Where was he?'

'In Gaucher Legoix's cellar. Enjoying their hospitality, it seems! We'll burn the place down round his ears for that!'

'And the bridge with it?' Caboche cut in coldly. 'I am the one who makes decisions round here.'

To her amazement Catherine felt a tremor run through the broken body she clasped so tenderly. Michel murmured painfully:

'I hid myself in their house . . . they did not know . . . I was there.'

'That's not true,' Catherine cried. '*I* was the one who . . .'

Here a powerful hand was clapped over her mouth and she felt herself lifted up off the ground. Caboche had picked her up and was holding her against his chest with one arm.

'Hold your tongue!' he whispered under cover of the din. 'Or I will be hard put to save any of you . . . if that's still possible.'

Half suffocated as she was in the butcher's grip, Catherine stopped screaming, but she went on imploring him while the tears rained down on to his hairy hand.

'Save him. Save him, I beg you. I would love you dearly for it. . . .'

'I can't. It's too late. Death can only be a merciful release to him in the state he is in. . . .'

Catherine watched horrified as he kicked the bleeding body at his feet.

'We have found him again! That's the main thing!' he cried. 'And now let's finish with him. Come here, Thomas Legoix. Let's see how you wield a cleaver, now you are rich and comfortable! Finish off the carcase for me!'

Cousin Thomas stepped forward. His face was also very red, and there were splashes of blood on his rich brown velvet robe. Notwithstanding his costly clothes, he had reverted to type and become a skinner again, with the same appetites as the rest. You could see this in the savage pleasure he took in the sight of spilt blood, the smile on his moist fleshy lips. He carried a butcher's cleaver which had already seen service that day.

Caboche felt Catherine's body go rigid in his clasp and realized that she was about to scream. He clapped his free hand over her mouth and whispered urgently to Thomas:

'Hurry up. Finish him off properly . . . for the child's sake.'

Thomas nodded and stooped over Michel. In a quick

merciful gesture Caboche moved the hand over Catherine's mouth over her eyes instead, completely covering them. She saw nothing, but she heard it all . . . the choking rattle of death, followed by a hideous gurgling noise. The crowd howled with delight. Wriggling like an eel she managed to squirm out of Caboche's grasp and dropped to her knees. What she saw made her eyes widen with horror and her hands fly up to her mouth. Michel's body, its head cut off, lay on the ground before her in a pool of blood which stretched to her knees, the life blood still pumping out of the severed neck. A little way off an archer in the green uniform of the Duke of Burgundy was calmly impaling the head on a lance.

Slowly the life seemed to drain from Catherine's bruised and weary body. She seemed to be turned to ice from head to feet. She began to scream, a thin ghastly scream which rose and rose to an intolerable pitch, and hung there, curdling the blood of all who heard it.

'Shut her up!' Legoix shouted to Caboche. 'It sounds like a dog who has smelt a corpse.'

Caboche bent and tried to pick Catherine up. He found that she was as if paralysed, frozen into a crouching position even after he lifted her up. Her whole body had gone stiff in a spasm of horror, her eyes were fixed and her teeth chattered, and still the unearthly scream went on. With a shaking hand Caboche tried to force her mouth shut. She turned dull, unseeing eyes on him. Her screaming ceased abruptly only to be replaced by the stertorous panting sound one hears in trapped animals. The child's anguished face had gone as grey as stone. A convulsion jerked her body in Caboche's arms. It was racked by atrocious pains, as if she were being stabbed by a thousand knives at once. There was a red mist in front of her eyes and a roaring in her ears which threatened to burst them. A crushing pain at the back of the neck made her cry out again, but feebly this time. Suddenly she went limp in Caboche's arms. She heard someone calling out:

'Loyse! Loyse!' but the sound seemed so remote it might have come from the depths of the earth.

After that there was only a black gaping hole into which Catherine felt herself fall, plummeting down like a stone. . . .

CHAPTER TWO

BARNABY THE COCKLESHELL MAN

MANY DAYS passed, long days in which dawn and twilight and night and day were all one to Catherine. She hung between life and death consumed by a brain fever which threatened to remove her from the land of the living. She was in little actual pain, but her spirit seemed to have left her body to join in long and wearying combat with the phantoms of fear and despair. From the depths of the abyss where she seemed to lie she continually saw re-enacted the appalling scene of Michel's death and the distorted faces of his killers weaving a fantastic saraband around the corpse. And when, as sometimes happened, light and peace of mind seemed on the verge of returning to her, suddenly unknown and often hideous faces would appear, which the child tried with all her feeble strength to push away.

Sometimes she seemed dimly to hear someone weeping, far away down a long dark tunnel at the end of which shone a faint speck of light. Catherine dragged herself along this endless tunnel in search of that speck of light, but the farther on she stumbled the longer the tunnel stretched in front of her.

Then one evening the mists parted, the things around her settled into place at last and took on clearly defined shapes. She had emerged at long last from the shadowy regions of unconsciousness. The surroundings in which she found herself were so strange that at first she took them to be merely an extension of her nightmare. She was lying in a dark low-ceilinged room, whose roof was a stone vault supported by rough pillars. The room's only light came from the fire which leapt high in the crudely fashioned chimney. A black cooking-pot, suspended from a hook over the flames, simmered away giving out a tantalizing smell of cooking vegetables. A skinny, ragged man sat on a three-legged stool near the fire and stirred the contents of the pot with a long wooden spoon. This man was Barnaby the Cockleshell Man.

Hearing Catherine's sigh he leapt to his feet and bounded across the room still holding the spoon. He bent over her anxiously, but the look of anxiety faded and the two deep lines either side of his mouth cracked in a smile when he realized that the child's eyes were not only wide open but apparently seeing clearly at last.

'Feeling better, eh?' he whispered, apparently fearful that he might bring on a relapse if he raised his voice. She smiled at him in reply and then asked:

'Where am I? Where is Maman?'

'You are in my house. Your mother is not far away. She will be here soon. As for how you come to be here, that's rather a long and complicated story which can wait till you are quite well again. The important thing for the moment is to rest and get back your strength. The soup will be ready in a moment.'

He went back to his cooking-pot. Standing over the flames he cast a bizarre shadow across the smoky room, but it no longer frightened Catherine. She made an effort to work out what she was doing in this cellar and how Barnaby had come to be her sick nurse, but her head was weak still. Falling back on the bed she closed her eyes and was soon fast asleep.

Barnaby had just finished skimming the soup when a woman appeared at the top of the flight of steps which went up to a narrow little door.

She was young and would have been beautiful had her skin not been so dark and her costume so strange. Her lithe slender body was dressed in a sort of dress of coarse stuff, anchored by a length of material draped round her hips. This material was of red and yellow striped wool. A sort of shawl across her shoulders protected her from the cold and her dark head was covered by a turban-like arrangement of coiled bands of cloth, one end of which passed under her chin. Two heavy plaits, dark as night and thick as a child's arm, hung below her turban.

Once more awake, Catherine regarded this strange apparition with astonishment. Her face was so dark-complexioned that when she smiled her teeth flashed dazzling white. Catherine noticed that her features were delicate and that she had magnificent black eyes. Barnaby came with her to Catherine's bedside.

'This is Black Sara,' he told her. 'She knows more secrets than a sorceress. She has been looking after you, and right well at that! Well, what do you think, Sara?'

'She has found her spirits again. She is cured,' the woman said. 'All she needs now is rest and good food.' Her thin brown hands meanwhile lightly touched the child's cheeks, brow and wrist, moving with the speed and delicacy of birds in flight. Then Sara sat with her arms round her knees on the ground beside her bed and gazed at Catherine thoughtfully. Meanwhile Barnaby drew on his shell-hung cloak and picked up his staff.

'Stay a little while,' he said to the woman. 'It is time for Mass at St Opportune and I don't want to miss it. All the tinsmiths of the neighbourhood are gathering for a service there, and they are sure to give generously.'

Barnaby left after suggesting to Sara that she taste the soup and give the invalid a good bowlful.

The next day, after a night of deep and peaceful sleep, Catherine heard the full story from her mother of what had happened on the Pont-au-Change after Michel's death. The risk of fire spreading had stopped the crowd setting the Legoix's house alight. Instead, they had looted and pillaged the building from top to bottom. Hearing what was going on, Gaucher Legoix had come hurrying back from the House of Pillars. His pleas and remonstrations only incited the angry mob, from whom Caboche's departure had removed any possible restraint, to further violence. The resentment which had been building up as a result of his cool attitude to the

Butchers' Guild now exacted a terrible revenge. In spite of his wife's tears and entreaties, joined with those of Landry and his father, they hanged Gaucher Legoix from his own shop sign and then threw his body into the river. Jacquette had then taken refuge with the Pigasse family, together with the unconscious Catherine, whom Landry had found and rescued. But soon the fury of the mob seemed to threaten Jacquette and her daughter too, and she had been forced to flee again with Barnaby's help. Landry, luckily, had gone to fetch him. First by river, and then along interminable alleys, the poor woman and her strange companion sought the safety of Barnaby's house in the Grande Cour des Miracles. She had stayed there ever since tending her daughter and trying to recover from the terrible ordeal from which she had just emerged. Gaucher's violent death had been a cruel stroke, but Catherine's critical condition left her little time to mourn. Her child was in danger. To which a new anxiety was soon added: Loyse had disappeared.

The last time anyone remembered seeing her had been at the moment when her younger sister lost consciousness, at the height of her brainstorm. She had been holding Catherine in her arms. Then a forward surge of the mob had swept Catherine from her. Landry turned up in the nick of time to rescue his friend. But Loyse had vanished in the midst of the angry crowd, which now hurled itself on the Sign of the Holy Tabernacle and tore it apart. No one knew what had become of her since.

'She could have fallen into the river,' Jacquette said, dabbing at her eyes which seemed perpetually swollen with tears, 'but then the Seine would have washed up her body. Barnaby goes to the morgue at the Grand Châtelet every day, but he hasn't found her yet. He is convinced she is still alive and goes on searching for her. All we can do is wait and pray. . . .'

'What will we do then?' Catherine asked. 'Stay here with Barnaby?'

'No. As soon as we have found Loyse once more we will

leave Paris and go to Dijon. As you know, your uncle Mathieu is a cloth-merchant there. As his only surviving relations, he can hardly refuse to take us in.'

Talking about her brother's house seemed to comfort the poor woman a little. It had been her parents' and she had spent her childhood in it and been married from it to Gaucher Legoix many years ago. It was the haven to which, in her grief, it seemed natural to turn for refuge and comfort. Grateful as she was to the Cockleshell Man for the generous way he had helped her, the good woman could not help regarding the bizarre world of the beggars, into which she had been so suddenly thrown, with mistrust and distaste.

Sara continued to look after Catherine. Her treatment consisted of cooling drinks and curious nostrums which she made the girl take to restore her strength. She obstinately refused to divulge how and with what they were made, though she did explain the properties of the infusions of vervain, which she made Catherine drink all the time as a sovereign remedy against all ills.

Gradually Catherine and even Jacquette grew accustomed to the presence of the dark-skinned woman. Barnaby had told them her story. Sara was born into one of the gipsy tribes which lived on the island of Cyprus. When still a young girl she had been seized by the Turks and sold in the market at Candia to a Venetian merchant who had taken her back with him to his own country. Sara had stayed in Venice for ten years, and it was there she learnt the secrets of herbal medicine. Then her master died and she was bought by a Lombard moneylender who had just bought a house in Paris. He was a cruel violent man. Sara was continually maltreated. Finally, one winter night, she ran away and was found by the pseudo-blind man, Maillet-le-Loup, in a church where she had taken refuge, trembling with cold and hunger. He took her back with him to his hovel in the Cour Saint-Sauveur, and there she had remained in the capacity of housekeeper ever since. Quite apart from her healing powers, which were always greatly in demand among the beggars, Black Sara could read palms. This gift sometimes led to her being summoned in great secrecy to some noble house. Moving about the town as she did and penetrating where many people never could, Sara learnt things about the town and Court. She knew endless stories too, and would spend hours at a time squatting beside the hearth between Catherine and her mother gossiping tirelessly in her soft sing-song voice while they shared out the herb wine which she made better than anyone else. Legends of some remote tribe, the latest Court scandal – all were equally grist to her mill. Almost every evening when Barnaby returned he would find the three women in their usual places, each deriving some sort of solace from the others' company. Then he would take his seat among this odd family which chance or fate had brought him, and in his turn recount the news and rumours from the outside world.

Once night had fallen and the Beggars' Kingdom woke to its riotous nocturnal life Barnaby's presence was essential to calm the fears of his guests. The fact was that the Grande Cour des Miracles became a terrifying place as soon as its inhabitants returned. And Barnaby's own corner of it was far from peaceful. From just before matins till the time when the trumpeter on watch heralded the dawn from one of the Châtelet towers and the guards were withdrawn from the gate, a sinister-looking rabble converged on the square, streaming out of their hovels and crowding along all the alleys. Then the cripples would stand upright, the blind would see and the supporting sores which touched hearts and generosity of the charitable would be whisked off in a flash, thereby enacting the nightly miracle which had given these places their name. Then the wild, turbulent mob would pass the rest of the night shouting, singing and feasting. There were at this time some 80,000 real or pseudo beggars in Paris.

The rule of the Kingdom of Thune was that everything found, begged or stolen in the course of the day should be consumed that same night. After all the day's harvest had been pooled at the feet of the King of Thune, the signal for the feast to begin was given. Whole animals were roasted over roaring

the girl Catherine gave an involuntary shiver of revulsion. What followed was worse still. This time Catherine kept her eyes tight shut as this repulsive creature threw the girl to the ground and took her publicly, there and then. But she could not help hearing the beggar girl's wild scream, and she realized then why Barnaby had forbidden her to so much as show her nose outside the house. When she opened her eyes again, the girl, who had fainted, was being carried away amid cheers and laughter. There was blood on her legs. . . .

She was beginning to grow restless after being shut up for so long. As her strength returned she felt an overpowering urge to run about, breathe in the pure air down by the river and feel the sun's warm caress on her skin. But Barnaby shook his head.

'Not till the day you leave Paris, my pretty. Till then it's dangerous for you to go out by day, and still more so by night.'

Then one day, Landry, who came almost every day to see Catherine, appeared hotfoot and breathless.

'I know where Loyse is,' he shouted as he burst through the door.

While wandering in his usual fashion about the city that afternoon, Landry had visited the Notre-Dame market to buy some tripe his mother wanted for supper. As a keen admirer of Caboche, the lad had gone straight to the shop kept by Mère Caboche, who specialized in offal. She lived in a narrow, dirty house in one of the less savoury alleys thereabouts. The whole of the ground floor reeked sickeningly of tripe. During the day the wares were displayed in front of the house, spilling out of large metal basins. Behind sat Mère Caboche in person, her scales on one side, and a metal fork in one hand, a quivering mountain of yellow fat. She was famous throughout the neighbourhood for her ugly temper, which her celebrated son had inherited, and inordinate fondness for the bottle.

When he reached the shop Landry had been surprised to find it closed and shuttered. If the door had not been half

T—C

open he would have thought the place uninhabited. But it so happened that a mendicant friar of the Order of Frères Mineurs, in his grey robe girdled by a thrice-knotted rope, was standing in the doorway talking to Mère Càboche, whose frowsty face could be clearly seen.

'Just a little bread for the brothers, my good woman,' said the friar, rattling his basket, 'today is the Feast of St John. Surely you will not refuse!'

'The shop is closed, Father,' retorted Mère Caboche. 'I am sick and I only have food enough for myself. Go on your way, Father, and pray for my recovery. . . .'

'But even so . . .'

The friar insisted. Some passing housewives stopped to place an offering in his basket. One of them said:

'The place has been shut for two months now, Father. No one round here can understand it at all. As for being sick, you should just hear the sort of psalms she sings in the evenings. Sick of work more like!'

'I can do as I please,' scowled Mère Caboche, making vain efforts to close the door again. The friar's sandalled foot was now wedged in the crack.

'How about a little wine then?' the friar suggested, inspired by the other woman's comments. At this Mère Caboche's face turned red as a beet under her yellow linen coif and she roared at him:

'I have no wine! To the Dev . . .'

'My child!' the scandalized friar expostulated, hastily crossing himself.

All the same, he did not remove his foot. People were beginning to collect outside the tripe-seller's house. The mendicant friar, Brother Eusebius, was well known to be the most persistent alms-seeker in the monastery. He had been ailing latterly and had not been able to make his usual rounds of the city. He was clearly intending to make up for lost time.

Landry was amused by the scene and had drawn nearer with the rest of the crowd, agog to see whether Mère Caboche's celebrated miserliness or Brother Eusebius's equally celebrated persistence would win the day. Most of the onlookers were merely amused, but there were others who fell to disputing the merits of the case, according to whether they supported the Church or Simon the Skinner. The din which ensued was further aggravated by a man drawing a cart, which got wedged between two houses in the narrow little street.

It was then that Landry, perched on a stone where he had climbed in order to see better, glanced casually upwards and caught sight of a pale face behind the single, upstairs window in Mère Caboche's house. One of the window's oiled-paper panes was torn just enough for the boy to recognize who it was, the person in question having leant forward to see what all the commotion was about. He waved and the furtive but unmistakable sign she made in return was enough to convince him that Loyse recognized him as surely as he had her. Then she vanished. Clambering down from his perch and quite forgetful of the tripe he had promised to buy his mother, Landry elbowed his way vigorously through the crowd and didn't stop running till he reached Saint Sauveur.

Catherine listened admiringly to Landry's story. Barnaby looked anxious.

'I might have guessed,' he said. 'Caboche was always after the girl. He must have taken advantage of the attack on the house to capture her and take her back with him. Now the old woman is guarding her. It won't be easy to get her away from them. . . .'

Jacquette Legoix had collapsed on the hearthstone and sobbed bitterly with her head in her skirts. Sara bent over her and stroked the thick blonde tresses, still barely streaked with grey, in an attempt to soothe her. But it was no good. . . .

'My child . . . my gentle lamb who wanted to keep herself pure for the Lord. He has taken her from me . . . The beast! Monster that he is! Alack, alack!'

Jacquette's heart seemed to be literally breaking with grief. Neither Catherine, shocked into silence by the news, nor the others, equally distressed though they were, were able at first to think of something consoling to say to her. It was Barnaby who finally persuaded her to raise her head, revealing a pathetic, red, tear-swollen countenance, streaming with tears. Appalled by her mother's grief and inwardly raging against Caboche, the fiend, Catherine threw her arms round her mother's neck.

'Easy or not,' said Barnaby, 'we must get Loyse away from Caboche. Heaven only knows what sort of misery the poor girl must be enduring at his hands.'

'But how do you propose to get her out of there?' Sara asked.

'Not single-handed, obviously! Mère Caboche only has to open her mouth to bring a whole crowd of people running to help her – there are all the people who want to win her son's favour, and all the others who are simply afraid of incurring his displeasure. Mâchefer is our only solution. He is the only man who can help us.'

Sara left Jacquette's side and went over to where Barnaby stood, propped on one leg, nervously chewing his nails. She murmured something to him in a voice pitched low so as not to be heard by the others, though not quite low enough to escape Catherine's sharp ears.

'Isn't there a risk that Mâchefer might want to be paid . . . in kind? Especially if the girl is pretty?'

'It is a risk we have to take. I hope we can stop him doing so. Anyway, we must cross our bridges as we come to them. What we have to fear at the moment is not Mâchefer but Caboche. The King of Thune must have almost as many men under him as the Skinner. He should be at his usual place now, outside the King of Sicily's palace. That's where he usually begs. Do you know him by sight, Landry?'

The lad frowned and grimaced:

'You mean the one who calls himself Colin-Beau-Soyant – the man with all the boils?'

'That's the one. Go and find him and tell him that Barnaby the Cockleshell Man wants him, and if he makes any trouble tell him I urgently need him to help me *load the dice*. Can you remember that?'

'Of course.'

Landry pulled his cap down over his ears and hugged Catherine, who was clinging to his hand.

'I want to go with you,' she said. 'It's so boring down here....'

'Better not, little one,' Barnaby interposed. 'You are much too easily recognized. There isn't another head of hair like yours in Paris! You would only have to lose your bonnet and that would be the end of everything. Besides, I wouldn't like Mâchefer to clap eyes on you, out there in the sunlight.'

As Landry ran up the steps and out through the low doorway Catherine felt a pang of regret as a ray of sunshine flashed briefly on the mildewed steps. It must be so lovely up there on this sunny June day! Barnaby kept promising that they would all leave Paris as soon as Loyse had been found. But that day seemed so slow in coming. Would they succeed in getting Loyse back, for one thing?

She felt rage swelling inside her when she thought of Caboche and her older sister. She had only a vague idea of what had been happening to Loyse, but she did know that she hated Caboche with all her heart. He had always been present when something awful happened in her life.

They did not have long to wait. An hour later Catherine saw Landry returning. He was accompanied by a man of such repellent appearance that she had not the slightest desire to leave the place in the chimney-corner, near her mother, where Barnaby had told her to stay. She had often seen Mâchefer at night as he presided over his subjects' merry-making, but at those times he had always been surrounded by the half-mocking, half-primtiive ceremony which befitted a beggar king. She had never seen him before in his everyday beggar's role. The man she saw now was fully a head shorter than Barnaby. He leant on two crutches and the filthy garment he wore was horribly distended behind by an enormous hump, which rose higher than his head itself. One leg, wrapped in pus-stained rags, was twisted under him and what could be seen of it looked like a running sore. The gleaming, wolfish fangs had been artfully blackened and looked for all the world as if nothing remained in his mouth but a few rotting stumps. Only one eye sparkled brightly, the other empty socket – Mâchefer's one genuine deformity – being hidden by a dirty bandage. At the top of the steps Mâchefer threw aside his crutches, straightened his crooked leg and leapt down the stairs with the agility of a youth. Catherine had to stifle an exclamation of surprise.

'What is it? The boy said you wanted to see me at once,' said Mâchefer.

'He spoke the truth. Listen, Mâchefer, we have not always seen eye to eye, you and I, but you are the chief here and you are known as a man who never betrays a friend. You may laugh when I tell you what I want you to help me do . . . it's a good deed!'

'Is this some kind of joke?'

'No, listen . . .'

Rapidly Barnaby explained the position to Mâchefer and outlined what he wanted him to do. The other man listened in silence, thoughtfully tearing off his false boils. When Barnaby had finished he merely asked:

'Is the girl pretty?'

Here Barnaby discreetly squeezed Jacquette's hand, sensing her to be on the verge of hysterics. But his voice was perfectly steady as he replied:

'Nothing out of the ordinary. Blonde, but too pale. Not your type . . . besides, she doesn't care for men, only for God. She's a future nun whom Caboche has kidnapped.'

'Some of them are quite pretty,' said Mâchefer meditatively, 'and Caboche is powerful at the moment. Going against him is a risky business. . . .'

'Not for you. What have you got to fear from Caboche? Power is notoriously short-lived, as you know.'

'Perhaps so. But what do I stand to gain from this business besides a beating?'

'Nothing,' said Barnaby curtly. 'Only fame. I have never asked you for anything, Mâchefer. I shall soon be returning to my own king, the Cockleshell King. How would you like it if I told Jacquot-of-the-Sea that Mâchefer-the-One-Eyed is only interested in his profit and won't help out a friend?'

This discussion was exasperating to Catherine, who was wild with impatience to see them get down to the task in hand. What was the point of all this talk when all that had to be done was to go round to Mère Caboche's house and take Loyse away by force. Mâchefer's meditations were gradually drawing to an end. Sitting on the lower step he rumpled his hair and pulled his ear, then hawked and spat five paces off. He rose to his feet and said:

'Very well. I am your man. Have to talk it over and see what can be done.'

'I knew we could count on you. Let's go and have a flagon of ale. We can go to Greedy-Ysabeau's and talk about this while we wait for nightfall. It's the Feast of St John, and there will be more money to be made tonight, round the bonfires, than during the day.'

The two men went off to the tavern in the square kept by a wild, unkempt creature who nevertheless had an enviable knack for bringing in the clientele. Jacquette watched them go, eyes round with horror, repressing a violent urge to weep.

'How can I entrust my daughter to a man like that?'

'The chief thing is to get her back,' Catherine said firmly.

Sara intervened once more. With a smile she drew the girl towards her and started to stroke the magnificent tresses which she had fallen into the habit of tending since Catherine's illness. The gipsy woman seemed to derive an almost sensual pleasure from handling the thick red-gold braids, brushing and smoothing them with gentle caressing movements.

'The child is right,' she said. 'She will always be right, especially where men are concerned. Because she will be beautiful enough to make a man die of love!'

Catherine stared solemnly at her without speaking. She was astonished to hear that she might be beautiful, because until then no one had ever suggested such a possibility to her.

People went into raptures over her hair, of course, and sometimes her eyes, but nothing more. Even boys had never mentioned the fact to her. Not Landry . . . nor Michel! The thought of the young man's death suddenly threw a dark shadow across the happy astonishment into which Sara's words had plunged her. After all, what difference would it make whether she was beautiful or not, since Michel would not be there to see her. He was the only one for whom she would have liked to be really beautiful. Now it was too late. She struggled against the desire to weep which swept her whenever she thought of him. The memory of the young man still hurt. It was a wound which would no doubt leave a sensitive scar.

'I don't care whether I am beautiful or not,' she said finally. 'I don't want to be beautiful. Men run after beautiful women and they hurt them . . . so much!'

In spite of the look of astonishment she read in Sara's eyes she did not explain herself further. She blushed suddenly, remembering the nocturnal scenes she had watched through the skylight, the brutish violence with which the more beautiful girls had been treated. Sara's eyes did not leave hers, as though this daughter of faraway tribes were able to see clearly what was going on in her young friend's mind. She forbore to question her, but merely smiled and said slowly:

'Whether you want it or not, you will be a great beauty, Catherine. You mark my words. Too beautiful for your own peace, perhaps. And you will only love one man, but you will love him passionately. For him you will starve and go thirsty, leave your bed and house. You will search for him along the highways and byways without even knowing whether he will be there to welcome you in the end. You will love him more than yourself, more than anything on earth, more than life itself. . . .'

'I won't! I will never love any man like that!' said Catherine, stamping her foot angrily. 'The one man I could have loved is dead.'

She broke off, afraid that she had given herself away by what she had just said, and looked nervously across at her mother. But Jacquette had not heard.

She had returned to her seat by the hearth and was sitting there telling her wooden rosary beads. Sara seized Catherine's hands in hers, pinioned her legs between her knees and lowered her voice several tones till it became a soft, insistent, soothing murmur.

'Thus it is written, nevertheless. Strange things are written in these small hands. I see a great, great love which will cause you much suffering and yet give you such raptures as the human heart can rarely have known. Many men will love you, and one in particular. . . . Oh!' She turned the girl's hands over palms upwards and examined them closely, her brow furrowed by lines. 'I see a prince . . . a real prince! He will love you and help you in many ways. But it is another whom you will love. I see him! He is young, handsome, of noble birth . . . but hard, so hard! You will often wound yourself on the thorns around his heart, but blood and tears are the bricks and mortar of which love is built. You will seek this man as a dog seeks its master, you will follow him like a hound on the scent of a great stag. You will have fame, fortune, love and everything. . . . But you will pay dearly for it all. And then . . . how strange! You will meet an angel!'

'An angel?' Catherine repeated, open-mouthed.

Sara let drop the girl's hands. She looked suddenly weary and old, but her eyes, which seemed to see far beyond the grimy walls, shone with light as though a bundle of tapers blazed in them.

'An angel!' she repeated ecstatically. 'A warrior angel carrying a flaming sword . . .!'

Feeling that Sara was losing herself in regions too remote for her to follow, Catherine shook her arm gently to bring her back to earth.

'And you, Sara? Will you return one day to your island at the end of the blue sea?'

'I cannot read the book of the future for myself, my pretty. The Spirit forbids it. But an old woman once told me that though I might leave my country for ever I would find my own people once again. She said that the tribes would come to me.'

When Barnaby returned he seemed in a high good humour.

'Well,' he said, 'the plan is drawn up, and everything has been decided. As soon as a favourable occasion turns up we will get Loyse back from Caboche.'

'Why wait? Why not tonight?' cried Jacquette. 'Hasn't she waited long enough already? And haven't I too?'

'Peace, woman,' said Barnaby somewhat roughly. 'We want to get her back without being killed ourselves. Tonight they will be lighting the bonfires for the feast of St Jean. The biggest bonfires are the one in front of the palace and the one on the quai. It will be impossible to do anything in the city itself, only a few yards from the bonfire and all the people who will come to see it. Besides, Caboche is captain of the Charenton bridge. He has men and weapons at his disposal there. He is more powerful than ever. Anyway, there are more preparations to be made. Once we have put our plan into action the town will become too dangerous for us. Caboche will be searching for us everywhere, even in the Cour des Miracles where he has spies. Once we have found Loyse we shall have to leave Paris.'

'We?' said Catherine delightedly. 'Will you be coming too?'

'Yes, little one. My time here is coming to an end. I am a Cockleshell Man. It's time for me to join my leader. The Shell King has summoned me to Dijon. We will travel together.'

He then outlined the plan which he had worked out with Mâchefer.

They would wait till a disturbance in some distant part of the town had attracted most of the local people away and then find some pretext for bringing old Mère Caboche out into the street, or at least making her open the door. Then, with the help of a few trusty companions, it would be child's play to kidnap Loyse. They would hurry to a warehouse beside the river and board a boat there which would take them up the Seine and Yonne rivers into Burgundy.

'I shall need your help till then, Sara,' Barnaby added. 'But afterwards you will be free to return. . . .'

The gipsy shrugged:

'I will stay with them if they want me to. It wouldn't be a great sacrifice. I've had enough of Maillet-le-Loup. He has got it into his head that he wants to sleep with me now and I have to fight him off every night. He gets more and more angry and now he has started threatening to make me dance for Mâchefer. You know what that means. . . .'

Barnaby nodded, and Catherine just stopped herself doing the same. She felt a righteous anger surge up in her. She had grown very attached to this strange doctor of hers and she realized that, for all her dark skin, Sara was beautiful enough for Mâchefer to want to add her to his harem. Slipping her hand into her friend's she turned a gaze on her as warm and golden as a summer day.

'You will never leave us, Sara? You will come with us to Uncle Mathieu's? Won't she, Maman?'

Jacquette smiled sadly. It seemed such a short while back that she had been gay and lively. Now the plump Burgundian woman seemed to grow more transparent-looking every day. Her cheeks were losing their colour and bloom, deep lines had appeared in the face which had been so smooth and fresh till tragedy struck her. Her laced bodice hung loosely over a shrunken bosom.

'Sara knows that wherever we are there will always be a place for her. Don't I owe my life to her?'

With one accord the two women, so different in every way, threw themselves into each other's arms and wept for each other's sorrows. Misfortune had made them akin. The solid bourgeoise felt as up-rooted as the child of the wind and great open spaces, the nomad of the world's great travel routes whose ancestors had followed the hordes of Genghis Khan. Feminine solidarity, which can be such a powerful force when there is no question of rivalry, was movingly demonstrated by these two women. Jacquette would gladly have welcomed Sara as a sister.

'That's enough tears and pretty speeches for one day! I'm hungry. And since we are all one big family now, let's sup as a family. I stole some cakes off Ysabeau-la-Gourmande. They are for you, my pretty,' he added, taking some appetizing golden cakes out of his pocket. It was a long time since Catherine, who was quite as greedy as the celebrated Ysabeau, had seen any like them. She bit into one eagerly, then swiftly pressed Barnaby's unshaven cheek with her honey-smeared lips.

'Thank you, Barnaby. . . .'

The old fellow was so astonished by this gesture that he almost dropped Catherine. He put her down and hurried across to the dark corner where he kept his pseudo-relics. He was heard to snort frequently. . . .

'Tomorrow they are taking the former Provost of Paris, Pierre des Essarts, to the gallows. The whole town will go to Montfaucon. That will be the moment . . .'

Mâchefer's shaggy head, without the false boils, poked round Barnaby's door. The Cockleshell Man was busy wrapping fragments of bone and putting scraps of paper with a few gothic characters on them into little brass boxes.

'Come in,' he said. Catherine was standing beside him, fascinatedly watching him at work. It was too late to hide her. Mâchefer had seen her.

'Who's that one?' he said, pointing at her with a large dirty finger.

'Sister of the Loyse who Caboche has got. Hands off, Mâchefer! She is what you might call my adopted daughter!'

The beggar king looked at the girl clinging to Barnaby's shoulder with astonishment in which there was a tinge of anger. Sara had just finished arranging Catherine's hair, and in the firelight the braids shone like coils of pure gold. Her eyes gleamed too, and she stood with her head thrown back as proudly as a little cock determined not to let Mâchefer see she was afraid. He stretched out a hand hesitantly, touched one of the plaits and grumbled:

'Old fox! I suspect that you have tricked me. If the older

sister has fulfilled the promise of the younger one she must
be a proud beauty.'

Barnaby's gnarled hand removed Mâchefer's.

'She doesn't look like her,' he said curtly. 'And this one is
too young. Let's leave it at that, Mâchefer. You had some
news to tell me. Do you want a drink?'

'I won't refuse,' said the other, lowering himself heavily
on to a stool. 'But it's a bit of luck for you that you belong to
Jacquot-de-la-Mer's band. Otherwise I wouldn't have thought
twice of cutting your throat to get my hands on these two
chickens. I like them young myself, they are tenderer then. . . .'

One of his hands played with a dagger passed through his
belt. The firelight reflected in his bloodshot eyes made him
look like a demon in human shape. Catherine stepped back in
terror and crossed herself. Barnaby shrugged and went on with
his work.

'So you go about frightening children now? Be quiet,
Mâchefer. We have more important things on hand, and you
know you are not as bad as you like to make out. Give him a
drink, little one . . . some wine.'

Not taking her eyes off this alarming personage for an
instant, Catherine filled a goblet of wine from the cask in the
corner. It was a magnificent Beaune wine, one of the casks
which Jean-sans-Peur had distributed among his butcher
friends and other allies in the flush of his demagogic zeal. This
particular barrel had originally been destined for the master-
butcher Saint-Yon but had somehow fallen into the hands of
the wily Barnaby, who reserved its use for special occasions.
Mâchefer drained two goblets straight off, wiped his mouth
and clucked appreciatively:

'Superb. . . . I have nothing to touch it!'

'You shall have the rest tomorrow, if we leave Paris then.
You won't even have to steal it. I make you a present
of it, and of my house into the bargain. Now, tell me your
news.'

His good humour restored by the prospect of acquiring the
cask of wine, Mâchefer willingly went on with his account.

Catherine, feeling reassured, sat on the ground between the two men.

The day the mob attacked the Hôtel de Guyenne and seized the Dauphin's followers it had also laid seige to the Bastille where Pierre des Essarts, former Provost of Paris, had taken refuge with a company of five hundred men-at-arms from his captaincy of Cherbourg. Stout and well-defended as it was, the fortress had been attacked with such ferocity that the Duke of Burgundy had finally decided to open the gates and surrender des Essarts. Under a heavy guard, des Essarts was taken to the Grand Châtelet, where he had been awaiting his sentence ever since. He was the last in a long line. Caboche had created a reign of terror in Paris. A visit to someone's house would be followed by arrests, pillaging and violence of all sorts. He was harassed by fear of the Armagnac party, now entrenched around the walls of Paris, and this fear led to a new outbreak of senseless bloodshed. On 10 June one of the men captured on 28 April had been killed in prison and then beheaded in the Halles market-place before his body was strung up at Montfaucon. On the same day, young Simon du Mesnil, squire trenchant to Prince Louis, was escorted to the Halles with de la Rivière and beheaded there, and his body hoisted up by the armpits. The fifteenth of June had been the turn of Thomeline de Brie, who had tried to defend the Char-enton bridge. And now it was the turn of the great Provost himself. On the following day, 1 July, he would be taken to the Halles to have his head chopped off.

'All Paris will be there,' Mâchefer wound up, 'apart from Mère Caboche, who is forced to stay indoors by her son to keep an eye on the girl. Her shop is still closed and she is drinking like a fish. The time to do the job is towards four o'clock in the afternoon. Everything is ready on my side. You keep a weather eye open here, and get your people organized. Our route will be via the Croix-du-Trahoir and the pig market and then along the river-banks. The rue Saint-Denis will be packed. Have you got a boat?'

'I am going to see about one. . . .'

Barnaby got up and carefully tidied away his wares, putting the fragments of bone in one bag and the little boxes in another. Mâchefer watched him with amusement.

'Which of the great saints are you busy putting in boxes at the moment?' he asked.

'St James, may Heaven forgive me! You know that I am a pilgrim from Compostela. . . .'

Mâchefer gave a great roar of laughter and slapped his thighs.

'You have been selling pieces of St James for so long he must be as big as one of Charlemagne's elephants! Why not choose a new saint?'

His companion's mirth left Barnaby unmoved. He looked at him with the genuine distress of a good merchant who does not like to hear his wares criticized.

'St James sells very well,' he said solemnly. 'I've got no reason to change.'

He put on his cloak, called to Sara, who was doing some mending with Jacquette in the next door room, and patted Catherine's cheek.

'Go and help the women, little one. I shall not be long.'

Catherine was eager to be allowed to help him find a boat, but Barnaby would not hear of it.

The following day the excitement in the air was noticeable even in the silent and sinister alleys leading into the Cour des Miracles. Everyone was out in the street, crowding round the Grand Châtelet and waiting for the condemned man to be led out. The sound of thousands of voices raised in execration reached their ears like the noise of distant thunder, blotting out the church bells which had been chiming the funeral obsequies since dawn. Barnaby's house had been seething with activity since first light. Just before leaving the house Barnaby packed his most precious possessions into several bundles, to which he added the personal effects of the women who were travelling with him. Landry was entrusted with the job of carrying these to the Quai Fort l'Évêque, where the powerful Guild of Watermen had some warehouses. Barnaby had booked places on a barge carrying a cargo of pottery up river to Montereau. A cargo of this type was safe from the attentions of the Armagnac soldiers who were in control of the river at Corbeil. All that was needed was a pass. . . . Landry was to take Jacquette to the warehouse and wait there for the others to arrive. Very unwillingly she had consented to allow Catherine to join the foray against the tripe-seller's house because she was the only person Loyse would be able to recognize among her rescuers. If they tried to stop her, she said, she would run away! Jacquette's own overwrought nerves made it impossible for her to be of the party. She was too easily upset and might thus be a danger to the rest.

'Nothing will happen to the child,' Barnaby promised. 'But don't on any account leave the warehouse. If all goes well we shall be there towards six, and the boat leaves at the vesper bell.'

'Don't worry,' said Landry. 'I will look after her. She won't move.'

The boy was feeling more than a little depressed. Catherine's imminent departure might well be the beginning of a long separation, and his heart bled at the thought of leaving the little friend whom he loved more than he would ever admit to himself. As for telling Catherine herself, the boy would have preferred to have his tongue cut off. But it was a melancholy prospect and Landry found that his eyes prickled in a funny way whenever he looked at Catherine.

She was looking very quaint. Barnaby had dressed her as a boy. She wore tight grey hose and shoes of stout leather, surmounted by a green fustian tunic and, despite the heat, a hood which closely framed her face and continued as a sort of little scalloped cape over her shoulders. This headdress completely hid her hair, which Sara had done up in tight little plaits so as to make it take up as little room as possible. The whole outfit became her marvellously well. She looked like a will-o'-the-wisp. She was not the only one to have altered her appearance, however. Barnaby himself was unrecognizable.

The cloak with the cockleshells had been rolled up in one of the bundles. Instead Barnaby wore a garment of brown stuff belted with a stout leather belt from which hung a large purse. A St James's medal hung on a chain round his neck. He wore a hood of the same material as his garment, so artistically and complicatedly draped about the shoulders that no one would have guessed that the said hood concealed the bulk of Barnaby's savings, whereas the bulging purse only contained loose change. Altogether, with the long pointed toes of his shoes protruding some six inches under his robe, he suggested a comfortably-off if not wealthy merchant who had retired from active business. Catherine was to pass as his grandson. Sara alone remained dressed in her usual bizarre costume because this dress of hers had a purpose to serve.

They all left the Cour Saint-Sauveur together, but when they reached the boundary of the beggar kingdom they split up into two groups and went their separate ways: Catherine, Sara and Barnaby took the rue-de-la-Monnaie Royale, while Jacquette and Landry headed for the Hôtel d'Alencon and the towers of the Louvre. Mâchefer and his men were already disposed about the city and along the fringes of the Notre-Dame market.

In spite of the danger which threatened herself and her companions, Catherine felt happier than she had since the death of Michel. It was lovely to walk about freely again and feel the hot sun. And then there was the excitement of an adventure, of a chase with human quarry. They would snatch Loyse away from that wild beast, Caboche.

The belfry of St Germain l'Auxerrois pealed out three o'clock as Landry and Jacquette passed it. When they went down towards the river in the heat of the day they found the banks almost deserted. The townspeople were doubtless all assembled along the route to the scaffold. There would be clowns and jugglers among the crowd as well as animal trainers, minstrels and story-tellers, for nothing drew such a throng as a fine execution. It was a holiday in which none of the ingredients of a real holiday were lacking. Death counted for so little.

Meanwhile Catherine and Barnaby, with Sara a few steps behind, also went down to the waterside but a bit further upstream. Crossing the Pont-au-Change evoked painful memories for Catherine. Her old house still stood, but its crumbling walls were cracked and dilapidated; the windows gaped open to reveal the emptiness inside and the handsome sign had been torn down. It was now no more than an empty carcase from which the spirit had fled. Catherine felt a lump rise in her throat. She screwed up her eyes as tightly as she could and wished she were miles away. Barnaby hurried along, squeezing the girl's hand a little more tightly in his own.

'Be brave,' he whispered. 'There are times when you need all the courage you have got. You will soon have another house....'

'Not another father,' she whispered, on the verge of tears.

'I was only seven when they took mine away. And when I think how he died I often think I would have given everything I had for him to be merely hanged.'

'What did they do to him?'

'What they usually do to forgers: they boiled him alive at the Morimont in Dijon....'

Catherine gave an exclamation of horror, but she stopped crying and went on in silence. Bravely she banished the dreadful memories which tore at her heart just when she most needed to be strong. When they reached Notre-Dame market she was able to pick out Mâchefer's men in all their different disguises. Some posed as soldiers, others as merchants, or even friars. They had all taken up positions round the market, as arranged. Mâchefer alone was in his usual beggar's costume. Barnaby discreetly pointed out Caboche's house, as tightly shuttered as ever.

'Your turn, Sara!...'

At a nod from Barnaby the gipsy woman walked slowly up the street, swaying her hips and humming softly. She had a tambourine in one hand and beat on it to keep time to her song.

She began almost casually, humming and beating time on her tambourine. But gradually her song increased in intensity, the melody speaking clearly through the incomprehensible gipsy words. The tune itself was bizarre, punctuated by silences and sharp wailing notes. Sara's slightly hoarse voice lent it mysterious depths of feeling and something of the power of a spell or incantation. Catherine listened quite carried away. One or two faces appeared at windows, while a few passers-by stopped to listen: all told, there could not have been more than ten people involved. Mâchefer went up to Barnaby on the pretext of begging for alms:

'If the old crone does not open up we will have to batter the door down. What do you say?'

Barnaby rummaged in his purse, and took out a sou which he dropped into the beggar's grimy hands.

'Certainly, but I would prefer to avoid that if possible. Battering down doors makes a lot of noise even if there *is* no one around.'

No faces appeared at the tripe-seller's windows. The house would have seemed quite deserted if they had not been able to make out faint sounds within. Catherine suddenly went white and leant against Barnaby.

'My God! ... There is Marion! ...' she exclaimed, cautiously pointing out a stout woman who had just come into sight at the end of the road. Barnaby raised his eyebrows.

'Who? The maid who—'

'Yes, the maid who brought the people in to our house and caused the deaths of Michel and Papa. Oh, I *can't* look at her!'

Overcome by revulsion, Catherine tried to break away. But Barnaby held her tightly by the hand.

'Now then! A good soldier doesn't desert in the face of the enemy, my little flower! I quite understand your not wishing to see the woman again. ... I'll wager she's not a pretty sight at the best of times. But you must stay where you are.'

'What if she recognizes me?'

'Disguised like that? I would be surprised if she did. Anyway, I suspect that she is in no condition to recognize anyone.'

The fat woman was in fact staggering from one house to the next, unable to keep a straight course. Catherine wondered what her mother would have said if she had seen her foster-sister now. Marion had changed a good deal in the past two months. She was fatter than ever and indescribably filthy. Her apron, once so white and stiffly starched, was rumpled and splashed with an assortment of meals and drinks. It barely covered a dress which was splitting at the seams, and fraying round the hem. Greasy locks of hair escaped from beneath a battered cap. She was stumbling along, oblivious to everything, her open mouth soundlessly forming words, her eyes glazed and her arms dangling at her sides. She didn't stop to listen to Sara. Indeed, she seemed not to see her at all, and passed on.

Sara's singing and dancing had reached a wild crescendo; filling the narrow lane between the houses which seemed to lean so dangerously towards each other overhead. Mère Caboche's door opened a crack and her red face peered out curiously. . . .

'Sara,' Barnaby whispered urgently, 'now's your chance . . .'

Breaking off her singing and dancing the gipsy leapt across to the threshold, wedged her foot in the door and cried:

'I can read the future in your palm, in clear water and in ashes. Two sous only! . . . Give me your hand, beautiful lady!'

Taken by surprise Mère Caboche tried to close the door. When she found she couldn't she began swearing like a trooper. But the more she screamed and shouted the more Sara insisted, promising her a golden future garlanded with roses, pleasant predictions to which Mère Caboche replied with a variety of unflattering observations on Sara's parentage and Sara herself. This brief verbal joust, however, had given Mâchefer's men time to assemble.

'Now, my lads,' cried the beggar king, 'forward!'

Barnaby pulled Catherine into the porch of a baker's shop. The baker himself must have been at the execution because his shutters were all down. Mâchefer's two dozen picked men rushed at the door. In a flash Mère Caboche was swept under the impetus of the attack into the far depths of her shop, while Sara, knocked off balance herself, rolled out into the alley where Barnaby helped her to her feet. She was laughing heartily.

'You aren't hurt?' Barnaby asked.

'No. Except that the blow Mâchefer intended for Mère Caboche missed its target and hit me in the eye. I shall have a fine black eye tomorrow. He has a blow like a battering-ram, that one. I thought he would knock my head off!'

Sara's left eye was already turning a ripe and alarming shade of blue, but it did not seem to affect her good humour. Meanwhile the beggars had overrun the Caboche household and the victim's screams were barely audible in the uproar. It seemed likely that the invaders had not contented themselves with merely hunting for Loyse.

A few minutes later Mâchefer reappeared carrying a young woman dressed only in a white chemise, her blonde hair flowing over her shoulders.

'Is this what you were looking for?' he asked.

'Loyse! Loyse!' Catherine cried, seizing the prisoner's limp hand. 'Heavens! She is dead!' A flood of tears poured down her face. Barnaby started to laugh.

'No, she is alive, little one. Just unconscious. But we must hurry. We can bring her round when we get to the warehouse.'

The girl remained quite inert, eyes closed and nostrils pinched. She was deathly pale with great violet shadows round her eyes. Her breathing was almost imperceptible. Sara frowned.

'You had better run then. She is too pale. . . . I don't like it.'

Mâchefer needed no urging. He started off, running through the city streets, leaving his men to loot the tripe-seller's house as they pleased. The three others raced after him. It was a headlong journey, but Catherine, who had dreamed so long of running about the streets during her stay in Barnaby's cellar, enjoyed it immensely. Besides, Loyse had been rescued, and they were all going away on a boat to see new countries and meet new people.

A great new adventure seemed to beckon. Already some of the scars of those recent tragedies seemed to be fading a little. Her flying feet took her rapidly past houses and crossroads, each with their fountain and votive cross. They crossed the Seine with one bound. Mâchefer, despite the slight but noticeable weight of Loyse, seemed to fly across it, and the other three had some difficulty keeping up. At last they reached the banks of yellow sand kindled by the sun. The doors of the watermen's warehouse closed behind them and they were safely hidden in the warm darkness within. Jacquette, who had been keeping watch for them, fell sobbing on Loyse, who was still unconscious. But Sara pushed her roughly aside.

'She needs care, not tears. Leave this to me. . . .'

Catherine, quite winded, but full of a deep contentment, flopped down on the sand to get back her breath.

An hour later, sitting beside Barnaby in the prow of the barge, she watched Paris unfold on either side. The tears which had flowed as she said farewell to Landry were still rolling down her cheeks. It had grieved her much more than she had expected. The girl realized for the first time just how large a place he had occupied in her life. As for Landry himself, he had been so moved that a great tear had fallen on to Catherine's cheek as they hugged each other for the first and last time. She felt as if her throat were being squeezed. Then Landry had promised:

'One day I will come and see you. I promise. I want to be a soldier and I shall take service under Milord of Burgundy. We shall meet again, I know we shall.'

He smiled and tried to brazen it out, but his heart was not in it. The corners of his mouth, which he struggled so valiantly to turn upwards, kept drooping again. At this point Barnaby decided to cut short the farewells and hauled Catherine aboard, seizing her under both arms. He carried her along like a parcel, weeping copiously and calling out repeated 'au revoirs', interrupted by bursts of sobbing. The sailors started pushing on the long poles which propelled them over the slimy riverbed, and the barge slowly drew away from the bank, gliding over the yellow water, swollen with sand and alluvial mud. Taxed to the uttermost by the effort of poling the barge upstream, the crew kept close by the river-banks instead of heading out into the middle of the river, where the current was strongest.

Another shadow hung over Catherine. This was Loyse's strange behaviour. After recovering consciousness the girl stared to begin with at the known and unknown faces leaning over her. She saw her mother in tears, her sister smiling at her. But instead of surrendering herself to the joy of finding them again and throwing her arms round her loved ones, she had shaken herself free of Jacquette's embrace and hidden herself in a corner of the warehouse among the barrels, bales of hides, pottery, piles of wood and grain.

'Don't touch me!' she cried. It was a cry so fierce that it cut her sister to the quick. Jacquette held out her arms in despair.

'My darling . . . My Loyse! It's I, your mother . . . don't you recognize your mother any more? Don't you love me?'

Huddled into her corner, Loyse looked like some small trapped animal. Her face seemed to be swallowed up by her huge, pale, terrified eyes and her hands were clenched so tightly over her breast that the knuckles showed white. A sob shook her voice.

'Don't touch me. I am unclean and vile . . . I am but dirt and filth and I can only disgust all virtuous women. I am no longer your daughter, Mother, but a slut, a fallen woman, the mistress of Caboche the Skinner! Go away, leave me alone!'

Jacquette tried to get closer to her, but Loyse shrank back, flattened against the dusty ground as if her mother's hand had been a red-hot iron. Sara intervened. She leapt on Loyse like a cat, and held her firm between her long, supple arms. There was no time to lose.

'*I* can touch you, child. It is a long time since I first made the acquaintance of this filth you speak of. You are not to torment your poor mother like this. It has only touched your body. Your soul is still clean since you did not want it to happen.'

'No!' Loyse screamed. 'I didn't want it to happen, but sometimes I found pleasure in his caresses. When his hands stroked my body, and he took me, I used to cry out in ecstasy. I used to desire him too. I, the girl who lived only for God, and wanted only God. . . .'

'How can you be sure you only want God till you have known earthly love, my child?' said Barnaby, shrugging. 'Now we have rescued you from all that, and we are going to take you away with us. The boat is about to leave. Unless you want us to take you back to Caboche?'

Loyse made a horrified gesture.

'No, oh no! I only want to die!'

'To kill yourself is a graver sin in the eyes of God than to submit to a man . . . even if you *did* enjoy it sometimes!'

'I want to destroy this shameful, vile body!'

'All you are doing is making us miss the boat. . . .'

And, quite calmly, Barnaby clenched his fist and struck Loyse on the chin, not too hard, but just hard enough to knock her out temporarily. Jacquette's indignant cry left him unmoved.

'We have lost too much time already. Dress her quickly and take her to the boat. Once under way we shall have all the time in the world to reason with her. But we must all keep a close watch on her to see she doesn't try to jump overboard.'

His orders were carried out to the letter. Now, more suitably attired, Loyse's unconscious form was placed in the sort of cabin at the back of the barge which gave shelter for the sailors. Sara and Jacquette lavished their attentions on her. The journey could now begin.

Seated on a coil of rope with his long legs stretched out before him, Barnaby contemplated Catherine. She sat looking straight ahead of her, her hands clasped round her skinny knees, tears rolling down her cheeks. She was greatly upset by what she had just heard. It reminded her of what she had seen in the Cour des Miracles. But Barnaby had used the word 'love'. Surely that couldn't be love, the thing she had seen in the Cour des Miracles, the thing Loyse spoke of with such loathing? Love was what she had felt the moment she saw Michel. A sweet constriction of the heart, a desire to be gentle and tender and say nice things. But Loyse screamed as if she had undergone torture, and seemed quite deranged.

Barnaby put his arm round her shoulders.

'Loyse will recover, little one. She is not the first person to undergo an experience like this since God created the world. But it will take her a long time, because she is narrowly pious and unbending in character. It will need a great deal of patience from everyone around her, but one day she will regain her

appetite for life. As for Landry, I am sure you will see him
again one day. He knows what he wants in life and he is one of
those who forge a path for themselves regardless of obstacles
and difficulties. If he wants to be a soldier with the Burgundian
army, he will be . . . believe me.'

Gratitude shone in the look Catherine turned on him.
Barnaby's affection for her was such that it instinctively understood and answered the questions she could not bring herself to
ask. She suddenly felt safe and contented. Barnaby leant forward pointing.

'See how beautiful Paris is. The largest and fairest city in
the world. But Dijon is not too bad either, as you will see. . . .'

The barge had passed under the Pont-aux-Moulins by now
and was gliding towards the great arches of the next bridge
along, the Pont-au-Change. They passed directly below the
house where the Legoix family used to live, and Catherine cast
a last look at the skylight through which Michel had tried to
escape, and then turned her head away. A little farther upstream a forest of pointed poles showed above the water. These
marked the foundations of the future Notre-Dame bridge.
Three weeks earlier in one of his rare periods of mental
lucidity, the king himself had driven the first pole into place
with a mallet, and his sons after him. Some faded wreaths of
flowers still hung from that pole.

All about them the towers and steeples of Paris soared up into
the sky. Bold arrowy church steeples stood out sharply against
the lacier outlines of bell-towers, the great roof of the House of
Pillars and the fine houses of noblemen whose gardens
stretched down to the river. Opposite the quai where the gibbet
and wheel stood empty of occupants, the square towers of
Notre-Dame stood out against a sky of molten gold. Farther
along came the St Pol harbour, where they unloaded grain from
flat-bottomed boats, and after that the King's Palace and gardens, and the slender turrets of the Hôtel owned by the Arch-
bishop of Sens. On the other side came the islands, the Île-
aux-Vaches and the Île-Notre-Dame, flat and green with
pasture land fringed by silvery willows. Catherine's gaze fell

next on the stout walls of the Celestins monastery separated by a narrow canal from the sandy little island called the Île Louviaux. This was the outer boundary of Paris, marked by the squat bulk of the Tour Barbeau. Grey and menacing under its pointed roof, the tower had been built in earlier times by Philip II, known as Auguste. A rampart connected the tower to the Bastille, and at night the great chain attached to it was fastened across the Seine. . . . A sunny June day and tall green trees relieved the scene of some of its military grimness, however. Even the stones seemed soft and friendly. Barnaby began to recite softly:

> 'She is crowned the Queen of Cities
> Wellspring of religion and learning
> Situated on the river Seine.
> Vineyard, woods, lands and meadows,
> All the goodly things of this mortal life
> Has she more than other cities do.
> All strangers now and evermore shall love her.
> For loveliness and jollity
> There is no city to rival her
> None can compare with Paris. . . .'*

'How pretty!' said Catherine, her drowsy head leaning against Barnaby's shoulder. Behind her the boatmen struck up a song to which they poled along rhythmically. There was nothing to do but let oneself be carried along towards a new destiny, leaving behind old memories and old griefs. All Catherine wanted to take with her of her old life was the image of Michel de Montsalvy, graven for ever on her heart, an image which she knew time would never rub away.

The green banks of the Seine slipped steadily by. Catherine felt herself drifting off to sleep. . . .

* From a poem by Eustache Deschamps.

Part One

THE ROAD FROM FLANDERS

1422

CHAPTER THREE

THE PROCESSION OF THE PRECIOUS BLOOD

THE INN at the Sign of the Flowering Mulberry was one of the most popular and crowded in Bruges. It stood on the Wollestraat, or Wool Street, between the Grande Place and the Quai du Rosaire, and thus catered to a large clientele of cloth and wool merchants, and merchants of all sorts from many countries. Its prosperity was clearly visible in the tall, sculpted and crenellated gable, in the gleam of its leaded windows of bull's-eye glass, in the tantalizing aromas which escaped from its immense kitchen resplendent with copper, tin and pottery, in the fresh dresses and winged caps worn by the servants, and above all in the round belly of the happy proprietor Maître Gaspard Cornelis.

Catherine was accustomed to the luxury of the Flowering Mulberry from other, earlier journeys. Just now all her attention was fixed on the bustle in the street below. Since early morning the whole town had been parading there in its holiday best.

Half dressed, her hair flowing untidily down her back, the young girl leant out of her window as far as she could, comb in hand, deaf to the recriminations of Uncle Mathieu, who had been grumbling away in the next room since daybreak. The cloth merchant, having finished his business in the town, had originally intended to leave for Dijon at dawn, but Catherine, after much argument, had finally persuaded him to stay over till that evening so that she could take part in the famous Procession of the Precious Blood, which was the most important feast day in the town.

She did not have too much difficulty in persuading her Uncle Mathieu. He grumbled for hours, insisted that feast days were simply there to make good people throw away their hard-earned gold by the shovelful, reminded her that there was business in Burgundy which would brook no delay, and finally allowed himself to be convinced – as indeed he always did, finding it impossible to refuse his ravishing niece anything. The good man had gallantly admitted defeat by making his pretty conqueror a present of a delicious white lace headdress and some gold pins to fasten it with.

Tired of shouting through the wall, and of leaning out of his window scolding the valets who were loading his latest acquisitions on to the mules, Mathieu Gautherin entered his niece's room. When he found her still only half dressed, and half out of the window into the bargain, he burst out:

'What! Still not dressed? The procession will be leaving the basilica in a minute and you haven't even done your hair!'

Catherine turned towards her uncle. Finding him standing there with folded arms, legs astraddle and cap askew above his fat red indignant face, she ran to fling her arms round his neck and cover his cheeks with little kisses, which was the sort of thing Maître Mathieu adored, though he would rather have lost an arm than admit it.

'I won't be a minute, Uncle. It's just that everything looks so lovely this morning!'

'Pah! One would think you had never seen a procession before.'

'I have never seen this one. And I've never seen so many beautiful clothes before! There isn't one woman who isn't wearing velvet or satin or brocade. They all have lace caps, and jewels, even the ones who were selling fish yesterday in the Watermarket.'

While she spoke Catherine hurriedly finished dressing. She pulled on a long dress of pale blue taffeta which was slashed in front to display a white skirt finely striped with silver, the same material which made the bodice under the deep pointed neckline of the dress. Then, hastily, she plaited and pinned up her hair and adjusted the crescent-shaped lace coif, one end of which went below her chin, accentuating the oval shape of her face. She turned to her uncle:

'How do I look?'

The question was unnecessary. Mathieu's affectionate glance reflected Catherine's beauty like a mirror. Sara's prophecy had come true. At twenty-one the girl was as ravishing a creature as one could imagine. Her huge eyes with their changing colour, lit up a face whose freckles had given way to a lovely velvety skin, pink and gold, and reminiscent of the petals of a tea rose. Her long golden hair was still the admiration of all. Catherine was not very tall, but her figure was perfect. Her proportions, grace, and curves, at once full and delicate, would have set the most exacting painter reaching for his brush. But to the great despair of Mathieu Gautherin, of his sister Jacquette and the rest of the family, Catherine, who had been besieged by a veritable army of suitors since the age of sixteen, still obstinately refused to marry. Her power over men seemed to amuse her, even to annoy her a little.

'You are youth and springtime incarnate,' said Mathieu sincerely. 'It seems a pity that no nice young man can look forward to the day when it will all be his. . . .'

'I don't see how *I* should gain by the arrangement. After a woman marries her beauty fades and loses its sparkle.'

Mathieu raised up his arms.

'What a way to talk! But my child—'

'Uncle,' Catherine interrupted gently, 'we shall be late.'

They left the room together. In the inn courtyard, where servants laden with plates and poultry raced to and fro, their caps fluttering, Mathieu gave some last instructions to his grooms. He ordered them to keep an eye on his packs and not go off drinking in some tavern, threatening the most brutal punishments if they disobeyed. Then, with a low and respectful bow from Maître Cornelis, uncle and niece stepped out into the street.

The crowd was biggest in the Place du Bourg, in front of the basilica of the Precious Blood.

As they drew nearer to the market-place Mathieu and his niece had difficulty in making headway through the crowd. Oblivious of the buzz of interest which her beauty excited in

the onlookers, Catherine walked with her nose in the air,
craning her head to see everything that was going on.

Around the square, the great houses, painted and decorated
like pictures in a missal, were almost hidden under cascades of
multi-coloured silken stuffs and costly tapestries woven of gold
and silver thread which had been brought out for the occasion
from the sombre interior to flash and gleam in the sunny
street outside.

Garlands of flowers were looped between house and house,
and the processional route was strewn with a thick carpet of
fresh grass, red roses and white violets over the uneven paving
stones. In front of the houses huge dressers, draped with
coloured brocades and velvets, displayed the family treasures.
Goblets and vases, gold and silver plates, richly chased and
studded with precious stones, testified to the wealth of the
family and solicited the admiration of passers-by, heavily
guarded meantime by muscular-looking valets.

Despite her efforts Catherine was unable to catch so much as
a glimpse of the old Roman basilica where the celebrated relic
was kept. A mass of banners like flames of embroidered silk and
multi-coloured pennants fluttering on the lances of the Flemish
nobility looked like a field of flowers swaying in the wind and
effectively hid the church from sight. Through the church's
wide-opened doors, however, great floods of music poured,
psalms chanted by stout Flemish throats against a background
of pealing organ music. She would have to make do with that!

After valiant efforts uncle and niece managed to find a place
for themselves in one of the best positions, at the corner of the
market-place. This corner faced the Ducal Palace and commanded a wide view over the vast market-place and the central
square of the town. Two women who were vigorously disputing over some old grievance of a coif lent but not returned had
had to be separated by some archers, thus leaving a gap in the
crowd of which Mathieu had quickly taken advantage. He had
thereby got access to the cornerstone of the market building
which would allow them, when the time came, to climb a little
above the sea of heads and see the Precious Blood carried past.

The last tenant of the stone, a tall figure dressed in saffron velvet and blessed with a doleful countenance, all vertical lines, was quite agreeable to moving up a little to make room for the young girl. He even twisted his lips into what might, at a pinch, be taken for a smile.

His clothes, edged with sables and lightly embroidered in silver thread, were of a certain elegance, but they gave off an unpleasant sweaty smell and Catherine felt obliged to move a little so as to put some distance between herself and the obliging burgess. Mathieu was not so fastidious. He soon struck up an animated conversation with his neighbour. It seemed he was a furrier from Ghent who had come to stock up in Russian and Bulgarian furs at the German trading post in the Hanseatic League. His conversation lacked coherence, however. It seemed as though he found the young girl's presence distracting. He stared at her continually. Catherine found this stare disagreeable and decided to ignore it. There was plenty to look at in the colourful crowd which packed the market square. Representatives of all the seventeen nations with trading posts in this great trading city rubbed shoulders there. Grimy Russian caftans bordered with priceless furs brushed against Byzantines in garments stiff with embroidery. The richly but discreetly dressed English rubbed shoulders with the cut velvets and shimmering brocades worn by the merchants of Venice and Florence whose opulence had a touch of *nouveau riche* about it and attracted thieves and pickpockets the way honey attracts flies. A huge yellow satin turban, round as a pumpkin and adorned in front with a white aigrette, towered above the heads of the crowd announcing the presence of a Turk. Finally, towards the far end of the market square, a skinny boy in a tight red costume walked nonchalantly to and fro on a tightrope high above the heads of the crowd, a long balancing pole in his hands.

Catherine just had time to observe to herself that he was undoubtedly the best placed to see what was going on when there was a blast of silver trumpets announcing the departure of the procession. At the same time all the bells in Bruges began to ring out and Catherine, laughing, clapped her hands to her ears to shut out the din of the belfry tower which seemed to be just above her head.

'It gets more and more difficult to buy English wool at a reasonable price,' Mathieu Gautherin was complaining. 'The Florentines buy it all up at exorbitant rates and then come here to sell their cloth at ridiculous prices. I must admit that the cloth is good and their colours brilliant but it's not right! Especially since the alum from the Tolfa mine means that they can fix the dyes for next to nothing. . . .'

'Bah!' his new friend agreed. 'We furriers have problems like this too. These Novgorod people insist on being paid in Venetian ducats now. As if our good Flemish gold weren't worth just as much . . . !'

'Sssssh!' said Catherine, bored by this mercantile talk. 'Here comes the procession.'

The two men fell silent and the bourgeois from Ghent made the most of the fact that the girl was absorbed in the approaching spectacle to edge a little closer to her. This meant he had to crane his head sideways to avoid having one eye put out by the lace horns of her high headdress. Catherine, her eyes like saucers, had forgotten about him. The procession was under way.

It was indeed a magnificent sight. The magistrates and all the city guilds were represented, each with their banner. Out of reverence for the relic they all wore crowns of roses, violets and marjoram which were in curious contrast to the well-nourished faces beneath.

A group of monks and a band of young girls in white dresses came immediately in front of the Precious Blood, whose approach was the signal for all present to fall on their knees in the dust.

To Catherine it seemed as though the sun itself had fallen from heaven in all its dazzling brilliance. The great canopy which four deacons carried above the bishop's head was of fretted gold. The prelate's cope and sparkling mitre were of cloth of gold, embroidered with gold thread and diamonds. He came forward slowly, seated on the back of a white mule, its harness and bridle also of gold, and carried the reliquary between purple-gloved hands against his chest. On its cover two kneeling angels were depicted, their enamelled wings glinting with pearls and sapphires. The crystal sides of the reliquary allowed the relic within to be seen, a small brownish-red phial: the Precious Blood of Christ, a few drops which Joseph of Arimathea had collected on Golgotha long ago. Thierry, Count of Alsace and Flanders, to whom the Patriarch of Jerusalem had given it in 1149, brought the sacred phial back from the Holy Land to Bruges.

Barely a minute after the girl got up from her knees, she was obliged to drop down again, this time in a deep curtsey.

'There is the Duchess,' said someone in the crowd.

A group of young women in sumptuous dresses followed the bishop's canopy. They all wore pale blue brocade encrusted with silver and pearls and tall pointed headdresses of silver cloth swathed in blue gauze. In their midst was a young blonde woman, slender and graceful, with a sad gentle face. The long ermine-lined train of her gold-flowered, blue brocade dress swept the flowers and foliage beneath her feet. Her headdress, starred with sapphires, looked like an arrow of pure gold. Jewels sparkled on her bosom and covered her wrists and her belt was formed of great nuggets of gold, almost barbaric in appearance because of the huge size of the gems with which it was studded.

It was the first time Catherine had seen the Duchess of Burgundy. She rarely came to Dijon but lived all the year round, with only her women for company, in the coldly sumptuous palace of the Counts of Flanders, at Ghent. Her husband could not bear the sight of her.

Michelle de France was the daughter of the poor mad king, Charles VI, and, more important still, sister of the Dauphin Charles who was generally rumoured to have been responsible for the assassination of the late Duke of Burgundy, Jean-sans-Peur, three years earlier. Philippe of Burgundy loved his father deeply and, the day he learnt of his death, the love which he had felt for his wife was extinguished for no other reason than that she was his enemy's sister. Since then Michelle lived only for God and for good works. The people of Ghent adored her and resented their liege lord's attitude towards so gentle and virtuous a woman. They considered it both unjust and excessive.

Looking at Michelle's wistful face Catherine instantly sided with the citizens of Ghent and told herself that Duke Philippe must be an idiot. Behind her the furrier from Ghent whispered to Uncle Mathieu:

'Our poor Duchess's life is one long martyrdom. Last year the Duke ordered great celebrations to mark the birth of his bastard son by the lady of Presles. Our good lady, who is childless through no fault of her own, wept for many days when she heard the news. But the Duke cared nothing for her tears and at once proclaimed the babe Great Bastard of Burgundy – as if it were something to be proud of!'

Catherine's impressionable heart swelled indignantly. She would have liked to fly to the assistance of the little Duchess, so unjustly spurned by her husband.

The Duke in person followed behind. He was on horseback, escorted by a troop of knights in full war harness, and formed part of the cortège of Count Thierry of Flanders, to whom Bruges owed the Precious Blood. As such he wore the armour of a past age. A coat of chain mail covered him from shoulders to knees, and on his head he wore a hood of mail under a pointed helmet which left only the severe pale oval of his face visible. A long, broad, flat sword hung at his side. In his steel-gloved right hand he held a lance from which fluttered a pennant in the Flemish colours. On his right arm he held a shield in the shape of an elongated almond. The lords around him were dressed in the same style and they formed an impressive forest of rigid and sinister black steel statues. Philippe's eyes gazed high above the heads of the crowd and seemed not to see anything. How haughty, remote and disdainful he seemed! Catherine, once more bent in a respectful attitude, told herself that he was definitely not a sympathetic character.

As she rose from her curtsey Catherine suddenly felt two shaking hands encircling her waist. She tried to shake them off

thinking that someone might have stumbled and seized hold of
her to retrieve their balance. But the furtive hands now
started creeping up her body to her breasts, which they greedily
seized. She cried out in a fury. Whirling round so violently
that her neighbours fell back and her headdress shook, she
found herself face to face with the furrier from Ghent who was
clearly stupefied by her reaction.

'Oh!' she cried. 'Filthy swine!'

Beside herself with rage, she gave him three tremendous
slaps on the face. His pale cheeks instantly flushed scarlet as
June poppies and he stepped back a few paces, raising his
hands to his face.

Catherine was on the warpath. Oblivious of her beautiful lace
cap, now trampled in the dust, with her gleaming mass of hair
streaming about her, she went after her assailant again, despite
her uncle's efforts to stop her.

'Niece, niece, are you mad?' cried the good man.

'Mad? Ask this sorry creature here, this common skin-
merchant here, what he has been up to! Ask him if he dares
tell you!'

The man sought refuge in the darkness of the market hall,
whence he evidently hoped to escape, but the crowd now blocked his passage. By now amused onlookers had joined in the
dispute, some siding with the furrier, some with the girl.

'Bah!' exclaimed a grocer as broad as he was tall. 'What's the
world coming to if one can't squeeze a girl's waist in the crowd
without causing a scandal?'

A young woman with a fresh, round face but haughty glint
in her eye leant forward to get a closer look at him.

'I'd like to see someone try and squeeze my waist!' she cried.
'The young woman was quite right. ... For my part, I'd
scratch the eyes out of anyone who tried to take liberties with
me.'

To scratch the furrier's eyes out seemed to be exactly what
Catherine, who had escaped from her uncle's restraining grip,
was attempting to do. Before long there was quite a commotion
at the corner of the market-place and none of the belligerents

noticed that the procession itself had stopped. A cold voice abruptly cut through the hubbub.

'Guards . . . seize these people who are disturbing the procession.'

It was the Duke in person. Halted at the corner of the market-place, he waited, a rigid figure in his steel armour. Instantly four men-at-arms of his personal guard pushed their way through the crowd. Catherine was pulled away from her adversary, who was defending himself as best he could, seized by two of the men-at-arms despite Mathieu's entreaties and dragged before Philippe of Burgundy's horse.

She was still furious. She struggled like a little demon, and by the time they managed to control her her hair was streaming all over the place. The collar of her blue dress had been torn off and one fresh, soft shoulder was bared. Her eyes sparkled angrily and her look clashed with Philippe's like steel on steel. They glared at each other for a moment, like two fighters measuring each other up, the one tall and haughty on his horse, the other defiant as a little fighting-cock, refusing to lower her eyes. Around them an anxious silence fell, broken only by the sobs of the unfortunate Mathieu.

'What happened?' the Duke asked curtly.

One of the archers who had hold of the terrified furrier answered:

'This fellow took advantage of the crowd to tease the girl a bit, sire. She slapped his face.'

Philippe's grey gaze passed briefly, with chilling contempt, over the furrier's ashen face and then returned to Catherine, who stood as before, with a haughty expression, obstinately refusing to utter a word. Sure that right was on her side, she was too proud to make excuses for herself in front of everyone, let alone implore forgiveness. She stood and waited. Philippe's cold voice rang out.

'Disturbing a procession is a serious misdemeanour. Take them away. I will take care of this matter later on.'

He leant across to the captain of the guard, Jacques de Roussay, and murmured a few words to him; then, wheeling his horse round, he once more resumed his place in the procession. The cortège moved on amid clouds of incense and the singing of sacred hymns.

The Captain de Roussay was obliged to wait till the end of the procession, a series of tableaux vivants illustrating scenes from the Old and New Testaments, before taking the prisoners away. His orders were to take them to the palace, and to do this he had first of all to cross the market square. Meanwhile Mathieu Gautherin tore his hair, wept unashamedly and collapsed on the cornerstone. The young woman who had taken Catherine's side in the dispute did her best to comfort him. He had tried to speak to his niece but been prevented by the bowmen. He pictured to himself with horrifying vividness the succession of disasters which might befall her. They would almost certainly consign the rash young woman to one of the palace dungeons. Then she would be tried and as likely as not hung, or even burnt alive, for sacrilege. As for him, they would doubtless pull down his house and banish him from his home town to wander the highroads with his family, begging his bread, always persecuted, always on the move till the time the Lord should see fit to take pity on him and gather him to His bosom. . . .

Catherine, on the other hand, had finally cooled down and now adopted an attitude of icy composure. The archers had tied her hands together and she stood there proudly, very upright, in her torn dress which revealed her bare shoulder, enveloped in clouds of hair, scornfully ignoring the comments, some flattering, some impudent and some frankly obscene, that her beauty called forth from the spectators. She was aware of all these people looking at her. She even found a certain secret amusement in observing how the captain of the guard blushed and looked away when she happened to catch him looking at her. Roussay was young, and the sight of his prisoner clearly disturbed him more than a little.

When the last tableau, representing a paunchy Daniel amid some highly fantastical beasts, had passed, he ordered the crowd to fall back and escorted his prisoners along at a good pace. They crossed the square almost at a run. Poor Mathieu, still weeping copiously, followed as best he could, his hood all awry and his fat face, swollen by tears, irresistibly reminiscent of a disconsolate baby's.

When he had got as far as the palace entrance, however, the lances of the guard barred the way and he was forced to give up his plan to accompany his niece. Heartbroken, he took his seat on a convenient stone and began to weep like a fountain, almost certain now that he would not see Catherine again till the time came for her to go to the scaffold.

Once inside the palace, Catherine noticed with some surprise that she had been separated from her adversary. The furrier was being taken by his guards to the left of the courtyard, whereas she was being conducted by Roussay himself towards the great staircase.

'Are you not taking me to the dungeons?' she asked. The captain did not answer. He was walking along like an efficient robot, eyes fixed straight ahead, face impassive under the raised visor of his helmet. Catherine could not know that, if he refused to look or even speak to her, it was only because he had not felt in control of his emotions since first laying eyes on that disturbingly lovely face. It was certainly the first time that Jacques de Roussay had hated doing his duty.

At the top of the staircase there was a long gallery, then a door opening into a sumptuously furnished room, next came another smaller room entirely hung with beautiful tapestries. Hidden in the tapestries was a door, which opened as if by magic when the captain pushed it.

'In here,' he said curtly.

It was only then that Catherine noticed with astonishment that the captain formed her sole escort at this point and that the soldiers seemed to have mysteriously vanished. On the threshold Roussay cut the rope which bound his prisoner's hands with a dagger, and then pushed her in. The door shut noiselessly behind her, and when Catherine turned to see whether her gaoler was still there, she couldn't believe her eyes: the door had disappeared, concealed in the pattern on the walls.

Sighing resignedly the girl looked about her. Her prison was a room whose small dimensions were compensated for by a rare splendour. Walls hung with cloth of gold threw into relief the sombre magnificence of a great bed entirely draped with black velvet. There was no coat of arms above the bedhead, but the curtains were held back by gold cords attached to griffons' heads of solid gold with emerald eyes. Near a high white chimney-piece, an ebony dresser held some gold and silver objects whose main purpose there seemed to be to set off a large goblet of sparkling crystal whose base and cover were of gold encrusted with large round pearls. An ebony coffer standing between two narrow Gothic windows held a basin of enamelled gold in which a huge armful of blood red roses had been placed.

Catherine advanced cautiously across the thick carpet, patterned in black and dark red, which, she would have been surprised to learn, had only just arrived from distant Samarkand, aboard a great Genoese caravel still berthed in the harbour at Damme. A large mirror reflected her image in passing: that of a young girl with sparkling eyes and tousled hair which shone brighter than the gilded walls. But her torn dress seemed to reveal more bare skin than was seemly. Embarrassed all of a sudden at the thought of all the people who had seen her so unsuitably dressed, she hunted about for a piece of cloth or something with which to cover her shoulders and bosom, but there was nothing to be found and she had to resign herself to covering her half-bared bosom with her hands.

She felt weary all of a sudden, and ravenously hungry. Catherine was one of those robustly healthy people whose appetite remains unaffected by even the most dire calamities. But there was absolutely nothing edible anywhere in this artfully sealed-up room with its invisible doors. Sighing deeply, she installed herself in one of the high-backed chairs of sculpted ebony which faced each other on either side of the fireplace. They were reasonably comfortable, thanks to their thick down-filled cushions of black velvet with gold tassels. Catherine curled up like a cat, relishing the comfort, and, since she had nothing better to do, was soon asleep. Her own fate worried her much less than the terrible anxieties which must now be assailing poor Uncle Mathieu. They couldn't have brought her to such a pretty room only to send her to the scaffold afterwards.

She woke with a start, a long while later, registering subconsciously a presence in the room. There, before her, stood a tall, thin young man, hands behind his back and legs slightly apart, watching her sleep. She leapt to her feet with a cry of surprise and alarm, and stood looking apprehensively at the newcomer.

The man before her was not a stranger, but the Duke Philippe in person.

He had changed his old-fashioned armour for a short black velvet tunic which matched the hose that showed off his long, thin, but muscular legs. His head was bare and he wore his blond hair cut very short above the ears. This severe costume only enhanced the youthfulness of his face. He certainly could not be more than twenty-six years old. He was smiling.

The smile deepened as Catherine, still half awake, dropped an awkward curtsey and exclaimed:

'Oh . . . sire, I apologize. . . .'

'You were sleeping so soundly that I didn't dare wake you. And there is no need to apologize. It was a charming sight.'

Pink with embarrassment as she observed Philippe's pale stare moving over her person, Catherine, remembering the state she was in, hastily covered her bosom with her hands. To accommodate this sudden fit of modesty the Duke moved a few steps away and shrugged faintly.

'Well, my pretty trouble-maker. Who are you, first of all?'

'Your prisoner, sire.'

'And what besides?'

'Nothing . . . since you call me "tu" so familiarly. I am not of noble birth, but neither am I low-born. I am not a servant. And just because I have been arrested is no reason to treat me like one.'

A half-amused, half-curious smile fleeted across Philippe's pale face. The girl's astonishing beauty had struck him at once, but now that he saw her more closely he was impressed by something more, a sort of intrinsic worth which he had not expected to find. However, he did not intend to let her see this and there was more than a suggestion of mockery about his smile when he asked:

'In that case I must ask your forgiveness, demoiselle. But would you mind telling me your name? I think I know all the pretty girls in the town, yet I have never seen you before.'

'Don't call me demoiselle, sire. I have told you I am not a demoiselle. And I don't live in this town. I came here with my uncle to buy cloth. . . .'

'Where are you from then?'

'I was born in Paris, but I have been living in Dijon since your friends, the Cabochiens, hanged my father who was a goldsmith on the Pont-au-Change.'

The smile faded from Philippe's face and his lips hardened in a thin line. Placing one leg on the corner of the coffer he half sat there and began pulling the petals off the flowers beside him.

'From Armagnac, eh? So that's why you cause disturbances during processions, is it? People of your sort should realize that they only come here at their own risk and peril, my pretty. In truth, seeing that you belong to the party which murdered my beloved father, it seems a strange piece of folly.'

'I am not an Armagnaque,' cried Catherine, flushed with anger. The Duke's attitude to her, at once insolent and subtly threatening, was beginning to exasperate her unendurably. It was not as though she had ever felt any sympathy for him. . . . Hoarse with fury she went on:

'I don't belong to any party. Your friends hanged my father because I tried to rescue one of your sister's attendants after she had been trying in vain to make you or your beloved father save him. Don't you remember? It happened in the Hôtel de Guyenne. Madame Marguerite was down on her knees, in tears, begging for Michel de Montsalvy's life to be spared.'

'Enough! Don't remind me of that incident! It was one of

the most terrible moments of my youth. I couldn't have saved Michel without implicating myself.'

'You couldn't save him,' Catherine snorted, 'but *I* tried to and I was nothing more than a little Parisian girl. Because of that my father was hanged, and my mother and I were forced to flee. We had to leave Paris and go to Dijon where my Uncle Mathieu is a cloth merchant. That's where I have lived ever since. . . .'

A silence fell between the two. Catherine, invaded anew by memories of those dark days, felt her heart beating like a drum. Philippe's sombre face was ominous. He would undoubtedly punish her insolence by having her thrown into his deepest dungeon, and Uncle Mathieu and her family likewise. Nevertheless, had the scaffold itself been standing in the middle of that luxurious room she would still have repeated every one of the words she had just flung so defiantly at the powerful lord of Burgundy. She even felt a certain quiet satisfaction in having done so. It was a sort of revenge for what had happened in the past. . . .

She took a deep breath, tossed back a lock of hair and asked: 'What are you going to do with me, sire? My uncle must be suffering great anxiety on my behalf, I am sure he would like to know . . . even if it should be the worst!'

Philippe shrugged angrily, and threw the remains of the rose he had been playing with out of the window. Dropping his nonchalant pose, he took a few steps towards Catherine.

'What am I going to do with you? Disturbing a procession certainly deserves some sort of punishment, but you are so angry with me already that I hesitate to displease you further. You see . . . I should like us to be friends in future. And, after all, a young girl is free to defend herself if someone attacks her. As for that man who dared . . .'

'Does that mean that that unfortunate man will suffer instead of me? In that case I suggest you pardon him, as I do. His action does not warrant so much publicity.'

To shake off the embarrassment she felt under the steady gaze of those grey eyes fastened on her face, she turned to the mirror and stared at herself in it, though without really seeing anything. The Duke's reflection, a whole head taller, appeared beside hers within that golden frame. Suddenly she shivered: two hot hands had seized her by both shoulders.

The mirror reflected two faces of a sudden equally pale. A strange light burned in the young Duke's eyes and his hands trembled slightly as he touched her silky skin. He bent close enough for her to feel his breath warm on her neck, and all the while, in the mirror, his eyes held her violet ones imprisoned.

'The peasant deserves to die a hundred times over for having dared to do what I cannot do myself . . . much as I would like to. You are too beautiful! I am afraid I might find it hard to find peace away from you. . . . When were you supposed to leave this town?'

'As soon as the procession had ended. Our baggage was ready, and the mules waiting.'

'Then leave as you had planned. Leave this very evening, and by tomorrow morning let there be as many leagues as possible between yourselves and Bruges. A safe conduct will open the town gates for you and assure your free passage along the roads. We will meet again at Dijon, whither I am returning shortly.'

Embarrassed and also vaguely disturbed by the hands which still held her, Catherine felt a strange emotion swell within her breast. Philippe's voice was at once brusque and warm, imperious and tender. She tried to fight against this fascination he was beginning to exert over her.

'Meet in Dijon? Sire! What can the high and mighty Duke of Burgundy do with a cloth merchant's niece except ruin her reputation?' she asked with a hint of insolence which stirred Philippe's blood. His hands left her shoulders and tangled themselves in her silky mane of hair. Then he stooped and buried his face in it.

'Don't play the coquette,' he murmured in a voice which grew hoarse. 'You are very well aware of the effect you have on me, and you are taking pitiless advantage of it. A prince's love does not necessarily bring dishonour. You know that I would do almost anything to gain you for myself. You would not be the daughter of Eve if you did not recognize desire in a man's eyes.'

'Sire,' she protested.

She tried to push him away, but he held her too tightly. Carried away by an overmastering desire, he stooped and kissed her on the nape, in that soft hollow where the neck is shaded by hair. Catherine trembled violently and gave a cry of protest: 'For pity's sake, sire! Don't make me have to slap your face too! I've had enough for one day!'

He let her go at once and moved a few steps away. His face was flushed, his grey eyes were clouded, and his hands still trembled. Then, suddenly, he burst out laughing:

'Forgive me! Fate must have willed that every man today should expatiate upon your beauty – a little too ardently. I am afraid I lost my head. I am beginning to understand that oaf of a furrier. It is partly your fault. . . .'

As he spoke, he crossed over to an ebony chest and took from it a long, hooded brown-velvet coat, lined throughout in priceless sables. He threw it rapidly round the girl's shoulder. She almost disappeared in the folds of the sumptuous garment. It covered the lovely shoulders and temptingly bared bosom which were proving too much for Philippe's self-control. All that was visible was the lovely head with its crown of golden hair. He gazed at her a moment longer in a sort of despair.

'You look more beautiful still! You had better go. Quickly, before the devil tempts me again. But don't forget that I shall find you again. . . .'

He pushed her towards the hidden door, which opened without Catherine seeing how. She saw a gleam of armour through the half-open door.

'Wait,' Philippe murmured.

He left the room alone; returning a few minutes later with a sealed parchment which he handed to his visitor.

'The safe conduct. Go quickly . . . and if you think of me only half as much as I shall be thinking of you I shall count myself happy.'

'I shall think of you, sire,' she said, smiling. 'But does your Excellency realize that you are still addressing me as "tu"?'

Philippe laughed again, a young, spontaneous, carefree laugh.

'I can't help it! Something inside me makes me address you as "tu" . . . Maybe because one day I hope to have the right to.'

With one hand on the door he kept her back a moment longer. His free arm drew her to him with tender violence, and before the girl could stop him, he stooped and kissed her half-open lips. Then he let her go.

'I wanted to so much!' he said by way of apology. 'Now go. . . .'

His hand brushed the dark velvet, expressive of the regret he felt at letting her go. She was halfway through the door to join the guard who was to escort her back to her uncle when he stopped her once more.

'Just a moment!'

Then, with a contrite smile:

'I don't even know your name.'

'Catherine, sire, Catherine Legoix,' she said, dropping so low a curtsey that her face was level with Philippe's knees. He stooped to raise her up once more, but she eluded him, with smiling agility, and followed the man-at-arms whose metal shoes rang hollowly on the marble floor. She did not once turn to look back at the Duke who watched her depart with a sigh. It was the first time Philippe of Burgundy had allowed a woman he desired to pass through his hands unscathed, especially one who had been closeted alone with him for so long. But this Catherine did not realize. Her head was in a whirl and, despite the little scene she had just enacted, she felt weary. She would have liked to climb into bed and stretch out between cool sheets. She felt no more warmth towards Philippe now than she had earlier on when the guards had first escorted her to the palace, but the short time she had spent with him had made a disturbing impression on her. His kiss, his expert hands, had between them stirred the deepest fibres of her being and awakened a mysterious longing which, once it had passed, left her feeling weak and a little ashamed, as if she had done something wrong.

At the end of the great staircase she found Jacques de Roussay waiting. His searching gaze added to her embarrassment. She felt suddenly as though Philippe's hands and lips must have left invisible marks on her skin. Instinctively she pulled the sumptuous coat higher round her shoulders and drew the hood down over her forehead. The Captain's eyes fastened on her lips so insistently that she pursed them up and, throwing her head back defiantly, stepped towards the stairs. He followed her without a word.

Only when they had reached the archway at the entrance did he decide to speak.

'I am under orders to escort you back to the Flowering Mulberry,' he said in a colourless voice, 'and then to see that you leave Bruges without hindrance.'

From beneath her hood Catherine flashed him such a dazzling smile that the young man blushed to the roots of his hair.

'What an honour! I suppose you aren't under orders to accompany us as far as Dijon too?'

'Alas, no—' he began, then suddenly changing his tone, he cried joyfully: 'Are you going to Dijon? Is that where you live?'

'Yes, indeed.'

'Oh, in that case I shall see you again. I am from Burgundy too, from the heart of Burgundy,' he added with such ingenuous pride that she smiled. It seemed as though this fellow wanted to get to know her better too. Catherine wondered silently whether, by the time she left Flanders, she would not have a rendezvous with the whole ducal army. . . . This thought put her in such a good humour that she was singing as she entered the inn. Mathieu Gautherin had collapsed in a chimney-corner, where he continued to weep, and quaff numerous flagons of beer, under the innkeeper's wary eye. Catherine's radiant appearance took him completely by surprise. He was expecting archers, black-robed judges, the executioner in person perhaps, and here was his niece, laughing gaily, dressed like a princess in a coat whose value was not lost on the merchant's experienced eye. One of the duke's officers, dressed up like a herald, followed the supposed prisoner like a proud little dog.

Everyone in Burgundy knew of the Duke's susceptibility to feminine beauty. Catherine's triumphal entry gave Mathieu Gautherin much food for thought. It looked as though the Duke and his niece had made peace. It remained to be seen just how far this peace-making had gone. As he shook his dozing valets and ordered them to finish loading up the mules he promised himself to keep his eyes open. He was one of those respectable citizens to whom a bastard, whether royal or not, is in no way a gift from heaven.

Despite her uncle's advice, Catherine refused to put her superb coat in one of the travelling chests. She had replaced her torn dress by a plain white one, made of that fine lightweight cloth woven by the women of Valenciennes. Her hair, which had been carefully plaited, was concealed by a coil of fine Flemish linen, one flap of which went under her chin and closely framed her face. On top of it all, though, she had replaced the famous velvet coat.

'If we meet any robbers,' Uncle Mathieu grumbled, still not altogether recovered from his ordeal, 'they will take you for a noblewoman and we shall be held to ransom. . . .'

But Catherine was so delighted with her magnificent coat that she refused to hear of parting from it.

'It would get spoilt, squashed into a chest. Besides, I shan't be allowed to wear it in Dijon. Maman would never hear of it, if only because it might offend the Dame de Chancey or the Dowager of Châteauvilain, who haven't got one like it. So I may as well make the most of it. . . .'

Proud as a queen in her sables, Catherine, ignoring the mild weather, took her seat on her mule. The merchant's little baggage-train followed behind de Roussay's charger as far as the city walls. At St Catherine's Gate, which de Roussay had commanded to be opened in the name of the Duke, they parted with a brief word of farewell, but as Jacques de Roussay bowed to the girl he murmured a hasty 'Till we meet again,' which made her smile. She did not reply. It was pointless. Now that he knew she came from Dijon, de Roussay seemed to be in a walking dream.

It was not to look at him again that Catherine turned round before passing through the heavily fortified gate. It was just to conjure up for a second the tall, thin, black silhouette of Philippe, and his pale face and burning eyes as he bent to kiss her neck. For the first time in her life Catherine had to admit that a man might have power over her. He intrigued and disturbed her all at once. The love of such a man should give some value to one's life – enough to make it worth living perhaps. . . .

Once they had gone through the St Catherine Gate she did not turn back. She adjusted her mule's step to that of Mathieu's and let herself be lulled by its trotting motion. On either side flat pasture-lands, intersected by canals, stretched to the horizon, interrupted here and there by clumps of trees or the weird silhouette of a windmill. Some sea birds, attracted by the brilliant moonlight, so bright that it seemed almost like day, streaked across the starry sky.

Catherine gleefully inhaled the salt air which a sea wind brought to her nostrils. She threw the hood back on her shoulders and unfastened her coat. It was a familiar horizon to which this road deeply rutted by cartwheels led, but lately it seemed to have taken on new colours.

As dawn broke Courtrai steeple rose from the flat countryside.

'We will stop at the Crock of Gold inn,' said Mathieu, who had not opened his mouth once for the good reason that he had been sound asleep on his mule. 'I am exhausted. We can stay till tomorrow. I have business to do with the merchants of this town.'

Catherine was sleepy. She saw nothing against this plan. . . .

On leaving Courtrai Mathieu Gautherin decided to pursue their journey with all speed. He felt that they had wasted enough time and he was eager to see the walls of Dijon again, with the towers of St Benigne and the slopes of Marsaunnay where he had a vineyard. Not that he had any fears for his house, which remained in the care of his sister, Jacquette, his niece, Loyse, and that Sara whom they had brought with them from Paris and whom Mathieu could not get used to even after all these years. Catherine, who was highly amused by this attitude of her uncle's, insisted that he was not only afraid of Sara, but secretly in love with her, and it was this that he could not forgive.

He kicked his mule, and pulled his hood well down, and set off as though the Devil himself were at his heels. Catherine trotted along beside him and the three valets rode behind them, two side by side and the third guarding the rear of the caravan. They had now left the estates of the Duke of Burgundy. Soon they would pass through those belonging to the Bishop of Cambrai and enter the property of the Comte de Vermandois, a fervent partisan of the Dauphin Charles. It would be as well not to delay at that point. It was the good merchant's eagerness to get this part of the journey behind him that explained his urgency.

They were at present travelling beside the upper reaches of the Escaut river towards Saint-Quentin. The road, winding along beside the water, was a pleasant one, between green hills, their soft curves spattered with white sheep. A scene which made it hard even to think of war.

Yet from time to time they passed through a ravaged village, which had been burnt to its foundations and where only a few tormented beams remained standing on the charred earth in eloquent testimony that this was not a peaceful country. And sometimes Catherine would have to look away as they passed a tree on which a corpse hung, like a monstrous fruit, among the tender new leaves.

The day was drawing to a close, and with the coming of twilight great clouds, dark as ink, were massing above the grassy summits. Catherine was suddenly struck by the chill in the air and shivered.

'There is going to be a storm,' said Uncle Mathieu, who had been studying the horizon for a moment. 'The best thing would be to put up at the next inn. Let us hurry. If my memory serves me right there is one where this road crosses the one to Peronne.' The mules, vigorously kicked in the sides, started to gallop just as the first drops of rain fell on the travellers. A moment later Catherine stopped dead, obliging her uncle to follow suit.

'What's the matter with you?' he scolded.

The girl calmly got off her mule, folded her coat and walked over to one of the baggage-mules which was carrying her travelling coffer.

'I don't want my coat to get spoilt. The rain would ruin it.'

'You would rather we all got a soaking then? If you had listened to me . . . but you always do just what you like! Night is falling, and so is the rain . . . I detest this sort of thing, it does terrible things to my rheumatism!'

Helped by Pierre, the oldest valet, who had always had a soft spot for her, Catherine implacably folded her coat away and took out another, whose coarse, thick, black material was sufficient protection against the heaviest downpour. She wrapped it round her and went back to her mule.

It was then she noticed something out of the ordinary. At this point along the river-bank the reeds were particularly thick, and formed, together with three large, gnarled willows, a sort of clearing or thicket protected still further by brambles. Something seemed to gleam strangely in the centre of this clearing, something black. Catherine ran down the river-bank towards the clearing.

'Well, what is it now?' Mathieu complained loudly. 'The rain is coming down with a vengeance. I don't know if you have noticed. . . .'

But Catherine wasn't listening. When she parted the reeds and leaves she discovered a man's body, motionless and giving no signs of life, lying face downward among the brambles. It was by no means unusual to find a body by the wayside in those troublous times, but the odd thing about this one was that it was not some humble peasant or other, but clearly a man of rank, a knight no less. This was evident from the black steel armour which covered him from head to foot, and which was now streaming with water, and from the sparrow-hawk emblem on his helmet. The man must have dragged himself out of the water. This was indicated by a greasy mark on the bank and the way his bare hands clutched at a bramble which he must have used to pull himself up.

Catherine did not dare touch anything, but stood looking disconcertedly at the large body lying at her feet. How had the knight met his death? There was no sign of a struggle or of a horse's hoofprints. His armour covered him so completely that the only part of him that was visible was his bleeding hands, both long and strong, with fine brown skin. But what struck Catherine about them was that the blood was still flowing. It occurred to her suddenly that he might not be dead after all. She knelt beside him and tried to turn him over, but he was much too heavy for her.

She was just about to call for help when Mathieu, who had got tired of wasting his breath scolding her, climbed off his mule and came to find out what was happening.

'By the Holy Virgin, what have we here?' he cried, amazed by the sight which met his eyes.

'A knight-at-arms, as you see. Help me turn him over. I think he is still alive. . . .'

As if to prove it the man in armour groaned faintly. She gave a triumphant cry.

'He's alive! Halloa there, Pierre! Petitjean and Amiel! Come here!'

The three valets came running. Between them they made short work of lifting up the wounded knight, despite his considerable stature and the weight of his steel carapace, and a moment later they had stretched him out in the soft grass by the side of the road. Pierre went off to look for Catherine's box of ointments and Amiel struck a flint to light a torch with. Night had almost fallen and it was becoming impossible to see anything.

The rain was not falling very heavily, but sufficiently hard to give the valet some trouble in lighting the torch. To complicate matters a wind was rising, but at last the torch took fire, reflecting redly off the wet armour. Stretched out thus on the grass, with his hands the only pale things visible, the dark knight looked like a giant carved out of basalt. Uncle Mathieu, forgetful of his rheumatism, sat on the grass and took the helmeted head on his lap to try and prise open the visor. This proved difficult because it had evidently been struck repeatedly and the hinge had jammed shut. Leaning over him, Catherine grew more impatient every moment, particularly as the wounded man was now groaning almost incessantly.

'Hurry,' she whispered. 'He must be suffocating in that steel cage.'

'I'm doing what I can. It isn't all that easy. . . .'

The visor did seem to be firmly stuck. Mathieu was sweating with effort. Seeing this old Pierre drew his knife and with infinite care inserted the point in the rivet which acted as a hinge. He bore down on the knife handle, the rivet gave, and the visor opened.

'Bring your torch,' Catherine ordered.

No sooner had the flickering light fallen on the face, with its closed eyes, than Catherine fell back with a scream, dropping the box of ointments.

'It can't be,' she stammered, suddenly white to the lips. 'It can't be!'

'What's the matter with you?' Mathieu asked her in surprise.

Catherine cast a desperate look at her uncle. The emotion which gripped her was so powerful that it left her almost bereft of speech.

'Yes! No! . . . I don't know!'

'Are you mad? What's all the mystery about? You would do better to help me get this helmet off instead of half passing out like that. He's bleeding. . . .'

'I can't . . . not just yet! Help my uncle, Pierre!'

The old servitor, looking anxiously from the girl to the wounded man, hastened to do so. Catherine sat down close by, pressing her trembling hands together. Huge-eyed, she watched her uncle and Pierre trying to uncover the head and face which was the very face of Michel de Montsalvy.

Shivering, huddling deeper into the coat which was already

sodden with rain, the girl saw the years melt away. The scenes which had brought her to death's door all those years before in Paris, now rose again before her with appalling clarity. Michel struggling with the butchers in the sumptuous apartments of the Hôtel de Guyenne. Michel, hands tied behind his back, proudly treading his *via dolorosa* amid the insults of the mob. Michel lying in the dark cellar gently describing his native region of France to an avidly listening little girl. . . . He had closed his eyes at one point, as though to remember it more clearly, and the wounded man's face, as it appeared framed in the black helmet, was strikingly reminiscent of Michel's at that precise moment. . . . With all her might Catherine struggled to ward off the hideous images which crowded in on her, especially that of Michel's handsome face, battered, swollen and smeared with blood and dust. The resemblance to the knight was extraordinary. The girl leant forward to get a better look, and convince herself that she was not dreaming. But no, the face was identical, pale, impassive, the darkened eyelids with their thick fringe of lashes tight closed over the unknown eyes. A thin trickle of blood ran down his forehead, and over his cheek as far as the corner of his tightly closed lips. From time to time his features tightened in a spasm of pain.

'Michel,' Catherine murmured in spite of herself. 'It isn't you, it can't be you?'

It was not he. But the resemblance was so exact that she was not convinced until Mathieu and Pierre finally got the helmet off. Instead of the golden locks which Catherine remembered so clearly, the hair which finally appeared was black as night, thick, straight and untidy. This reassured her, though in fact the different coloured hair did not in any way lessen the resemblance. Except perhaps that this face was, if anything, more beautiful than Michel's. And harder.

'We can't leave him here. We are all wet through, and the young mistress is not too well either by the sound of things,' said Pierre, who had noticed Catherine's teeth chattering, something of which she herself seemed oblivious. 'We can carry him between the four of us as far as the inn.'

'He is far too heavy with all this weight of armour,' said Mathieu.

They rapidly removed the armour. Then the young man was wrapped in coats, and with poles and rope a sort of stretcher was fashioned, on which they laid him. Catherine had recovered somewhat from the shock she had received and now she stanched the blood, which was flowing from a scalp wound, and placed a dressing over it, held in place by a scarf.

While this was going on the wounded man did not once open his eyes, but he groaned when they took off his armour, and again when they lifted him on to the improvised stretcher.

'One of his legs must be broken,' said Pierre, probing the swollen limb with his skilful old fingers.

When they set off once more Catherine refused to climb back on to her mule. She wanted to walk beside the stretcher. One of the man's hands lay on his breast, outside the covers. This hand drew her like a magnet and it was not long before she succumbed to the temptation to hold it in her own. It was cold and damp and drops of blood still stood out along the deep scratches. Catherine carefully wiped it with her handkerchief and then kept it in hers. Between her soft palms the large masculine hand soon grew warm again.

Hurry as they might along the last part of the road, the night was pitchy black, and the little band was soaked to the skin by the time the lantern hanging above the door of the Inn of the Grand Charlemagne flashed ahead of them in the night.

An hour later they were all safely installed and the wounded man lay in the depths of a large bed, curtained in red serge. Standing as it did at an important crossroads, the inn was, fortunately, one of the best in the region.

The arrival of the wounded knight had thrown the inn into confusion because there was hardly anywhere for him to sleep. A caravan of merchants travelling towards Bruges had taken up almost all the rooms. Finally, however, a room was found for him and a bed hurriedly made up for Catherine in a small room near by. Mathieu, for once, would have to be content with the stable, and sleep on the straw with his valets.

'It's not the first time and I doubt that it will be the last,' he said philosophically. He was more concerned about the condition of the man they had found by the wayside. He was still unconscious. The wound on his head, no doubt caused by a heavy blow from the weapon which had dented his helmet, was still bleeding.

Their entry into the Grand Charlemagne had not gone unobserved by the travellers who were seated at their meal round the table in the main room. As a result, Mathieu and Catherine received a visit shortly afterwards from a highly unusual personage. At Bruges and in other markets the cloth merchant had met many Moslems, and the sight of a turban was no surprise to him. But the man who appeared at the door of the room where the wounded man lay was far from typical in every possible respect.

He was thin and supple, but so small that his face seemed to be suspended somewhere about halfway between the towering and voluminous red turban he wore and his feet, which were shod in matching red shoes and pretty blue stockings.

A billowing robe of indigo damask covered him to the knees. It was belted by a wide sash of fine linen draped about his waist, from whose folds the heavily chased hilt of a dagger protruded. But this costume, striking as it was, paled to insignificance beside the man himself. His thin, and indisputably youthful face was paradoxically decorated with a long snowy beard, above which a small, delicately chiselled nose protruded. He came forward and bowed low before the merchant and his niece, his slender hands crossed on his chest.

'May Allah preserve you!' he said in silky but slightly lisping French. 'I learnt that you have a wounded man with you and here I am! My name is Abou-al-Khayr, I come from Cordoba and I am the greatest doctor in the whole of Islam.'

The word 'doctor' checked the wild peal of laughter which Catherine had been on the point of uttering. The immense dignity of the little turbaned man, who did not seem to be remarkable for his modesty, had something irresistibly comic about it, a fact of which he appeared quite unaware.

'We have indeed got a wounded man . . .' she began. But, raising a hand, the little doctor imposed silence on her. He then said severely:

'I am addressing this honourable old gentleman here. Women are not permitted to speak in our country.'

In her annoyance Catherine reddened to the roots of her hair, while Mathieu in his turn had to suppress a strong urge to laugh. But this was no moment to discourage wellwishers.

'There is indeed a wounded man in there,' he answered, bowing in his turn. 'A young knight we found by the river-bank who seems to be in a sorry state.'

'I will examine him.'

With his two black slaves, one carrying a large painted cedar chest and the other a pitcher of chased silver, following at his heels, Abou-al-Khayr went into the chamber where the knight lay. In his red-curtained bed, which, together with the fire-place, took up all the available space, he looked even paler than he had earlier on. Pierre stood beside him mopping at the still bleeding wound with a pad of material.

'This gentleman is a doctor,' Mathieu explained to Pierre, whose eyes were popping in astonishment.

'God be praised! He has not come a moment too soon! The wound still bleeds.'

'I will deal with that at once,' said the Arab, signalling to his slaves to place their burdens on the table by the bed. Raising both arms, he shook back his wide sleeves and quickly felt the wounded man's head.

'No fracture,' he said at length. 'Simply a broken blood vessel. Go and bring me some hot coals in a pot.'

Pierre ran out of the room while Catherine took his place at the head of the bed. The little doctor looked at her disapprovingly.

'Are you this young man's wife?'

'No I don't even know him. But I shall stay here all the same,' the girl said decisively. This little man, who apparently had no great affection for women, would not succeed in chasing her away.

Abou-al-Khayr sniffed disdainfully but said nothing more. He rummaged in his chest, which, now that it was opened, displayed rows of shining steel instruments and a profusion of phials and little pottery jars in bright colours, black, green, red or white. He took out an object shaped like a tiny seal, with a bronze handle superbly wrought in the shape of birds and leaves. After carefully wiping this instrument with a little pad of wool, on which he had poured a few drops of some acrid-smelling liquid, Abou-al-Khayr placed it in the pot of glowing coals which Pierre had just brought in. Catherine's eyes opened wide in horror.

'What are you going to do to him?'

The little doctor was clearly loath to speak to her, but he was also congenitally incapable of keeping silent when an explanation of one of his actions had been demanded.

'Oh, ignorant woman that you are, does it not leap to the eye? I am going to cauterize the wound to seal up the vein. Your own fools of doctors employ this practice. . . .'

With a steady hand he grasped the bronze handle of his instrument and held the red-hot metal up to the wound, which had now been cleaned of the armour grease still adhering to it. Catherine closed her eyes and dug her nails into the palms of her hands. But she couldn't shut out the wounded man's scream or the nauseating smell of burnt flesh and scorched hair.

'A sensitive young fellow!' commented the doctor. 'I barely touched the wound so as not to leave too large a burn.'

'If someone touched your temples with a piece of red-hot metal,' cried Catherine who was gazing wide-eyed and horrified at the young man's contorted face, 'what would you do?'

'I would say it was an excellent idea, if by doing so a vein was sealed and my life was saved. You may now observe that he is no longer bleeding. I shall anoint the wound with a miraculous ointment and in a few days' time there will only be a small scar, for the wound itself is small. . . .'

Taking a little green pot, gaily painted with fantastic flowers, from his chest, he delicately scooped out a little of the ointment it contained with a gold needle and applied it to the cut. Then, with a little square of fine cloth, he crushed the balm over the wound and with fantastic dexterity began enveloping the young man's head in an astonishing helmet of bandages to hold the compress dressing in place. It completely concealed his hair and one end passed under his chin like a woman's coif. Catherine watched him at work with passionate interest. Since the balm had been applied to his wound the young man had stopped groaning. A pungent and yet agreeable smell filled the room.

'What is this balm?' she asked.

'We call it Matarea balm,' the little man explained curtly. 'It comes from Egypt. Has the young man any other wounds?'

'I think he has a broken leg,' said Mathieu, who had stood in silence during the last operation.

'Let's see it!'

Completely disregarding the young girl's presence, the doctor threw back the coverlets and sheets exposing the young man's naked body. He had been undressed by Mathieu and Pierre before placing him in the bed. The effect of this total nudity on Mathieu was to make him blush to the eyebrows.

'Leave the room, Catherine!' he commanded, taking his niece by the arm and directing her towards the door. The little doctor stopped him with a ferocious look.

'What ridiculous Christian prudery is this? A man's body, together with that of a horse, is Allah's most beautiful creation. This woman will one day give birth to men like this. Why, therefore, should the sight of his body be offensive to her? The ancient Greeks made statues of naked men with which they ornamented their temples.'

'My niece is a virgin,' replied Mathieu, who still had Catherine by the wrist.

'She won't be for long. She is too beautiful for that! I do not like women. I find them silly, noisy and childish. But I can recognize beauty when I see it. This young woman is a master-

piece in her style. . . . As is this young man. Have you ever
seen anything more perfect than this fallen warrior ?'

Abou-al-Khayr's aesthetic appreciation, which Mathieu did
not seem disposed to share, did not stop him working away as
he talked, and he was now feeling the broken leg with extreme
care and delicacy. Mathieu had reluctantly let go of Catherine,
and stood looking at the brown body whose skin shone faintly in
the candlelight with unwilling fascination. Catherine had taken
her place at the head of the bed again and watched as well. As
the little doctor went on with his work he continued to sing the
praises of male beauty in his flowery and lyrical fashion. In this
case, however, what he said was true. The wounded knight was
magnificently built. Under his bronzed skin long, supple
muscles were outlined with anatomical precision, and against
the white sheet his powerful shoulders, hard narrow flanks and
flat belly, and thighs bulging with muscle, stood out in striking
relief. Deeply troubled by the sight, Catherine felt her hands go
cold while a faint blush mantled her cheeks.

Helped by his slaves, Abou-al-Khayr seized the leg to
stretch it, and re-align the broken bones. Then, suddenly,
Catherine heard:

'If that brute weren't hurting me so, I might think myself in
Paradise, for you are surely an angel. . . . Unless, that is, you
are the Rose herself stepped straight out of the pages of Lorris's
old Romance ?'

She saw two black eyes, of a sable blackness to which fever
lent a disturbing sparkle, gazing up at her. Now that he had
regained consciousness, and his eyes were open, the resemblance
to Michel was fantastic – so much so that the girl could not
resist asking him, in a voice which shook slightly:

'In Heaven's name, sire . . . tell me your name!'

The drawn face, which was sweating with pain, contracted
in something which might have been a smile. It finished up as a
hideous grimace, but a flash of brilliant white teeth made up for
this.

'I would rather find out who you are, but it would be
churlish to make so lovely a lady repeat the same question

twice. My name is Arnaud de Montsalvy, Lord of the Châtaignerie in Auvergne, and I am Captain in the service of the
Dauphin Charles.'

In order to see the young girl better the wounded man tried
to raise himself on one elbow, drawing a furious protest from
the little doctor:

'If you don't keep still, my young Lord, you will be lame for
the rest of your life!'

Arnaud's black eyes, which had been fastened on Catherine,
now rested with amazement on the doctor's turban and on his
two strange acolytes. He crossed himself hurriedly and tried to
snatch his leg from the hands which held it.

'What is this?' he cried angrily. 'An infidel dog, a Moor?
How dare he touch a Christian knight without fear of being
skinned alive?'

Abou-al-Khayr gave a sigh which indicated a deep weariness
with this attitude. He slid his hands deeper into his sleeves and
bowed politely.

'The noble knight would doubtless prefer to lose a leg? I do
not think there is another doctor in the place. Also I deeply
regret having stopped the rapid flow of his precious blood a
little while ago. Unworthy dog that I am! I should have left it
to bleed away to the last drop!'

The half-angry, half-ironic tone of the little doctor's voice
sufficed to calm the young man. He suddenly burst out laughing.

'They tell me your compatriots are clever men! Besides, you
are quite right. I have no choice. Carry on with your work. I
will see that you are royally paid for it.'

'What with?' Abou murmured, once more rolling back his
sleeves. 'You had nothing with you but your armour when the
worthy cloth merchant found you.'

Mathieu, for his part, was beginning to think that the wounded man stared too boldly at his niece. He slid between them and
began to tell the knight how they had found him by the bank of
the Escaut, and how they had removed his armour and brought
him to the Grand Charlemagne. Then the young man, now
grown suddenly grave and thoughtful, related his own story. He

had been sent as ambassador to the Duke of Burgundy by the Dauphin, and he had been travelling through the countryside with one squire to accompany him when they had both been set upon and attacked on the other side of the river by a band of robbers, half Burgundian and half English, who had hurled him from his horse, robbed him and hit him over the head before throwing him into the river, where they doubtless expected him to drown. Miraculously, despite the weight of his armour, he had succeeded in swimming as far as the opposite bank, thanks largely to an opportune sandbank. He had dragged himself up the bank with one last burst of strength and lost consciousness. As to his squire, he had no idea what could have become of him, and supposed that he must have been killed by the bandits.

'I am sorry if he was,' he said sadly. 'He was a fine boy.'

While he spoke, Abou-al-Khayr went on with his work, occasionally interrupted by groans, half of pain, half of rage, from his patient. Patience was clearly not the outstanding quality of Arnaud de Montsalvy.

Catherine, meanwhile, devoured him with her eyes. It was as though heaven had performed a special miracle for her by resuscitating the man she had never ceased to love, and would never forget. Between Arnaud and herself a bond had been forged with each passing moment, each look they exchanged, strengthened and deepened. Every time the wounded man's feverish eyes fell on her, which was often, she felt as though something exploded inside her. Her cheeks grew hot. Clearly the knight had but one desire: to be left alone for an instant with this young girl, whose beauty, as he made no attempt to hide, had dazzled him. So he protested violently when the doctor raised a little gold cup to his lips in which he had mixed a mysterious draught. He tried to push it away.

'My dear young knight,' said the Moor severely, 'if you wish to recover your strength quickly you need sleep. This will help.'

'My strength? But I must leave tomorrow! There is the Dauphin's message . . . I must go to Bruges.'

'You have a broken leg. You must stay in bed,' cried Abou-al-Khayr.

'Besides,' Catherine interpolated gently, 'it is possible that you might not find the Duke at Bruges any longer. He is on his way to Dijon, where he had many things to attend to. And Dijon . . . is where we are going ourselves.'

As she spoke Arnaud's sombre gaze lightened.

When she finished he stretched out his hand to seize hers, but found he had hold of Mathieu's garment instead, and frowned. Then he regained his good humour, smiled, and declared that nothing would make him happier than to travel with her.

'I suppose,' he added, 'that it would be possible to find a litter.'

'We will see about that tomorrow,' interrupted Abou. 'Now drink this!'

A few minutes later, under the influence of the powerful opiate, the knight's eyes closed and he slept peacefully. Everyone left the room save one of the blacks whom the doctor left in attendance on his patient. The two slaves were both dumb, a fact which diminished the likelihood of their quarrelling with the patient. As the doctor confided to Mathieu, he was a patient who seemed to be as irascible as 'a scorpion disturbed in its hole'.

Catherine was the last to leave, sighing regretfully.

Abou-al-Khayr's company proved much more amusing than Catherine would have supposed, notwithstanding his obstinate refusal to acknowledge her presence. He was, in fact, a young man despite the long white beard, which, he explained to Mathieu, was the distinguishing mark of doctors, professional men and other Islamic notables. In the Moslem countries middle-class men were entitled to wear a shorter beard, which could be dyed blue or green. The whiteness of this fine beard, and its maintenance, were a constant preoccupation to the Cordoban doctor, who lavished much care upon it; as, indeed, he did upon his entire person, which was of a fastidious cleanliness. He complained bitterly of the lack of comfort in Christian sanitary installations.

'Those bath-houses of yours,' he said scornfully, 'would be considered fit only for slaves in Cordoba.'

But, despite this drawback, he was prepared to concede that Christianity had its good side, that it was of great interest, and provided a doctor with a huge field for experiment because people hacked each other to pieces far more often than they did in Islamic countries. Especially in the kingdom of Cordoba, where things were too peaceful for much medical progress to be made.

'Here one can find corpses at every crossroads,' he concluded with an air of great satisfaction. Despite his age, he had travelled widely, from Baghdad to Kairouan, from the sources of the Nile to Alexandria, always in search of the same thing – knowledge. His plan now was to seek the Court of the powerful Duke of Burgundy, the great Duke-of-the-Western-world, whose fame was already spreading across mountains and seas.

'This encounter means I shall no longer pursue my journey to that town by water,' he told Mathieu. 'I shall travel with the wounded man and thus I shall be able to keep an eye on him till we reach Burgundy. He has need of it. But we shall not leave for two or three days. This inn is not too bad a place, it seems.'

It appeared that the little doctor had a soft spot for good food. He was now tucking hungrily into a chicken, cooked with herbs, which he washed down with copious draughts of local wine, overlooking the precepts of the Koran in favour of the celebrated vineyards of Sancerre.

'In that case we will meet at Dijon,' said Mathieu, who was also tucking in to a hearty meal, 'because my niece and I and our servants will be leaving tomorrow. We are already overdue at Dijon.'

Catherine did not join in the meal. She had drunk a bowl of milk and was nibbling absent-mindedly on a honey cake. These last words, however, instantly brought her out of her reverie.

'It would be more amusing if we all travelled together,' she said.

At this Mathieu, for no apparent reason, flew into a rage.

'No!' he shouted, thumping his fist on the table. 'We leave tomorrow! If you must know, I didn't much like the way that knight looked at you. And as for you, there you were smiling at him, almost making advances to him, upon my word! And it is high time you told me where you met him before!'

'I shouldn't pin too many hopes on that,' Catherine said coldly. 'I have nothing to say, except that I have never seen the knight before. He is very like someone I used to know once, that's all! And now, good night, Uncle Mathieu!'

Dropping a hurried curtsey to the cloth merchant and his new friend, she hastened across the room before Mathieu could catch up with her, climbed the wooden stairs and then went down the narrow passage leading to the bedrooms. All the doors opened on to an outside balcony. She stopped in front of Arnaud's room, where a little light showed under the door. She felt a passionate longing to go in and look at him as he slept. Her own little room was at the far end of the balcony, opposite the room which was occupied by this fascinating wounded knight.

She stood there for a moment, buffeted by the wind and sleet. The rain splashed right into the gallery itself. The storm really had risen now and a fierce wind was blowing, whipping up the surface of the puddles down below. The spray looked like clouds drifting across the ground; tormented trees writhed this way and that in the gale. Catherine shivered under the coat which she had thrown over her shoulders.

She loved this wild weather tonight. The fury of the elements matched the other storms which raged within her. She was a little frightened by the violence of the passions which had so suddenly been unleashed in her. She had never before felt this wild longing to be near, to touch, to embrace a creature of flesh and blood. In a few seconds the old Catherine, who met the passionate avowals of the young men of Dijon with such cool composure and unconsciously cruel laughter, had turned into a passionate woman for whom a man's love had suddenly become the whole meaning of existence. Even that Catherine who had trembled with pleasurable distress when Philippe of Burgundy kissed her was far away. . . .

What would Mathieu say if he found her in Arnaud's room? Catherine put that awkward thought out of her mind by telling herself that he was sleeping in the stable, and would therefore not be likely to come up again. Why should he? No longer able to resist the longing which impelled her, she put her hand on the latch of the door and went in.

CHAPTER FOUR

THE WOUNDS OF LOVE

ARNAUD AND the black slave were both asleep. The great body of the Sudanese was stretched across the hearth, curled up like a large dog. The wounded man lay motionless on the bed. The bandages round his head looked like a helmet, but snow-white. The odd contraption made of strips of wood and linen bandages soaked in flour paste which the Cordoban doctor had strapped round his broken leg meant he had to lie stretched out flat on his back – lending his stillness a rather corpse-like air. Catherine paused for a moment and leant against the bed to get a closer look at the sleeping face with its closed eyes. A wooden bench strewn with red cushions stood alongside the wall. She tried to pull it closer to the bed, but it was too heavy for her, so she merely sat down upon it, letting her hands fall loosely clasped on her lap.

The sound of the wounded man's slightly laboured breathing filled the room. He did not appear to be in pain. As she gazed silently at him Catherine decided that he really was handsomer than Michel. This was possibly because he was more of a man, more virile, whereas Michel had been little more than a boy. He looked about twenty-three or four. Under the somewhat bizarre headdress the Moor had concocted for him, the harsh but infinitely pure lines of his face stood out as clearly as though they had been carved. With its haughty nose and square, determined chin, blue-shadowed now by an unshaven stubble of beard, it was a face with no trace of softness about it apart from a set of uncommonly long thick lashes. But it had considerable charm. Catherine had still not recovered from the shock of finding just how powerfully his charm acted upon her. She was still bewildered by the strangely disturbing feeling which welled up from deep inside her. It swept her body, irresistibly, bringing sudden inexplicable blushes to her cheeks.

A burning log fell out of the grate in a shower of sparks, and rolled in front of the hearth. Catherine got up and put the log back on the fire with a pair of tongs. The black slave stirred, muttering something unintelligible in his sleep, but Arnaud had not moved. With a sigh the girl leant against the back of her seat. The fury of the storm seemed to have passed. The rain still drummed a tattoo on the roof but inside the little room it was cosy and sheltered.

Little by little the monotonous patter of falling rain set Catherine's head nodding, and soon she was fast asleep stretched out along the bench. She did not see the door open and the little doctor's immense turban appear. His sharp eyes darted about the room, resting briefly on the wounded man and then, having made certain he was asleep, they moved on. A curious expression came over his leathery features as his eyes fell upon Catherine sleeping on her bench. His first impulse was to go across to her and wake her up, but halfway across the room he stopped and shrugged. His lips curled in an ironic smile and he left the room as quietly as he had entered it, shutting the door softly behind him.

Nor did Catherine know that the little doctor, meeting Mathieu in the gallery, had expressly forbidden him to go into the knight's room, explaining that his feverish condition made him a light sleeper. The cloth merchant went down to his straw bed in the stable without suspecting for a moment that his niece was sleeping in the knight's room.

Towards four-thirty in the morning Catherine opened her heavy lids. Day was breaking and in the inn's poultry-run a vociferous cock was trying to persuade everyone that he was crowing the sun back into existence. Arnaud had not moved by a hairsbreadth from his position of the night before, and the Nubian slave still slept, snoring doggedly in front of the cold ashes of the fire. Catherine got up, stiffly, grimacing slightly. She went silently over to the window and opened it to look out.

The rain had stopped, though there were still great shining puddles on the ground in which the rosy morning sky was mirrored. The trees and leaves all looked as though they had just been varnished. There was a smell of warm stable and wet earth, a good country smell which the young girl drew in with long delighted breaths. She stretched herself with the slow graceful movements of a cat, yawned, then calmly began undoing her plaits to let her hair loose in the cool air. She ran her hands through it, shook it out, and fluffed it up, happily enjoying its silky feel against her skin. Then she closed the window and went back to the bed.

The wounded man still slept soundly, eyes shut, his firm lips turned down slightly at the corners and a fine line drawn from the corner of each nostril. He looked so young and touching like that, so disarming, that Catherine surrendered to an irresistible impulse. She slid to her knees by the bed, and leant her cheek against the brown hand which lay palm upward on the bed-cover. The hand felt warm, but its skin, hardened by the daily handling of weapons, scraped a bit. Catherine pressed her lips to it with a passion which took her by surprise. There was a lump in her throat, and she wanted to laugh and cry all at once. But, more than anything, she wished that this moment of intense sweetness could last for ever. The world around her seemed to vanish away, leaving only Arnaud and herself locked together in a charmed circle against which dull reality crashed and crumbled away. For a moment he was hers, hers alone. . . .

Absorbed in the enchantment of the moment Catherine did

not notice the hand stirring under her lips, and another hand
stretch out and stroke the mass of hair spread out over the bed.
But when the two hands suddenly came together and cupped
her face, raising it up, she realized suddenly that the wounded
knight had woken. He lay on his side, half raised on one elbow,
and looked steadily at her. Then he began drawing her slowly
towards him. She gave a little cry and tried to free herself.

'Messire . . . let me go . . . please. . . .'

'Sssh!' he said. 'Be quiet!'

Subdued by his authoritative tones, she fell silent and stopped struggling. She had neither the desire nor the strength to do
so. Her heart thumped so wildly in her breast that she could
hardly breathe. She was hypnotized by those passionate black
eyes which were coming nearer and nearer to her own. The
young man's hands no longer held her face. He clasped her now
in both arms, pulling her hungrily towards him on the bed. . . .

When he held her against him, pressed against his hard chest,
Catherine shivered from head to foot. Arnaud's brown skin was
damp with a fine sweat. He smelt of warm bed, fever and something else which she could not quite place, possibly the balm
which had been spread over his wound. He was breathing hard
and the sound filled his willing captive's ears. She heard him
curse between clenched teeth when his immobilized leg got in
the way. She did not try to resist. Unconsciously she had waited
all her life for this moment. . . .

But she moaned when his hard mouth swooped on hers,
forcing it open with the ferocity of a starving man. A peal of
bells rang out in her head, a joyful carillon as ancient as the
earth itself. Without even being aware of it, she yielded herself
to the hands which moved over her, searching out the truth
about her young girl's body.

For a man so close to death only the night before, Arnaud de
Montsalvy evinced a remarkable vigour. He wasted no time on
niceties or pretty speeches. His quick, masterful movements
were those of a soldier for whom every minute counts. And yet,
in this violence of his which robbed her of all will to resist,
Catherine found an extraordinary gentleness. She gave herself

up to him, completely abandoned, and already contented. Their kiss seemed to go on for ever, became more passionate, arousing the girl's blood to madness. She was no longer aware what Arnaud was doing. He unfastened her bodice and unlaced her dress. It was not until his lips left hers, and he buried his head between her breasts, that Catherine found she was half naked in his arms. But the sight of her own flesh, rosy in the dawn light, still rosier in contrast with the black hair which emerged from Arnaud's turban, did not embarrass her in the least. It was as though, from all eternity, she had been created merely to give herself to this man, as though she had been made for him alone, for his pleasure and happiness.

With greater gentleness now he undressed her with one hand and caressed her with the other. His fingers seemed to hesitate before each new discovery. Then, in joy and wonderment, they closed fiercely on each new conquest. He murmured broken, disconnected words which Catherine did not understand. Then, for a moment, his face came near to hers. She saw his features harden with desire, his flashing black eyes seek hers.

'How beautiful you are!' he groaned. 'How sweet and soft and rosy!'

Passionately he sought her mouth again and pulled her supple body under him, arching her round waist. Catherine moaned again. A soft moan which was almost a call.

Suddenly in the inn courtyard a great shout was heard:

'Catherine! Catherine! Where are you?'

'Heavens! My uncle!'

Brusquely recalled to her senses, Catherine sat up, pushing the young man away. For the first time she became fully aware of her nakedness, of the door which might open at any minute, of the Nubian who was beginning to stir and would soon be awake. Crimson with shame she tried to pull on her clothes and disengage herself from Arnaud's embrace. Surprise had made him let her go for an instant, but now he was pulling her towards him again, with a groan:

'Stay here, with me! . . . I want you! I'll kill anyone who comes in.'

'I can't! Oh, let me go, for God's sake!'

Supple as an eel, she somehow managed to slip out of the bed. While she pulled on her clothes with shaking clumsy fingers, she kept on looking at him. He was so white! His face was drawn like a famished wolf's and his hands, without his realizing it, stretched out to her in a pathetically imploring gesture. All his strength and violence seemed to have drained out of him. He was just a man cheated of a pleasure, which his hands had not been strong enough to clutch on to. Then, abruptly, and quite unexpectedly, he started to laugh gaily.

'I won't always be bed-ridden, my beauty! I shall find you again! By St Michel, I believe you have driven me out of my mind!'

'Please forget what has happened, messire, I beg you,' Catherine implored him as she finished lacing up her dress. 'You made me lose my head. . . .'

Once again he burst out laughing. A clear, gay, young laugh which laid him out flat on his back again. Then it stopped as suddenly as it had begun, as he stared at Catherine again with a gravity in which there was a challenging, passionate note.

'Forget that I saw your eyes change colour, and felt your body tremble under my hands? Forget your beautiful body and the sweet taste of your lips? If I lived to a hundred that would be asking too much of me. Catherine . . . your name is music to my ears, and you are the loveliest woman born of woman. The only woman I want. . . .'

Torn between a desire to hear more and fear of angering her uncle, Catherine hesitated before leaving the room. Then she took a step towards the door. Arnaud implored her:

'Go then, if you must . . . but, first, give me one more kiss, just one!'

She was just about to go back to him when the little doctor's black slave, now wide awake, stood up and began raking the ashes to try and start the fire going again. He paid no attention to them and did not even look their way. Catherine went to fling herself into the knight's arms when a clatter of horses' hooves outside checked her. They heard the rattle of armour; instantly on the alert, Arnaud turned away from Catherine:

'What is that? There are armed men down there. . . .'

She ran to the window and looked down into the courtyard. There she saw a company of soldiers which appeared to have just ridden in. There were about ten of them, and over their armour Catherine recognized the half-black, half-grey gold-embroidered tabards worn by the men of Philippe of Burgundy's bodyguard. The fronts of their tunics were embroidered with the Duke's arms and motto: 'I shall have none other.'

'They belong to the Duke of Burgundy's bodyguard,' she said. 'There is an officer with them. . . .'

Just then a tall knight, crested with white plumes, dismounted and went up to Mathieu Gautherin, who was nervously pacing about the courtyard with Abou-al-Khayr at his side. The girl recognized the newcomer's slightly nervous manner and resonant voice.

'Why, I believe it must be Messire de Roussay!' she went on. Arnaud grimaced.

'A plague on't, my darling! You are well informed about these accursed Burgundians. Upon my word, you seem to know them all!'

'You forget that I live in Dijon and that I am a subject of the Duke's.'

Meanwhile, down in the courtyard, Jacques de Roussay went up to the cloth merchant, and his loud voice boomed out on the still morning air.

'I am happy to have found you, Maître Gautherin. I was looking for you, in fact.'

Mathieu bowed so low he almost fell over, momentarily forgetting all about his niece, whose absence he did not trouble to explain.

'For me? But this is a great honour indeed!'

'For you, and your lovely niece. Monseigneur Philippe was suddenly afraid that you might meet with undesirable company along the road, especially when you are travelling through the parts which are infested with English and do not belong to

Burgundy. Therefore he sent me to escort you and demoiselle Legoix as far as Dijon.'

Catherine heard no more because behind her a voice of thunder roared out:

'Legoix . . . who is called Legoix here?'

Whirling round she saw Arnaud sitting up in his bed, his face whiter than the sheets. His eyes flashed fire and he was beginning to push back the covers with a shaking hand, ready to leap out. When the black slave saw this he ran and threw his powerful arms round him to hold him down. Imprisoned by those black arms, Arnaud struggled like a maniac.

'Who bears this accursed name?' he shouted. 'Who is called Legoix?'

'Why . . . I am, messire. It's my name. I am called Catherine Legoix.'

'You!'

In a few seconds the knight's face expressed first stupefaction, then fury, then a look of implacable hatred which transformed his features. His jaws stood out and his lips curled back on his white teeth like those of a beast about to spring and bite. He looked at her as if he had suddenly seen her for the first time and there was not a trace now, in his black eyes, of the passion she had seen there such a little while before.

'Your name is Legoix,' he said, in a voice where anger simmered just under control. 'Then tell me . . . are you related to those Parisian butchers who made . . . such a stir a few years ago?'

'They were my cousins, but—'

'Be quiet! Don't say another word. But get out!'

'What!'

'Get out, I tell you! Get out before I throw you out! One black day of despair I vowed to kill everyone who bore that name. I won't kill you because you are a woman . . . but I don't want to see you again, ever!'

Catherine stood there, stunned and uncomprehending, as his fury exploded around her. A few minutes before this very man had been murmuring and holding her in his arms, gazing at her with eyes full of passion; and now, in a senseless metamorphosis, he had become her enemy. . . . He rejected her. . . . He spoke again, between clenched teeth.

'Listen to me carefully. I had a brother . . . a wonderful brother whom I adored. He was in the service of Louis de Guyenne. During Caboche's riots the butchers got him and slaughtered him. They cut off his head like an animal in the slaughter-house. He was young, handsome and honourable, he never did anyone any harm, but they cut his throat like a pig's. And the man who killed him was a butcher called Thomas Legoix. Now you know. . . . So be gone with you, and pray to God that we never meet again. . . .'

There was so much fury, and so much anguish, in the young man's voice that Catherine's eyes filled with tears. Such a disappointment was too cruel to be borne, and the sudden destruction of that universe of love which had grown up around this meeting was too brutal! First to find a dream one had thought buried for ever, and then to see it vanish in this absurd fashion! How could he accuse her so brutally of Michel's death, when it was she who had risked and lost everything for an unknown boy? She tried to defend herself.

'Have pity, messire, listen to me and do not condemn me without hearing me first. Don't you know what actually happened on that dreadful day when your brother died? Don't you know—'

Arnaud's voice interrupted her brusquely and pointed towards the door.

'I know only too well. Get out . . . you disgust me, the sight of you makes me feel sick! Besides, they are waiting for you down below. Did I not hear that knight who has just arrived announce that the Duke of Burgundy had sent him to protect you? What an honour, what courtesy! It's not difficult to see what sort of a woman you are, my beauty! The Duke Philippe is said to fancy women like you.'

'I am nothing to the Duke Philippe,' Catherine protested angrily, scarlet to the roots of her hair. 'On the contrary, he actually had me arrested a short time ago. What can you be imagining about me?'

Arnaud's laugh was even more insolent than his words.

'Imagining? He can't have had much difficulty in winning your favours if my own experience is any guide. You are a good whore and you don't set too high a price on your charms. . . .'

Catherine's cry was that of a wounded animal. Tears started from her wide open eyes and streamed down her cheeks and neck. She stretched out trembling hands towards the knight.

'For pity's sake, messire. What have I done to you that you should treat me so? Don't you understand?'

'What?' said Arnaud sarcastically. 'That you could happily climb into bed with me only a few hours after getting out of the Duke's? Who knows? Perhaps you were acting under instructions? That attack – and that dramatic rescue last night – were perhaps all part of a cunning plot. And your role was to wheedle the purpose of my mission out of me while I was in the throes of passion. Congratulations! I must admit that you all but succeeded. Upon my word, you drove me out of my senses for a moment! It must be that I haven't often met whores as attractive as you. Now, be gone with you! I have told you that I don't want anything more to do with you. . . .'

Mad with rage now, forgetting the passion which the knight had awakened in her, Catherine stalked with clenched fists up to the bed. 'I won't go until you have heard me out . . . and apologized to me!'

'Apologized? To a whore?'

He spat the word at her. At this cruel attack the girl fell back, and put her hands over her face as if he had hit her. Her courage and her anger seemed to have abandoned her all of a sudden. The whole gentle romance had turned into a grotesque and humiliating farce. It was no use arguing, she realized, because Arnaud was blinded and deafened by fury. She turned away, her hands hanging limply at her sides, and went towards the door. She was about to open it when a sudden surge of pride made her turn back for a moment. Her elegant little head was

thrown proudly back under the magnificent mane of hair which
formed an untidy halo around her face. She fixed scornful eyes
on the young man. Propped on one elbow, his head lowered a
little, all his muscles tense with anger, he looked like a wild
beast about to spring despite the absurd white turban which
had got a bit disarranged by recent events, and detracted somewhat from the ferocity of his appearance.

'One day,' said Catherine coldly, 'you will go down on your
knees in front of me to beg my forgiveness for your words.
Arnaud de Montsalvy, Seigneur de la Châtaignerie. But you
will get neither pardon nor mercy from me. Your brother was
good and gentle and I loved him. Adieu. . . .'

She was about to leave the room when a violent blow made
her to stumble. She managed to lean against the wall in time to
stop herself falling. A large pillow, hurled by an expert marks-
man, had just hit her in the back. It took more than womanly
dignity to subdue Arnaud when he had flown into a rage.
Astounded, she turned to look at him. He was sitting up in bed,
shouting with laughter, and looking at her with eyes which
sparkled with malice.

'Next time you dare speak of my brother, you little slut, I
will strangle you with my own hands,' said he, holding his
large brown hands towards her. 'Thank the Lord that I cannot move. The name of Montsalvy shall not be sullied by lips
like yours, and women of your sort. . . .'

He would have gone on but his angry diatribe was cut short.
Catherine ran to the bed and dealt him a stunning blow across
the face.

The dressing had been knocked awry and the wound on his
temple had opened again, letting a thin trickle of blood fall on
his stubbly cheek. Beside herself with rage and indignation
Catherine had forgotten that he was wounded and struck him
with all her strength; the sight of his blood flowing calmed her
down, but did not cause her the slightest twinge of regret or com-
punction. He had insulted her basely and she had been far too
patient with him. She felt obscurely happy at having been able
to inflict pain on him. She could even have wished it were

greater. She would have liked to lash out at him with her teeth and nails and gouge out those insolent eyes in which, for the moment, surprise had taken the place of contempt. Mechanically, Arnaud raised a hand to his cheek, now much redder than the other. To all appearances it was the first time such a thing had ever happened to him and he could not get over it. The slap had reduced him to silence and Catherine, realizing this, contemplated him with satisfaction.

'Like this,' she said sweetly, 'you will remember me much better, messire. . . .'

Dropping a curtsey, she left the room with all the majesty of an outraged queen, leaving the knight to his own thoughts. But she did not go far. She was at the end of her strength. When the door closed behind her, she leant against the wall trying to quieten down a little. She could hear Arnaud swearing hideously on the other side of the stout wooden door, but this left her unmoved. What did his fury matter to her now? What mattered was that he had inflicted a cruel wound on her, one which made her want to scream out in pain. What had happened between them was irrevocable. Love could never bring them together again. They were destined to hate each other for all eternity, and all because of a misunderstanding which Catherine was too proud ever to try to clear up. He had refused to hear her explanation and so he would never learn the truth. Besides, even if he had heard it, his pride of caste would have led him to reject it as a fabrication on the girl's part. She took little sobbing gasps and tried to get her breath back. She closed her eyes for a second. The wild beating of her heart seemed to slow down a little. A little peace welled up from deep within her, calming the tempest. . . . When she re-opened her eyes the little Arab doctor was standing in front of her, looking solemnly at her from under the huge turban which looked like a giant peony. Catherine was astonished to see so much understanding in the Moor's tranquil gaze.

'The road of true love is paved with flesh and blood,' he quoted gently. 'You who pass that way must raise the hem of your skirts.'

The young girl hurriedly dashed away a tear which hung on her cheek.

'Who said that?' she asked.

Abou-al-Khayr shrugged his shoulders and put his hand on the door knob. He was a good half head shorter than Catherine, turban included, but his dignity was such that he seemed immensely tall.

'A Persian poet who died many long years ago,' he replied. 'His name was Háfiz and he understood the workings of men's hearts. He understood women's hearts less well and was to suffer as a result. . . . But I see that this time the tables are turned, young woman, and it is you who suffer. You have come up against a man as beautiful and dangerous as a Toledo blade, and you bleed. . . . I would not have believed it, by Allah, for looking at you both I thought that you were destined to form one of those rare and blessed couples which are so rarely encountered.'

'You were wrong,' Catherine sighed, 'and so was I. I too believed for a moment that he was going to love me. But he hates and despises me. I can't tell you why. He says he never wants to see me again.'

The little doctor burst out laughing, taking no notice of the indignant look Catherine gave him. She found his merriment ill-timed to say the least.

'Háfiz also said: "It is to be feared that those virtuous and pious ones who scoff at drunkards may one day find themselves chanting their prayers in the tavern." He detests and desires you. What more can you ask? When a woman kindles a man's desire she can always be certain of meeting him again one day. You must know that an angry man lets his speech, that wild mare, run on unbridled. The voices of the tempest within him shriek much too loud for him to hear the rather muted voice of reason. Go and join your uncle, who is beginning to worry about you, and leave me to deal with this difficult man in here. I shall stay with him and accompany him to the Duke of Burgundy. I will also try and find out what is going on in that obstinate head of his. Go in peace, young woman.'

Without another word Abou-al-Khayr bowed to Catherine and then, making a sign to his black servant who stood a little way off looking like an ebony statue, he went into the room. Catherine, pensive but a little comforted, went back to the room in which she had spent so little time to start putting her rumpled appearance to rights. Mathieu was still calling her name from the courtyard below. She leant over the balustrade and called:

'One moment, Uncle, I'm just coming.' Then she went back in again. A few minutes later, dressed in a fine brown wool dress under the Duke's splendid coat, with her braids hidden under a close-fitting silk hood which gave her the look of a young monk, she swept majestically down the stairs into the courtyard, followed by the half-angry, half-delighted gaze of her uncle and the frankly admiring one of young Roussay. The Burgundian captain was clearly delighted to see the girl again and he leapt forward to hand her down the last step and help her across the puddles left behind by the storm.

With a distant smile Catherine let her fingers rest on the hand outstretched to her, and went up to Mathieu, who was watching the scene with his arms akimbo and his hood standing up on end as was its wont.

'Good morning to you, Uncle. Did you sleep well?'

'Where have you sprung from?' Mathieu grumbled, dropping a hurried kiss on his niece's proffered brow. 'I have been looking for you for hours.'

'I went for a walk, but the grass was wet and I had to change my clothes. Are we leaving?'

'You seem to be in a hurry now. I thought you were in such a state of anxiety about our last night's discovery . . .'

Catherine flashed a dazzling smile at her uncle and then, raising her voice sufficiently to make it carry as far as a certain window, which stood open just above her head, she replied: 'We have found him a doctor, so there is nothing more we can do for him. We need not carry our charity towards him any further. Let us leave now – I am in a hurry to get home.'

With a firm step she went towards the mules which stood

waiting, saddled and ready to leave. She allowed Jacques de Roussay to hold her stirrup for her instead of old Pierre, thanking him with a smile and a pretty speech: 'Many thanks, messire. I am grateful to Monseigneur Philippe for having sent you to us. It is a great honour, and a pleasure, too, since it means we shall be travelling companions.'

Crimson with pleasure the young man remounted and gave his men the signal to depart. Catherine's gracious remarks had opened wide a door which up till then he believed firmly closed to him. This courtesy of the Duke's was only too clearly a sign of the value he set on the beautiful Dijonnaise, and Jacques had no doubt that Catherine was destined, in the none too distant future, for his master's love. But a woman always has the right to pick and choose, and there was nothing to prevent the young captain from trying to press his own suit while the voyage lasted.

He shortened his horse's step to fit in with the mule's, and tried to pursue the conversation which had got off to such a good start. But Catherine suddenly seemed to have been struck dumb. She replied in monosyllables to all his overtures, keeping her eyes downcast and her face expressionless. Jacques de Roussay soon grew resigned to travelling in silence, and had to content himself with admiring her ravishing profile, framed by its sumptuous fur hood.

Reassured by his armed escort, Mathieu Gautherin fell quietly asleep in the saddle, rocked by his mule's rhythmical gait. The grooms and soldiers followed behind. Catherine, locked in her silence and her thoughts, was trying to remember Arnaud's glowing face when he spoke to her of his love. It had all been so sudden. She felt as giddy as if she had been drinking too much rough wine. She would need the domestic tranquillity of her home and the calm familiar presence of her mother and sister and Sara before she could get back to normal. Especially Sara. She always understood everything, and could read what was going on in Catherine's mind as clearly as if it were an open book. She could always explain everything too, because there wasn't a woman alive who understood men as well as she did. A violent desire to see her again took hold of Catherine. She would have liked to spur on her mule, and ride off ahead of the others without stopping till she saw the walls of Dijon.

But in front of them the Flanders road stretched on interminably. . . .

Part Two

THE GUARDIAN OF THE TREASURE

1422–23

CHAPTER FIVE

MESSIRE GARIN

E ARLY MASS was just ending in the church of Notre-
Dame in Dijon. Outside, the hot July sun was already
flashing off the many spires of the ducal city. But inside it was
so dark that it was hard to see. Dark at the best of times, the
large Gothic church was made darker still by the heavy black
draperies which hung across all the arches. There were black
draperies hanging in all the churches and in front of many of
the private houses at that time, because Burgundy, for the
past week, had been mourning its Duchess. Michelle de
France had died suddenly, in her palace at Ghent, on 8 July –
so suddenly that there was talk of poisoning, though veiled
talk to be sure.

People whispered that the young Duchess had been doing
everything in her power to bring about a reconciliation between
her husband and the Dauphin Charles, and that the Queen
Isabeau, her terrible mother, did not approve of this reconciliation between her son-in-law and a son she loathed. It was
she who had introduced the Dame de Viesville into her daughter's retinue, the lady whom everyone accused secretly of having
brought about Michelle's untimely departure from this life.
The Duke Philippe had left hurriedly for Ghent, leaving
Dijon in the care of his mother, the Dowager Duchess Marguerite of Bavaria, Isabeau's cousin – cousin and enemy.

Catherine thought about all this as she knelt beside Loyse
and waited for her to finish saying her usual interminable
prayers. Since she had been living in Dijon, Loyse had been
seized by a profound devotion to the strange black statue of the
Virgin which belonged to Notre-Dame. The statue was carved
of dark wood. It was so old that no one seemed to know how
long it had been there, and it was known variously as Our Lady

of Succour or Our Lady of Good Hope. She would spend long hours kneeling in the chapel in the south transept, contemplating this stiff little figure with its long, sad Roman Virgin's face and rigid little Child Jesus, barely visible among the scintillating gold ornaments and the brilliance of a forest of tapers. Catherine also venerated the ancient Madonna, but she found it hard to get used to these long periods of kneeling. It was only to please Loyse, and also to avoid drawing acrimonious recriminations upon herself, that she complied.

Loyse was dreadfully altered since the flight from Paris. In this withered spinster who seemed much older than her twenty-six years, Catherine had difficulty in recognizing the gentle young girl of the Pont-au-Change, the one whom her father used to refer to tenderly as 'my little nun'. The first days after they had rescued her from Caboche had been the worst: Loyse had avoided her family, huddling in a corner and refusing to let anyone touch her. She did not even answer when she was spoken to. She tore the clothes they dressed her in and threw handfuls of ashes into the food she was given. When, that is, she was not living off brackish water and mildewed bread. Under her wretched dresses she wore a horsehair belt, studded with little steel points, which lacerated her tender skin. Jacquette Legoix was in despair, envisaging the day when Loyse, in her fanatical desire to expiate her sin, would demand to be walled up for ever, like Agnes du Rocher, the St Opportune recluse to whom she had so frequently taken bread and milk in the old days. The poor woman spent night after night praying and weeping. When she slept badly her slumber was disturbed by frightful dreams. They were always the same ones: she saw her daughter kneeling in a coarse woollen dress, surrounded by bricklayers who were gradually building a wall around her. A wall which was to separate her for ever from the rest of humanity, burying her alive in the midst of her fellow men. There she would be no more than a suffering body at the bottom of a filthy hole, exposed to cold, frost and the suffocating summer heat, in a cell barely large enough to allow her to lie full length, and ventilated by no more than a narrow slit.

Catherine remembered the heartbroken cries her mother used to give in the middle of the night.

She would wake with a start, and even the neighbours would cross themselves in their beds. But Loyse would listen without so much as a muscle moving in her expressionless face. The girl seemed to have lost her soul. She behaved like a social leper. Her self-loathing had reached such a pitch that she did not dare go to a church to confess and be absolved of this sin of the flesh which she dragged about with her like a ball and chain. This state of affairs went on for about a year. . . .

Then, one autumn day in 1414, a pedlar passed through the town. He had come from the north, and he stopped off for a while at Mathieu's to sell the women some needles. He sat himself down for a bit of a rest, and to pass the time he began to describe how Caboche had taken refuge with some of his men in Bapaume. Unfortunately for them the town fell into the hands of the Armagnacs shortly afterwards, and Simon the Skinner and his lieutenants were strung up without more ado by the enemy.

The pedlar never understood why, at the end of his tale, the tall pale blonde girl who had been listening to it so intently should have burst out laughing – but such a laugh as he hoped never to hear again from mortal lips.

From that day on Loyse had changed. She had agreed to dress properly, though still all in black, like a widow; and, though she still wore her spiked belt, there was no more talk of becoming a recluse. The following Friday she fasted all day, and then went alone to Notre-Dame where she prayed for a long time to the Black Madonna before finding a priest and asking him to hear her confession. After that she took up a normal life again, if a life which was one long series of penances and mortifications could be called normal.

'She will go into a nunnery one of these days,' said Sara nodding wisely. 'She will return to her old ambition.'

But she was wrong. Loyse no longer wished to enter a convent because she had lost the virginity she wanted to offer the Lord. She was once again within the fold of the Church, but she still thought herself unworthy to live among women who were completely dedicated to God. Unfortunately Loyse had extended her self-loathing over the rest of humanity, and in the neighbourhood where they lived her sour disposition was feared as much as her virtue and exemplary piety were admired.

While Loyse finished her prayers, Catherine yawned slightly and gazed round the church. Her abstracted glance fell upon a long masculine form standing not far from her in the same pew. The man was praying with a touch of arrogance, standing up, his arms folded across his chest. ... With his head thrown back and his eyes fixed on the sparkling altar, he gave the impression of speaking to God as an equal. He seemed far from humble. In fact there was even something a bit challenging about his bearing. Catherine was surprised to see him there, especially at this early hour on a weekday morning. Messire Garin de Brazey, Lord Treasurer of Burgundy, Keeper of the Ducal Crown Jewels, and bearer, into the bargain, of the title of Squire to Monseigneur Philippe, a purely honorary title but one which added great lustre to this prominent bourgeois, was one of the richest men in Dijon. As such, he only went to Mass on Sunday and feast days, and then always with a certain pomp and splendour.

Catherine knew him by sight through having passed him in the street several times, and also having met him in her uncle's shop when he came to buy materials there. He was a man of about forty, tall and thin, but solidly built. His face, with features as clearcut as those on an antique coin, would have been handsome but for the unattractively sardonic grimace which lifted the corners of his thin lips. His mouth was like a sabre slash across his smooth, close-shaven face. His large black hood, part of which passed under his chin, was fastened with a beautiful gold brooch in the shape of St George. It not only hid his hair, but cast a dark shadow across his pale face. It found a sinister echo in the black kerchief which hid Messire Garin's left eye. This eye had not seen long service. The Keeper of the Jewels had lost it at the age of sixteen, at the battle of Nicopolis, during the foolhardy crusade against the Turks on which he had accompanied Jean-sans-Peur, then the Comte de Nevers. The young squire had been captured along with his lord and his loyalty at this hour of great danger had led to his subsequent wealth and ennoblement.

Garin de Brazey was an enigma as far as the women of Dijon were concerned. An apparently confirmed bachelor, he ignored them all despite their many and brazen advances. Rich, not unattractive, in good standing at Court and generally considered as something of a wit, he would have been received with open arms by any bourgeois family or member of the lesser nobility. But he appeared not to notice the smiles showered upon him and continued to live alone in his magnificent mansion in the town, surrounded by his servants and valuable collections of *objets d'art*.

When, at last, Loyse had had enough, Catherine hurried after her, but she could not help noticing that the Treasurer's single eye was fixed upon her. As they left the chapel the two young women were swallowed up in the darkness of the church, which deepened the farther they went from the halo of light surrounding the Black Madonna. They walked behind each other, picking their way along cautiously, because in those days the floor, which was constantly being dug up for burial purposes, was dangerously uneven, and there were holes and cracks in it where people often fell or sprained an ankle.

This was precisely what happened to Catherine as she followed behind Loyse. She was just reaching out towards the holy water stoup when she tripped over a broken flagstone and fell flat on the ground with a cry of pain.

'How clumsy you are!' Loyse complained. 'Can't you look where you are going?'

'I can't see anyway, it's too dark,' Catherine protested. She tried to get up but gave up with a slight moan. . . . 'I can't get up, I must have twisted my foot. Help me.'

'Allow me to assist you, demoiselle,' said a grave voice which seemed to come from a long way above the girl's head. Catherine saw a tall silhouette bend towards her. A hot, dry hand took hold of hers to pull her up to her feet and at the same time a strong arm encircled her waist and supported her securely.

'Lean on me as much as you want. . . . There are some servants of mine waiting outside who will take you back to your home.'

Loyse had run on ahead and opened the great church door, letting in a dazzling ray of golden light, which was all the sunshine that filtered under the massive overhanging porch outside. Catherine could now see the face of the man who had helped her out: it was Garin de Brazey.

'Oh messire,' she said with some embarrassment, 'there is no need to go to so much trouble. . . . My foot feels a bit better already. In a few minutes I am sure I shall be able to walk perfectly well.'

'But I thought I heard you say you had twisted it?'

'It hurt so much at first I thought I had, but now the pain seems to be going. It really is much better. Thank you very much, messire. . . .'

In the porch she disengaged herself from the arm which still supported her, and blushingly dropped Garin a pretty, if slightly uncertain, curtsey.

'I beg your pardon, messire, for having interrupted your prayers,' she said. Something which resembled a smile crossed de Brazey's face.

In the full light of day, the black bandage over his eye took on a rather melancholy air. He was dressed in black from head to foot. Altogether he was a slightly intimidating spectacle.

'You did not disturb anything,' he replied briefly. 'However, a look of confusion sits charmingly on such a pretty face.'

It was not a compliment so much as a calm and sincere statement of fact. The Keeper of the Crown Jewels bowed slightly and went across to the far corner of the square, where a groom in purple and silver livery stood holding a black, spirited-looking horse. Catherine saw him vault lightly into the saddle and ride off in the direction of the rue des Forges.

'If you have finished simpering at strangers,' Loyse said sarcastically, 'perhaps we could set off home. You know Maman is waiting for us, and Uncle Mathieu needs you to help him with the accounts.'

Catherine followed her sister without a word. It was not very far from the church to the house in the rue Griffon where Mathieu Gautherin had his home and shop. Catherine craned her neck as she went out of the church to get a better view of the quaint iron figure perched high above the façade of the parish church with its elaborately and skilfully sculpted gargoyles. His function was to strike the hours on a large bronze bell. This iron figure, known to everybody as Jacquemart, had been taken many years earlier by Duke Philippe the Bold, grandfather of the present Duke, from the steeple of the church at Cambrai to punish the inhabitants of that town for an attempted revolt. Since then Jacquemart had become a familiar landmark in Dijon, and one of the most important inhabitants of the town. Catherine never failed to give him a friendly glance up there in his little tower.

'Are you coming or not?' said Loyse impatiently.

'I'm coming. I'm just behind you.'

The two young women, still walking one behind the other, were now skirting the precincts of the ducal palace. As soon as she caught sight of the palace chapel spire, encircled halfway up by a crown of gold fleur-de-lys, Loyse crossed herself piously. Catherine did likewise, and then the two of them turned down into the narrow, winding rue de la Verrerie. Loyse was striding along at a smart pace, and seemed in a worse humour than usual. Evidently the chance meeting with the Sire de Brazey had put her in a bad mood. With the sole exception of Uncle Mathieu, who did not care to inquire too deeply into what her feelings towards him might be, Loyse hated and despised men both singly and *en masse*.

Catherine, not wishing to exasperate her further, hurried along as best she could despite the slight twinge of pain she felt each time she put her foot down. They went down the short rue de la Draperie and then turned into the rue de Griffon, which led out of it. A moment later Catherine and her sister were crossing the threshold of Uncle Mathieu's shop at the Sign of the Great St Bonaventure.

Ever since her return from Flanders Catherine had been nagged by an odd feeling, as though she were living in another person's skin which did not quite fit her. She had found it very difficult to settle down again into the tranquil domestic routine which had been so lovingly and carefully built up over the years. She felt oddly but profoundly uncomfortable in the quiet comfortable, middle-class existence into which she had been born.

And yet it had been such a trivial thing which had set the wheels of Fate in motion, precipitating her from the tranquil monotony of her familiar world into the future whose far horizons were still blurred and unknowable. That slap on the Ghent furrier's face seemed to have been the signal for Fate to step in. On the one hand that slap had delayed their departure from Bruges, and on the other all but thrown her into the Duke Philippe's arms. Then, in its turn, this delay had led to their timely discovery and rescue of the wounded knight. For a moment it had seemed to Catherine as though the portals had been thrown open upon a dazzling, glorious future, but then, to the sound of another slap on the face, those doors had swung shut again. From slap to slap the wheel might have seemed to swing full circle, but Catherine knew that this was only the beginning. Something would happen soon to alter the whole course of her life.

To reassure herself of this she had only to look at the gaudy parrot dozing on its gilded perch in one corner of her room near the window. It was a magnificent bird with blue plumage tipped with scarlet. A page had brought it round one morning with the Duke's compliments. Uncle Mathieu had been sorely tempted to send the bird straight back. Catherine laughed to herself, remembering the scene of the bird's arrival, and her uncle's angry astonishment when confronted by this exotic creature whose round, arrogant eyes transfixed him with a far from kindly stare. On learning that the bird was a present for

Catherine sent by the Duke himself Mathieu had gone purple with fury.

'Monseigneur Philippe does us great honour,' he said to the expressionless page who stood waiting for someone to relieve him of his burden, 'but my niece is still a maiden and ought not to accept such valuable gifts.'

It was difficult to convey his real meaning in such a way as not to offend the Duke, but the page seemed to understand what he was getting at well enough.

'I cannot take Gedeon back!' he said. 'It would be an insult to Monseigneur.'

'But what about me?' Mathieu protested. 'Monseigneur insults *me* by supposing that my niece can accept his attentions. A young woman's reputation is a fragile thing.'

It was then that Gedeon, who was getting bored with the conversation, added his voice to the argument. He opened the immense red beak, which gave him a vague resemblance to Uncle Mathieu in profile, and shrieked:

'Long live the Duke! . . . Long live the Duke!'

Mathieu had been so astounded on hearing the bird speak that he had let the page go without making another attempt to detain him. Catherine, choking with laughter, took the parrot up to her own room. He was still shouting away at the top of his voice. Since then Gedeon had become the pet, and delight, of the entire household, including Uncle Mathieu. The two of them argued furiously for hours.

Catherine smoothed her hair in front of her mirror and was about to hurry downstairs when she heard a horse's hooves in the road below her window. She ran across to the window and looked out. The animal had stirred up a thick cloud of dust as it went by because the streets of Dijon had not yet been paved. But soon she recognized Garin de Brazey riding slowly along between the rows of houses where busy housewives could be seen passing to and fro behind the windows. She barely had time to recover from her surprise when the Treasurer looked up, caught sight of her, and saluted her gravely. Blushing, she returned the salutation and withdrew into the far corner of her room, not quite knowing how to interpret this second meeting following so hard on the heels of the first. Had he come to buy cloth? But no, the sound of the horse's hooves were already becoming fainter. Distractedly smoothing her skirt of almond green linen with its single band of white ribbon trimming, she went downstairs to join her uncle.

She found him in the little study where he kept his account books. He was hunched over the black oak desk, a quill behind his ear, busily entering up figures in a huge parchment-bound account book. Next door, in the shop itself, his assistants were at work unpacking a large consignment of cloth which had just arrived from Italy. Seeing that Mathieu was much too absorbed to pay any attention to her, she went to help old Pierre put away the lengths of new materials. There were brocades from Milan, and Venetian velvets. Catherine liked nothing better than fingering these sumptuous fabrics, destined for the backs of the nobility or the rich bourgeoisie. It was unlikely that she would ever wear anything so costly herself. She was particularly attracted by a ravishing pale-pink brocade interwoven with silver thread in a pattern of fantastic birds.

'Isn't this beautiful?' she exclaimed, holding a length of it up in front of her. 'How I would love to wear this!'

Old Pierre's private opinion was that nothing was too good for Catherine, and he watched her with an indulgent smile.

'Ask Maître Mathieu for it!' he suggested. 'He might even give it to you. And if I were you I should ask him for that one over there too. You would look very well in it.'

He pointed to a Venetian cut velvet with a design of large black flowers on a glittering gold ground, and Catherine was just about to pounce on it with a cry of admiration when they heard Mathieu's voice, scolding:

'Leave those stuffs alone! They are fragile and very expensive!'

'Oh, I know,' said Catherine, with a sigh, 'but, seeing this shop is the only place where I can touch cloth like this . . .'

With a wave of the hand she gestured towards the cupboards full of neatly piled bolts of silken stuffs, lengths of brightly coloured satins and soft textured velvets. Other cupboards held large pieces of lace, fine and delicate as cobwebs, veils from Mossoul, flowered shot silks from Persia, light rustling taffetas. Still others held the wool cloth of Champagne or England, soft white woollen stuff woven by the women of Valencienne, the supple Florentine materials, soft and almost as lustrous as satin.

Deftly Mathieu whisked the pink brocade from his niece and the black and gold velvet from Pierre and started piling them up on a large square of sturdy white cloth, adding a good selection of gold and silver cloth, and several coloured satins, striped, embroidered and plain, all of which he selected from the new shipment.

'These have all been sold,' he explained, 'and must be put on one side. It is an order for Messire de Brazey, which he will send for later on. As for you, my girl, go and finish adding up the week's takings and stop day-dreaming. I have to go out and I want everything to be in good order when I get back. Oh, and you might make out the Dame de Châteauvilain's bill, which she has asked for! And see that they measure out the length of turquoise diaper which the wife of the Sire du Toulongeon is waiting for.'

With a sigh of regret Catherine left the shop and took her uncle's place in the cubby-hole. Those heavy tomes full of Roman numerals bored her to tears, although she found some pleasure reading about the far-away places from which the cloth had come, with their romantic, evocative names. But since her return from Flanders a brown face would rise up unbidden all too often before the huge crackling yellow pages, and Catherine would feel near to tears. All of a sudden there seemed to be an impossible gulf between the Dauphin's squire and the niece of a Dijonnais cloth merchant. And, besides, Arnaud hated and despised her; and then, on top of that, there was the war which put them both in opposite camps. But this particular morning Catherine was not thinking about Arnaud. Dipping her quill into the ink, she set to work courageously. All she was thinking about at that moment was that beautiful pink brocade which she yearned to possess, and also why the Keeper of the Crown Jewels, who always dressed in sombre black, should suddenly have decided that he would look better in pink?

Despite what he had said, they did not see Uncle Mathieu again all that day. Towards dinner-time he sent word that he would not be home till supper, but supper came and he had still not arrived. When at length he returned he summoned his sister Jacquette and they both went into his large high-ceilinged room and remained closeted in there for hours without a word of explanation.

When she opened her eyes the next morning Catherine saw that Sara was sitting by her bedside waiting for her to wake. This surprised her. As a rule it was Loyse who woke her, giving her an unceremonious shake to rouse her in time for the early morning devotions. But this time there was no sign of Loyse and the sun was high in the sky.

'Today is an important day, my lamb,' the gipsy woman said, holding her chemise out for her. 'You must hurry up and get dressed. Your uncle and your mother want to speak to you.'

'What about? Do you know?'

'Yes, I know, but I have promised not to tell you.'

Catherine was consumed with curiosity. But she was well aware of her power over her old friend. She began wheedling the truth out of her.

'Is it something nice? Surely you can tell me if it is something I will like. . . .'

'I really don't know. It might be and yet it might not. Why not get up and find out?'

Sara bustled about, pouring some water into a bowl and laying out a clean napkin. Catherine ignored the chemise which Sara proffered her and bounded out of bed just as she was, as naked as the day she was born. People were in the habit of sleeping naked in those times. She had never felt the slightest embarrassment in front of Sara, who was a sort of second mother to her.

The tall gipsy woman had not changed a bit with the passing

years. She was still beautiful, and as brown-skinned as ever. Though she was nearing forty, there was not one white hair in her mass of black tresses. She was merely a bit fatter, the easy life she had led at Uncle Mathieu's having cushioned her lithe, feline body with a comfortable layer of fat. But her spirit was as wild as ever, and as independent. Sometimes she would disappear for two or three days at a time, and no one had any idea where she had gone, with the possible exception of Barnaby. . . . But he knew how to keep a secret, and in that dangerous turbulent world where he had chosen to live, despite Catherine's entreaties, everyone knew how to hold their tongues.

While she rushed through her preparations with unaccustomed haste, Catherine, who generally liked to dawdle and take her time, noticed Sara gazing thoughtfully at her.

'What's the matter?' she asked. 'Do you think I look ugly?'

'Ugly? You must be fishing for compliments! You know very well you don't look ugly. Perhaps it would be better for you if you did. It's not always a good thing for a girl to be too beautiful. As a matter of fact, I was thinking that not many men, once they'd had a look at your body, would be able to resist you. And yet someone so expressly formed for love must necessarily bring death and suffering in her wake. . . .'

'What do you mean?'

Sara often made strange remarks, and as often as not refused to explain them in any way. It was as though she had been speaking to herself, but out loud. That was what happened this time.

'Nothing,' she said curtly, handing the girl the green dress she had been wearing the day before. 'Get dressed and come downstairs.'

When Sara had left the room Catherine hurriedly finished washing and dressing, tied her plaits with a ribbon which matched her dress and went down to the big room where Sara had told her her mother and uncle were waiting to talk to her.

She found Mathieu sitting in his chair, looking grave and

T—F

anxious. Jacquette was sitting opposite him on a bench, saying her beads. Neither of them spoke.

'Well, here I am!' Catherine said. 'What has happened?'

They both looked at her for a moment, so attentively that Catherine had the feeling that they were seeing her for the first time.

She saw a tear shining in her mother's eyes and ran across to her. She knelt down beside her, put her arms around Jacquette's waist and leant her cheek against her bosom.

'Maman . . . you are crying? What has happened?'

'Nothing, nothing, my darling. Something which may bring you great happiness.'

'Happiness?'

'Yes . . . perhaps. But your uncle will explain.'

Mathieu had abandoned his chair and was now pacing to and fro about the immense room, which took up almost the length and width of the house. His step seemed heavier than usual and he appeared to be trying to make up his mind about something. At last he stopped in front of her and said:

'Do you remember those stuffs which arrived from Italy yesterday? The ones you liked so much? A pink brocade—'

'Yes,' said Catherine. 'The ones Messire de Brazey has ordered.'

'Exactly. Well, if you still want them, they are yours.'

'Mine?'

Had Uncle Mathieu gone mad all of a sudden? Why should a man as important as Garin de Brazey suddenly take it into his head to make such a costly gift to the niece of one of his tradesmen? Catherine looked from her uncle to her mother and glanced rapidly about the familiar room as if to reassure herself that this was not all a dream. Both of them were watching closely for her reactions.

'But . . . why?' Catherine asked again. Mathieu turned and walked across to the window, looked out, pulled a leaf off the basil which was planted in a pot on the window-sill and then walked back to his niece.

'Because Messire Garin has done us the honour of asking for

your hand in marriage. I went to see him yesterday and he outlined his proposition to me. I must say I cannot see anything against it. It is a great honour, as I said, a little unexpected perhaps, but still a great honour!'

'Now, now,' Jacquette interrupted. 'Don't try to influence the child.'

'I am *not* trying to influence her,' Mathieu said impatiently. 'I am by no means certain myself that this marriage is altogether desirable. I find it a bit worrying, as a matter of fact. All I said was that it is a great honour, and that's neither more nor less than the truth. What do you think, my child?'

The girl was struck dumb. After all, it was a pretty astonishing piece of news. All of a sudden, since the day before, de Brazey seemed absolutely determined to enter her life. She was too fond of getting to the bottom of things not to put some more questions to Mathieu.

'*Why* does Messire Garin wish to marry me?' she asked.

'He loves you apparently,' said Mathieu, shrugging his shoulders. 'There's nothing strange in that. He told me he had never seen a more beautiful girl, and I know there's more than one man of a like mind. Well, what shall I tell him?'

Once more Jacquette interrupted.

'You are going too fast, Mathieu! All this must have come as a complete surprise, and a shock to the poor child! You must give her time to get used to the idea. . . .'

Get used to it? Oh yes, it would certainly take some getting used to! In the mirror of her memory Catherine saw Garin de Brazey's reflection, his cold face, single eye and impressive, almost frigid manner. He was like a figure in a tapestry suddenly come to life. One cannot marry a figure in a tapestry.

'I appreciate the honour he has done me,' said Catherine quickly, 'but I would like Messire de Brazey to know that I have no wish to get married. I don't love him, you see . . . but there is no need to tell him that.'

'You refuse him?'

Mathieu was flabbergasted. He had been expecting surprise, disbelief, perhaps even a little excitement. A proposal of marriage from such a rich, powerful man would surely overwhelm a shy young maiden with surprise and delight. But that such an offer should be rejected so positively and spiritedly was enough to appal anyone. Catherine, who was now sitting by her mother, holding her hand, seemed neither overwhelmed nor particularly moved. Her lovely, candid eyes were quite untroubled and clear, and her voice was quiet, even as she replied, gently:

'Of course I refuse! I have always refused all the other people who wanted to marry me because I didn't love them. I don't love Messire de Brazey any more than them, so naturally I shall refuse him too.'

This faultless logic did not seem to impress Mathieu, whose face darkened. The deep line between his brows grew deeper still. He paused for a moment, then added:

'Has it occurred to you that you would be the richest, most beautifully dressed woman in Dijon? You would live in a magnificent house, you would have any number of those fine clothes you dream of, jewels fit for a queen, servants, you would go to Court—'

'—and,' Catherine interrupted, 'I would have to sleep every night beside a man I don't love, who repels me even. No, Uncle, I can't accept such an offer. The answer is no.'

'Unfortunately,' said Mathieu, not looking at his niece, 'you have no choice in the matter. You must marry Garin de Brazey. It is an order.'

At these words Catherine's admirable composure vanished. She leapt up to face Mathieu, resplendent with a rage which made her eyes flash and her cheeks pink.

'An order? And from whom, may I ask?'

'From the Duke himself. Read this . . .'

From a casket on the table Mathieu Gautherin took a large parchment scroll, with the ducal arms on it, and handed it to the girl.

'Garin de Brazey gave me this at the same time as he formally asked for your hand in marriage. You will be the Dame de Brazey before the summer is out. . . .'

Catherine spent the rest of the day locked in her room. No one disturbed her there. Uncle Mathieu had given orders for her to be left alone, after the wild and furious outburst with which she had greeted the news of the ducal edict. Even Sara had disappeared to the mysterious place where she went from time to time, without warning or explanation. Catherine sat on her bed, her hands clasped in her lap, and thought over what had happened, with only Gedeon to keep her company. The parrot, possibly realizing instinctively that his mistress was going through some crisis or other, was silent. Head on his breast, eyes half closed, the bird seemed to be asleep on its perch, and it made a brilliant splash of colour against the bare wall of the room.

The fury she had felt a few hours earlier had abated somewhat, but Catherine still seethed with rebellious thoughts. She had believed that the Duke thought well of her and wished to be kind to her, but then he did extraordinary, incomprehensible things like this: marrying her off to Garin de Brazey, who was not only a man she did not love, but one whom she barely knew. And his way of setting about it disgusted her. Did Philippe think she was some chattel of which he could dispose at will? She was not even a subject of his and she had said as much to Mathieu.

'Monseigneur Philippe is not my liege lord. I don't have to obey him and I shan't!'

'That would mean ruin and prison for all of us. . . or perhaps worse. You forget that I am a subject of the Duke's, and a loyal one. You are my niece and you live under my roof. Therefore you are a vassal of his whether you like it or not. . . .'

It was unanswerable. Catherine, angry as she was, was well aware of this, but she could not resign herself to being delivered, bound hand and foot as it were, into the Treasurer's hands – she, Catherine, the girl who till then had always managed to keep out of men's clutches, and who had sworn to continue doing so. There had been Arnaud, to be sure, and her bitter-sweet encounter with him. But, seeing that happiness with him was denied to her for ever, Catherine had made a vow on the journey back from Flanders: she would never belong to anyone but that fiercely tender man who had so swiftly ravished her heart, and so nearly her body too.

Other men's faces flashed through Catherine's fevered mind: Garin, with the sombre black bandage over his eye, the young Captain de Roussay, so desperately in love with her that he might, at a pinch, be prepared to risk a rash enterprise on her behalf. For a moment Catherine considered eloping with the young soldier. Jacques, she was sure, would snatch at the chance, even at the risk of incurring the Duke's anger. That would be an infallible way of escaping from de Brazey. But, once in de Roussay's power, she would be obliged to grant him the reward he would be expecting and which was already consuming him with hopeless desire. Catherine had no more wish to belong to de Roussay than to de Brazey. In either case it meant yielding to a man other than Arnaud.

Then another face rose up before her – Barnaby's! The cleverest man in the world at getting out of difficult situations! Had he not smuggled her out of a besieged Paris, rescued Loyse from Caboche, and escorted them safely to Dijon across country devastated by war and swarming with ferocious gangs of mercenaries and bandits ? He was a man who could perform miracles. The upshot of her long, solitary hours of thought was that Catherine decided to pay Barnaby a visit. It was no use waiting till he decided to pay his respectable bourgeois friends a visit. There was no time to lose.

They did not see much of Barnaby at the quiet house in the rue du Griffon, mainly because it *was* so quiet. Despite his advancing years, the elderly vendor of pseudo-relics still liked to live as dangerously as he always had. He would not consider leaving his own strange, disturbing, but vivid and colourful world. He would put in an appearance from time to time, shambling, sarcastic, nonchalant, carrying off his filthy rags with kingly arrogance. First he would stretch out his long legs in front of the blazing fire, then, later on, under Mathieu's abundantly stocked table. Mathieu, who was fond of him without quite knowing why, never failed to invite him to stay for a meal.

Barnaby would stay for several hours, chatting to Mathieu about this and that. He invariably knew what was happening throughout the length and breadth of the duchy and was often able to give the merchant information which proved of considerable use to him in his business – such as news of the arrival of a Genoese or Venetian boat at Damme, or of a caravan of Russian fur-dealers at Châlons. He also knew all the court gossip, the names of the Duke Philippe's mistresses and exactly how many times the Dowager-Duchess had lost her temper that week. Then he would take his leave, pinch Catherine's cheek, gravely salute Jacquette and Loyse, and return to his nocturnal way of life. Both Mathieu and Catherine were well aware that Barnaby was one of the right-hand men of the sinister Jacquot-de-la-Mer, the Cockleshell King, but neither of them mentioned the fact in public, and when, as sometimes happened, Loyse's sharp tongue let slip some reference to their friend's rather undesirable profession, they would both hurriedly tell her to hold her tongue.

Towards evening Jacquette, worried by Catherine's silence and long seclusion in her room, brought her up a bowl of soup, some slices of cold beef and a pitcher of milk. The girl had eaten nothing since morning. She thanked her mother sweetly and to please her she took a little soup, ate a slice of beef and drank a sip of milk, although she had absolutely no appetite. But it did her good. Almost at once she felt her spirits reviving, her mind seemed clearer and her body more relaxed.

'You mustn't take it so hard, sweetheart,' said Jacquette, smiling at her. 'This offer of marriage is really rather a good thing when you think about it. A lot of girls will envy you, and not a few grand ladies too. And you may find that Messire Garin improves on closer acquaintance. He is not bad-looking. You may well grow to love him, and whatever happens you will be spoiled and pampered. . . .'

The good woman's eyes strayed towards the bundle of shimmering cloth which Mathieu had ordered to be taken to his niece as a tempting reminder of the good fortune which awaited her. Catherine had tossed it contemptuously on to a chest in the farthest, darkest corner of the room. Jacquette's tone, which was both humble and tremulous, upset the girl and she jumped up and embraced her mother.

'Don't worry about me, Maman. . . . It will all be all right, and, as you say, everything may come right of its own accord.'

Completely misunderstanding the drift of Catherine's remarks, Jacquette went back to the kitchen feeling greatly comforted, and reported to her brother that the child was growing more amenable and no longer said 'no' quite so emphatically and categorically.

Nothing, however, was farther from Catherine's mind than surrender. She had simply wished to allay her mother's fears and give herself more scope for action. When she had eaten her light meal, she went and lay down on her bed to wait for it to get dark. She heard her uncle Mathieu go out, as he did every evening, to hand over the keys of the St Nicholas Gate which it was his responsibility to guard and maintain, to the Vicomte-Mayeur or Mayor of the town.

Soon afterwards she heard him come in and lock and bolt his own doors, and shortly after the bellringers of St Jean sounded the curfew bell. From then on the streets were given over to prostitution, theft, brigandry and every kind of malpractice.

Catherine still lay motionless on her bed. She heard the stairs creak as her uncle went up to bed, then Loyse scolding the servant girl and old Pierre humming to himself as he climbed up to his attic. Little by little silence settled over the house. Sara still had not come in. Catherine knew she would not be back before dawn, assuming she came back the next day at all.

When the only sound to be heard was Uncle Mathieu's smothered snoring, Catherine slipped out of bed, pulled on a brown dress which she had chosen specially for the purpose, braided her hair tightly and covered it with a close-fitting hood and then, throwing a loose cape round herself which completely hid her figure, she crept down the stairs. She knew from long experience how to descend them without making the steps creak, and also how to slip the bolts and turn the keys in the locks without making a sound, thanks partly to Sara's careful oiling of them from time to time. A few minutes later she was out in the street.

CHAPTER SIX

THE TAVERN OF JACQUOT-DE-LA-MER

CATHERINE WAS not easily frightened, and besides it was a brilliantly clear night. The sky was velvety black and sprinkled with stars that sparkled as brightly as the diamonds on the Black Madonna's coat. Nevertheless, it took some courage to walk deliberately into the town's most disreputable district, where even the Watch dared not go.

'If you ever need me,' Barnaby had once confided to her in secrecy, 'you can find me at the bawdy house. It belongs to one Jacquot-de-la-Mer, who is a Sergeant of the Mairie. He is also the chief of all us beggars and vagabonds. I am telling you this because I know you are no chatterbox and because I believe the day may come when you will need help. If I am not there you can send someone to find me at the hostelry of the Porte d'Ouche, where I also go from time to time, though not so often.'

Catherine had no idea what a bawdy house was until she mentioned the subject to Sara one day. The gipsy woman believed in calling a spade a spade and maintained that truth is a hundred times better than hypocrisy in the education of young girls.

'A bawdy house,' she explained, 'is a house where silly girls sell their bodies to men for money.'

At the time Catherine had felt that this information told her everything she needed to know about the matter, but now she thought of Sara's words again as she skirted along as close as possible to the double-gabled houses of the rue du Griffon, trying to conceal herself in the dark shadows under the eaves and to avoid the centre of the narrow, twisting street where there was more light.

When she reached the Place de la Sainte Chapelle she plucked up her courage and ran straight across it as far as the Cross which stood in the middle, where she paused for breath. The Cross flung a long shadow across the square, flanked on one side by St John and on the other by Mary Magdalene, their stone faces set in eternal contemplation of the Divine Agony. Having got her breath back, Catherine edged round the bastions of the ducal palace. It was reassuringly dark in the shadow of its towers, but she had to be on the look-out for the archers on watch, whom she could just distinguish by the faint gleam of their helmets. Starting to run again she darted down the rue des Forges, where the blacksmiths' wretched hovels still gave out a smell of burning wood, scorched leather and armour grease. This street was extraordinarily narrow, and it was famous for the number of fires which began there, started by the blazing fires in the forges.

On the doorstep in front of each house stood a large leather bucket which was used to fetch water up in case of fire. Catherine knew this, but in her hurry and anxiety she forgot about the buckets, tripped over one, crashed down on the ground and swore like a trooper. Swearing was not a habit of hers, but this once she found it really eased the pain.

At the spot where the narrow alley joined the Bourg, the town's largest and busiest commercial street, it widened out to form a little square, just big enough to accommodate a pillory comfortably. There was no one in it at the moment, but it was not an agreeable sight. Catherine looked the other way and was about to hurry on when she felt someone grab her by the corner of her cape and screamed. A shapeless shadow emerged from a dark corner, grunted, and then burst out laughing while a pair of hands grabbed her round the waist under her cape.

Catherine was almost paralysed by fright, but she had a reflex of self-defence. Twisting her supple waist, she wriggled like an eel right out of the clumsy hands which were trying to hang on to her. Leaving her cape behind she ran blindly on as fast as she could, trying to master her terror and keep her head. She *must* reach the Beggar King's tavern!

But she could not help hearing that someone was after her. Close behind she heard the dull thud of running bare feet and the panting of the man in pursuit. The night was growing blacker and the labyrinth of streets through which she ran seemed to have become impenetrably dark. She choked on the stench of open sewers, old rubbish and bad meat which rose up and almost made her sick. In those days no one troubled to remove slops and rubbish until there was so much that it got in the way of passers-by. Then they would throw whatever the cats and dogs rejected into the Ouche or the Suzon.

In the shadow of a doorway a bundle of rags moved and stirred, and Catherine was horrified to see another shadow fling itself after her with a crazy giggle. A nameless horror invaded her. She forbade herself to turn back and tried desperately to run faster, but in her blind haste she did not look where she was going. She tripped against a pile of rubbish from which a smell of rotten fish rose up, flung up her hands to support herself, felt the damp stones of a wall in front and leant against it, faint with fear, breathless, eyes closed. ... Her pursuers were upon her. ...

She felt the same hands which had seized her before grab her once more round the waist. They began to squeeze and feel her eagerly. A sour smell reached her nostrils. The man must have been very tall because he blocked out the sky behind.

'Now then,' came a hoarse whisper in her ear, 'what's all the hurry about? Where are we rushing off to in such a state? A lover's tryst?'

As soon as the man spoke he lost his terrifying ghostly quality, and this rallied Catherine's spirits a little.

'Yes,' she stammered faintly. ... 'That's it ... a tryst!'

'Your tryst can wait. ... I can't. You smell young, and clean. ... You must be a dainty morsel indeed! Mmm! Your skin is soft!'

Feeling sick with revulsion, Catherine stood helpless as the man's hands fumbled about her bodice, pausing when they reached her throat and shoulders just at the point where her tucked collar ended. The man's breath stank obscenely of cheap rancid wine and decaying teeth, and his skin felt as hard as if it had been burned. His hands groped for the neckline of her dress, caught hold of it, and were just about to rip it open when a squeaky voice which appeared to issue from the earth beneath them, piped up nasally.

'Slowly there, my friend! ... I saw her too, remember! Fair's fair!'

The giant who had hold of Catherine relaxed his grasp slightly in his astonishment, and turned round. The bundle of rags which Catherine had seen moving in the doorway now stood behind him, a short squat tattered shape in the darkness, hung with fluttering rags. Catherine felt her assailant's muscles tighten ominously. He was just about to strike out when the other man added:

'Come now, Dimanche-l'Assommeur, don't be nasty! You know what sort of reception you would get from Jacquot-de-la-Mer if he found you had beaten up his best friend. Let's share the girl. ... I'll wager she is a rare ... morsel! As you know, I can see in the dark like a cat!'

The beggar grunted again, but did not protest. Instead he held his captive all the tighter and said:

'Oh! It's you, is it? Be on your way, Jehan des Écus! Girls are not for the likes of you!'

The bundle of rags did not seem to find this argument convincing. His laugh sounded again, grating and sinister, reminding the girl irresistibly of the noise made by a gibbet's creaking, rusty chains.

'That's what you think! I may have boils and a hump back, but I'm as good as the next man in bed. ... Take the girl to the house with the gable and we'll strip her clothes under the porch. Jacquot-de-la-Mer always says you can't tell what a girl's like while she has a stitch on her back. ... Come on now!'

His voice had the authoritative ring to it of a man who is accustomed to being obeyed. And the man called Dimanche-l'Assommeur would probably not take long to be persuaded.

But, luckily, Jehan des Écus had repeated the name of the Beggar King twice over, and the familiar name had roused Catherine out of her terror. She decided to play her trump-card. At all events nothing could be worse than the fate which awaited her at the hands of these two monsters.

'You speak of Jacquot-de-la-Mer,' she said in a voice which she tried to keep steady. 'It is he whom I am on my way to see and you are . . . keeping me waiting.'

Instantly the giant's paw loosened its hold and the other man came closer for a better look. With an astonishingly powerful grasp for such a twisted fellow, he pulled her free of Dimanche's hands.

'What do you want with Jacquot? You aren't one of his usual girls. They are all at work now!'

'I have to see him,' Catherine cried, almost in tears, 'it's very important! If you are his men you must take me to him, please!'

There was a moment's silence. Then Jehan des Écus drew a sigh of real regret.

'That puts things in quite a different light,' he said. 'We can't stop you if you are on your way to see Jacquot. But it's a bloody shame! Come on, Dimanche, pull yourself together. We've got to escort this little virgin . . . you are a virgin, ain't you? You can always tell. . . . If you weren't you wouldn't have made such a fuss about giving two lusty beggars a bit of fun.'

Too shaken to speak as yet, Catherine started off again, walking between the two men who were still faceless shadows to her. She was no longer afraid. She realized obscurely that she was quite safe as far as the chief's house, and that these two bandits constituted a sort of bodyguard. The giant's huge shadow kept her company on one side, while the other man limped painfully along, stumbling over the uneven cobbles, on the other.

The alley began sloping downhill, plunged between two houses, and became a sort of tunnel between two high-walled gardens. At the far end of the lane a fantastic-looking construction came into sight, which proved, when they drew closer, to be formed by two tumbledown houses. A light was shining behind one of the shutters in defiance of the curfew. They could hear a woman's voice singing, or rather chanting, a strange dirge in a foreign tongue.

As they drew nearer to the house the song became more distinct. At times the singer's voice soared up to an almost unbearably high note, and held it for a moment before once more taking up the strange harsh melody. At her side Catherine heard Jehan des Écus give his peculiar creaking laugh.

'Ha, ha! . . . Jacquot is having a party . . . good, good!'

When they reached the house a shadow emerged from the doorway. Catherine saw an axe-blade gleam.

'The password?' said a rough voice.

'Hard and fast!' said Jehan des Écus.

'All right. You may go in.'

The door swung open, revealing the interior of Jacquot-de-la-Mer's famous tavern, meeting-place for the underworld of Dijon. The good citizens of the town spoke of it only in hushed voices, crossing themselves with pious horror. It was hard to understand at first just why the Vicomte-Mayeur should allow such a den of iniquity to survive.

Any of the respectable ladies of Dijon would have fainted on the spot had they known that their worthy husbands sometimes sneaked off to the forbidden house to purchase the charms of some handsome wench. But Jacquot knew how to pick his girls, and his house could stand comparison with the most celebrated stews of the day. As a good businessman he believed before everything in keeping his clients happy. . . .

At first glance Catherine only registered a kaleidoscopic pattern of vivid colours. A babel of voices, laughter and music rose up to meet her, but this soon died away as the inmates gazed open-mouthed at the strange spectacle presented by the beautiful young woman, white-faced and hair flowing untidily, and her two sinister companions, posted one on either side. Meanwhile Catherine took a closer look round this huge, low-vaulted chamber, reached down a short flight of steps. At the far end of the room there was a huge chimney in which three whole sheep at once were slowly rotating on spits. There were

benches and large tables of grease-stained wood standing about,
all crowded. A wooden staircase spiralled up to the roof at the
far end of the room. The drinkers were a motley collection.
There were drunken soldiers, and round-eyed youths, students
or apprentices who had come to the tavern to see a bit of low
life. Two old crones supervised the food cooking on the hearth.
And all round the room, on the benches, on the clients' laps, or
even sitting on the tables among the pools of spilt wine and the
pewter mugs, there were scores of girls, most of them with their
bodices half unlaced, some of them completely naked. Their
bodies made pale highlights in the dark smoky atmosphere. The
light from tapers and the blazing fire flickered over pale skins,
satiny-textured dark ones, and then over the red, flushed faces
of the drunken men, glowing as richly as rubies in the sun.

The momentary astonishment caused by their sudden entrance passed. The bacchanal was in full swing again before
Catherine and her escort had reached the bottom of the steps.
The dancing and shouting started up again. A girl with a brown
body and large breasts climbed up on to a table and danced
there, writhing and twisting suggestively in the midst of a forest
of outstretched hands. For a horrified moment Catherine
thought she must have stumbled into hell, and closed her
eyes.

Memories of similar scenes, dredged up from the depths of
her mind, paraded before her. They were the orgies she had
witnessed in the Grande Cour des Miracles, when she hid in a
corner of Barnaby's old shack and peeped out of a skylight.
Such sights had merely surprised and vaguely disturbed the
child she was then. But now she was amazed and disgusted to
find that they excited a strange, dubious pleasure in her.

The woman who had been singing a little earlier on now
began another song, and at the harsh, low, nostalgic sound of
her voice Catherine's eyes flew open again. This woman,
wearing a flame-coloured satin dress and gold spangles in her
hair, sat on the stairs at the far end of the room with a group of
men around her. A lute player accompanied her, leaning
towards her as she sang. She sang with her eyes closed, her

hands clasped about her knees, and Catherine gave a barely perceptible start of surprise as she recognized her. This was decidedly a night of discoveries. The woman was Sara. . . .

She had not noticed Catherine, and had she done so it would probably have made no difference, because, as the girl quickly noticed, she was intoxicated. But drunk with an intoxication in which wine acted only as the conductor by which Sara, gipsy that she was, could blot out the real world around her and return in spirit to her faraway tribe and savage life. Catherine listened entranced. Sara had often sung her to sleep, especially in the early days of their exile to Burgundy, but never with quite this hoarsely passionate voice, or this unbearable burden of grief. . . .

In the woman before her, sunk into a trance-like state, Catherine saw the wild young girl she had once been, the child born in a nomad caravan, on the way from distant Asia. Her features alone were the features of Catherine's companion and friend of every day. She was not surprised or shocked at discovering the secret of Sara's repeated disappearances, or at finding her here in this low place, taming these beasts with human faces, these men of Jacquot's, with the simple magic of her voice. . . .

A man's figure stepped between her and the singer. A tall pale man, so white-faced that he looked as if his skin had been bleached by remaining a long time under water. Once, many years earlier, Catherine had seen a drowned man's body taken out of the Ouche. The stranger before her was exactly the same colour, and this supernatural aspect of his appearance was enhanced by a pair of greenish, glaucous eyes. Thick, hooded eyelids like a tortoise's concealed these disturbing eyes most of the time. A short, loose, mouse-grey garment flapped about his bony form, on which the skin hung as limply as a sodden rag. His slow, sleep-walking gestures added to the ghostliness of his appearance.

'Who is this ?' he asked, pointing a long white skinny finger at Catherine.

Dimanche-l'Assommeur's appearance was not improved by

the taper-light, which showed up his pock-marked face and the angry red weal of the executioner's brand on one cheek.

It was he who replied:

'A little wild she-goat we found in the street. She says she wants to see you, Jacquot.'

The Cockleshell King's long, sinuous, colourless lips stretched even wider in a grimace which was almost recognizable as the smile for which it was intended. His hand brushed Catherine's chin.

'Pretty!' he exclaimed appreciatively. 'Is it my reputation as a lady-killer which brings you here, my pretty?'

'No,' said the girl crisply. Gradually she was regaining her aplomb and composure. 'I have come here because I wanted to see Barnaby. He told me to seek you out if ever I needed him. And I need him now!'

The unpleasant gleam which had appeared momentarily in Jacquot's eyes was extinguished as his heavy lids drooped over them. Ugly, twisted little Jehan des Écus tossed back his red elf-locks and tattered felt hat and darted a quick look at Catherine.

'I know who you are now. . . . You are the niece of that donkey Mathieu Gautherin, the beautiful Catherine . . . the fairest virgin in all Burgundy! I don't regret now having let you slip through my fingers because you are destined for a greater man than I. Had I touched you I would have risked my neck. . . .'

An expressive gesture accompanied the little man's last words. Catherine realized with surprise that, in spite of the nervous tics which contorted his face, it was finely formed and he had beautiful eyes.

'Risked your neck?' she asked with genuine surprise. 'Why?'

'Because the Duke wants you for himself, and he will have you! Still, when all is said and done, perhaps I should have given in to my desires after all! First you, then the gallows! It might be a wonderful way to shorten one's life! You are certainly worth it!'

Jacquot-de-la-Mer must have found the conversation

growing tediously long. His hand slowly descended on Catherine's shoulder.

'If you want to see Barnaby, go up the stairs over there. He is in the attic at the top of the house. He is in bed because he took a bad tumble over Chenôve way three days ago. You may have difficulty getting through to him because he must be dead drunk by now. Wine is the only medicine he believes in.'

Guided by the landlord's hand Catherine climbed the first few steps. As she passed Sara her dress brushed against the gipsy's, but Sara's eyes were closed again and she was singing her heart out, lost in her inner world, a thousand leagues from the thieves' den.

The attic was shut off by a rickety door made of uneven planks. Candlelight gleamed through it. Catherine had no difficulty opening it. A simple push was all that was needed, but it was so low she had to bend double to pass through. She found herself in a dark, windowless little cell under the beams of the steep roof. A straw pallet was pushed under a massive beam, and on it Barnaby was lying, a pitcher of wine close at hand and a tallow candle spluttering and smelling unpleasantly in a pewter dish beside him. His face was very flushed but he was clearly not drunk. His eyes were quite clear as they gazed, in astonishment, at the girl.

'You? But what are you doing here . . . my little pigeon? And at this time of night?'

He raised himself on one elbow and modestly pulled his tattered shirt over the matted grey hair on his chest.

'I need your help, Barnaby. So I came to find you as you said I should,' said Catherine simply, sitting down at the foot of the mattress whose straw stuffing stuck out through a number of holes.

'Are you wounded?' she asked, looking at the dirty bandage flecked with greasy balm and bloodstains which was bound round Barnaby's forehead.

He shrugged indifferently.

'Oh, it's nothing. Some rough fellow hit me with a spade

because I asked him to let me help him count up his savings. It's almost healed.'

'You will never change,' Catherine exclaimed with a sigh. She was neither shocked nor surprised by this admission. Perhaps that was because of the joyous gleam in her friend's eye, which always, magically, seemed to make everything he said quite harmless and even amusing. The fact that Barnaby was a thief, if not worse, made no difference to Catherine. He was her friend, and that was the only thing that mattered. That apart he could do as he pleased. To salve her conscience, however, she felt obliged to add a few warning words.

'If you don't take care you will find yourself at Morimont one of these days with Maître Blaigny on one side and a stout hemp rope on the other.'

With a careless wave of the hand, Barnaby dismissed this unpleasant picture from his mind. He took a good swig of wine, set down the pitcher, wiped his mouth on his sleeve and then settled back comfortably into his ragged covers.

'Come on, now, out with it . . . tell me what brings you here! Though I think I already know what it is!'

'You know?' said Catherine, in honest astonishment.

'I know this much – the Duke Philippe has ordered you to marry Garin de Brazey. And in order to persuade this rich, important fellow to accept the niece of one Mathieu Gautherin, tradesman, he has settled a big dowry on you. The Duke Philippe always knows what he is about. . . .'

Catherine's expressive eyes were saucer-like, almost perfectly round, with surprise. Barnaby had a matter-of-fact way of putting things that made it seem perfectly natural for a beggar to know just what was going on in the Palais des Princes.

'How do you know all this?' she stammered.

'I just know it, and let's leave it at that. And one thing more, little one. You must understand that if the Duke wishes to marry you off it is only because, in a town like this where the bourgeoisie are powerful, it is better that his mistress should be a married woman rather than a young maid. The Duke is a prudent fellow and he always knows how to turn a situation to his own advantage.'

'I just don't understand,' said Catherine. 'Messire de Brazey doesn't seem to me to be the stuff from which willing cuckolds are made.'

This was no more than the truth, and Barnaby was struck by her logic. He scratched his head and made a terrible face.

'I see your point, and in truth I do not know why he should have chosen his Treasurer sooner than another man, except perhaps that he isn't married. Garin de Brazey is just the man in every respect save that he is uncommonly difficult to handle. Perhaps the Duke could not find anyone more suitable among his loyal followers. It's obvious that the thing he hopes to accomplish by this marriage is to introduce you into Court circles. I suppose you have accepted. It is not the sort of offer one turns down.'

'You are wrong about that. To date I have refused.'

Carefully and patiently Catherine described her adventures in Flanders to her old friend. Sensing that this was not the moment to keep anything back, she told him exactly what had happened; how she had met Arnaud de Montsalvy, how, finding an old beloved memory come to life again in him, she had fallen in love at first sight, and how Mathieu's summons had torn her from his arms just as she was about to give herself to him. She talked and talked, without effort or embarrassment, and quite frankly and openly, omitting nothing. Sitting on one corner of the mattress, with her hands clasped round her knees, her gaze lost in the dark shadows of the attic, she seemed to be telling herself a beautiful love story. Barnaby held his breath so as not to break the spell. He realized that for the moment Catherine had forgotten he was there.

When the girl stopped talking, silence fell between them both. Catherine turned her gaze on her old friend again as he meditated, head sunk on his chest.

'If I understand aright,' he said finally, 'you have refused Garin de Brazey because you want to keep yourself pure and inviolate for this young fellow who hates and despises you and

only just prevented himself killing you because you are a woman
. . . or, more likely, because he was wounded and couldn't see
how he would get away with it in a place like that inn where you
were staying. Are you quite sure you aren't a bit soft in the
head ?'

'Soft in the head or not,' Catherine said shortly. 'That is
how things stand. I don't wish to belong to any other
man.'

'I should just like to hear you say that to the Duke,' Barnaby
groaned. 'I wonder what he will think ? Anyway, how do you
expect to get rid of Garin ? He is much too loyal a servant of the
Duke's to be shaken off easily . . . and besides you are too pretty
to be relinquished without a struggle. If you refuse, you will
only bring the Duke's wrath down upon your head, and the
heads of your entire family. He isn't famous for his sweet
nature, that Duke of ours. So what then ?'

'That's what I came to see you about. . . .'

Catherine stood up and stretched herself, feeling cramped by
her sitting position. Her slender figure seemed taller in the rosy,
dancing candlelight. Her resplendent golden hair enveloped her
in a sort of radiance which suddenly made the old man's heart
ache.

The girl's beauty was almost blinding, and Barnaby, more
anxious for her than he liked to admit, had a presentiment that
she was one of those rare women for whom wars are fought, for
whom men kill themselves, and who rarely bring happiness to
the men who possess them, so dangerous is any sort of
excess. It is never a good thing to stand out so far above the
norm. . . .

He drained the pitcher of wine and then threw it aside carelessly. The pitcher broke and some fragments rolled into the far
corners of the room.

'What do you expect me to do ?' he asked quietly.

'I want you to make this marriage impossible. I know you
have the means . . . and the men too. There must be some way
of preventing the marriage without my having to refuse directly,
or Garin de Brazey having to go against his master.'

'Which he wouldn't be prepared to do in any case, sweetheart. I see only one solution. For you or Garin. I don't suppose you are prepared to die, are you?'

Catherine shook her head, speechlessly, her eyes fixed stubbornly on her dusty shoes. Barnaby was not misled by this silence.

'Well, that leaves him! That's it, isn't it? In order to remain faithful to some silly love affair you condemn a man to death in cold blood. . . . And probably several others with him, because you don't suppose that once the Treasurer is dead the Duke Provost will simply sit there twiddling his thumbs?'

Barnaby's voice cut mercilessly into the girl's heart with the searching precision of a surgeon's knife. He forced her to see herself and her motives clearly, and she was ashamed of what she saw. The glimpses that this strange night had given her of her innermost self were rather terrifying. Nevertheless, if Garin's death were the only thing which could save her from a marriage which both terrified and frightened her, she was ready to accept it in cold blood. She signified as much to Barnaby, and her icy resolution astounded the old man.

'I don't wish to belong to that man. Do what you like, but get rid of him.'

Once again there was silence, dense and solid as a mass of earth, between the girl enclosed in her steely resolve and the beggar, who was bewildered by what he had just discovered about her. In fact Barnaby felt closer to her now; he found her easier to understand. It was a little as though this child he loved were his own daughter instead of the daughter of quiet working folk. How could the worthy Gaucher and his devout wife Jacquette ever have given birth to this little wild animal in petticoats? Barnaby smiled inwardly at their consternation had they but known. He finally smiled outright.

'I'll see what I can do,' he said at length. 'Now you had better go home. Did you have any trouble getting here?'

As briefly as she could, Catherine described her encounter with Dimanche-l'Assommeur and Jehan des Écus and how she had finally managed to make them release her.

'They sound like an excellent bodyguard,' Barnaby approved.
'I'll tell them to see you home again. Don't worry. You can trust
them now that it is I who appoint them your guardian angels.'

Sure enough, a few minutes later Catherine left Jacquot's
tavern with the same ruffianly companions, one on either side of
her. She left Sara asleep on the stairs. Her return was as peaceful as her journey there had been eventful. Whenever a
frightening shadow appeared one or other of them would
murmur a few words in the beggars' incomprehensible argot,
and the shadow would melt back into the darkness.

The wind was rising, and a storm seemed to be in the offing
by the time the two beggars took their leave of their protégée at
the top of the rue Griffon. Mathieu's house was visible from
there and Catherine no longer felt afraid. Besides, she was now
on such good terms with her ferocious mentors that she was
able to bid them farewell sweetly. Jehan des Écus spoke up on
behalf of them both. He seemed to be the brains of that odd
team, while Dimanche provided the brute strength.

'I generally beg outside the door of St Benigne,' he said.
'You will always find me there should you need me. You are
Barnaby's friend already, and you shall be mine too if you so
wish.'

His hoarse creaking voice took on strangely gentle modu-
lations during this little speech, and this finished the job of
wiping away any bad memories of their first encounter that
evening. She knew that an offer of friendship from a beggar is
always sincere, since nothing obliges him to make it, just as a
threat from him should never be taken lightly.

The front door barely squeaked as Catherine pushed it open.
She ran upstairs without making a sound and got into bed.
Uncle Mathieu was still snoring.

What remained of the night was too short for Catherine to
get her full ration of sleep. She did not hear Notre-Dame ring
out the end of the curfew and she ignored Loyse's brusque
shaking which was intended to get her up in time for Mass.
Loyse finally departed in a fury, vanquished by her sister's
profound lethargy and predicting her eternal damnation.

Catherine, oblivious of everything but the downy comfort of her pillow, dropped straight off to sleep again.

It was close on nine o'clock when she finally went downstairs to the kitchen. The atmosphere in there was stormy.

Jacquette was ironing the family's clothes on a trestle table by the hearth, using a hollow flat-iron in which she put a shovelful of glowing embers from time to time. There were beads of sweat on her brow under the white linen coif and she pursed her lips in a way which Catherine knew well. Something must have displeased her. She was obviously raging inwardly. The way she attacked the linen sheet with her iron pointed to a temper barely kept under control. Loyse sat by the window with her back turned to her. She was winding thread on to a spindle, also without speaking a word. Her thin fingers twisted the flax quickly, and the thread wound around the spindle which stood beside her. Studying the expression on her face Catherine came to the conclusion that she and her mother must have had words.

To her great astonishment she saw that Sara had returned home. The gipsy woman must have returned at daybreak. Dressed in her usual dark-blue fustian dress with a big white apron wrapped round her waist, she was busily peeling a huge basket of brussels sprouts for soup. She was the only one who turned round when Catherine entered the room, and she winked at her knowingly. The passionate girl of the night before slept once more deep within this strange woman and there was not a trace of her to be seen on that familiar face. But Loyse too had seen her sister come in and she whispered maliciously:

'Bow down, slaves, here comes the high and mighty Dame de Brazey . . . who deigns to leave her chamber to inspect her scullions.'

'Hold your tongue, Loyse,' said Jacquette coldly. 'Leave your sister alone.'

But it took more than that to silence Loyse when she had something on her mind. Dropping her spindle, she jumped up and stood in front of her sister, hands on hips and mouth twisted unpleasantly.

'Too grand to get up at dawn now are we? The dirty chores, the early morning Mass are for humble people like me and your mother! While you mince about putting on airs like a princess, imagining yourself already married to your one-eyed Treasurer.'

Jacquette threw her iron angrily down on the hearth. She had gone red to the roots of her still blonde hair. But Catherine intervened before she could launch into a tirade.

'I slept badly,' she said with a slight shrug. 'I stayed a little longer in bed than usual, that's all. It isn't a crime, and I shall work a little later tonight to make up for it.'

Turning her back on Loyse, whose contorted face distressed her, Catherine quickly embraced her mother and bent over to pick up the flat-iron she had dropped. She was just about to fill it with hot embers when Jacquette spoke up.

'No, Cathy . . . you mustn't do these chores any more. Your fiancé doesn't wish you to. You must start learning how to behave in your new station in life, and there isn't too much time left as it is.'

Catherine's temper rose instantly.

'What do you mean? My fiancé? I haven't accepted his proposal yet. Anyway, if he wants to marry me that much he must take me as I am.'

'You have absolutely no choice in the matter, my dear, a page came from the Dowager Duchess only this morning. Until your marriage you must leave this house and go and live with the Dame de Champdivers, who is married to the Duke's Chamberlain. She will educate you to take your place in Court life, and teach you fine manners and courtly ways.'

As her mother spoke Catherine's rage grew. Jacquette's red eyes betrayed her distress and the flat tone of her mother's voice added fuel to her fury.

'Not another word, Maman! If Messire de Brazey wishes to marry me I can't stop him, since it is an order from Monseigneur Philippe. But nothing will ever make me leave my own family to go and live with other people, or leave this house for a place where I shan't feel at home and where people will look down on me. I absolutely refuse!'

Loyse's sarcastic chuckle was the last straw for Catherine. She whipped round and confronted her furiously.

'Stop laughing like an idiot! If you must know, the idea of this marriage makes me feel ill and the only reason I am accepting is to spare you the consequences of a refusal. If I had only myself to think of I should have crossed the frontier of Burgundy by now, on my way back to Paris . . . to our own home!'

The two sisters would probably have come to blows, as Loyse was still laughing unpleasantly, if Sara had not slipped between them. She took Catherine by the shoulders and steered her well away from her sister.

'Calm down! You must listen to what your mother says, child. She is quite right. You only make things worse for her by taking it all so badly.'

Jacquette had in fact collapsed on the hearthstone and was sobbing with her head in her apron. Catherine could not endure seeing her mother cry and she ran towards her.

'Don't cry, Maman, please! I'll do what you want. But you can't ask me to leave home and go and live with a lot of strangers. . . .'

The last remark was both an entreaty and a question. Large tears rolled down Catherine's cheeks as she buried her face in her mother's neck. Jacquette wiped her eyes and gently stroked her younger daughter's blonde plaits.

'You will go to the Dame de Champdivers for my sake, Catherine. Don't you see – Messire de Brazey will want to visit you every day, once your banns have been published, to pay his court. He can't come here! The house isn't worthy of him. He would be embarrassed.'

'Too bad,' said Catherine bitterly. 'He can always stay at home!'

'Now, now . . . he would be embarrassed, as I said, but I would be even more so! The Dame de Champdivers is elderly, and kind, from what I hear, and you will not be unhappy with her. You would learn suitable manners. And besides,' Jacquette added sadly, forcing a smile, 'you will soon have to leave this house for your husband's in any case. This will act as a transitional stage, and then, when you move to Garin de Brazey's house, you won't feel quite so lost. Anyway, there is nothing to stop you from coming here as often as you like.'

Catherine listened in despair as her mother recited what appeared to be a well-learnt lesson. Uncle Mathieu must have harangued her for hours to reduce her to this state of hopeless resignation. But it was pointless arguing with Jacquette in her present condition. And if Barnaby came to her assistance, as she hoped he would, all this would soon be no more than a bad dream. She capitulated.

'Very well then, I'll go to the Dame de Champdivers. On one condition. . . .'

'What is that?' asked Jacquette, who couldn't decide whether she should rejoice at her daughter's prompt submission or lament that it should have come about so rapidly.

'That Sara comes with me.'

When she finally found herself alone with Sara that night in the family's communal room, Catherine decided that the moment had come to put words into action. It was no longer the moment for secrets and reticences because they would have to leave the very next day for the beautiful town house where their future hostess lived.

Without wasting a moment Catherine told Sara about her expedition of the previous night. Sara did not even raise her eyebrows on finding that the secret of her disappearances had been found out. She even smiled faintly, because she understood, from the tone of the girl's voice, that she not only did not blame her, but actually rather sympathized with her.

'Why are you telling me this tonight?' she asked.

'Because I want you to go back to Jacquot's tonight and take a letter from me to Barnaby.'

Sara was not a woman to argue, or show astonishment. Her only reaction was to take a dark cloak from her coffer and wrap it round herself.

'*Dame!*' she exclaimed.

Catherine scribbled a few hurried words, read them through carefully, and then sanded the wet.ink.

'You must act swiftly,' she wrote to Barnaby. 'You are the only one who can help me, and you know how much I hate the man we spoke of. . . .'

Satisfied with her note, she handed the folded paper to Sara.

'There,' she said. 'And hurry.'

'Barnaby will have your letter in a quarter of an hour. Keep the door open for me.'

She slipped out of the room as soundlessly as a shadow, and although Catherine strained her ears she could not hear the lightest footstep or the door creak ever so faintly. Sara seemed able to vanish into thin air at will.

Gedeon, on his perch, with his head buried in his chest, dozed with one eye closed and the other open, watching his mistress occupying herself in an unusual fashion for this time of night. She was rummaging in chests and taking out piles of dresses. She held them up to her for a moment, then she threw some on the ground and laid others on the bed.

This unexpected bustling about encouraged the bird to go through its tricks, since it was clearly not yet time to sleep. Gedeon shook himself, fluffed out his gleaming plumage, stretched out his neck and squawked:

'God save the Duke!'

He did not get a chance to repeat the cry. One of Catherine's discarded dresses, thrown by an unerring hand, landed on top of him, completely blinding him and half suffocating him into the bargain.

'I hope the Duke goes to the devil . . . and you with him!' the girl shouted angrily.

Sara returned towards midnight. Catherine sat up in bed waiting for her, having snuffed out all the candles.

'Well!' she asked.

'Barnaby says all goes well. He will let you know at the Hôtel des Champdivers what he has decided to do . . . and what you will have to do too.'

CHAPTER SEVEN

MOTHER OF A ROYAL FAVOURITE

A RAY OF blue and red sunlight, flecked with gold, streamed from a high stained-glass window representing St Cecilia holding a harp, and enveloped Catherine, who stood motionless in the middle of the huge room with a seamstress crouched at her feet, her mouth bristling with pins. It barely lit up the sombre garments of an elderly lady, dressed entirely in brown velvet trimmed with marmot, despite the heat outside. She was sitting bolt upright in a high-backed oak chair, supervising the fitting. Marie de Champdivers had a gentle face with delicate features, and a faded blue gaze which her double-pointed headdress of priceless Flemish lace softened prettily. But the most striking thing about her was the look of profound sadness which seemed to belie her indulgent smile. In Marie de Champdivers one sensed a woman consumed by a secret grief.

In the hands of the best seamstress in the town the pink and silver brocade which Garin de Brazey had chosen had become a queenly garment in which Catherine's beauty blazed so brightly that her hostess felt quite uneasy. Like Barnaby, the old lady felt that such physical perfection carried more seeds of destruction with it than promises of happiness. But Catherine was looking at herself in the mirror of polished silver with such childlike delight that Madame de Champdivers took good care to keep her sombre reflections to herself. The shimmering, supple cloth which flashed like a river at sunrise fell in graceful folds from her slim waist and fanned out behind in a short train. The dress was extremely simple. Catherine had refused the least ornament, claiming that the cloth itself was ornament enough. The deeply cut neckline, in a wide V-shape, descended as far as the sash which was placed just below the bosom. The neckline revealed the silver cloth of an underdress, on which a flower pin of pink pearls, each one perfectly round, glowed softly. This was the first costly gift from Garin to his fiancée. There were more pearls twined round her silver cone-shaped headdress, with its swathing of pink gauze, and round the girl's slender neck. The dress was cut low behind as well, showing her shoulder-blades. The long sleeves, however, fitted her arms closely to halfway down her hands.

Marie de Champdivers spoke up in her measured tones:

'That fold on the right needs to be raised a bit . . . there, under her arm, it doesn't hang right. That's much better! You look dazzling, child, but one glance in the mirror must have convinced you of that!'

'Thank you, madame,' said Catherine, smiling and pleased despite herself.

During the month she had been living at the Champdivers' she had seen her fears and prejudices melt away, one by one. Her aristocratic mentor treated her without either haughtiness or sarcasm. She had received her like a young lady of noble birth, without in any way making her feel conscious of her humble origins, and Catherine for her part had found in this good and gentle woman a friend and true counsellor.

She was much less taken with the master of the house. Guillaume de Champdivers, Chamberlain to the Duke Philippe and Member of his Privy Council, was a dry, abrupt, old man. His look made Catherine feel uneasy. The expression was like a horse dealer's sizing up the points of a good filly. There was something of the trafficker in human flesh about this self-controlled, silent old man who never raised his voice and who stepped so noiselessly that he always appeared at one's side without warning. Through Sara, Catherine had learnt of the strange origins of his considerable fortune, and how the one-time stable master to Jean-sans-Peur had risen to the position of Chamberlain and Counsellor of State. Some fifteen years earlier, Guillaume de Champdivers had handed over his ravishing fifteen-year-old only daughter, Odette, to his master, Duke Jean. She was not destined for the Duke himself, but to become the mistress, keeper, ever-vigilant companion and also, it must be admitted, spy, over the unfortunate King Charles VI, who was ravaged by insanity. Thus, by a scandalous piece of horse-dealing, quite devoid of pity or shame, the chaste, gentle girl had been delivered to an unhappy lunatic whose former good looks were gradually disintegrating in filth and vermin. For as long as his bouts of madness lasted, sometimes for weeks or even months on end, no one could persuade him to let himself be washed.

But then, just as Jean-sans-Peur was congratulating himself on having got the King's weak mind firmly under his control, he found that he had in fact brought him the one thing which could soften and sweeten the royal sufferings: a woman's tenderness. Odette had loved her unfortunate prince and she had become a guardian angel to him, the gentle, patient, loving fairy whom nothing can dishearten. A little girl was born of this strange love affair. The King had recognized her as his daughter. She was given the name de Valois. And the people of Paris, who hated their unworthy ruler, the fat Isabeau, were not mistaken, in their simple common sense, in their summing-up of Odette. Spontaneously, and tenderly, they had christened her 'The Little Queen'.

Nevertheless, deep in the heart of Marie de Champdivers, bereft of her only child for fifteen years, a wound remained which had never healed, though she never displayed it in any way, and hid the bitterness she felt towards her husband beneath a smile.

Thus, enlightened by Sara, Catherine had spontaneously found a place in her heart for the old lady without in the least suspecting what deep compassion she inspired in return. Marie de Champdivers knew too much about Court life and about men in general not to have understood, the moment she first laid eyes on Catherine, that her task was not so much to form a fitting wife for Garin de Brazey as a worthy mistress for Philippe of Burgundy.

As Sara entered the room, with a tray balanced on one arm, the seamstress got to her feet and stood back some distance to admire her handiwork better.

'If Maître Garin isn't satisfied,' she said with a broad smile, 'then he must truly be a hard man to please! By the Holy Mother of God, did anyone ever see a lovelier bride? I will wager that Messire Garin, who got back from Ghent just this morning, will be hurrying round to kneel before his future lady and—'

Marie de Champdivers cut short the good woman's flow of chatter with a single gesture, knowing full well that it would be hard to stop her if once she got going.

'You have done very well, my good Gauberte, very well indeed! I will let you know whether Messire Garin is pleased in due course. Now please leave us.'

At a glance from the old lady Sara accompanied the seamstress to the stairs. Catherine and her hostess were left alone. With a pretty, graceful movement Catherine sat down on a velvet cushion at the old lady's feet. Her smile had vanished and it was replaced by a frown so melancholy that Marie de Champdivers stroked her forehead with a finger as if to smooth it away.

'The news of your betrothed's return does not appear to fill you with excitement and pleasure, my dear? Does Garin displease you? Don't you love him?'

Catherine shrugged.

'How can I be expected to love him? I hardly know him; apart from the morning he helped me to my feet in Notre-Dame, I have only seen him once, and that was here, the evening I first arrived here. Since then he has been in Ghent with the Duke to attend the Duchess's funeral. And besides . . .'

She stopped, stumbling for a moment over the difficult avowal she was on the point of making, then plunging on regardless, '. . . besides, he frightens me!'

Marie de Champdivers did not answer at once. Her hand lingered on the girl's forehead and her gaze lost itself in contemplation of the coloured reflections made by the stained-glass window as if she hoped to find an answer there to this unformulated but unanswerable question.

'And . . . what about the Duke?' she asked, after a barely perceptible pause. 'What do you think of him?'

Catherine raised her pensive face abruptly. A sparkle of girlish malice flashed in her eyes.

'A very attractive young man,' she said with a smile, 'but a little too conscious of the fact. A fine gentleman, well spoken, gallant with the ladies and skilled in the little games of love and courtship . . . or so rumour has it, at least. In short, an accomplished prince. But—'

'But?'

'But,' Catherine finished, laughing gaily, 'if, as they say, he is only marrying me off to get me all the quicker into his bed, he is making a mistake!'

Astonishment brought Marie de Champdivers back sharply from the melancholy regions where her imagination had been wandering. She looked at the girl with comical surprise. So Catherine knew what awaited her? And not only that, but she was actually planning to send the Duke packing like any ordinary suitor after he had staked his all to win her?

'Do you really intend to?' she asked at length. 'Intend to refuse the Duke, I mean?'

'Why not? When I marry I intend to remain faithful to my husband as well as to my marriage vows. Therefore I shall not become Monseigneur's mistress. Let him seek his consolation somewhere else.'

Marie de Champdivers smiled this time, though a little sadly. If only her Odette had shown a little of this quiet, cheerful courage, a little of this sturdy resolution, when she had been handed over to Charles, so many things might have turned out differently! But then, she had been so young. No more than fifteen, whereas Catherine was more than twenty.

'Messire Garin is a lucky man,' the old lady said, with a sigh. 'Beauty, virtue, faithfulness. . . . He will have all that the most exacting man could ask.'

Catherine bowed her head and became serious all of a sudden.

'I wouldn't envy him too soon. Who knows what the future may have in store for him.'

T – G

She kept her own counsel about the little scribbled note which Sara had brought to her that morning with her breakfast. The note was from Barnaby. The Cockleshell Man informed her both of Garin's return and also that everything was ready for that evening.

'You must try to keep the person in question with you until after the curfew,' Barnaby wrote. 'That should not be too difficult for you.'

The day was drawing in by the time Garin de Brazey crossed the threshold of the Hôtel des Champdivers. From behind the little leaded window-panes of her bedchamber, Catherine watched him leap from his black horse with a strange tight feeling round her heart. As always he was dressed entirely in black, impassive, chilly, but rich-looking, thanks to a heavy gold chain set with rubies which hung round his neck and a huge blood-red carbuncle which flashed in his hood. A valet followed behind, carrying a chest with a cover of purple cloth fringed with gold.

As soon as she had seen the tall black figure disappear into the house, Catherine left the window and sat down on the bed to wait till she was summoned. It was hot, in spite of the thick walls which kept the place cooler than most. But the girl shivered in her silver embroidered dress. She felt a sudden terror seize her now that the moment had come for her to confront the man whom she had already condemned to death. Her hands were icy, and she shivered all over in a sudden panic. With chattering teeth but burning cheeks she looked about her, wildly seeking some refuge or way of escape, because the mere idea of seeing Garin again, of touching his hand perhaps, left her feeling suddenly drained of strength, and weak to the point of fainting.

Muffled but ominous noises throughout the building reached her ears. With a great effort she dragged herself from her bed towards the door, where she stood, leaning against the wall to steady herself. She was no longer capable of sane thought. She was nothing but animal terror. Her hand tightened over the elaborately wrought door handle so convulsively that the metal edges bit into her forefinger and a drop of blood stood out. But her hand was shaking so violently that she was unable to open the door. It opened nevertheless and Sara appeared. She gave a little cry when she caught sight of Catherine standing there, white to the lips.

'What are you doing there? Come! They have sent for you.'

'I . . . I can't,' the girl stammered. 'I can't go down there.'

Sara gripped her by both shoulders and shook her like a rag doll. Her features in her brown face hardened till they looked like a tribal mask, carved from some rare and exotic wood.

'When one has the courage to wish for a certain thing, one must then have the courage to face up to it,' she declared roundly. 'Messire Garin awaits you.'

She softened a little when she saw tears well up in the large violet eyes. Letting go of Catherine, she walked across to the dressing-table, shrugging, and damped a linen cloth in the silver pitcher standing on it. Then she mopped the girl's face vigorously. Soon her natural colour returned to her cheeks. Catherine took a deep breath. And Sara did likewise.

'That's better! Now come along with me and try to put a good face on things,' she advised, taking Catherine by the arm and steering her towards the stairs. Incapable of showing any reaction by now, the girl let herself be escorted docilely.

The table had been laid for dinner in the large apartment on the first floor and stood against the chimney-place, where there was no fire at present. As she went in Catherine saw Marie de Champdivers sitting in her accustomed chair, and in the window embrasure she caught sight of her husband conversing quietly with Garin de Brazey.

It was the second time she had met the Lord Treasurer under the Champdivers' roof, but it was the first time she had felt the shock of finding his single eye fixed appreciatively upon her. When he had come to the Hôtel in the rue Tâtepoire the night of Catherine's arrival he had been too preoccupied to pay any attention to her. He had said a few trivial words, so banal that Catherine could no longer remember what they had been. He had spent almost the entire evening arguing with Guillaume de Champdivers, leaving his future wife to her own devices, and to the kindly solicitude of Marie. Catherine had been grateful for this indifference because it dispelled any lingering scruples she might have felt on his account.

Assuming that this evening would be a repetition of the other, she made her way across the room to bid them good evening. When they saw her coming, however, they both stopped talking and rose to their feet. Catherine's lowered eyes prevented her seeing the look of wondering surprise which spread across their faces and to which Garin gave poetic expression:

'A summer dawn is not more beautiful. You are a wonderful sight, my dear.'

As he spoke, his tall figure bent in a low bow, one hand on his heart, in answer to the girl's curtsey. Champdivers bowed too, a smile of satisfaction on his ferret's face. A girl of such exceptional beauty should be able to attach Philippe le Bon's fickle heart to herself for a long time, and Champdivers foresaw a long succession of honours and profits in recognition of the services rendered. He all but rubbed his hands. . . .

Garin, with an abrupt gesture, summoned the valet who had accompanied him and who now stood waiting in a corner, still holding the little purple velvet casket. The Treasurer opened it. All the light blazing from the tall iron torch-bearers seemed to be concentrated in the contents of the basket. With his long dexterous fingers, Garin drew out a heavy magnificent gold necklace, as massive and long as an order of chivalry. The links in the shape of flowers and leaves were studded with immense purple amethysts, of rare brilliance and purity, and with flawless orient pearls. There was a general cry of admiration as this marvel appeared, followed a second later by a matching pair of ear-rings.

'I dote on this violet colour, which is that of your eyes, Catherine,' he remarked in his slow, ponderous way. 'It suits your golden hair and clear skin. So I had this necklace made for you at Anvers. The stones come from a faraway chain of mountains, the Ural mountains on the borders of Asia. The successful completion of this necklace represents an enormous amount of courage and dedication on the part of men who have never known what it is to be afraid, and I would like to see you wear it with pleasure . . . because the amethyst is the stone of virtue . . . and chastity.'

As he laid the necklace across Catherine's trembling hands, she flushed deeply.

'I will wear it with pleasure since it is a gift from you, messire,' she said in so faint a voice that not everyone heard her clearly. 'Would you like to fasten it round my neck ?'

There was something comic about the Treasurer's horrified gesture of refusal, but it proved salutory to Catherine, who was on the point of swooning away.

'With that pink dress ? What an idea, my dear! I shall see that you have a dress made which will set off these amethysts as well as possible. Now, give me your hand.'

From the bottom of the casket Garin took a simple ring of twisted gold which he slipped over the girl's third finger.

'This,' he said gravely, 'is the token of our betrothal. The orders of Monseigneur the Duke are that we should marry at Christmas, as soon as the period of Court mourning is ended. He hopes to be present in person at the ceremony, which is indeed a great honour. He may even be a witness. Now take my arm and let us go to the table.'

Catherine obediently let herself be escorted. She still felt bewildered, but the sickness of a short while back seemed to be lifting. Garin had a way of organizing things and events which made them a little less frighteningly mysterious. One sensed that everything was easy for this rich and powerful man. All the easier because there was not a jot of feeling in either his words or his actions. Whether he was bestowing a King's ransom's worth of jewels or slipping the ring on her finger which would bind them together for life, the tone of his voice remained exactly the same. His hand was steady. His eye stayed cold and lucid. As she took her place beside him at the table where they were to share the same silver plate, Catherine caught herself wondering involuntarily what the life of such a man could be like.

He was an intimidating man, but his character seemed calm and even, and his generosity without limit. The girl reflected that there might even have been some agreeable aspects in such a marriage if, as there must be in any marriage, there were not the irritating, depressing question of conjugal intimacy, especially since she still nursed deep within herself the painful memory of the Inn of the Great Charlemagne, a recollection so wounding that only to think of it brought tears to her eyes.

'You seem distressed?' Garin's voice murmured beside her. 'I can imagine that a young woman does not take a step like this without a little apprehension. But there is no need to get things out of proportion. Married life can be quite a simple matter and even a pleasant one if one is only prepared to take a little trouble over it.'

He was obviously trying to reassure her, and she thanked him with a pale ghost of a smile, embarrassed by his attentiveness. Her thoughts suddenly flew towards Barnaby and what he might mean by 'Everything is ready'. What had he planned? What trap was he going to spring for this man before her, whose death would be followed by such grave consequences to herself? Catherine imagined him hidden in the shadow of a doorway, invisible in the darkness like Dimanche-l'Assommeur and Jehan des Écus had been the other night. In the crystal ball of her imagination she saw him suddenly materialize out of the shadow, a flash of steel in one hand, and fling himself on the horseman, forcing him out of his saddle. Then she saw him strike an inert body over and over again.

To free herself of this unpleasantly vivid picture, Catherine tried to interest herself in the conversation of the two men. They were talking politics and the women were neither expected nor invited to join in. Marie de Champdivers ate, or rather pecked away in silence, with her eyes on her plate.

'There are some serious loopholes in the Burgundian nobility,' her husband was saying. 'Several of the great families refuse to recognize the treaty of Troyes and think ill of Mon-

seigneur for having signed it. Among others the Prince of
Orange, the Sire de Saint-Georges, and the powerful Châteauvilain family, refuse to acknowledge the English heir and the
other clauses in the treaty which are deleterious to France. I
myself must admit to a certain repugnance.'

'Who does not?' Garin replied. 'It seems that his grief over
his father's death affected the Duke so deeply that he forgot
that he is primarily, despite all that has happened, a prince of
the French blood. He is aware of my feelings on this matter and
I have not concealed from him what I think about the treaty:
a scrap of paper which disinherits the Dauphin Charles in
favour of the English son-in-law, the conqueror who has been
devastating the country and covering us with shame and dishonour ever since the battle of Agincourt. Only a woman as far
gone in debauchery as this dreadful Isabeau, rotten to the core
with vice and greed, could have sunk so low and demeaned
herself to the extent of proclaiming her own son a bastard.'

'There are moments,' said Champdivers, nodding, 'when I
find Monseigneur's actions hard to understand. How can one
reconcile this great regret he expresses at not having been able
to fight at Agincourt along with the rest of the French nobility
with his subsequent action which almost invites the English to
enter the country? Could King Henry V's marriage to Catherine
de Valois, his late wife's sister, have been sufficient to make him
change his mind? I don't think so. . . .'

Garin turned aside for a moment to dip his greasy fingers into
the bowl of scented water which a valet held out to him.

'Nor do I! The Duke hates the English and fears the military
genius of Henry V. He is too good a knight not to genuinely
regret his absence from Agincourt and a disastrous, bloody but
heroic day of fighting. Unfortunately, or perhaps fortunately
from the point of view of this part of the country, he thinks in
terms of Burgundy rather than in terms of France, and if ever
he thinks of the fleurs-de-lys it is to reflect that the French
crown would have been far better placed on his own head than
on that of the unfortunate Charles VI. In the gamble of war
and politics he hopes to come off the winner in the long run

because he is rich, whereas the English are always short of money. He is making use of Henry V instead of the other way round. As for the Dauphin Charles, the Duke has never doubted his legitimacy at heart, but his hatred of him and his own ambitions find expression in this rejection.'

Guillaume de Champdivers took a deep draught of wine, gave a comfortable sigh and settled back comfortably into his cushions.

'They say that the Dauphin is doing everything in his power to win Burgundy over to his side again and that he recently sent a secret envoy here. Did some misfortune befall the envoy?'

'So it seems. Near Tournai Captain de Montsalvy was set upon and left for dead by a band of robbers who were as likely as not in the pay of Jean de Luxembourg, our military leader who is on the side of the English. He managed to escape, thanks to the timely assistance of an infidel, an Arab doctor who happened to be there, God knows why, and who took excellent care of him according to reports.'

Catherine's attention, which had been wandering a little during this exchange between the two men, was suddenly riveted. She drank in what Garin was saying. But just then he stopped talking to select some Damascus plums from the large platter in front of him. She could not resist asking him:

'And . . . what happened to this envoy? Did he succeed in seeing the Duke?'

Garin de Brazey turned towards her, half surprised, half amused. 'Your interest in my discourse, which some might think a little austere for a lady, comes as an agreeable surprise to me, Catherine. No, Arnaud de Montsalvy has not managed to see the Duke. His wounds delayed him for some time, and by the time he was able to resume his journey once more the Duke had long since left Flanders. Furthermore, Monseigneur has sent word that he had nothing to say to him. From the latest report it would seem that the captain has returned to the Château of Méhun-sur-Yèvre, where the Dauphin's Court is assembled, to complete his recovery.'

The Lord Treasurer seemed to be thoroughly well informed

about the actions and deeds of the Dauphin's entourage, and
Catherine longed to ask him further questions. But she felt
that it would be a mistake to show too much interest in an
Armagnac captain, so she merely said:

'Let us hope he has more success next time.'

The rest of the meal seemed to her to drag on tediously. The
two men were now discussing financial questions, and Catherine
understood nothing of them. Marie de Champdivers dozed in
her chair, still erect as ever. Catherine, for her part, took refuge
in her thoughts and did not come back to earth till Garin rose
to his feet and announced that he was about to leave.

The girl glanced at the window. It was not quite dark yet. It
was too early to let Garin depart. Barnaby had been insistent
that it should not be until after the curfew had sounded.
She cried hastily: 'What, messire, would you leave us so
soon?'

Garin began to laugh, and, leaning towards her, looked at her
with amused interest.

'This really is a night of surprises, my dear! I had not supposed that my company was so agreeable to you.'

Was he really pleased, or was his remark intended to be
mainly ironical? Catherine decided that this was not the
moment to worry about that, and she got out of the situation
with a clever evasion.

'I like to hear you talking,' she said, modestly lowering her
eyes. 'We still scarcely know each other. Unless you have some
business elsewhere or are finding this evening tediously long,
why don't you stay a little? There are so many things I want to
know about! After all, I know nothing at all about the Court, or
the people there, or the way one should behave. . . .'

She had gone too far, and she cursed herself for being so
clumsy; she was aware of the astonished looks directed at her
and did not dare look at her hostess for fear of the disapproving
expression which must have appeared on her face. To thus
solicit a man's company must have struck the good lady as the
height of immodesty. But the master of the house came
unexpectedly to her assistance. He was delighted to see a

marriage in which he had such interest getting off to such a good start.

'Stay awhile, my dear friend, since you have been requested to do so so prettily! Your home is not far from here. And I do not suppose you are afraid of thieves!'

With a smile in his fiancée's direction, Garin sat down again. Catherine gave a sigh of relief, but she did not dare look at the man whom she was betraying in this fashion. She despised herself for this part she was forced to play, but the love which sustained her was stronger than the pricks of conscience. Anything was better than belonging to a man other than Arnaud!

When Garin finally took leave of Catherine and his hosts an hour later, the curfew had sounded three-quarters of an hour before and it was pitch dark. Catherine watched stony-eyed as Garin rode off into the night, to a sudden and violent death. But, since it is not so easy to quiet a rebellious conscience, she did not close her eyes once that night.

'Garin de Brazey is only slightly wounded and Barnaby has been arrested.'

Sara's voice woke Catherine from the half-sleep into which she had fallen since dawn. She saw the gipsy standing beside her ashen-faced, with dull eyes and trembling hands. She did not quite catch the meaning of what she was saying at first. She seemed to be saying something absurd and incredible. . . . But then Sara repeated the terrible words to Catherine, who gazed at her appalled. Garin de Brazey alive? Somehow that did not seem quite so serious now and Catherine even felt a little relief on his account. But Barnaby arrested?

'Who told you this?' she asked in a faint voice.

'Jehan des Écus! He came round here to beg this morning with his bag and staff. He couldn't tell me any more because just then the cook came over to listen to what we were saying. That's all I know.'

'Help me to dress then!'

Catherine had just remembered the advice the young beggar had given her – to seek him out at the entrance to St Benigne if she should ever need him. This was the moment, if any! In a flash she was dressed and her hair arranged. As the whole house was in an uproar she decided to go out without making too many excuses. The news that Garin had been the victim of an attack had spread like wildfire through the town with everyone adding something to it in the telling. Catherine had only to say that she was going to the churches in the town to offer up thanks to God for having spared her fiancé's life for Marie de Champdivers to give her permission to go out with Sara.

As they hurried through the Bourg they saw the housewives calling from window to window across the street, or gathering in little groups in the shadow of the painted metal shop-signs to discuss the latest rumours. No one seemed really surprised by the news about Garin. The Lord Treasurer's rise to wealth and power had been too rapid and his delight in ostentation too obvious not to have made him many enemies. But Catherine and Sara did not stop to listen to the gossip. They were approaching the town ramparts and the immense buildings which comprised the abbey of St Benigne, one of the largest in France. Catherine could think of nothing but what she was about to learn from Jehan des Écus. Her heart ached.

There were few people about in the square outside the church and the entrance to the abbey. A handful of people were going into the church. High up in the tall octagonal towers built of new stone the colour of thick cream, the bells were tolling the funeral knell. The two women had to wait while a funeral procession wound its way slowly across the square into the church. Monks, in black serge robes, carried a litter on which the dead man lay, his face exposed. The family and a few mourners followed behind: not many people in all since this was not an important funeral.

'I can't see Jehan,' Catherine whispered behind her veil. 'Yes, there he is! In the entrance . . . that monk in a brown habit. . . .'

The beggar had donned the brown habit of a mendicant friar, and with his bag slung over one shoulder and staff in hand, he was soliciting alms for his monastery in a nasal sing-song voice. As Catherine went up to him, she saw that he had recognized her by the way his eyes sharpened under the dusty hood. She went close to him, placed a coin in his outstretched hand and murmured rapidly:

'I must speak to you, at once.'

'As soon as these loud-mouths have gone into the church,' said the pseudo-monk in the same way. '*De profundis clamavi ad te, Domine!*'

Once the funeral cortège had gone into the church he drew the two women under the shadow of the large porch.

'What do you want to know?' he asked.

'What happened!'

'That's simple enough! Barnaby wanted to do the job by himself . . . it was a private matter, he said, and far too risky to involve any of the other lads. Not that it mightn't have been worth the risk to us, considering how much jewellery the Treasurer usually has about his person! But that's Barnaby for you! All he would allow me to do was keep an eye open for him. I tried to persuade him to take l'Assommeur with him, to be on the safe side, you understand? Brazey is still a young man and Barnaby is getting on a bit. But you might as well try to reason with a stone wall! He is as stubborn as a bishop's mule. So we had to do as he said. My job was to keep watch over towards the Bourg while he hid behind the fountain at the street corner. I saw a man coming, with one groom behind. I whistled to warn Barnaby and then hid myself. As the Trea-surer rode by the fountain Barnaby leapt upon him with such force that he knocked him off his horse. They wrestled on the ground for a bit while I kept an eye on the groom. But he wasn't a brave fellow. Poor coward that he was, he took to his heels at once crying out for mercy! . . . Then I saw Barnaby. I was just about to step forward to help him throw the body into the Ouche. I had even collected some large stones together, when I saw that it was the other man, Garin. . . . Barnaby was still lying there on the ground, moaning away like a woman in labour.'

'It seems to me that *that* was the moment to come to his assistance, if any,' Catherine cut in dryly.

'I was just about to, to be sure! Only, just as I was getting out my knife to fight it out with Garin, the Watch came marching out of the rue Tâtepoire. Brazey called out to them and they came pelting towards us. I only just had time to make myself scarce. There were rather too many of them for one poor solitary beggar to take on,' he finished with a contrite smile.

'What have they done with Barnaby?'

'I saw a couple of fellows pick him up and drag him away, none too ceremoniously. He was as quiet and still as a dead pig, but he wasn't dead. . . . I could hear him breathing! Anyway, I heard the officer of the Watch order them to take him to prison. That's where he is now . . . in the Château of the Gens d'Armes. You know the one I mean?'

Catherine nodded. She was nervously twisting the corner of her velvet-covered Book of Hours between her fingers, feverishly searching her mind for some solution to the most pressing problem – how to get her old friend out of prison.

'We must get him out of there!' she said. 'He must be freed somehow.'

A mirthless smile raised one corner of the pseudo-monk's twisted mouth. He shook his wooden pan in the direction of three housewives who were passing by, in bonnets and aprons. They looked like three stall-holders from the Bourg market-place who had come to say a prayer or two between sales.

'He'll get out of there all right, but perhaps not the way you mean! They'll take him for a stroll to the Morimont for a nice chat with Monseigneur's chief "butcher"!'

The action with which he accompanied this last remark was singularly explicit. With his forefinger Jehan went through the motion of slitting his throat. Catherine turned pale.

'If anyone is responsible for this affair, it is I,' she said decisively. 'I can't let Barnaby die like that, in my place! Is there any way we can help him to escape . . . with money? Lots of money?'

She was thinking of the jewels Garin had given her, which

she would gladly sacrifice. The word money had an instant effect on Jehan. His eyes started to sparkle like flames.

'That might be possible! Only I don't think Jacquot-de-la-Mer will be much help to you, fair Catherine. You are not very popular with him at the moment! They are saying that you have got one of their best men into trouble and all for some silly woman's nonsense! In other words, I suggest you keep well out of their way for the time being. Nobody would listen to your explanations and you might come to harm. Jacquot's not the gentlest of men when he's rubbed up the wrong way!'

'But what about you?' Catherine begged. 'Won't *you* help me?'

Jehan did not answer at once. He thought for a moment, then shrugged:

'Yes. I'll help you. Because I'm the sort of fool who could never say no to a pretty girl! But what can you and I do between us?'

Speechlessly, Catherine bent her head to hide the tears which filled her eyes. Sara tugged her sleeve and discreetly drew her attention to three women who were just then entering the church, and were staring curiously at the odd trio they made. Jehan shook his pan at them and begged for alms in a nasal whine. Once the women had gone he whispered:

'You had better not stay here. . . . I'll think it over and see if I can't come up with something. After all, they haven't executed Barnaby yet . . . and that accursed Treasurer is still alive. . . .'

The reference to Garin suddenly checked Catherine's tears. An idea had come to her. A crazy idea perhaps, or at least a desperate one, which often amounts to the same thing. She took Sara's arm.

'Come,' she said, in such a decisive voice that the gipsy was startled.

'Where, my love?'

'To see Messire de Brazey. I must speak to him. . . .'

Without giving Sara time to protest, Catherine turned and left St Benigne. When she came to any decision she always acted upon it at once without stopping to weigh up the pros and cons. Hurrying along behind her Sara breathlessly tried to persuade her that such a visit, on the part of a young unmarried girl, was not at all seemly, that the Dame de Champdivers would undoubtedly scold her severely, and that Catherine was endangering her reputation by visiting a man, even if he were her fiancé. Catherine hurried on without listening, her eyes fixed on the ground and a worried frown creasing her brow.

Leaving the church of St Jean behind on her right, she turned down into the narrow rue Poulaillerie, where the air was loud with the cackling and squawking of hundreds of hens, geese and ducks. The low, picturesque houses with their brightly daubed signs and ancient Hebraic emblems harked back to the days when this street was part of the Jewish quarter. Garin Brazey lived at the far end of the town, a large and imposing mansion, surrounded by high walls, which stood on the corner of the rue Portelle, where the goldsmiths had their glittering, enticing shops.

As she came out into the market-place the tripe-sellers' cauldrons were bubbling away on all sides. Catherine held her nose to shut out the nauseating smell of blood and fat. The market was in full cry, and it was hard work pushing one's way between the butchers' stalls which spread out over half the street and the peasant women's baskets overflowing with vegetables and fruit. There was a festive atmosphere about the place, which usually delighted Catherine. But this particular morning she found that the noisy, lively scene irritated her unendurably. She was just about to turn into the rue de la Parcheminerie when the figure of a man caught her eye.

He was large and powerfully built, with long arms and a slightly crouching walk so that he looked rather like a big monkey. His grey hair, cut in a square bob, showed beneath a red frieze hood. He was dressed entirely in reddish leather. He moved slowly forward, pointing with a long white stick to the goods he wished to buy, and the merchants, in nervous haste, hurried to place them in the basket which was carried by a servant who followed behind. The sight of this man made

Catherine shudder, but it was Sara who suddenly gave expression to the thought in both their minds.

'Maître Joseph Blaigny,' she whispered.

Catherine did not answer and turned her head away. For it was indeed the public executioner of Dijon doing his marketing. . . .

The injured man's face was a pale dot at the far end of the chamber, which seemed enormous and very dark to Catherine. Tall shutters of painted oak were half drawn across the high, mullioned windows, set with panes of glass, and they shut out almost all the sunlight. When she first entered the room, behind a valet, she had to pause for a moment to let her eyes grow accustomed to the darkness. A faraway voice addressed her, slowly:

'What an unexpected pleasure, my dear! . . . I would not have dared hope for such solicitude on your part. . . .'

His voice expressed irony, surprise and a little contempt all at once, but Catherine did not stop to consider what the master of the house might be thinking of her visit. Now that she was there, the main thing was to carry out the strange mission, which had brought her thither. She took a few steps forward. As she went forward she found she was able to distinguish the things around her better and she began to take in the details of the plain but sumptuous décor. Garin was lying in a large bed which stood in the farthermost corner of the room, opposite the windows. The bed was entirely hung with purple velvet, quite plain and unadorned, save for the silver cords which held back the heavy curtains. The Seigneur de Brazey's arms were emblazoned above the bedhead, together with his enigmatic motto, 'Never', repeated several times over. 'A motto which seems to refuse something or someone, but who and what?' thought Catherine.

Garin watched her approach in silence. He wore a robe of the same colour as the bed, as much of it as could be seen under the bedcovers and a large throw of black fur. He was bareheaded apart from a small bandage on his forehead. It was the first time

Catherine had seen him without a hood, and she felt as though she were face to face with a complete stranger. Against this pale face and short silver-streaked brown hair, his black eye-patch stood out more starkly and noticeably than it did under the shadow of a voluminous hood. Catherine felt her confidence ebbing as she crossed the slippery black marble floor, stepping wherever she could on the little islands of safety provided by an archipelago of rugs in muted colours into which her feet sank luxuriously without making a sound. There were few pieces of furniture in this room, whose stone walls were hung with purple velvet like the bed. They included an ebony credence which held a collection of exquisite and finely carved ivory statuettes, a table, standing between two X-shaped chairs drawn up near a window, on which a chessboard of amethyst and silver sparkled in the light, and, most striking of all, a large ornate chair made entirely of solid silver and crystal. It stood slightly raised above floor level on a dais whose two steps were covered with carpet. A veritable throne . . .

It was this lordly chair, whose raised platform brought it to the height of the bed, that Garin signed to the girl to sit in. She went up to it with slow, hesitant steps, but her courage returned a little when she sat down and could grip the two silver arms firmly with both hands. She coughed to clear her throat and asked:

'Are you badly hurt?'

'I was beginning to wonder whether you had lost your voice. Really, Catherine, ever since you entered this room you have been behaving like a criminal in the dock. No. I am not seriously wounded, thank you. A slight stab wound in one shoulder and a bump on my head. In other words, nothing serious. Are you satisfied?'

Catherine suddenly felt sick at having to pretend to a solicitude she did not feel. She knew she could not keep up the pretence much longer. What was the point of hiding behind the convenient screen of polite sentiments when there was a man's life at stake?

'You said just now,' she remarked, throwing back her head

and looking him straight in the eye, 'that I looked like a criminal in the dock, and in a way you were right. I have come here to ask you to see that justice is done.'

The Treasurer's black brows climbed above the kerchief and single eye. His voice took on a harsher, steely tone.

'Justice? For whom?'

'For the man who attacked you. He did it on my orders. . . .'

The silence which fell between the silver chair and the velvet curtained bed was as heavy as the executioner's axe. Garin had not blinked an eyelid, but she noticed that he had grown still paler. Catherine, with both hands gripping the crystal chimerae which finished off the arms of her chair, had not bowed her head. She simply waited, trembling inwardly at the thought of what he was about to say, of the words which would issue out of that tight-lipped mouth and stony face. The humming of a bee suddenly filled her ears, driving out the sounds of the street outside, which seemed to have grown fainter in any case, and shattering the oppressive silence of a moment before. The girl was suddenly afraid, with a child's unreasoning fear. Garin de Brazey still said nothing. He just looked at her, and there was more intensity in the gaze of that single eye than in a thousand other looks. . . . The girl's body tensed itself for flight, ready to bound away. Then, abruptly, the wounded man spoke. His voice was colourless, empty of emotion, almost indifferent. He merely asked:

'You wanted to kill me? Do you hate me so much then?'

'I have nothing against you, personally. It is the marriage I hate and which I wanted to destroy. Once you were dead . . .'

'The Duke Philippe would have instantly chosen someone else. Do you suppose that I would have agreed to give you my name, and make you my wife, except at his command? I scarcely know you, and you are of exceedingly humble birth, but . . .'

Catherine interrupted him furiously, red to the ears:

'You have no right to insult me. I won't allow it. Who do you think you are, anyway? Your father was only a goldsmith, like mine!'

'I am not insulting you. I am simply stating the facts, and I would be grateful if you would allow me to finish. It is the least you can do, after last night's incident. As I was saying, you are of poor and humble birth, but you are beautiful. I would even go so far as to say that you are the most beautiful girl I have ever seen – and doubtless that the Duke has seen either. My orders were to marry you, with one aim only: to bring you to Court, and the bed of the man for whom you are destined!'

In one spring, Catherine was on her feet, standing over the sick man as he lay on his back.

'I won't! I refuse to be handed over to the Duke like a thing, or a serf!'

Garin signed to her to be silent and sit down again. His hard mouth curved in a thin smile at this childish display of rebelliousness, and his voice softened a little:

'We are all to a greater or lesser degree Monseigneur's serfs. Your wishes, like mine,' he added, with a trace of bitterness, 'are quite unimportant. Let us be quite frank with each other, if you don't mind, Catherine. It is the only thing which can stop us hating, and waging a tedious and unpleasant battle against each other. Neither you nor I are powerful enough to gainsay the Duke's commands or desires. Now his desires, or rather his desire, is you. You must face the true facts of the matter even if my putting it so bluntly comes as a shock.'

He paused for a moment as if to take breath, picked up a silver cup which stood on a table by the bed, along with a pitcher of wine and a platter of fruit, drained it off at a draught and held the platter out to the girl, who automatically took a peach from it. Garin resumed:

'If either of us refuses to go through with this marriage which is being forced on us, the result will be the scaffold for me and prison or perhaps worse for you and your family. The Duke doesn't like people to go against him. You have tried to have me killed, for which I willingly forgive you because you did not know what you were doing. But even if the scheme had succeeded and I had been killed by the fellow's dagger, you would still not have been freed. Philippe would have chosen someone else to put the ring on your finger. He always does what he has set himself to do, remember that, and he lets nothing stand in his way.'

Catherine bowed her head in defeat. The future seemed blacker and more threatening than ever. It was like being caught in a spider's web which her inexperienced hands were too feeble or clumsy to destroy. Or in a slowly circling whirlpool such as sometimes appear in rivers, which was sucking her slowly but inevitably into its whirling vortex. ... Without daring to look at Garin, she added:

'Does that mean that you, a knight, will stand quietly by while the woman who bears your name is seduced by the Duke? Won't you do anything to prevent that happening?'

Garin de Brazey shrugged and leant back against the silken pillows piled behind him.

'I have neither the desire nor the power to do so. Some men might even think it an honour. Not I, I admit. And obviously if I loved you the whole business would be much more painful. ...'

He stopped as if searching for words. His attention remained fixed on Catherine's face, however, and she blushed, feeling ill at ease again. She raised her head defiantly.

'But?'

'But I don't love you any more than you love me, my dear child,' he said softly. 'So you see that you need not feel any remorse on my account. I am not even angry with you for having plotted my death.'

Suddenly reminded of the purpose of her visit, Catherine decided to take the bull by the horns.

'Prove it then!'

'Prove it?'

Garin's face showed his surprise. He knitted his brows and his pale cheeks flushed. Afraid that he might fly into a rage, Catherine hurriedly explained:

'Yes ... please! The man who attacked you is an old friend of mine, almost my only friend. He is the man who rescued us after my father's death, and helped us flee from Paris, and brought us safely here. I owe him my life as do my mother and sister. . . . He only did this out of love for me. He would jump into the fire if I asked him to. He mustn't die because of my stupidity, please! Do something for him. Pardon him, make them free him. . . . He is an old, sick man.'

'Not as ill as all that!' said Garin with his thin smile. 'He is still vigorous enough, I can vouch for that!'

'Forget him! Pardon him. . . . You are powerful. You can save an unfortunate man from the gallows. I would be so very grateful to you!'

Overcome by her longing to save Barnaby, Catherine left her chair and flew to the bedside. She fell on her knees beside the prostrate man, raising a face wet with tears to him, and stretched out her trembling hands. Garin pulled himself up a little and leant over for a moment towards the pretty tearful face in which huge wet violet eyes sparkled like precious jewels. His features had hardened, and his nose looked suddenly thin and pointed.

'Get up!' he said hoarsely. 'Get up at once! and don't cry. . . . I forbid you to cry in my presence!'

His voice throbbed with suppressed anger, and Catherine was so startled that she automatically obeyed, rising to her feet and stepping back a few paces with her eyes fixed on the man's angry face. He tried awkwardly to explain his outburst.

'I hate tears! I can't stand seeing a woman weep! Now go! I will do everything you ask! . . . I will arrange a pardon for this brigand! . . . But go! Go at once, do you hear!'

He sat up in his bed and pointed towards the door. Catherine was alarmed and mystified by Garin's sudden display of temper. She walked across to the door with nervous little steps and hesitated for a moment before going out. Then she summoned up her courage and spoke again.

'Thank you,' she said simply.

Feeling greatly comforted, though a little uneasy about Garin's odd behaviour, Catherine returned with Sara to the Champdivers' mansion, where the mistress of the house then proceeded to deliver the expected homily on the discretion and modesty befitting a true lady and, still more, a young unmarried girl. Catherine heard her out without a murmur, inwardly happy at the turn events were taking. It never occurred to her to doubt Garin de Brazey's word. He had said that he would have Barnaby set free and she was certain that he would. It was just a question of time. . . .

But unfortunately for Barnaby, the Treasurer's request for a pardon arrived too late. The old beggar had been put to the torture to discover the motive for his deed and it had killed him. He died on the rack without confessing. Jehan des Écus brought the news to Sara the following morning.

Catherine locked herself up in her room and sobbed heart-brokenly all day, mourning her old friend and reproaching herself bitterly for having sent him to such a cruel and pointless death. Her mind was full of old memories: Barnaby in his cockleshell cloak, selling his false relics at the entrance to St Opportune; Barnaby in his cavern in the Cour des Miracles, cobbling his clothes or arguing with Mâchefer; Barnaby leading the attack on Caboche's house; Barnaby in the barge which took them down the Seine, his long legs stretched out in front of him, reciting poetry. . . .

That evening Sara brought Catherine a little, carefully wrapped packet from Garin de Brazey. When she opened it she found it contained only a dagger on whose horn handle a cockleshell was carved. She recognized it at once – it was Barnaby's dagger, the one which he had used to stab Garin. . . . On the note which accompanied it, there were just three words: 'I am sorry,' was all Garin had written.

Catherine held the crude weapon in one hand for a long, pensive moment. Her tears had suddenly stopped. Barnaby's death marked the end of one chapter of her life, and the beginning of another. The horn handle grew warm in her hand, just as though it had left Barnaby's grasp only a moment before. Slowly Catherine walked across to the little coffer of carved wood her Uncle Mathieu had given her and placed the dagger in it. Then she knelt before the little statue of the Black

Madonna which stood, flanked by two candles, in one corner of her room. With her head in her hands she prayed for a long while, trying to calm the agitation of her heart.

When she got up again she had taken a decision. In future she would not fight against her destiny. Since there was nothing else she could do, since everything seemed to be in league against her, she would marry Garin de Brazey. But no power in the world, not even the Duke Philippe, could stamp out the love which had taken complete possession of her heart. It was a hopeless but unwavering passion. She would never stop loving Arnaud de Montsalvy.

CHAPTER EIGHT

MADAME DE BRAZEY

ALTHOUGH SHE wore an ermine surcoat wrapped closely over her silver-blue brocade dress and had a cloak lined in the same fur thrown round her shoulders, Catherine felt chilled to the marrow and she had to press her lips together to stop her teeth chattering out loud. The December cold nipped cruelly in the little Roman chapel at the Brazey château in spite of thick carpets everywhere and velvet cushions scattered under everyone's feet. The priest looked frozen stiff in his gorgeously glittering chasuble, and the little acolytes kept rubbing their noses furtively on their sleeves.

The marriage ceremony was brief. Catherine heard herself answer 'Yes' to the priest's questions as though in a dream. Her voice had sunk to a whisper and the old man had to lean forward to catch her responses. Garin, for his part, had spoken up in a calm, indifferent voice.

From time to time Catherine's glance strayed to this man who was now her husband. The bitter cold of this midwinter day seemed to affect him no more than the knowledge that he had just taken a wife. He stood beside her, arms folded, his one eye fixed on the altar with the oddly challenging expression which had so struck Catherine at their first encounter in Notre-Dame. His black velvet, sable-trimmed clothes seemed no thicker than usual and he was not wearing a cloak over his short doublet. He wore no jewellery either, except for a large tear-shaped diamond of astonishing brilliance which a golden leopard, pinned to the folds of his hood, held between its paws. When he removed his gloves to take Catherine's icy fingers in his, she was surprised to find how warm his hand was. Garin had been standing so stiff and motionless throughout the Mass that he might easily have passed for one of the many statues which adorned the church.

When she got to her feet after the Elevation, Catherine felt her cloak slipping off, and she was just about to clutch at it when two swift, gentle hands replaced it quickly round her shivering shoulders. Turning round a little way she thanked Odette de Champdivers with a smile. The months that had passed since Barnaby's death had brought her one new friend; the Champdivers' daughter had returned home.

Three months earlier the unlucky Charles VI had at last reached the end of his agonizing calvary. He died in his young mistress's arms, in the solitude of his Hôtel Saint-Pol. Finding herself now quite alone and increasingly the target for Isabeau's malice and ill-will, both of which seemed all the greater now that the Queen's obesity had rendered her all but impotent, the 'Little Queen' had returned to her native Burgundy. A spontaneous friendship had grown up between the gentle young woman who had been the mad King's guardian angel and the proud and beautiful creature whom she found living in her parents' home. Odette knew why Garin was marrying Catherine, she knew with what motive Philippe had decided to turn the little bourgeoise into a great lady, and she sincerely pitied her friend. She had herself known the terror of being handed over to a stranger, but Heaven had at least shown her the mercy of letting her love this unknown man, notwithstanding his insanity, and she had loved him far more than she could even have supposed possible.

But would Catherine be able to love Philippe, the arrogant sensualist who let nothing stand in the way of his desire? Odette, in all the wisdom of her thirty-three years, doubted it very much.

The Mass was ending and Garin held out his hand for his wife to lean on. The old oak chapel doors creaked slowly open, framing a winter landscape white with snow. A gust of wind swept through the church, fluttering the flames of the great yellow wax candles which stood on the altar and sending a shiver through the handful of people present at this almost clandestine marriage. A group of frozen peasants, with their noses blue and hands red and raw with cold, were standing, huddled against each other for greater warmth, outside the main door and they all now began shouting 'Merry Christmas!' But without much conviction, for they longed to return to their homes. Garin plunged a hand into the deep purse he wore at his belt, drew out a fistful of golden coins and threw them into the snow. The peasants shouted and flung themselves excitedly after the money, almost coming to blows in the process.

All this had a curiously unreal, almost sinister air. Recalling the cheerful, happy ceremonies she had attended when her uncle Mathieu's colleagues married, and the rollicking peasant weddings in the wine country, Catherine told herself that this was easily the most depressing wedding she had ever been to. Even the sky seemed to reflect the general mood. It was yellowish-grey and leaden, heavy with snow to come, and the ravens croaking as they flew by only intensified the gloom of the occasion. . . .

Her face was stung by the icy air and it hurt when she breathed. Catherine had to bite her lips to stop herself crying. If it had not been for Marie de Champdivers' and Odette's warm friendship she would have felt dreadfully lonely on this the most important day in a woman's life. Neither Jacquette, Loyse nor the good Uncle Mathieu had been accorded the honour of an invitation to the wedding, for all Catherine's tearful entreaties.

'It is impossible,' was all Garin would say. 'Monseigneur

would object to their presence, even though he cannot personally attend. You must try to make everyone forget your lowly birth, and to do that you must start by forgetting it yourself.'

'I wouldn't be too sure of that!' Catherine cried furiously. 'As if I ever could or would forget my mother, or sister, or uncle, or any of the people I love! And there is something else I want to make quite clear. If you try to stop me inviting them to this so-called house of mine I shall go and see them, and nothing on earth, not you nor anyone else, will stop me.'

Garin shrugged wearily.

'You may do what you like . . . as long as you are discreet about it.' This time she did not even answer him. For eight days the future bride and groom did not speak a word to each other. Catherine was sulking. Her ill-humour, however, had not the slightest effect on Garin, who seemed in no hurry for a reconciliation. It was a cruel blow to the newly-wedded bride not to have her mother and uncle there on that day. She was not impressed by the arrival of envoys from the Duke Philippe, who had been detained in Flanders. These were the nonchalant, elegant Hughes de Lannoy, a close friend of Philippe's, whose insolent stare did little to put Catherine at her ease, and the young but unbending Nicolas Rollin, who had been appointed Chancellor of Burgundy only a few days before. It was only too clear that both men were only there to acquit themselves of a disagreeable duty, and this despite the fact that Rollin was Garin's closest friend. Catherine knew that he strongly disapproved of the marriage.

A banquet awaited the twelve wedding guests in the main hall of the château. This room, which was hung with Arras tapestries to keep out the storm raging outside, was not large by prevailing standards, nor, indeed, was the château itself. It might have been more accurately described as a manor house. The main part of the building abutted on to a massive tower and small turret. The table, however, which stood before a leaping fire, was covered with a silk damask cloth and laid with a sumptuous service of silver-gilt. The Lord Treasurer could not have borne, even for this modest wedding feast, to have fallen short of his usual standards of pomp and elegance.

As soon as she entered the room Catherine went across to the fire to warm her frozen hands. Sara, now promoted to be her chief maid, helped her off with her cloak. Catherine would gladly have handed over as well her tall silvery headdress, from whose sapphire-studded crescent there floated a cloud of fragile lace. Her head throbbed with migraine. She felt chilled to the core of her being. She did not dare look at her husband.

The interest Garin had shown in her during the visit she paid him after Barnaby's attack had not even lasted till their next meeting on the following day. In fact, since then Catherine had scarcely seen him at all, because he had accompanied the Duke Philippe on several journeys, notably to Paris, where Philippe had gone about the time of the sudden death of the King of England, Henry V, which had occurred at the end of August. The victor of Agincourt died at Vincennes of a fistula, leaving a child only a few months old, his son by Catherine of France. With his usual caution Philippe of Burgundy refused an invitation to become Regent of France and returned to Flanders without waiting for the dead King's funeral. There he remained even after news reached him of the death of King Charles VI, because, as a French prince, he had no intention of being made to feel small by the new Regent, the Duke of Bedford. Garin de Brazey had stayed there with the Duke, but each week a messenger would arrive from him bearing some gift or other: a jewel, a work of art, a book of hours richly illuminated by Jacquemart de Hesdin, and even a pair of Karaman greyhounds, famous as superlative hunting-dogs. But there was never so much as a short note with the gift. Marie de Champdivers, on the other hand, received regular letters instructing her as to the preparations for the marriage and rules of polite behaviour which it might be necessary to teach the bride-to-be. Garin returned eight days before the wedding, just in time to stop Catherine inviting her family.

The wedding banquet was a sad affair in spite of Hughes de Lannoy's efforts to lighten the atmosphere. Catherine, who was

sitting beside Garin on the seat reserved for the lords of the
manor, scarcely touched the food which was placed before her.
She ate a morsel or two of a superb Saône pike, cooked in herbs,
and a few sugar-plums. The food stuck in her throat when she
swallowed, and she hardly spoke a word during the meal. Garin,
meanwhile, ignored her completely, as, indeed, he ignored all
the other ladies present, leaving them to chat among themselves.
He talked politics with Nicolas Rollin, displaying a passionate
interest in the Chancellor's forthcoming embassy at Bourg-en-
Bresse, where the Burgundians and the followers of Charles V I I
were to try to come to terms, in accordance with the ardent
wishes of the Duc de Savoie, who sincerely hoped for peace.

As the time passed Catherine's distress increased, and by the
time the sweetmeats, consisting of bowls of preserves, pieces of
nougat and sugared fruits, were brought in by valets in purple
and silver livery, she felt as though her nerves were about to
snap and was forced to hide her trembling hands under the
table-cloth. In a few moments, when the company had risen
from the table, the ladies would accompany her to the bridal
chamber and leave her there quite alone, face to face with this
man who now had complete power over her. At the mere
thought of touching him Catherine's skin prickled under her
silk clothes. Desperately, and with all her might, she struggled
to banish the memory of an inn in Flanders, of a face, a voice
and a passionate, imperious kiss. Her heart stopped beating
when she thought of Arnaud and their all-too-short moment of
love. Anything that Garin could do that night, anything he
might say, would be no better than a pathetic parody of that
most precious moment of her life. Knowing as she did, beyond
any shadow of doubt, that in Arnaud she had met the real love
of her life, the man for whom God had created her, how could it
be otherwise, she thought bitterly. A minstrel was singing now,
accompanying the graceful movements of a dozen or so dancing-
girls on his harp:

> My true love, my mistress and my joy,
> Now that I must be parted from you,
> I have only a memory to comfort me. . . .

The melancholy words brought tears to the young woman's eyes. They seemed to echo her own heart's lament so closely that it was almost as though the minstrel had borrowed her voice for a moment. . . . She looked at the young man through a mist of tears, saw that he was very young, thin and blond, with knobbly knees and a childish face. . . . Then Hughes de Lannoy's mocking voice broke the spell and she hated him for it:

'What a mournful ditty for a wedding night!' he cried. 'By Heaven, young man, haven't you some sprightly roundelay with which to serenade a newly wedded pair?'

'It's a pretty song,' Garin intervened. 'I don't know it. Where did you hear it, minstrel?'

The young singer blushed like a girl, bent his knee humbly and doffed his green bonnet where a heron's feather fluttered. 'From a friend of mine, if it please your worship, who heard it across the Channel.'

'An English song? I don't believe it,' said Garin contemptuously. 'Those people only compose drinking-songs!'

'If it please your worship, the song comes from London, but it is French. Monseigneur Charles d'Orléans composes ballads, songs and odes in his English prison to while away the long and weary hours. This one became known outside the prison walls and I was lucky enough to hear it. . . .'

He would have gone on if Hughes de Lannoy had not drawn his dagger and vaulted over the table with his arm flung up to strike the unfortunate minstrel. 'Who is this who dares to pronounce the accursed name of Orléans in Burgundian country? Cursed fool, you shall pay dearly for this!'

Beside himself with rage, Philippe's hot-blooded friend was about to strike the minstrel when Catherine rose to her feet, unable to restrain her feelings a moment longer.

'Enough, sir knight! You are under my roof and this is my wedding supper. I forbid you to shed innocent blood here! A song must be judged on its beauty, not its origins.'

Her voice, which trembled with indignation, rang clear as a trumpet call. A silence ensued. Dumbfounded, Hughes de Lannoy let his arm drop harmlessly to his side. His eyes and those of all the other guests were riveted on the young woman. She stood very erect, her fingertips resting on the table, chin held high, still glowing with anger but clothed in such dignity that no one present dared even to express surprise at her behaviour. Catherine's beauty had never blazed so brightly as at that moment. All the men present were struck, in a moment of revelation, by the majesty of her bearing. The girl might come from a cloth-merchant's shop, but the imperial beauty of her face and body was worthy of a queen.

With a strange light shining in his pale-blue eyes Hughes de Lannoy slowly sheathed his dagger, released the minstrel and approached the table. He smiled and bent one knee:

'Forgive me, gracious lady, for having allowed myself to be carried away by anger in your presence. I crave your pardon and a smile. . . .'

When she found all these eyes fixed on her Catherine's confidence ebbed again as fast as it had come. She smiled at the young man with a touch of embarrassment, and turned in confusion towards her husband.

'It is rather to you, messire, that any apologies are due. Forgive me for having spoken in your stead. But I hope you will—'

Garin had risen to his feet, and taken her hand to cut short her apologies and extricate her from an awkward moment.

'As you so rightly said, this is your house . . . and you are my wife. I am happy that you should have acted thus because you were completely in the right. Let us assume that our friends agree, and that they now give us permission to retire. . . .'

The blood which had flooded Catherine's cheeks with pink as suddenly ebbed away again. Her hand trembled in Garin's. Had the dreadful moment finally arrived? Her husband's expressionless face certainly did not call to mind the sweet effusions of love, but it was towards their bridal chamber nevertheless that he was leading her.

The guests followed behind, led by six musicians playing on flutes and viols. In her anguish Catherine looked quickly round at Odette, who was following a little way behind, escorted by

Lannoy. She saw warm affection and pity in her expression.

'The body is unimportant,' Odette had told her while helping her to dress that morning. 'The moment of physical union is a painful one for almost all women, even when they are in love; and yet, when they are not, it does sometimes happen that they fall in love later.'

Catherine had turned aside at this point to take her headdress from one of the maids. In spite of her close but still recent friendship with Odette, she had not yet resolved to confide in her and tell her of her secret passion for Arnaud de Montsalvy. She had the feeling, a silly one perhaps, that the moment she put her secret into words the already shadowy, distant figure of the young man would become more shadowy still, and she would have broken the spell which bound her to this beloved enemy of hers.

> Now that I must be parted from you,
> I have only a memory to comfort me.

The words of the plaintive song echoed through her mind. They seemed especially poignant now, as she saw the door before her opening to let her pass through. Soon it would close behind her. She had reached the threshold of the bridal chamber. . . .

Odette was the last to withdraw, leaving Catherine alone to wait for her husband's coming. A last sisterly kiss, a last smile, soon hidden as the door swung to behind her, and the young woman had disappeared. Catherine knew that Odette had to leave Brazey that very evening to return to her château at Saint-Jean-de-Losne, where her daughter was waiting for her. In spite of the snow and the bitter cold, not many of the guests were to remain at the château that night. Most of them preferred to return home. Only Guillaume and Marie de Champdivers were staying, on account of their age. It wasn't much, but even so their presence under the same roof was a slight comfort to the young bride. She was far from regretting the departure of Lannoy and Rollin, however.

Sitting up in the great bed whose tapestry hangings depicted hunting scenes, she listened intently to the sounds of the château preparing for sleep. Gradually the place fell silent, the last noises muffled by the thickness of the walls. Soon the only sounds to be heard in the large, gloomy room were the fire crackling in the huge stone chimney-place and one of the dogs yawning at the foot of the bed. The other dog slept, its head stretched out on its paws.

That very morning new hangings had been put up round the bare stone walls of her rather austere-looking bedchamber. These veiled the narrow windows and shut out the desolate view of snowy plains under a black sky. Several of the brown bearskins which Garin liked had been scattered over the floor, and with this extra layer of protection from the cold, the circular tower room took on a more comfortable and luxurious appearance. Two whole tree trunks had been sawn up to build the huge fire in the chimney, and the heat it gave out was so fierce that Catherine could feel the perspiration trickling down her back. Her clenched hands were still icy cold, however. She strained her ears to catch the sound of steps in the passage.

Under Odette's supervision, her maids had dressed her in a sort of nightdress of white silk, gathered up round the neck by a gold ribbon. Its sleeves were so wide and loose that they slipped back to the shoulder if she raised her arm even slightly. Her hair had been plaited in two thick braids which hung down over her bosom and trailed over the red damask counterpane.

Although she was watching the door closely, Catherine neither heard nor saw Garin enter the room. He stepped suddenly and noiselessly out of a dark shadowy corner and crossed the floor, walking on the fur rugs as silently as a ghost. Catherine stifled a scream, and nervously pulled the covers up round her neck.

'You frightened me: I didn't see you come in. . . .'

He said nothing, but came closer still and mounted the two steps which led up to the bed. His dark eye was fixed intently on the frightened young woman, but his tight lips were not smiling. He looked even paler than usual. Covered as he was

from head to foot in a long black-velvet robe, he struck a
funereal note which seemed rather out of place. He was like
an evil spirit or ghost doomed to haunt this lonely château.
With a little moan of terror Catherine closed her eyes and
waited for his next move.

Then she felt his hands touch her head. She realized that
Garin was undoing her plaits. His hands moved deftly and
gently. Soon her loosened hair slipped over her shoulders and
down her back like a familiar, comforting coat. He seemed in
no haste. Catherine finally nerved herself to open her eyes
again and found him studying a long golden lock which he held
in his hand and dangled so that it glistened in the firelight.

'Messire,' she stammered.

He signed to her to be silent. Still without looking at her he
went on contemplating the silky lock of hair. Then abruptly
he said:

'Get up.'

She did not obey at once, not understanding what he
meant. So he took her gently by the hand and repeated, 'Get
up.'

'But—'

'Obey me! Come! Don't you realize that you must submit
yourself entirely to me henceforth? Or didn't you understand
what the priest was saying?'

His voice was cool and unemotional. He was simply stating a
fact. She climbed obediently out of the bed and padded across
the bearskins in her bare feet, hitching up the silk nightdress in
one hand so as not to trip over its trailing hem. Garin had taken
her hand again. He led her towards the fire. The expression on
his face was unfathomable. Catherine's heart pounded under
her ribs. What did he want from her? Why had he made her
get out of bed? She dared not ask.

When Garin's fingers went up to her throat and untied the
gold ribbon she felt her cheeks flame, and closed her eyes,
shutting her eyelids tightly as though they could form a protective screen. Then she no longer felt his hands upon her.
Instead she was aware of the white silk sliding off her shoulders

T—H

and falling in a heap round her ankles. The heat of the fire
struck fiercely on her bare skin.

Several minutes passed. Red spots danced before Catherine's
tight-shut eyes. The fire was beginning to scorch her thighs
and stomach. Garin did not touch her. He remained silent. She
was not even aware of his presence. Her consciousness of her
nakedness, however, despite her closed eyes, made her suddenly try to hide her body with her hands. She was stopped by a
brief command, at which she opened her eyes again:

'No!'

Then she saw him. He was sitting in a tall oak chair a few
feet away, with his chin resting on his hand, looking at her.
There was a curious expression, compounded of rage and
despair, on his face. The look was so intense that Catherine had
to turn away her head. She noticed that his shadow, blackly
outlined and so magnified by the firelight that it towered up to
the old vaulted stone ceiling, seemed as precisely etched as an
engraving. It struck her as somehow touching and even a little
comic. Then shame flooded her as she became aware of herself
being inventoried, bit by bit, by this man's appraising steady
gaze. She said plaintively, 'Please . . . the fire is burning
me.'

'Move away a little.'

She did so, stepping out of the white silk heap on the floor
and going across to him with innocent provocativeness, thinking to stop him playing this unkind, frightening game with her.
The heat of the fire seemed to have warmed her body and
excited it strangely. She had known this deep mysterious
thrilling within her, this strange half-entranced state, once
before. Catherine's healthy young body was clamouring for
the kisses and caresses which were its due. But Garin de
Brazey did not move a muscle as he sat in his high-backed
chair. He simply stared at her. . . .

Catherine felt suddenly furious, and sick with shame. She
was on the point of turning and running to the bed, where she
would be able to pull the curtains and covers around her and
hide her mortification. But he must have sensed her mood.

His fingers closed round her wrist in an iron grip, forcing her to stay beside him.

'You belong to me! I can do what I like with you. . . .'

His voice had thickened a little, but the hand which gripped her wrist was quite steady. He seemed oddly unmoved by the feminine beauty which stood unveiled before him. His free hand went up and touched her averted face, still crimson with shame, and then slid with a long lingering movement round one breast and along one hip and thigh. It was not a caress so much as the appreciative gesture of a connoisseur as his fingertips appraise the fine grain of a piece of marble and a statue's consummate purity of line. He did not repeat the movement, but Catherine started as his warm fingers touched her skin. His hoarse voice was heard again:

'A woman's body can be the most beautiful or the ugliest thing in creation,' said Garin. 'It gratifies me that yours should possess such splendour.'

Then he rose to his feet and released her bruised wrist. Catherine, her eyes wide open this time, watched him in astonishment as he crossed the room and opened the door.

'Sleep well,' he said quietly.

He vanished into the darkness as silently as he had entered. Catherine watched his dark form merge as if by magic with the shadows of the night. She remained where she was, standing alone in the middle of the huge room, while she slowly recovered from her surprise. Though she would not admit it to herself, she felt deeply disappointed. Then, catching sight of her shadow on the wall, she remembered her nakedness and raced across the room and jumped into bed, her heart beating wildly. Once she found herself in the warmth and comfort of her silken pillows and soft coverlets she suddenly, irrationally, began to weep.

When she stopped crying some time later, the fire had burnt out and the headache which had threatened her during the wedding-feast seemed to have returned with redoubled strength. Catherine got slowly out of bed, her eyes red and swollen and her head throbbing painfully. She found her nightgown lying near the fireplace and slipped it on. Then she bathed her face in a silver bowl which stood beside a pitcher of orange-flower water on a nearby chest. The cool water made her feel better. The room was as still and silent as the grave, and a feeling of intense loneliness overcame her. Even the dogs had gone. They had followed Garin out, no doubt. She had not noticed them leave the room. Feeling slightly calmer, she got back into bed. Then she settled herself comfortably against the pillows and tried to review the night's events dispassionately.

The happenings of this strange wedding night had taught her more about herself than had the past ten years. She had learnt that henceforth she would need to be wary of her body and its unpredictable reactions and demands. When she yielded to Arnaud's embraces, she was able to explain this lapse as the result of her immediate, irresistible love for him. But what about this evening? She didn't love Garin, and was not attracted to him in the least . . . yet she had been within a hair's-breadth of imploring him to take her in his arms. Her body had shown itself hungry and demanding, inhabited by strange urges whose existence she had hitherto scarcely even suspected.

She did not even try to guess the motives for her husband's behaviour. It really was impossible to make head or tail of it!

The following day was Christmas Eve. A frail piping music woke Catherine from her sleep. The curtains had been drawn back to reveal a gloomy winter landscape, but the fire leapt up merrily in the grate. Before it, with a greyhound lying at his feet, sat Garin, in one of the high-backed oak chairs. He was still wearing his black velvet robe, as though he had just got up. As Catherine started up in bed he smiled thinly.

'Those are the oboes of Advent playing, my dear. Tradition has it that they play here all day until midnight. You must make haste to receive them. I will summon your women.'

Still half awake, Catherine watched bewildered as her maids ran gaily into the room to wish her good morning. They all seemed very cheerful and tripped about the bed, one holding out a loose dressing-gown lined with fur, another her slippers, and a third a mirror. But their mischievous glances kept straying across to where Garin sat, composed and erect in his chair. He surveyed all this cheerful bustle with an indulgent air, playing to perfection the role of newly married husband enjoying watching his beloved wife at her morning toilet. Catherine did not know whether to laugh at this humbug or lose her temper with him.

Sara alone maintained her imperturbable calm. She came in last, bringing with her the dress which Catherine was to wear that day, the one following her wedding. It was a gown of honey-coloured wool embroidered with silken wheatsheafs in the same colour, each one outlined with a delicate gold thread. Its wide sleeves, neckline and hem were bordered with a band of sable in a rich brown colour. The underdress was of plain honey-coloured satin. The headdress, which completely concealed Catherine's hair, consisted of a double band of sable encircling a tall cone of embroidered cloth from which a matching veil fluttered. A broad belt of chased gold kept the folds of her dress in place just below the bosom. And a necklace of topazes, interlaced with gold wheatsheaves, completed the outfit, which Sara helped her mistress put on with the ceremonious gestures of a priest before the altar of some pagan goddess.

The gipsy woman's face was glum, however, and she did not utter a word while Catherine was dressing. Garin had retired to see to his own toilet, and the two women could have spoken freely to each other had it not been for the mischievous swarm of young maids darting about the room. When Catherine was ready Sara dismissed them with a wave of the hand and then turned towards the young woman with an anxious expression.

'Well?' she asked. 'Are you happy?'

The abruptness of the attack took Catherine by surprise. Sara seemed in a savage mood. Her black eyes searched the face of the new Dame de Brazey as though she hoped to read something in it. Catherine frowned.

'Why shouldn't I be? Or rather, why should I be? I didn't get married to be happy? Or didn't you know?'

'I know. I merely want you to tell me what happened during

your wedding night. The first experience of physical love is so important, especially for a woman. . . .'

'It all went well,' said Catherine cryptically. She had determined not to admit to a living soul, not even to Sara, what a humiliating experience she had undergone the previous night. Her pride rebelled at confessing, even to her old confidante, that her husband, after contemplating her in all her naked splendour, should have returned to spend the night in his own room without vouchsafing her so much as a kiss. Sara however was not so easily fobbed off.

'All that well? You don't look very tired for a woman on the morning after her wedding night. You haven't even got shadows under your eyes.'

Catherine lost her temper at this and stamped her foot.

'I would like to know what all this has to do with you. I am as I am! Now leave me in peace. I must go down to join my husband.'

The young woman's exasperation drew a faint smile from Sara. She laid her brown hand on Catherine's shoulder. Then, pulling her towards her, she dropped a quick kiss on her brow.

'Please to God you are telling the truth, my angel, for then I need no longer worry about you. Would to God you had found yourself a real husband! But I doubt it.'

Without explaining herself further Sara opened the bedroom door, after enveloping Catherine in the voluminous brown velvet coat which Duke Philippe had given her and which she had carefully saved. Then she escorted her down the tower's cold, draughty stone stairway to where Garin was waiting outside the château. When he saw his wife he hurried forward to give her his hand.

A group of young lads gaily clad in red and blue stood opposite the tower entrance playing their oboes, blowing into their instruments with their cheeks puffed out like apples. The appearance of the young châtelaine only served to increase their ardour, and they blew and puffed all the more vigorously. A pale watery sun filtered weakly through the clouds.

Catherine played her new role of châtelaine conscientiously

all that day, to the accompaniment of the Advent oboes. At sunset she went with all her household and villagers to the little Brazey church to light brands at the altar lamp, after which everyone was supposed to return home and light their own fires with this sacred flame. She stood beside Garin and watched while the traditional yule log, a huge slice of tree trunk, was set alight in the chimney-place in the main hall. Then she helped him distribute a length of cloth, three silver coins and a large loaf of bread to each of the peasants as a Christmas gift. At midnight she heard the three Masses celebrated, according to tradition, in the chapel of the château, the very one where she had been married the day before. Then she returned to the château for the meal which awaited them.

She felt weary by the end of this long and crowded day. Nightfall had reawakened her doubts and fears. What would happen tonight? Would Garin behave as strangely as he had the night before, or would he finally claim his conjugal rights? He had been perfectly normal, even good-humoured, during the day. He had smiled at her frequently, and as they left the table after the midnight supper, he had presented her with two pearl bracelets as a Christmas present. But sometimes Catherine caught his look fixed so strangely upon her that it chilled her to the soul. At those moments she could have sworn that he was wrestling with some dark and terrible secret. But what was it? And against whom was his dark fury directed? She behaved as sweetly and submissively towards him as the most captious husband could have desired. The Lord Treasurer of Burgundy's heart seemed to be a most baffling enigma!

Catherine's fears, however, proved groundless. Garin escorted her to the door of her bedchamber, but that was all. He wished her good night, then, inclining his tall figure slightly, dropped a quick kiss on the girl's forehead. The kiss was hurried and to all appearances casual, but Catherine could not help noticing that his lips were burning hot. Sara's eagle eye had not missed one of these strange manifestations of conjugal intimacy but she forbore to comment on them.

The next day, her face expressionless, she told Catherine

that her husband had been called away suddenly to Beaune on some business of the Duke's. He sent word that he apologized for making such a hurried departure and asked that his wife should return to Dijon some time that day and instal herself in the house in the rue de la Parcheminerie. There she should await her husband's return, which might not be for some little time since he had received orders to accompany the Chancellor, Nicolas Rollin, on his journey to the Duke of Savoie. Garin would send someone from Beaune to collect his luggage and would not be returning before his departure. He asked Catherine to settle into her new home on her own.

The young woman promptly obeyed, somewhat relieved by this new turn of events and delighted by the thought of such unexpected freedom. At midday she seated herself with Sara beside her in a litter closed in with stout leather curtains, and left the little château at Brazey for the ducal capital. It was not quite so cold as it had been and the sun seemed to have decided to shine for a while. Catherine thought happily that the next day she would be free to go and see her mother.

CHAPTER NINE

THE PHILOSOPHY OF ABOU-AL-KHAYR

ON St Vincent's day, 22 January, Catherine and Odette de Champdivers were guests at the great traditional sucking-pig banquet which her uncle Mathieu gave every year in his vineyards at Marsannay. Similar feasts were being held all over Burgundy in honour of the vineyard workers, whose patron saint was St Vincent.

It had been early morning when the two young women left the Brazey mansion, where Odette had been staying for a few days, and night had fallen by the time they reached Marsannay. A large escort of servants surrounded the closed litter where they sat talking excitedly like two schoolgirls on holiday. To keep warm they had ordered two footwarmers, metal receptacles filled with hot coals, to be placed in the vehicle.

Catherine had almost forgotten that she was now a married woman. Almost a month had elapsed since Garin's departure. She had taken possession of her husband's magnificent house and her own sumptuous apartment with childlike glee. Day after day had been spent merely discovering its many wonders. She was a little surprised to find herself such a rich and great lady. But she had not forgotten her family in her new station of life and she often went round to the rue de Griffon to see her mother and uncle Mathieu, and kiss them, and then took in the rue Tatepoire on her way back so as to chat with Marie de Champdivers for a moment. She was always affectionately received at Uncle Mathieu's, particularly now that Loyse had left home to enter a convent.

Her sister's marriage had had an odd effect on the elder Legoix daughter. The world, whose sight she had more or less tolerated until then, had suddenly become abhorrent to her. The thing which she found hardest to accept, it seemed, was the thought that Catherine, now that she was obliged to submit to a husband's authority, had gone over to the other side of the fence, into that world full of men which she hated so much. About a month after her sister had taken up residence with the Champdivers Loyse announced her intention of entering as a novice into the convent of Bernardines de Tart, a particularly strict order which followed the inflexible trappist rule of the Abbey of Cîteaux. No one had dared oppose this decision, which seemed final. Uncle Mathieu and his sister were even vaguely relieved by it. Loyse's character was growing more shrewish every day, and her temper, which had never been very good, had become appallingly savage. Jacquette, moreover, had been growing more and more anxious about the gloomy future which seemed to be in store for her elder daughter. A nunnery, for which she had yearned ever since childhood, seemed the only place where Loyse might find peace and serenity. So they had allowed her to join the white-robed flock of the future brides of Christ.

'It is just as well,' said Uncle Mathieu dryly, 'that Our Lord is infinitely patient and infinitely meek . . . because he will find he has a difficult bride to deal with there.'

And from the bottom of his peace-loving heart the good fellow breathed easier when the forbidding, chilly figure of his niece had stopped haunting the great St Bonaventure church. He and his sister settled into a comfortable existence, just the two of them, and Mathieu savoured the pleasures of being spoilt and cosseted to the full.

Catherine and Odette found the village of Marsannay in a high state of excitement. They had been preparing for the feast for days past. All the snow had been zealously swept from the one and only main street. The finest lengths of cloth and most brilliantly coloured pieces of stuff which could be found in the marriage chests had been hung in front of all the houses, even the poorest. Winter leaves and berries, silvery mistletoe which had been gathered at great risk in the topmost branches of an old oak tree, and prickly holly decorated the doors and windows. A strong smell of roasting pig floated out over the countryside. They had slaughtered all the fattest pigs for the banquet, as that worthy animal would provide all the meat for the feast.

Uncle Mathieu being, together with the monks of Saint-Benigne, the richest vineyard proprietor in Marsannay, no less than ten pigs had paid with their lives for the lavish repast to which the cloth-merchant had invited all the harvesters who would be coming to pick his purple grapes when the next harvest came round. Although he didn't like to throw his money around, Uncle Mathieu was a rich man. To wash down the meal he had ordered six barrels of Beaune wine to be set aside, both Beaune de Nuits and de Romanée.

The feast began about midday. The solemn High Mass had ended late, and everybody was both thirsty and hungry. Catherine and Odette took their places at the table presided over by her mother. Jacquette glowed with happiness in a splendid gown of crimson satin lined with grey squirrel which had been a gift from her daughter. At the other table Mathieu, all puce velvet and black fox, with his hood over one ear, was spurring on the drinkers, who were in no need of encouragement as it was. The talk crackled merrily, enlivened with many a joke and sally inspired by the excellent wine. From time to time they struck up a verse or two of some old song. There was an atmosphere of innocent, good-humoured gaiety in which Catherine joined wholeheartedly. It was agreeable to be enjoying oneself, to be young, and beautiful, as the bold looks of some of the young men present attested.

Suddenly, just as the scullions, four abreast, carried on the roast pigs all golden and glistening in their crackling skin, a deafening uproar broke out at the door. A group of men, late arrivals no doubt, were all struggling to get into the room first. A volley of oaths, bellowed out at the top of their lungs, was heard, in the midst of which a high-pitched voice could be heard protesting furiously.

'What's all this?' cried Mathieu, thumping his fist on the table. 'Hallo there! Stop that brawling! There's room for everyone here.'

With an explosion as loud as that of a champagne cork leaving the bottle, the group on the threshold burst into the room. Catherine looked on in astonishment as they dragged forward a kicking struggling human form which looked uncannily like an enormous pumpkin standing on short little legs, the only difference being that this pumpkin was shouting away in a foreign tongue.

'See what we found by the wayside, Maître Mathieu,' cried one of the vineyard workers, a huge rogue with a face the colour of wine lees. The fellow stretched out an arm, picked up the little man without apparent effort and set him down on the table, just in front of Mathieu. Then he grabbed the pumpkin, which had slipped down and so covered the little man's face and neck, and tugged at it. The white beard and ferrety face of Abou-al-Khayr, the little Cordoban doctor, appeared. The former was as white as ever, while the latter was scarlet with rage and suffocation.

'Have you ever seen such an ugly monkey?' cried the labourer with a great guffaw. 'I found him going along the road with two great devils, both black as Satan, all three of them as cool as you please perched on their mules. I thought you would like to see these freaks before we throw them into the river. It isn't often one gets the chance of a good laugh!'

'But it's my friend of the Grand Charlemagne inn!' cried Mathieu, who instantly recognized the Moorish doctor. 'It is the great Abou-al-Khayr in person! Fool! Imbecile! So you want to throw my friends in the river, do you? What did you think you were doing, in God's name! What did you think you were doing?'

He hastily helped Abou-al-Khayr down off the table and found him a chair and a glass of wine, which the little doctor drained at a gulp, such was his agitation. It took him a little time to recover after his alarming experience, but gradually the colour returned to his face. He made no attempt to conceal his pleasure and relief at finding Mathieu.

'I thought my last hour had come, my friend. May Allah be praised that I fell into your hands! And if it isn't too late to save my servants I should like to stop them being thrown into the river too!'

At an order from Mathieu the labourer responsible, a little bewildered by this sudden turn of events, was shepherded towards the door, while the little doctor rearranged his clothes and adjusted his turban according to the prescribed manner, helped by Jacquette, who was deeply astonished by the wide range of her brother's acquaintances. By now Abou's sharp eyes had lighted on Catherine, who was standing a little to one side, not daring to come closer. The sudden appearance of the Cordoban doctor had set her heart beating wildly. Garin had said that the Arab had attached himself to Arnaud de Mont-salvy. He would doubtless be able to tell her many things about the man who haunted her heart and mind.

The excitement which had been occasioned round the table by the little doctor's sensational entry was subsiding. Ensconced in a chair piled high with cushions, supplied with a pewter pitcher and goblet, Abou-al-Khayr was putting the finishing touches to his restored good-humour. His gaze, which had been fixed on Catherine with an almost embarrassing insistence, now returned to the table and the vast dishes which Mathieu was hastening to place before him. . . .

But the good man was stopped dead, knife and fork poised in mid-air, just as he was about to launch himself on the fattest of the roast pigs. For, with a wild scream of horror, Abou-al-Khayr had leapt to his feet, pushed back his chair which fell to the ground with a thunderous crash and rushed as fast as his legs would carry him as far as the chimney-corner, where he remained crouching, whiter than his beard, trembling in every limb and moaning with terror.

'Come, come now!' cried Mathieu. 'What's the matter with him now? Don't run away like that, my friend! Come, and let's finish off this roast together. What has frightened you?'

'Pork! . . .' Abou exclaimed in a shaking voice. 'Pork! . . . The unclean animal! . . . Accursed, forbidden meat! A true believer may not even go near the table where the disgusting animal is being devoured!'

Round-eyed and startled, Mathieu stared first at the little doctor, who was still trembling with fright, and then back at the innocent pig, looking so succulent on its dish.

'What do you mean? My pigs aren't unclean!' he protested crossly.

It was Odette who saved the situation. She left her seat and came over to where Mathieu was standing. Catherine saw that she was having some trouble keeping a straight face.

'At the court of King Charles I once met a heathen sorcerer of this man's race. Madame the Duchess of Orleans, who was a good Christian herself, was hoping that his magic arts might be of some use in curing Monseigneur. This man always refused to eat pork, which his religion regarded as unclean.'

'The prophet has said: "You may not eat the flesh of the unclean beast," ' came Abou's querulous voice from the corner. Mathieu gave a deep sigh, threw down his knife and fork, and rose to his feet.

'Very well,' he said to his sister. 'Tell them to put some fat capon on to roast, and prepare a tasty fish dish or two. My friend and I will take a cup of wine together in my study while we wait for the meal to cook. Please carry on your meal without us.'

And to Catherine's great chagrin Abou and Mathieu went off together. So it was her uncle who would hear the little doctor's news while she herself was burning to ask him questions! She vowed to herself that she would not leave Marsannay that night without first having a chat with him, even if it meant displeasing her uncle.

There was no question of displeasing Mathieu, as it turned out. While she was watching the labourers dancing after the meal was finished and the great hall had been cleared of tables, she felt someone plucking at her sleeve. She looked round and found the doctor standing at her side.

'It was you I was seeking along this accursed road,' he said in a low voice.

'I return to my house in Dijon tomorrow morning,' she replied. 'Come with me unless you are afraid of a woman's hospitality . . .'

Abou-al-Khayr smiled, then bowed low, murmuring:

'Allow me to kiss the dust before your door, O Queen, as does the sky itself . . . in the words of the poet. I can only say that I should be happy to follow you if you will also accommodate my two slaves, who appear to have been rescued in the nick of time.'

At dawn the next morning Catherine's litter set off for Dijon once more, conveying the doctor and the two young women. The whole countryside seemed to be still snoring!

When they reached Dijon Odette took leave of her friend to go and see her mother, with whom she planned to spend two days before returning to Saint-Jean-de-Losne. Catherine did not try to detain her. The former King's Favourite seemed to have something on her mind. Besides, Catherine knew that Abou-al-Khayr would not talk to her as long as Odette was there. On the homeward journey he had not spoken three words together.

Her return to the house in the rue de la Parcheminerie

flanked by two black slaves caused something of a stir. All
Catherine's serving-women instantly lifted up their skirts in
both hands, ready to take to their heels, while the men drew
back crossing themselves. An imperious glance from their
young mistress stopped them in their tracks. In a month she
had succeeded in making herself almost as respected as Garin
himself. Dryly, she ordered Tiercelin, the steward, to have the
Griffon Room made ready for the distinguished guest, and to
have two mattresses taken up there for his servants to sleep on.
After which she herself, with the utmost ceremony in order to
show how much store she set by this guest, conducted her
visitor to his apartment, preceded by valets carrying torches.
While this was going on Abou-al-Khayr was silent, busily
examining the people and things around him.

Catherine left him at the door of his room, after telling him
when the next meal would be served. He gave a deep sigh and
took her by the arm.

'If I read the signs aright, things have changed greatly,' he
asked gently. 'You are married?'

'Yes . . . a month ago.'

The little doctor shook his turbaned head. All of a sudden he
seemed very sad.

It was late that afternoon when they finally met again.
Catherine found she could wait no longer. She had lunched
alone because Abou-al-Khayr, on the pretext that the journey
had tired him, asked for his meal to be served in his apartment.
In fact he really wanted more time to think before his conversation with the young woman. When he came at last to her
apartment in answer to a message she had sent by a page, he
stood for a moment watching the flames flickering and dancing
in the tall and elaborately and finely carved white stone chimney-place. Catherine was at the end of her patience. 'Talk to
me, for pity's sake! Your silence is torturing me. Please . . . tell
me about him,' she begged.

The Arab shrugged sadly. Actions, he thought, seemed to
speak louder than words in Catherine's case.

'What is the point now that you are married? What difference can it make to you now what my friend does? When I first saw you together I had the feeling that you were bound to each other by an indissoluble bond. I believe that I can read men's eyes, and in yours I thought I saw a great love. But I should have remembered that a woman's eyes are deceptive. I seem to have read wrong,' he said bitterly.

'No, you didn't. You read the truth. I loved him and I still do. I love him more than I love myself. But he hates and despises me.'

'That's quite another thing,' Abou smiled. 'One could write volumes about the Seigneur Montsalvy's capacities for scorn and contempt. When a wound cuts deep into the flesh the flesh heals, but a scar remains and nothing on earth can remove it. Take a doctor's word for it. It grieves me very much to find you married. You women are strange creatures. You call the world to witness that you are consumed by a great love and then you calmly go and offer your body to another man!'

Catherine was losing patience. What did he mean by wasting time philosophizing about the feminine soul when he knew she was pining to hear news of Arnaud?

'I dare say the women in your country are free to choose which man's bed they shall be placed in? It is different here. I married because I was ordered to.'

She briefly described the circumstances of her marriage to her guest. She told him about the formal command from Philippe and the motive which lay behind it. But she didn't feel brave enough to tell him that as yet her husband had not touched her. What would be the point? Sooner or later, when Garin returned, he would claim his rights.

'So,' said the doctor when she had finished her story, 'your husband is the same Garin de Brazey who accompanies the Chancellor of Burgundy to Bourg? It is indeed strange that the Duke's choice should have fallen on him. He is as obscure as the night and as inflexible as iron. His character seems as rigid as his spine. He doesn't suggest an indulgent husband to me.'

Catherine dismissed this comment, which recalled the one

Barnaby had once made, with a wave of the hand. She had not sent for him to discuss Garin. And at last Abou-al-Khayr agreed to tell her what she longed to hear.

He had not left Arnaud de Montsalvy's side since the incident in the Flemish inn. They had stayed together at the Grand Charlemagne until Arnaud's wounds and injuries had healed.

'He fell sick of a high fever after you left and became delirious. And a highly instructive and interesting delirium it was too, but I won't go into that now. By the time we finally set off again the Duke of Burgundy had left Flanders for Paris. There was no question of following him there, as we would never have escaped with our lives.'

Little by little, in his high singsong voice, the Moorish doctor told of Arnaud's slow return to health, and eventual return, in a highly irascible frame of mind, to the Dauphin his master. Abou spoke of the Dauphin's warm welcome of them and of the many marvels of the château of Méhun-sur-Yèvre, airiest and most fantastic of all the feudal dwellings, a lacy confection in gilt and stone which Charles had inherited from his uncle Jean de Berry, who had been the most lavish and luxury-loving Maecenas of his day. He spoke of the warm affection and loyalty which united Arnaud de Montsalvy to the Dauphin's other captains in a knightly brotherhood-at-arms. His descriptions were so vivid that Catherine felt she could almost see these friends of Arnaud's. First there was young Jean d'Orléans, the most attractive and knightly of all the royal bastards, whose fraternal affection for the Dauphin dated from their childhood. Then came the square, rough-hewn shape of the redoubtable Étienne de Vignolles, nicknamed The Terrible One because of his ferocity in battle, a soul of bronze in a body of iron. And next to him, his *alter ego*, a jolly but irascible fellow from the Auvergne, Jean de Xaintrailles, ruddy and solid as a chestnut. There was also another Auvergnat, Pierre de Ciac, a sly bully of a man who was said to owe his fame and fortune in war to a pact with the Devil, to whom he had sold his right hand. There were many others besides, lords from inscrutable Languedoc, doughty Auvergne, sentimental Touraine and lively Provence, all those, in short, who remained faithful to the rule of one king, one faith and one law even in adversity. Abou-al-Khayr also dwelt rather wickedly on the charms of the pretty women who thronged the Court, describing them with what seemed like sly relish. Charles VII, who was almost as fond of women as his cousin of Burgundy, liked to fill his Court with these fresh young damsels. To hear Abou-al-Khayr on the subject one might have supposed that these delicious creatures only awaited a signal from Arnaud de Montsalvy to fall into his arms. And foremost among them was the dazzling daughter of the Marechal de Séverac, a ravishing brunette with eyes 'as long as a night of love'.

'You can leave that part out,' said Catherine, exasperated by these raptures which the devilish Abou was assuming for her benefit.

'Why?' said Abou, with well-feigned surprise. 'Surely it is only right and proper that a young, healthy man should employ his strength in the search for pleasure. As the poet says, "Grieve not for what is past nor fear what is to come, but enjoy the present, for that is the purpose of life." '

'And my purpose here, I suppose, is to hear all about Messire de Montsalvy's conquests! Tell me what happened next!' Catherine cried furiously.

Abou-al-Khayr smiled winningly at her and stroked his snow-white beard.

'Then the Dauphin was crowned King, and that was an occasion to remember! There were banquets and jousts which I watched from the window of the lodging which my friend discovered for me, where I received many visits in the course of my stay in that city, particularly from the Sire de Ciac.'

By now Catherine had reached the limit of her patience. She could feel nervous tears welling up into her eyes. 'For pity's sake!' she begged, in such a tragic voice that the little doctor finally took pity on her. He rapidly sketched in the events of the past few weeks, the jousts in which Arnaud and 'The Terrible One' had taken part together: then he mentioned his appointment as escort to King Charles's emissaries on their journey

from Paris to Bourg-en-Bresse. These included the Chancellor
of France, the Bishop of Clermont and Martin Couge de
Chardaignes, a relative of Arnaud's. Finally he described the
departure of the envoys, which was followed at a discreet distance by his own.

He had obviously not been able to personally attend the
delicate and complex negotiations presided over by the Duke of
Savoy. But every evening he would see Arnaud return in a
slightly worse humour. As Nicolas Rollin went on implacably
detailing the Burgundian peace terms, which added up to a
formidable list of demands, the young man's rage had steadily
increased. He insisted that the peace terms were unacceptable,
and day after day he had the utmost difficulty in restraining
himself from leaping at the throat of the insolent Burgundian
who had the audacity to insist not only on a public apology from
Charles for the murder of Jean-sans-Peur, but also on a dis-
pensation absolving Philippe from the homage which any vassal
owed to his king, even when that vassal was the Duke of Burgundy. And he demanded finally the surrender of a good half of
the land which the English had not yet conquered. Rollin's
evasiveness and humiliating secretiveness had whipped the
hot-tempered Captain's fury to boiling-point . . . and with it his
hatred of Duke Philippe.

'He hates him,' said Abou pensively, 'as I have yet to see one
man hate another . . . and I am not sure that you are not somewhat to blame in all this. For the moment the Duke of Savoy
has succeeded in obtaining a truce between the protagonists
and the promise of further talks, which are to start on 1 May.
But I know one person who is determined not to let this truce
stand in his way.'

'What does he want to do?'

'To come and challenge the Duke Philippe in person.
Engage him in single combat . . . above all in a combat to the
death!'

Catherine gave a fearful cry. If Arnaud so much as challenged the Duke he would never leave the town alive! Who had
ever heard of a ruling prince taking up arms against a mere

knight in single combat ... particularly in a combat to the death ? She bitterly reproached the doctor for having deserted his friend while he was still in such a distraught state of mind. He should have reasoned with him, shown him that he would be committing suicide in trying to put such a project into action and restrained him by force if necessary. ... Abou-al-Khayr nodded his head.

'It is about as easy to stop Messire Arnaud as to stop a stream gushing down a mountainside. He will do as he says. The reason for my coming hither, on the pretext of visiting an old and very learned Jewish scholar who lives in seclusion not far from this town, is that you alone can do something to help him.'

'But what can I do ? I am all alone, without forces or power ?'

'Philippe loves you ... at any rate Arnaud thinks so, and with some reason to judge by what you have just told me, only Arnaud believes that you have been his enemy's mistress for some while now. When he has thrown down his crazy challenge, your hand will be the only one influential enough to protect him from the fury of the Burgundians. It is hard to refuse anything to the woman one loves – especially when you have yet to make her entirely yours.'

'Where is Arnaud now ?'

This was the first time she had ever spoken out loud that name which she had so often murmured softly to herself, for the sole pleasure of rolling its two syllables on her tongue.

'He is still at Bourg. The envoys are about to leave. Your husband will be returning presently and Arnaud is to accompany the Bishop of Clermont to the King at Bourges. Then . . .'

There was no time to lose. Arnaud's irascible character was not overburdened with patience. He was one of those people who, once they have decided upon a certain course of action, forge ahead without a thought for the consequences. Catherine was glad to hear that Garin would soon be returning, because it meant that it would not be long before she was presented at Court. She must have access to the Duke, and the sooner the better.

Catherine's thoughts were broken into by Sara, who came in carrying Gedeon in his cage which she had just been cleaning. Abou-al-Khayr jumped up with a scream of delight and rushed over to look at the bird. He started tickling him under his beak and poured out a torrent of words in his native tongue, which sounded both soft and guttural at once. Catherine was about to warn him of the bird's fearsome beak, as Gedeon was not renowned for his patience or good manners, when, to her astonishment, she noticed that the bird was bobbing up and down on his perch as coyly as a girl being wooed. He swung his head from side to side, strutted up and down, and cooed as softly and tenderly as a dove. He and the little doctor made a bizarre love duet. Eager, no doubt, to display the range of his accomplishments, Gedeon suddenly broke off his tender aria to shout at the top of his voice:

'Glory . . . to the Duke!'

Then, rolling a beady eye at his mistress, he shrieked with a touch of defiance: 'Garin! . . . Horrible Garin! . . . Horrible! Horrible!'

'Merciful heavens!' Catherine groaned. 'Who can have taught him to say that? If my husband hears him he will wring his neck!'

Abou-al-Khayr laughed heartily. He held out his hand and the bird hopped on to it and sat there, quite docile.

'Give him to me! We are already such good friends. And no one will hear him in my room. I'll teach him to swear in Arabic!'

The parrot allowed himself to be taken away, not only without protest but apparently with considerable satisfaction. He had begun practising his scales again with renewed vigour. Watching the pair leave the room from her position by the fire, Catherine reflected that the parrot and the doctor made an unusually well-matched couple. Abou's turban and Gedeon's head feathers were of just the same brilliant scarlet. Just as the door was about to close behind them she asked: 'Why should you suppose that your friends' feelings towards the Duke Philippe have any connexion with me?'

A mocking smile wrinkled the little doctor's face. With the parrot still perched on his wrist he bowed slightly and said:

'The sage wrote: "The eyes can sometimes be mistaken." He did not mention the ears. Some men talk in their sleep. What they say is often very interesting and instructive to anyone who happens to be there. May the peace of Allah be with you, rose most fair!'

Garin returned home two days later. He seemed harassed, nervous and in a thoroughly bad temper. He greeted Catherine with a preoccupied air, dropping a hasty kiss on her brow, and then told her, as though it were a thing of little importance, that she must be ready to be presented in a very short time to the Dowager Duchess.

'You will be admitted as one of her ladies-in-waiting, which will put the finishing touches to your social education.'

If he was at all surprised at finding the Moorish doctor who had so greatly excited the curiosity of the people of Bourg during his stay there now actually resident in his house, he gave no sign of it. Catherine for her part introduced Abou-al-Khayr as an old friend of her uncle's, and Garin seemed delighted to meet him. He received him with a courtesy and generosity which charmed the little doctor.

'In this century of ours where men tear each other to pieces like wild beasts and think of little else but looting, stealing and destroying things, a man of science whose mission is to alleviate the sufferings of our poor human bodies seems like a gift from God,' he said to him in greeting. He invited him to stay in his house for as long as he liked, and approved of Catherine's choice of rooms for their guest.

'That room on the first floor of the west wing, it would not be difficult to have a laboratory set up there should you decide to stay here for some time, or perhaps permanently.'

To Catherine's surprise and indignation, for she considered him as bound by loyalty to Arnaud, Abou-al-Khayr thanked Garin effusively and accepted. When she reproached him with this later, he said:

'The sage saith: "You will serve your friend more effectively under your enemy's roof, but you must not let him pay for the bread you eat." '

After this, seeing that Garin had retired, he went to his room to say his evening prayer.

The young woman was satisfied with this explanation. Besides, she was in fact delighted to have Abou under her roof. With him there she could talk about Arnaud to someone who knew him well, and had remained at his side for months on end. With the Moorish doctor's help she would get to know him better. He could tell her about his daily life and what things he liked and didn't like. It was as though a particle of Arnaud himself had come to the Hôtel de Brazey. Now he would no longer be just a memory stored in the shadowy recesses of her mind, a painful and inaccessible image. Abou's presence lent life and substance to this shadow, and the hope which she had stifled for so long of seeing him again burgeoned anew, stronger and more vivid than ever.

When her women helped her prepare for bed, Catherine took a new and intense pleasure in the beauty of her own body. While Sara stood behind her combing out her golden hair till it shone as brightly as the gold comb which the gipsy used for this purpose, her other women washed her with rose water and then elaborately scented her body, using different scents for its different parts. Sara, whose long years in the Venetian merchant's household had made her an expert in perfumes and their properties, used to supervise this ritual and choose the different scents which Catherine used. Ten years spent in the shop of an apothecary and spice merchant are liable to teach one a lot of useful and curious information. But strangely enough it was only recently that Catherine had discovered this talent in her old friend.

The maid would place a few drops of violet essence on her hair and eyes, powdered orris root on her face and bosom, marjoram behind the ears, spikenard on her legs and feet, rose on her thighs and stomach, and finally a little musk in the folds of the groin. It was all so delicately and lightly done that when

Catherine moved she felt herself enveloped in a cloud of fresh, delicious but subtle fragrance.

The big polished mirror, in its elaborate gold and Limoges enamel frame, reflected back a charming picture, all rose pink and pale gold. It was such a ravishing sight that Catherine's eyes sparkled proudly. Her present mode of life and the fact that she was a very rich woman did at least ensure that she could take care of her looks and groom her beautiful body to become an irresistible magnet, a delicious trap for the man she loved. She longed for Arnaud with all the ardour of her proud heart, and all the passion and vigour of blooming youth. There was nothing she would stop at to get him back. For the ecstasy of holding him in her arms once more, as vanquished by desire as he had been at their first meeting, she was even prepared, if the need arose, to commit a crime.

When Perrine, the young maidservant who was entrusted with the task of preparing and applying the perfumes, had finished, she too stood back a little distance to admire the enchanting vision of womanhood reflected in the mirror with its aureole of candle flames from the masses of slender wax tapers which lit the bedchamber.

'By rights the master should be head over heels in love,' she murmured to herself. But Catherine heard. The reference to Garin, who was so far from her thoughts just then, brought her back sharply to earth and made her shiver. Stretching out a hand she impatiently seized the dressing-gown which had been placed on a nearby chest. It was a sort of long, loose tunic with wide sleeves and a low neck-line. The cloth of which it was made, a gold tissue embroidered with flowers in brilliant colours and fantastic shapes, had been brought by a Genoese vessel from Constantinople. She wrapped it quickly round her and slipped her feet into the little matching slippers which had been made with the remnants of the gold stuff. Then she dismissed her servants.

'Leave me now, all of you!'

They obeyed, Sara included. But before closing the door behind her Sara turned and tried to catch Catherine's eye in the hope that the command did not include her. But Catherine stood motionless in the middle of the room, staring into the fire and did not turn round. With a sigh Sara left the room.

When she was alone the young woman went over to the window and opened the heavy painted and gilded wooden shutters, whose decoration echoed the motifs on the ceiling beams. Looking down into the courtyard outside was like looking down a well. There was not a light to be seen. Garin's windows were quite dark. She suddenly felt like calling Sara back and sending her to see what her husband was doing, but pride prevented her. Heaven knows what Garin would think if she sent someone to him! One minute she longed for his presence and the next she would be praying that he would not visit her that night. She both feared and desired him. But Catherine tortured herself to no purpose, for Garin de Brazey did not knock on her door that night, or on any of the nights which followed. And she, quite unreasonably, felt aggrieved and injured.

During the time which elapsed between his return and Catherine's presentation to the Dowager Duchess, Garin de Brazey had the pleasure, for so he seemed to regard it, of introducing his young wife to all the hidden treasures and marvels of his house. While Garin was away Catherine had made herself thoroughly at home in her own apartments, and she had visited and admired the section of the house set apart for receptions and social life. She had seen over the main hall with its carved and gilded ceiling and walls hung with superb Arras tapestries interwoven with gold thread showing scenes from the lives of the Prophets. Then she had toured the suite of rooms leading off it, slightly smaller, most of them, but no less luxuriously decorated and furnished. In every one the walls were of that rich crimson shade which seemed to be Garin's favourite. They were decorated lavishly with gold and silver and set about with a profusion of *objets d'art* and things chosen either for their beauty or novelty. There were innumerable samples of the goldsmith's art, some of rare beauty, priceless books, their covers studded with precious stones, enamelled caskets, gold, bronze or crystal statues. The floors were strewn with rugs so thick that Catherine's feet seemed to sink into them up to the ankles, and there was a collection of musical instruments, all carved from the rarest and most costly woods. Catherine had also visited the immense kitchens, where everything seemed on a scale required to feed an army, and toured the gardens, with their rose-beds enclosed by clipped borders and the stables and the store-houses where the household's provisions were kept. But she had never once set foot in the east wing of the house. This was reached through a solid heavy oak door with massive iron hinges which was always kept locked. Nor had she seen her husband's apartments. This wing stood at right-angles to the long gallery which, with its coloured glass windows, ran the whole length of the first floor of the house.

When Garin picked up a blazing torch and opened the mysterious oaken door Catherine realized at last why it was kept so carefully locked. The whole east wing of the building, which appeared to be of great antiquity and was lit only by narrow slit windows, was really a sort of enormous warehouse where the Lord Treasurer stored the shipments of merchandise which were constantly arriving from the farthest corners of the globe and which he would then dispose of at a handsome profit through his many agents. In addition to and quite apart from his many distinguished and honorific posts, it seemed that Garin also operated a thriving and far-flung business empire. Though necessarily secret and hampered to some extent by the interminable wars, it had none the less proved highly lucrative.

'You see,' said Garin, half serious and half ironic as he escorted her through rooms crammed with every conceivable sort of merchandise, 'I am letting you into all my secrets, in the hopes, I need hardly add, that you will feel free to take anything you need or like from here at any time.'

She smiled her thanks and followed him, her eyes round with wonderment and admiration, as he guided her through his vast storehouse of treasures. One of the rooms was piled to the roof with carpets, rolled up one on top of the other, and they gave out a heavy, musky scent, suggestive of sunshine and

distant lands. The light from Garin's torch brought their
glowing colours to life for a moment. There were carpets from
Asia Minor, from Smyrna, Brousse and Kulah, recognizable
by their warm colouring of deep blues and greens contrasted
with rich reds and purples. Others, in more delicately blended
shades, were from the Caucasus. Then there were Persian
carpets from Herat, Tabriz, Meshed or Kashan, blossoming
with all the flowers of an imaginary garden, superb Bukharas,
brilliant rugs from Samarkand, and even some of the loosely
woven Khotan silk carpets from fabulous China.

Other rooms held cloth of gold from the Euphrates, costly
furs, sables, ermine, fox and vair from Mongolia, saddles and
harnesses from Kerman, jasper from Kara-Shahr, lapis lazuli
from Badakhshan, uncarved ivory from the African jungle,
white sandalwood from Mysore. Then there were spices worth
their weight in gold, among them ginger from Mecca, cloves
from China, cinnamon from Tibet, black pepper, cumin and
nutmeg from Java, white pepper from Cipango, pistachio nuts
from Syria, all of them packed in bags piled in great pyramids.
The odour of all these spices combined was so strong that it
made Catherine's head reel. She felt the first warning throb
of a migraine. The whole place was rather like a magical cave,
in whose dark depths something would suddenly catch the
light, a bright scrap of cloth, perhaps, or a gleam of metal, the
creamy whiteness of a piece of ivory or the opaque green of a
fragment of jade. When they reached the far end of the last
room Garin, who had carefully locked the door into the
gallery after they passed through it, drew back a plain green
cloth curtain to reveal a low door which he then unlocked with
a key which hung from his belt. Catherine found herself for
the second time in her husband's room, standing behind the very
same silver and crystal chair where she had undergone such agonizing moments on that previous occasion before her wedding.

'I still have a few more treasures to show you,' Garin said.
She allowed herself a little nervously to be led towards the
bed. Then Garin went round the back of this massive piece of
furniture and showed her another door normally concealed by

the velvet curtains round the bedhead. It led into a little round tower room. Three huge iron chests with massive padlocks took up almost all the available space. Garin put his candlestick down on a slab let into the wall and then, with an effort which made the veins on his forehead stand out sharply, struggled to open one of the chests. In the gloom Catherine could just make out the yellow effulgence of a mass of gold coins.

'There's a king's ransom in there, should it ever be needed!' said Garin with an oblique smile. 'The second chest is full of gold too. As for this one . . .'

He wrenched back the heavy lid to reveal a dazzling Aladdin's hoard of flashing gems of every possible size, colour and shade, some mounted and others unset. In one corner of the chest a number of little caskets, each covered with purple velvet, stood neatly piled on top of each other.

There were turquoises from Kerman, round Coromandel pearls, Indian diamonds, Kashmir sapphires, emeralds from the Red Sea. There were orange corundums as well, transparent blue aquamarines, milky opals, blood-red carbuncles and golden topazes. But not a single amethyst.

'All the amethysts are in the caskets,' Garin explained. 'There is no finer collection in the whole world. Not even the Duke's! I think he even envies me them a little. . . .'

He gazed at the jewels with a glint in his eye. He seemed all of a sudden to have forgotten Catherine's presence. The light reflected off the jewels on to his face in a curious coloured pattern which gave him a little of the look of some weird demon. Then he plunged his long dry hands suddenly into the blazing heap of gems and drew out a large barbaric-looking necklace made of enormous crudely cut turquoises, set in a sort of heavy gold lattice formed by intertwined serpents. Before Catherine could stop him Garin threw the necklace round her shoulders. His hands, which were trembling as with a sudden fever, struggled to fasten the clasp at the nape of her neck. The necklace was so heavy that Catherine felt as if someone had tied a lead weight round her neck. It was also much too long to fit within the modest neckline of the gown she was wearing, a simple one of brown velvet bordered with a narrow band of marten fur. Garin's hands still shook.

'It doesn't look right! It doesn't look right!' he complained between clenched teeth.

He looked quite wild. His black eye blazed uncannily, and the deep lines round his mouth seemed to have deepened farther still. Then he suddenly abandoned the necklace clasp and clutched at the neckline of Catherine's dress, wrenching at it violently. The cloth ripped open with a dry little sound and Catherine cried out in alarm. The fever which had taken hold of Garin, however, seemed to leave him as suddenly as it had come. He was quite calm again as he slipped the torn dress off her shoulders, leaving her naked to the waist. He still smiled his curious sidelong smile. . . .

The necklace now hung correctly. The gold lattice covered Catherine's shoulders completely and hung down over her bare breasts, half concealing them.

'That's much better!' Garin said with an air of satisfaction. 'I am afraid you can't be expected to go about half naked to show this piece off at its best . . . though it does look quite marvellous against your skin, like that. But keep the necklace, if only to make up for the torn dress. I must apologize for that, my dear. But, as you know, I cannot abide faults of taste.'

A long velvet stole, which she wrapped round her torn dress, allowed Catherine to return to her room without attracting the notice of her maids. She carried the necklace in both hands. By the time she finally reached her room she was shaking like a leaf. Fortunately Sara was not there. Catherine hurriedly took off her torn dress and threw it into a corner. She had one more proof of the fact that one never knew with Garin what might happen from one moment to the next.

At supper that night he was cold and distant, and such words as he addressed to her were of the most banal description, to do with the weather they had been having. Then he escorted his wife to her room without more ado, kissed her normally and turned on his heel.

'Why don't you ask him to explain what he is up to?' Sara asked as she helped her mistress undress. 'I think you have a right to know. I felt all along that there was something odd about this marriage, but I didn't realize that it was as bad as this! Still a virgin after more than a month of marriage! I know your husband has been away most of that time, but still . . .'

'But you guessed that something was wrong. Don't you remember how you questioned me the morning after my wedding-night?'

'I knew your husband had not stayed with you for long that night. But I imagined that he would have visited you frequently since. How could one have guessed that he would behave like this? It's incredible!'

After the necklace incident and the cheerless meal which had followed it, Catherine had been so angry that she had not tried to hide her state of mind. Feeling herself spurned and humiliated by Garin's complete indifference, she had finally decided to tell Sara the truth about their conjugal relations, such as they were. Sara heard her out with an expression of comical amazement, hands on hips.

'What? Nothing? Nothing at all?'

'Almost nothing. On our wedding-night he came into my room and made me get out of bed and take my clothes off. And then he stared at me for a long time, as though . . . as though I were one of those ivory and alabaster statuettes he has in his room. He told me that I was very beautiful . . . and then he left. He has never come back. Perhaps he doesn't find me attractive.'

'Are you mad?' Sara cried, her eyes kindling. 'Not find you attractive? Why, silly girl, you only have to look at yourself in the mirror! There isn't a man alive who could resist you if you really set your cap at him. That husband of yours is made of the same stuff as the others! Do you mean to tell me that he took off your nightgown, looked at you standing there all naked . . . and then went quietly off to bed at the other end of the house? Why, I have never heard of anything so ridiculous! It's enough to make him the laughing-stock of the whole kingdom!'

As she spoke Sara shook out the dress which Catherine had just taken off and laid it out across the bed to brush it before putting it away. Catherine watched her with a disillusioned expression on her face.

'I don't see why? He may very well only be keeping to the Duke's bargain. He married me it is true, but Philippe may easily have made him promise never to touch me.'

'Do you really believe that? Well then, just you explain, my poor child, what man worthy of the name would accept such a bargain without feeling eternally disgraced in his own eyes? Anyway, a great prince like the Duke Philippe would never stoop to such a suggestion. No, there can be only two possible explanations. One is that Messire Garin does not find you attractive, which seems impossible. And the other is that your husband is not a real man. After all, he had nothing to do with women before his marriage. He has never been known to have a mistress, or a love affair of any sort. He had to be ordered to do so before he would take a wife. Perhaps . . .'

'Perhaps?'

'Perhaps he is inclined the other way. . . . It is a common enough practice in Greece and Italy where I come from. Many women there are forced to go to their graves untouched because there are men who prefer young boys to them. . . .'

Catherine's eyes grew huge.

'Do you mean you think Garin is like that?'

'Why not? He has travelled a great deal, especially in the countries of the Levant. He might well have become addicted to this shameful vice out there. At all events, we must get to the bottom of this mystery.'

'I don't see how,' said Catherine, with a shrug.

Sara put down her brush and came towards her, looking at her with eyes which had narrowed to mere slits.

'I told you that if you really wanted a man enough no one worthy of the name would be able to resist you. Well, now you must show him that you do want him. After all, you have done nothing so far to attract your husband.'

'But I don't want to attract him!' the young woman protested. 'I would like to find out why he behaves as he does, I admit, but that is not at all the same thing as giving myself to him. . . .'

Sara flashed her a look of such withering contempt that it left Catherine rooted to the spot. Then she shrugged and turned her back. Catherine had never known Sara look at her like that before.

'You are not a real woman!' the gipsy woman said contemptuously. 'To tell the truth you are well matched, the pair of you! No woman, no *real* woman that is, would allow herself to be so humiliated without trying to find out why. It is a question of pride.'

'No it isn't. I just love someone else. That's all.'

'Oh yes, I know you want to keep yourself pure for some young fellow or other who won't have you at any price! And you really think you can succeed? Silly little fool! How long do you suppose you can hold out against the Duke? Would you rather wait till your husband, since that seems to be his role, hands you over to him all trussed and ready like a fat little goose? You accept this slave's role then? I'll tell you something: if you had a little of my blood in your veins, a little honest red blood all hot with pride and arrogance, you would go and throw yourself into your husband's arms and force him to do his duty by you . . . if only to pay this Philippe of Burgundy back as he deserves! But it isn't blood which flows in your veins, it's water! Wait till you are handed over then, poor thing, it's all you deserve. . . .'

Catherine could not have been more shattered if she had been struck by a thunderbolt than she was by Sara's outburst. She stood there, with her arms hanging at her sides, not quite knowing how to react. Sara suppressed a smile, before adding with deadly gentleness.

'And the worst part of it all is that you are secretly pining to go and have it out with your husband – because if there is one thing you are not ideally suited for it's chastity! You are really as cross as a turkey-cock!'

This second of Sara's comparisons borrowed from the

poultry-run had the effect of spurring Catherine out of her state of stunned surprise. She instantly flushed to the roots of her hair and angrily clenched her fists.

'So I deserve no better than to be handed over like a fat little goose, do I? And I'm as cross as a turkey-cock, am I? Well, we shall see about that! Go and fetch my women!'

'What are you going to do?'

'Wait and see! You were right about one thing: I am very cross indeed! I want a bath, at once, and all my perfumes! . . . And let me tell you that if you don't succeed in making me irresistible somehow or other I shall have you flayed alive when I get back.'

'If it only depended on me,' cried Sara, laughing as she ran to ring the bell, 'your husband would be in mortal danger!'

A few minutes later Catherine's women arrived, breathless. The silver bath was filled with lukewarm water and Catherine immersed herself in it for a few minutes. Then they massaged her from head to toe, powdered her all over and Perrine performed her rite with the perfumes under Sara's watchful eye. Sara herself took charge of Catherine's hair. While the other maids busied about their various tasks she brushed and brushed the long silky hair till it gleamed like gold and crackled when she touched it. She left it hanging loose down Catherine's back. Then Sara dismissed the maids, intending to complete Catherine's toilet on her own.

'What shall I wear?' Catherine asked, looking questioningly at her once the women had left the room.

'You will wear what I tell you to wear,' said Sara, who was now busy dressing Catherine's hair in a long shining horse's tail, secured on top of her head with a gold bracelet studded with turquoises. She clearly took considerable pleasure in her handiwork, and kept smiling mysteriously to herself.

A few minutes later Catherine left the room holding a candle in one hand to light the way. Perrine had brought word that Garin had not yet retired for the night. He was talking about medicine to Abou-al-Khayr. . . . Catherine hurried along the corridors wrapped in a great taffeta coat lined with pale grey fur, with matching slippers on her feet. She wanted to get to Garin's room before he did.

When she reached the heavy oak door which led to her husband's room there was no light to be seen underneath it. She raised the latch and peered into the darkened room. Then she lifted up her candle, stepped in, and quickly shut the door behind her. All was well. . . .

She went round the room lighting the torches which the valet had left ready with her candle. Presently the large, luxurious room was ablaze with light. The silver and crystal chair glittered like a jewel, but it was the bed which attracted Catherine. Slowly and a little fearfully, she climbed the two velvet-covered steps and stood there looking at the sober but sumptuous bed. Germain, the valet, had turned back the covers, and she paused for a moment wondering whether to slip between the violet silk sheets. But, remembering Sara's advice, she remained as she was, standing by the bed. Then she heard a quick footstep approaching along the gallery.

When Garin opened the door of his room the first thing he saw was Catherine standing beside his bed, head thrown proudly back, looking at him. She was still wrapped in the silk coat. His gaze left her for a moment to range round the room with its blazing candelabra, then returned to her with undisguised astonishment.

'What are you doing here?'

Without a word she let her coat slip down to her feet and stood there, stark naked but for the barbaric necklace he had given her a few hours earlier. She smiled at him challengingly. Her pale slender body stood out sharply against the dark bed hangings, the golden nimbus of hair drawn back so as to reveal her long supple neck. She looked like some pagan goddess.

Garin blenched, staggered as though transfixed by an arrow and then leant against the wall with his eyes closed.

'Go away . . .' he stammered hoarsely. 'Leave me . . . at once.'

'No!'

He could no longer conceal the fact that he was profoundly agitated. He could not recover his self-control. With a feeling of triumph Catherine observed the distress into which this normally icily calm man had been thrown. She abandoned her last reserve of modesty. Silently, on bare feet, she came across the room towards him, smiling, and irresistible.

'I won't go,' she said. 'I am staying here because this is where I belong, as your wife. Look at me, Garin! Are you so frightened of me?'

He murmured, without opening his eyes:

'Yes. I am frightened of you. . . . Don't you understand that I cannot touch you, that I haven't the right to do so? Why torture me by tempting me to do something forbidden? Leave me alone, Catherine, please!' But instead of obeying him she came still closer, slipping her arms round his neck in spite of his protests, and pressed her body against him, enveloping him in her scented warmth. She touched his white face with her lips. Garin, standing with closed eyes, looked like a martyr nailed to the whipping-post.

'I won't leave you till you have made me your wife, as you have every right to do. I don't care a fig for Philippe's orders. They are wicked and unnatural and I repudiate them. I am your wife, and if he wants me he must take me as you have made me. Look at me, Garin.'

She heard him groan softly, and once more he tried gently to push her away. But this time he did look at her. And he saw the face of his enchanting temptress close to his own, with parted lips and eyes soft with promise. He felt each curve of her young, supple body against him. The golden goddess of a moment before, whom he had almost believed to be a figment of his imagination, had come to offer herself to him, and she was maddeningly desirable. He lost his head. . . .

Seizing Catherine in his arms he stumbled across to the bed and flung her down on the velvet bedcover. Then he threw himself on top of her. He moved with such violence that Catherine had to suppress a scream. She shivered fearfully as she felt herself swept and bruised by a hurricane of passionate, savage caresses. Garin's hands mauled her rather than caressed her, and his mouth covered her with hungry kisses from her knees up to her throat. He grunted like a famished beast as his fingers kneaded her soft, female flesh. Gradually, as the girl abandoned herself to the frenzy of the man's caresses, she felt the stirring of desire and pleasure in her own body. At first she moaned softly under Garin's exploring, impatient hands but then her body relaxed, yielding itself expectantly to the promise of still greater delight. Her groping hands unfastened Garin's doublet and lingered caressingly on his chest, which was lean, hairy and hard as oak. The canopy of the bed seemed to be spinning above her head. . . . Suddenly, she gave a cry of pain; Garin, almost beside himself with desire, had bitten the soft skin below her right breast. . . .

Her cry had much the same effect on her husband that a jet of icy water might have done. He released her abruptly, stood up and then sprang to the end of the bed, where he stood looking at her, wild-eyed. He was panting, his face was scarlet and there was a ferocious brilliance in his gaze.

'You made me lose . . . my head. Now go! You must leave me!'

She held out her arms to him, trying to bring him back to her. She felt angry and dismayed that he should still be trying to elude her.

'No, Garin! Come to me . . . please! For the love of Heaven forget about the Duke. . . . Come back to me! We could be happy together. I know we could!'

But he gently pushed away her outstretched arms and began fastening his doublet with trembling hands. He shook his head. His face. was regaining its accustomed pallor. Catherine was suddenly convulsed by sobs. Angry tears sprang from her eyes.

'But *why*? Tell me why? You find me desirable. I know . . . you have just proved that you want me. So *why, why*?'

Garin slowly sat down on the edge of the bed. He stroked her lovely tearful face with infinite gentleness and then laid his hand on her golden head. Catherine heard him sigh. She cried out brokenly:

'You can't make me believe that this cruel, inhuman restraint you have imposed upon yourself doesn't make you suffer too! You can't make me believe that! I know you are unhappy. And yet you go on stupidly and obstinately making us lead this absurd, unnatural life. . . .'

Garin suddenly looked away. Leaving the rosy figure stretched out upon the bed, he walked over to a shadowy corner of the room. She heard him sigh once more. His voice took on a strange gentleness in which the note of suffering sounded all the more poignantly for being restrained and held in check.

'There is such sorrow in my heart!' he murmured.

'Life was once so beautiful!
Such sorrow that my laughter has turned to tears!
Even the birds of the forest are moved by my lament, and
  mourn!
O love so wondrous fair that you rob me of my resolve!
But what am I saying, poor fool, in the heat of my rancour?
He who seeks happiness in this life must lose it in the next, alas!
For ever, alas!'

Catherine listened, astonished, as he spoke these lines. She wondered at their meaning.

'What is that?' she asked.

Garin gave her a pale smile.

'Oh, nothing . . . forgive me! A few lines by a German poet who went on the Crusades, and whom the Emperor Frederick II made his protégé. He was called Walther von der Vogelwiede. You see, I am like our friend Abou-al-Khayr. I love poetry too. Now I must leave you, Catherine. Sleep here, if you wish to. . . .'

Before Catherine could stop him he had crossed the room and vanished into the darkness of the long gallery. She heard his footsteps grow fainter. . . . She was suddenly consumed with rage. Slipping to the foot of the bed she seized her coat and slippers. Then she wrapped it round her and ran back to her own room. As she slammed the door behind her Sara, who had been dozing on a stool near the fire, gave a jump and then, recognizing Catherine, stood up and looked inquiringly at her.

'Well?'

Catherine tore the necklace off and threw it angrily across the room, as far as she could. Then she stamped on her silk coat. There were angry tears in her eyes.

'Well . . . nothing!' she sobbed. 'Absolutely nothing!'

'It isn't possible!'

'Yes it is, I'm telling you!'

Catherine's nerves finally cracked. She sobbed on Sara's shoulder without even bothering to put her clothes on again. Sara waited till she had grown a little calmer, her brows knitted in a worried frown. When her sobs were quietening a little she lightly touched the spot where Garin's bite had broken the skin, and a little drop of blood could be seen.

Now quite exhausted, Catherine let herself be put to bed like a child. Then, while Sara attended to the tiny abrasion, she told her exactly what had passed between Garin and herself, ending with this despairing cry:

'He is so much stronger than we thought, Sara! And so much in control of himself! Nothing in the world will make him break the promise he has made the Duke!'

But Sara shook her head.

'It isn't that. I am sure that he was on the point of breaking that promise, and that you almost won the day. I suspect there must be something else, but what can it be?'

'Well, how can we find out? What can I do now?'

'Nothing. Wait. Time will tell, perhaps. . . .'

'Anyway,' said Catherine, snuggling into her pillows, 'don't expect me to go through another experience like that!'

Sara bent over and kissed her. Then she drew the curtains round the bed and smiled.

'Shall I go and fetch the whip for that punishment you promised me?'

It was Catherine's turn to laugh now and the laugh did her a great deal of good. The humiliation she had suffered that night began to seem less grievous as her body relaxed and revelled in the comfort of her bed. It had been an interesting experience, but perhaps it had not ended so badly after all . . . seeing that she didn't love Garin.

These comforting reflections did not prevent her having bizarre dreams that night in which Garin and his exasperating secret played by far the largest part.

Catherine was not wearing the turquoise necklace – to which she had in any case taken a violent dislike – when, with her hand on her husband's, she was ushered into the room in the Ducal Palace where the Dowager Duchess was waiting. Garin knew too much about Marguerite of Bavaria, mother of Philippe le Bon, to allow his wife to wear anything more elaborate on this occasion than a simple grey velvet dress over a silver underdress which matched her tall pointed headdress. The headdress was so high that Catherine had to bend her head to pass through the door. She wore only one jewel, but an exceedingly beautiful one. It was a superb amethyst, framed by three magnificent and lustrous pear-shaped pearls, and Catherine wore it hanging on a fine gold chain round her neck.

The reception-room which formed part of the Duchess's private suite of rooms was not particularly large, and it was chiefly furnished with some carved chests and a group of chairs near the window where the Duchess herself was sitting in a tall chair emblazoned with her personal coat of arms. Some black velvet cushions were scattered about on the flagged floor for the maids-of-honour to sit on.

Though she was more than fifty, Marguerite of Bavaria still retained many traces of the beauty which had once been famous. The carriage of her graceful head was still superb, and it helped to give her not particularly long neck a positively swan-like air. Her cheeks no longer had the roundness of youth, and her blue eyes had faded a little, but their expression remained direct and imperious. The fold of her slightly thick lips indicated a stubborn, forceful character. Her nose was long but finely chiselled. She had beautiful hands and a tall, stately figure.

Marguerite of Bavaria had been in mourning ever since her

husband's death. She wore unrelieved, but sumptuous, black. Her black velvet dress and headdress were banded with sables. A magnificent gold necklace, in the shape of a garland of acanthus leaves, gleamed under the black veil which hung from the headdress and veiled the Duchess's neck. This strict observance of mourning was inspired not so much by regrets for her dead husband as by this tall, haughty woman's ceaseless preoccupation with the prerogatives of her own high rank. Marguerite had found the gay, charming Duc d'Orléans a great deal more attractive than the surly Jean-sans-Peur, and the French court had always rumoured that he had been her lover. It was common gossip in well-informed circles that it had been jealousy still more than ambition, which drove Jean-sans-Peur to the assassination of the Duke. But, be that as it might, Marguerite's tight-shut lips had never disclosed their secret. She was an excellent mother to her son Philippe, and a devoted and disinterested collaborator in matters of state. Burgundy was safe and thriving in her firm, capable hands and Philippe could devote himself to the northern provinces without a moment's unease.

Four of the Duchess's six daughters were seated round their mother, forming a little inner circle amid the maids-of-honour. They were working with her on the same piece of embroidery, a huge battle standard in red silk embroidered with a white St Andrew's cross. Catherine instantly recognized the Duc de Guyenne's young widow, Marguerite, among them, and she derived a sort of pleasure from the thought that the girl who had tried to save Michel de Montsalvy during the riots in the Hôtel de Saint Pol should be sitting there. She attached a sort of superstitious importance to this meeting. Now twenty-nine years old, the young Duchess had not greatly changed. She was a little stouter, but her white skin was perhaps more dazzling than before. She was three years older than her brother Philippe and the oldest of the family.

Beside Marguerite's full-blown beauty, her sister Catherine seemed oddly colourless. She was so slender as to be almost transparent and always dressed soberly, like a nun, in dark dresses and plain wimples which left only her narrow ferret's face visible, with its timid anxious eyes. Catherine was the unlucky one of the family. Her first betrothal at the age of ten, to the Comte Philippe de Vertus, had come to an abrupt end six years later when she learnt, just before the marriage should have taken place, of her fiancé's heroic death in the muddy field of Agincourt. Another match, this time with the heir to the Duke d'Anjou, had been contemplated, but then Duke Jean's violent death at Montereau had thrown the pair into opposite camps and put an end to the projected marriage. Since then Catherine of Burgundy had refused all her suitors.

The two other Princesses, Anne and Agnes, respectively nineteen and sixteen years old, were still young girls, and they did not aspire to be anything more than pretty, fresh and gay, though the poor folk of Dijon were already singing the praises of Anne, whom they reverently described as an angel dropped from Heaven.

They both greeted Catherine's curtsey with an open smile which went straight to the young woman's heart.

'So this is your wife, Messire Garin,' said the Duchess in her deep voice. 'We must compliment you on your choice. She is indeed beautiful, and yet she retains the modesty and decorum suited to such a young woman. Come here, my dear. . . .'

Catherine, with a beating heart, went up to the Duchess's chair and knelt beside it with her head modestly bowed. Marguerite smiled, noting with an approving eye the details of the young woman's dress, particularly its modest neckline, and above it the young woman's blushing face. She was aware of the rather special regard which her son entertained towards this girl and this did not displease her. It was normal for a prince to have mistresses, and, though her pride had at first flinched from the prospect of such an honour being bestowed upon a girl of humble birth, still she now noted approvingly that this young bourgeoise had all the bearing and elegance of a great lady, and she was undeniably a peerless beauty.

'We shall be pleased to number you henceforth among our ladies-in-waiting,' she said graciously. 'The Mistress of the

Robes, the Dame de Châteauvilain, to whom we will introduce you presently, will explain your duties to you. Now, curtsey to our daughters and then take your seat on this cushion by our feet, next to Mademoiselle de Vaugrigneuse.'

She indicated a young girl with a mean face richly dressed in blue and silver brocade which did not flatter her yellow, liverish complexion. The young girl thus indicated assumed a disdainful little curl of the lip as she moved away from the cushion assigned to Catherine, which did not escape the Duchess's sharp eyes.

'We would like it to be remembered,' she added, without raising her voice, but in such a cutting tone that the girl in question flushed to the roots of her hair, 'that birth is not the only thing that counts in this sinful world of ours and that our favour can easily replace it. It is the prerogative of princes to elevate modesty to whatever rank they please, just as it is within their power to raze the proud and arrogant to the ground.'

Marie de Vaugrigneuse allowed the rebuke to sink in, and she even managed a smile in response to Catherine's timid one.

Pleased with the way she had dealt with this situation, the Duchess now turned towards Garin.

'You may leave us now, messire. We wish to discuss certain domestic and feminine matters with your young wife which we know are not diverting to a man's ears.'

The Duchess had been born and brought up in Holland and she had absorbed the solid, housewifely virtues of the Dutch, their love of orderliness and a well-run home. She was not above taking an active interest in the running of the palace, and she kept an eye on the expenses of her household, the kitchens and even the poultry-run. She knew almost exactly how many sheets she had, how many turkeys, and whether the money spent on candles was reasonable or not. She had a fondness for strange animals. A pet dolphin had been raised in a pool in the palace gardens and the Duchess lavished her most tender care on a porcupine for whom she had had a little niche built at the bottom of the staircase of the New Tower. She also owned a huge parrot, a handsome white cockatoo with a pink crest which a Venetian traveller had brought back specially for her from the Moluccas islands. At that very moment a page entered carrying the resplendent but bad-tempered bird on its gilded perch, and it provided a ready-made subject of conversation between the Duchess and Catherine. Catherine admired the bird's vivid plumage with an unfeigned enthusiasm which won Marguerite's heart, and she talked about Gedeon in reply to the countless questions with which the curious Duchess plied her. The Duchess had christened her bird Cambrai after the town where she and Duke Jean had been married. She laughed heartily at the story of Gedeon's misdeeds and at the account of his banishment to the little Moorish doctor's room.

'You must bring both the bird and his keeper to see us,' said Marguerite. 'We are as curious to see one as the other. And perhaps this heathen doctor may be able to do something for our ailments, which are indeed numerous.'

The Duchess was so delighted with her new lady-in-waiting that when the collation was brought in by the head cooks she ordered that Catherine should be served first. There was 'galant' to drink, a decoction of heated, perfumed and pungently spiced wine which the late Marguerite of Flanders had made fashionable and which she had enjoyed preparing with her own hands.

Catherine forgot her shyness in this benevolent and sympathetic atmosphere. She felt she could be happy in this setting even though two or three of her high-born companions, such as Marie de Vaugrigneuse, might look askance at her. She nibbled two custard tarts and drank a goblet of the punch with relish. Garin had told her that the Duchess approved of hearty appetites like those of her own countrymen.

They had finished the collation and a footman was just taking away the remains of the meal when a page entered with a message for the Duchess. He told her that a horseman from the Duke's Grande Écurie had ridden with all speed from Arras with a message for her.

'Bring him here!' Marguerite commanded.

A few minutes later they heard rapid steps of armour-shod feet echoing along the flagged floor of the ante-room. A moment later a man entered, dressed in the green cloth uniform, reinforced with steel plates, which was worn by members of the Duke's House. He was not very tall but unusually powerfully built. The page escorted him to the Duchess and he knelt at her feet. He had removed his dusty helmet and carried it under one arm. Now he took a roll of parchment bearing the ducal arms from out of his tunic and gave it to the Duchess, bowing his head respectfully as he did so. This head, with its thick crop of square-cut black hair, seemed strangely familiar to Catherine. As she stared at it her first reaction of astonished disbelief gave way to a joyful certainty. Could it really be he? Might it not be the effect of some trick of the light, or of her imagination? And yet that profile, with its aquiline nose, was just like the one she remembered so clearly from all those years ago.

'You have come direct from Arras?' inquired the Duchess.

'Direct, madame, and I await Your Grace's commands. Monseigneur the Duke himself urged that I should make all possible haste. The news I bring is of considerable importance.' The tone of the stranger's voice was easy without being familiar.

Listening to that voice, now a little deeper than she remembered it, Catherine's last doubts vanished. This cavalry officer of the Duke's was none other than Landry Pigasse, her childhood friend.

He had not seen her. He had not so much as glanced once in the direction of the whispering, rustling group of maids-of-honour. He was simply kneeling there waiting for further instructions. Catherine needed to summon up all her newfound training in courtly etiquette to prevent herself flinging her arms round her old friend and confidant and thereby shocking everyone present. Alas, what Catherine Legoix could do with impunity was forbidden to the Dame de Brazey, especially under the Duchess's eye.

The Duchess had taken the parchment with its great red seal and was unrolling it slowly, holding it in both hands. With knitted brows she studied what appeared to be a short enough missive.

Her face sharpened a little and her lips tightened. The onlookers' curiosity turned to anxiety; it must be bad news.

The Duchess dismissed Landry with a wave of the hand. He stood up and backed his way out of the royal presence. Catherine watched him go with a sigh, but she promised herself that she would find him again as soon as possible. . . .

Marguerite of Bavaria sat in silence, one elbow leaning on the arm of her chair and her chin propped in her hand. She appeared to be thinking deeply. A moment later she sat up again and looked round, first at her women, and then at her daughters.

'Ladies,' she said, slowly and solemnly, 'it is important news indeed which our prince and son sends us. We feel it is not too soon to pass it on to you. Monseigneur has sent for two of his sisters to join him as soon as possible and it will be necessary for some of you to accompany them.'

This news was greeted with excited, curious murmurs among the ladies. Meanwhile the Duchess turned towards her elder daughter and looked at her earnestly.

'Marguerite,' she said, 'it is your brother's wish that you should once more enter the state of holy matrimony. He has given your hand in marriage to a rich and noble lord, a man of ancient lineage and fair name.'

'Who is he, Mother?' asked Marguerite, who had grown slightly paler.

'You are to marry Arthur of Brittany, Comte de Richemont. And you, Anne,' the Duchess went on, turning towards her young daughter with ill-concealed emotion.

'I, Mother?'

'Yes, you, my child. Your brother has chosen a husband for you too. He intends to marry you at the same time as your sister, to the Regent of France . . . the Duke of Bedford.'

The Duchess's voice faltered over these last words, but this was covered by the young girl's horrified exclamation:

'I must marry an Englishman?'

'He is your brother's ally,' said the Duchess, with an effort, 'and his policy demands that the bonds should be tightened between our family and that of . . . King Henry.'

A harsh, powerful voice resounded from the other end of the room.

'The King of France is Monseigneur Charles and the Englishman is no better than a thief! If it were not for that damned whore Isabeau's proclaiming her son a bastard there would be no two ways about it!'

A tall, robust figure of a woman had just marched through the door in the manner of one accustomed to finding them open automatically at her approach. She had the build of a foot-soldier, draped in a flowing scarlet gown, and the soft wings of white muslin which framed her face only further accentuated her masculine cast of features and slight moustache. The Duchess, far from showing annoyance at this outspoken interruption, watched her approach with a smile. Everyone at Court knew that the noble Lady Ermengarde de Châteauvilain, the Duchess's Mistress of the Robes, was allowed the privilege of speaking her mind, and that she was implacably opposed to the alliance with England and would have been quite prepared to voice her convictions on the subject in the midst of the English Court if she had felt her opinions merited so much attention. She hated the English and allowed no one to remain in ignorance of that fact. Indeed, more than one doughty warrior had retreated in alarm and confusion before the immensity of her wrath.

'My dear,' the Duchess said gently, 'unfortunately there *is* some doubt about Charles's birth.'

'Not in my mind, and I am as proud a Frenchwoman as I am a Burgundian! So this little ewe-lamb is to be handed over to the English butcher, is she?' she remarked, extending toward the Princess a hand as large as a plate but surprisingly finely shaped. The poor girl needed no encouragement to break down. She was already quietly weeping, quite oblivious of protocol.

'The Duke wishes it, my good Ermengarde. As a good

Burgundian, you know that his wishes must be obeyed.'

'That's just what makes me so furious!' said Dame Ermengarde, seating herself heavily in the chair which Anne de Bourgogne had just vacated in order to kneel at her mother's side. Suddenly her eyes fell upon Catherine, who had been looking at her open-mouthed since she entered the room. The large but comely hand now pointed towards her.

'Is that our new lady-in-waiting?' she asked.

'It is indeed Dame Catherine de Brazey,' said the Duchess, while Catherine curtseyed to the Dame de Châteauvilain as deeply as her importance seemed to require. The latter studied her, replying to her obeisance with a brisk nod of the head, and then remarked good-humouredly:

'A pretty recruit! Forsooth, my dear, if I were your husband I would mount a strong guard round you! I can think of more than one gentleman here who will soon be scheming to get you into his bed as quickly as he can!'

'Ermengarde!' said the Duchess reproachfully. 'You are embarrassing the child.'

'Bah!' Dame Ermengarde exclaimed, with a wide grin which displayed a formidable array of strong white teeth. 'A compliment never killed anyone, and I dare say Dame Catherine has heard a few in her time.'

The good lady would undoubtedly have gone on in this vein a while longer, for she was fond of tales of gallantry and bawdy jests. But the Duchess Marguerite hurriedly intervened and told her ladies that they should all begin packing their travelling chests for their forthcoming visit to Flanders. Meanwhile she asked them to leave her alone with her dear friend the Dame de Châteauvilain, with whom she had many important matters to discuss.

Catherine dropped her curtsey with the others and left the room determined to seek out Landry at once. But as soon as they entered the gallery Marie de Vaugrigneuse plucked her by the sleeve.

'I dote on this velvet you are wearing, my dear. Did you buy it at your uncle's shop?'

'No,' said Catherine sweetly, mindful of what Garin had told her, 'your grandfather's donkeys brought it for me all the way from Genoa.'

CHAPTER TEN

ARNAUD DE MONTSALVY

CATHERINE WENT to look for Landry as soon as she could but she did not succeed in finding him. The quarters of the ducal cavalry were near the stables, in a part of the palace where a lady-in-waiting could not go without the Duchess's consent. Besides, she was told by the squire to whom she applied for information that Landry Pigasse was only staying a short while in Dijon. He was resting at that moment but would be in the saddle again that very evening to carry some dispatches which had just arrived from Chancellor Rollin in Beaune. He would certainly have crossed the city boundaries before the curfew.

Catherine did not dare pursue the matter further. But she reminded herself on the way home that if she were one of the ladies who accompanied the Princesses to Flanders she would surely have further opportunities to see her childhood friend there. She vowed that this time nothing would stop her. She had been overjoyed to see him again because, apart from anything else, he was one of the few links which connected her to the past, to the days when they still lived in the shop on the Pont-au-Change, to the streets of Paris which she remembered so vividly and the terrible day of the citizens' revolt.

During the weeks which followed, however, she had little time to dwell on reminiscences of those days. She had first of all to attend the Dowager Duchess, who had taken a fancy to her and called upon her services more and more frequently, requiring her at the palace almost every day. Catherine found that she, together with Marie de Vaugrigneuse, the Duchess's god-daughter, had been placed in charge of their mistress's wardrobe. This proximity led inevitably to an occasional unsheathing of claws, and some barbed exchanges. There was little love lost between the two young women. Catherine would gladly have done without this little private war, for the other girl inspired only contemptuous indifference in her, but her character was not such that she could patiently suffer the constant pin-pricks to her pride which Marie administered. Uncle Mathieu's cloth and Grandfather Vaugrigneuse's donkeys formed the principal ammunition in this war. Grandfather Vaugrigneuse's rise to the nobility had been quite recent. He had made his fortune in a somewhat clandestine, but very profitable, fashion, smuggling with the help of the invaluable donkeys.

Another thing which took up a great deal of the young women's time was their imminent departure for Flanders, and the preparations for the Princesses' double wedding. The wardrobe being her responsibility, Catherine was actively concerned with the two Princesses' trousseaux. She helped them choose the materials and styles for their dresses. She bullied Dame Gauberte, the worthy seamstress, with the vigorous assistance of Ermengarde de Châteauvilain. She had had the foresight to make an ally of the formidable Mistress of the Robes by a gesture as discreet as it was endearing. This was the gift of a superb length of crimson and gold Genoese velvet which she had found in her uncle's shop and which delighted the Countess. Ermengarde had, it seemed, a strong partiality for bright colours and particularly for bright red, which she seemed to think added to her natural dignity. The length of velvet and Catherine's own enchanting smile, together with her undeniable taste in clothes and domestic appointments, had placed the Countess very decidedly on the side of the Lord Treasurer's young wife.

As for the new lady-in-waiting's private existence, however, that passed without incident. Life with Garin slipped by peacefully and uneventfully, each day much like the one before. The Treasurer did not entertain much and did not like to make too much display of his great wealth, being well aware of the jealousy and envy which great riches incite in others. If he tended towards a show of luxury and ostentation in the privacy of his various homes, that was purely for his own personal pleasure, and the gratification of his eyes alone. To large banquets and noisy, crowded festivities, he preferred a quiet game of chess by the fireside, reading a book, contemplating his collection of rare *objets d'art*, and, recently, the company of Abou-al-Khayr, whose learning and Oriental wisdom pleased him.

The two men frequently had long discussions together. Catherine sometimes joined in, but more often than not they made her yawn with boredom, because, unlike Garin, she was not interested in the mysteries of medicine and the dangerous and subtle science of poisons. The little Moorish doctor was not only a remarkably skilled medical practitioner for that age. He was an even more remarkable toxicologist.

At length the time arrived for the two Princesses, Marguerite and Anne, to leave Dijon with their retinue. It was towards the end of March when the long train of horses, hackneys, carts and baggage mules passed through the Guillaume Gate. They soon left the fortifications behind them, and it was not long before Dijon, its fantastic skyline fretted with towers and steeples, which looked like a forest of spears at a distance, had faded from sight.

The gaiety usually to be found in expeditions of this sort was, Catherine noted without much surprise, totally missing from this one. The Duchess Marguerite's health had taken a turn for the worse of late and she had had to abandon the idea of accompanying her daughters, as she had originally intended to do. The Countess Ermengarde was travelling as her representative, and was to act as chaperon to the two Princesses.

Comfortably ensconced in her saddle, enveloped in an enormous maroon pelisse lined with red fox, which doubled her already impressive girth, Ermengarde de Châteauvilain ambled along at Catherine's side. Neither of them spoke, being too busy admiring the fresh green foliage on the trees, inhaling the sharp early morning air and enjoying the sunshine – sunshine which was so little seen in the town's twisting, narrow, dirty streets. Catherine had always enjoyed travelling, even on short distances, and this journey reminded her of the one she had made with her Uncle Mathieu the year before and which had been so rich in incident and adventures.

The Countess Ermengarde also enjoyed travelling but for different reasons. There was the satisfaction of being able to gratify her insatiable curiosity about people and places. She also liked the horses' slow, tranquil pace along the endless roads, which allowed her to nod off comfortably, and she found that these siestas in the open air gave her an agreeable sense of well-being and sharpened her appetite.

The Duke of Burgundy awaited his sisters at Amiens, where the double marriage was to take place. These marriages were the outcome of many months of negotiations and talks with the English Regent and the Duke of Brittany. He had deliberately chosen this episcopal city because, since it was neutral, in theory at least, this arrangement would cause least offence to the Duke of Savoy, with whom protracted peace negotiations were still going on. But the real reason for the choice was that the Bishop of Amiens was a loyal servant of the Duke and in Amiens he felt as if he were in his own country.

As the two Princesses and their retinue reached the Somme, after a long but uneventful journey across the devastated country of Champagne, Countess Ermengarde's conversation was reduced almost entirely to curt, unladylike but expressive monosyllables. The reason for the good lady's wrath was the fact that, wherever the lavish, glittering royal cortège passed, they saw only starving and ragged men, women and children, their features wasted by hunger and their eyes glittering wolfishly. The English and their thieving soldiery had spread misery, hunger, fear and hatred wherever they went. The winter now drawing to an end had been a terrible one. The famine caused by the destruction of entire crops by fire had ravaged the countryside for hundreds of leagues around and decimated the population. Those villages which had not been razed to the ground were quite empty of signs of human habitation. The journey, which Catherine had found so pleasant while they were travelling through Burgundy, now became an interminable nightmare. The young woman shut her eyes with a stricken heart when she saw the armed escort using the wooden shafts of their lances to beat back a little group of half-starved people who had made the mistake of asking for their charity. Whenever this happened, however, Princess Anne intervened indignantly, reproaching the soldiers bitterly for their hard-heartedness. Her own generous heart was touched to the quick by the sight of so much suffering, and wherever they went she would give, give, and give still more, till her purse and hands were empty, leaving a shining trail of sweetness and compassion behind her. If Garin had not respectfully but firmly opposed the notion she would undoubtedly have distributed the thirty thousand gold écus carried by the mules along the route. This money represented a part of the Princess's dowry of a hundred thousand écus which had been exacted by the English duke. The size of this dowry contributed to Dame Ermengarde's increasing bad temper.

'What more does the greedy goddam want?' she demanded of Catherine when the walls of Amiens at length came into view. 'He comes here unlawfully, unasked, and bleeds this country of its last drop of blood. He takes to wife the sweetest, loveliest and most virtuous of our princesses, and yet he is still asking for gold when he should be down on his knees kissing the dust in thanksgiving for the favour Heaven has shown him! I boil with rage, Dame Catherine, I literally boil with rage to see our Duke extending a friendly hand to this country's ancient enemy and, not content with that, giving him his own sister too. . . .'

'I think he only does it to revenge himself on King Charles. He hates the King bitterly.'

'To revenge himself, perhaps, but also in the hope of usurping his throne,' the Countess complained. 'That sort of behaviour is disloyal in a vassal! Even when the vassal is a prince and trying to forget his obligations. It is dishonourable behaviour and that is all there is to it!'

A smile flitted rapidly across Catherine's lips, chapped by the icy wind which had arisen and was driving the clouds pell-mell before it high above the spires and towers of Amiens.

'Those are dangerous words, Countess,' she said slyly. 'They could be dangerous both for you and for me if the Duke were ever to get wind of them.'

But the look with which that good lady fixed her was so open, honest and proud that Catherine felt herself reddening under it.

'The Duke is perfectly well aware of my views, Dame Catherine. A gentlewoman does not stoop to deceit, not even for a Duke of Burgundy! What I am saying to you now I would be equally ready to say to him!'

Catherine could not help admiring her. Fat, stentorian-voiced, and faintly comical though she was, Ermengarde nevertheless came of a great and noble line, and this high breeding was something which no amount of excess fat or eccentric behaviour could ever disguise. Her greatness and dignity were instinctive and they triumphed over all the pettier human frailties. She was a loyal friend, but she could also be a formidable enemy. It was far wiser to be her ally.

When they reached Amiens the Princesses went to meet their brother, who awaited them in the Bishop's Palace. Their retinue meanwhile sought their lodgings in the houses which had been set aside for them. Ermengarde, naturally, accompanied her two young charges, while Catherine and her husband installed themselves in a house which stood a stone's throw from the large white stone cathedral, and whose back windows faced on to a tranquil canal. This house, which, although not very large, was extremely comfortable, belonged to one of the town's most important cloth-merchants with whom the Lord Treasurer had close business ties. Garin had sent his steward Tiercelin and his valet and secretary on ahead, together with Catherine's women, the latter under Sara's supervision. They had taken the bulk of their baggage with them, under armed escort, and when Catherine entered the cloth-merchant's house she was delighted to find that nothing had been overlooked which might have added to her comfort. A fire blazed in the hearth, her bedroom was comfortably appointed and hung with embroidered tapestries, her bed had been made and a huge bunch of violets in a painted faïence bowl lent their delicate fragrance to the scene. A meal was prepared for them in the principal room.

This lodging of theirs, modest though it was, was a rare luxury and privilege in a grossly overcrowded town where any form of accommodation fetched an inflated price. The large retinues of the Dukes of Brittany and Bedford, the Comte de Richemont and the Earls of Suffolk and Salisbury had overrun the town. More than one burgher of Amiens had been reduced to crowding into one small room with his entire family and all the servants in order to leave more room for the followers, most of them arrogant and ill-mannered, of all these lords who had come to parley with the Duke Philippe.

Every house had an escutcheon at its windows, and innumerable pennants and banners fluttered on the evening air. The device of the Duke of Brittany, black ermine tails on a field argent, covered all the houses to the east of the Bishop's Palace, while the blood-red perpendicular stripes of the Comte de Foix covered the western sector of the town. The south part belonged to the red Lancastrian rose of the Duke of Bedford. The English Duke and his followers, together with those of the Earls of Suffolk and Salisbury, occupied quite half the town. The Burgundians were crowded together in the northern sector and the servants of the Bishop of Amiens had to fit in wherever they could.

Despite her weariness, Catherine did not sleep that night. All night long the town echoed with singing and shouting and trumpet fanfares of such vigour that they left the houses shaking. This was but the prelude to the magnificent and lavish feasts which the Duke Philippe had promised. And added to the din outside was her own nervous condition. Garin had visited the Bishop's Palace that evening in answer to a summons from his master. On his return he paid a call on his wife, who had just gone to bed. She was chatting to Sara while the devoted gipsy woman brushed and folded away the clothes her mistress had been wearing that day.

'You will be presented to Monseigneur tomorrow night, during the ball which is being given to celebrate the betrothals,' he said briefly. 'I wish you good night.'

On the following evening the Bishop's Palace glowed in the dark as ruddily as if it were on fire. The barrels of blazing pitch on the battlements, together with the gold and crimson light which streamed through its tall Gothic windows, cast a lurid glare over the intricately carved white masonry of the nearby cathedral, enveloping its statues and carvings with a sort of unearthly radiance. A cascade of silken stuffs fluttered down to the ground from every embrasure and every pillar carried its silken banner. In the market-square, where the guards were having trouble controlling the crowd of idlers and sightseers, the townsfolk could see a vividly coloured fresco unfolded before their eyes. There were lords and knights in doublets coruscating with precious gems, taking cautious steps in their absurdly elongated pointed shoes, some of which were so long that their owners wore the points fastened to their belts with little gold chains. Some of them sported great embroidered hoods or immensely long jagged-edged sleeves which trailed as far as the ground and which they flaunted with superb effrontery. The ladies wore their most elaborate finery under the airy fantastic superstructure of their horned, pointed head-dresses. These were edged by single or double rolls of cloth or fur and swathed in clouds of lace or mousseline. They too sparkled with jewels, and walked along trailing the heavy satin, velvet, brocade or lamé trains of their festive gowns behind them. Separated from the crowd by a double row of guards in full armour, these dazzling apparitions strolled nonchalantly towards the celebrations in the palace like so many unknown stars glittering for an instant in the torchlight before being engulfed by the dark maw of the palace doorway. All round the market-square the windows were thronged with sightseers, and it was as bright as daylight, thanks to the Duke's liberality with torches and candles.

Catherine stood watching the apparently unending stream of guests from one of the palace windows. She had come there that afternoon with her own women and the coffers which contained her gown and jewels for the ball. The Mistress of the Robes had insisted that the responsibility of making a last-minute inspection of Catherine's clothes for her presentation to the Duke should be hers alone. For greater security, and to ensure that Catherine did not show herself, either from boredom or curiosity, to the assembled guests before the appointed time, Ermengarde had locked her into her own room while she went off to supervise the dressing of the two Princesses. Catherine's own toilet had been completed long ago and she stood gazing out of the window in the hopes that this would make the time go faster. . . .

'I can't help wondering whether Madame Anne and Madame Marguerite will pardon you your beauty tonight. For beside you I am afraid their beauty is eclipsed as are the stars beside the sun. It really isn't done to look so beautiful, my dear! It's indecent, almost scandalous!'

Ermengarde had looked genuinely vexed, but her praise was none the less sincere for that. For once, however, Catherine found no pleasure in these compliments. She felt unaccountably sad and weary, and she would gladly have taken off her wonderful gown to snuggle down in her white bed above the green canal waters. She had never felt so lonely.

In a little while Garin would be coming to fetch her. He would take her by the hand and conduct her to the great hall where the guests were now assembling. There she would curtsey to the Duke Philippe, his sisters the Princesses, and to their future husbands. She would again be seeing those grey eyes whose inscrutable calm she had once fleetingly disturbed. She knew that Philippe was waiting to see her and that this evening was to see the fruition of his powerful, unwavering desire for her, but this thought gave her no pleasure. That this high and mighty Duke should long to possess her, should even

love her after his fashion, did not excite her in the least. She
had noticed one couple in particular amongst the many who
streamed into the palace. They had seemed very young, the
chevalier little more than a boy, as fair as Michel de Montsalvy
had been, clean-shaven and radiant in his dark-blue satin
costume. He led a ravishing girl-child by the hands, as blonde as
himself, her hair wreathed with a simple circlet of pink roses
as fresh as her pink moiré gown. From time to time the boy
would lean towards his companion and whisper something in
her ear which made her smile and blush, and Catherine
could imagine the squeezing of hands going on, the sweet
whispered exchanges, the ardent, hungry kisses. Those two
might have been alone in the world. He did not look once at
the many dazzlingly gowned, often glowingly beautiful
women who surrounded them. Her mischievous eyes did not
once leave his face. They loved each other with all the ardour
of the very young and it would not have occurred to them for
an instant to hide their passion. They were happy. . . .

Against the yardstick of this blithe happiness Catherine
measured the emptiness of her own existence. A yearning but
lonely heart, a travesty of a husband who dressed her in fine
clothes only to throw her into the arms of another man, the lust
of strangers which did not interest her in spite of the many
restless nights when her whole body ached to be appeased and
satisfied and the blood seemed to boil in her veins. And finally
the contempt of the one man she loved. . . . It was a sad
reckoning.

'Your husband is here, Dame Catherine,' she heard the
Countess saying behind her. She had not heard the Mistress of
the Robes enter the room, but there she unmistakably was, a
garish but impressive figure in a red and gold velvet gown and
a headdress almost as tall as a cathedral spire. She seemed to
overflow into all the space available and almost hid Garin, whose
black-clad form loomed darkly near the door.

He stepped forward, studied Catherine for a moment and
then announced:

'Excellent!'

'Better than that!' Ermengarde corrected him. 'Breath-taking!'

The word was apt. Catherine was breathtaking that night because of her calculated simplicity. Her plain black velvet dress, caught in under the bosom by a wide belt of the same material, was free of all ornament but for a flash of cloth of gold lining the long, long sleeves. In contrast to this absolute severity of cloth and cut, the daring neckline showed off her dazzling skin all the more triumphantly. It was cut low and square in front, baring her bosom as low as decency allowed and just covering the points of her shoulders. Behind, it plunged to a point below her shoulder-blades. The immensely long sleeves, in contrast, reached almost to her finger-tips. There would be many women as daringly gowned, but none of them, thanks to the dark matt texture of her dress, would look as naked as Catherine. The other daring touch which the Countess of Châteauvilain had thought up was that Catherine should not wear a headdress. Her magnificent mane of hair hung loose on her shoulders as simply as a young girl's. A single jewel, but one that took the eye with its brilliance, flashed on the girl's brow, held in place by a thin gold circlet which was concealed under her hair. It was a black diamond, as fascinating as an evil star. This jewel, of matchless brilliance, was Garin's most prized possession and the most valuable gem in his collection. He had bought it several years before in Venice from the captain of a caravel which had just returned from Calicut. He had paid dearly for it, but not so dear as the exceptional beauty of the stone would seem to have warranted. The sailor had seemed eager to get rid of his black jewel. He was a sick man and his ship had been badly damaged during its last voyage.

'Every storm on earth seemed to be in league against us while I had this cursed pebble in my possession,' he told Garin. 'I shall be glad to get rid of it. It brings bad luck! Every mis-fortune that could befall a ship has haunted me since we set sail – even to the plague itself, which struck us off Malabar. As a good Christian I feel it my duty to tell you that this is an unlucky stone, as unlucky as it is beautiful! I might perhaps have kept it, for I must die soon and luck matters little to me now, but the price of it will make my girl a good dowry. . . .'

Garin paid, and pocketed the diamond. He was not at all superstitious and did not believe in bad luck, which was exceptionally strong-minded for a man of those times. The only thing that interested him was the beauty of this incomparable jewel, which, so the Venetian captain confessed, had been stolen from the forehead of an idol in a temple lost in the depths of the Indian jungle.

Catherine knew the diamond's history, but she was not afraid of wearing it. On the contrary, it fascinated her, and when Sara had placed it on her brow earlier that evening she had indulged in strange fancies about the heathen statue whose brow it had once adorned.

'The time has arrived to go into the great hall,' said the Mistress of the Robes. 'Monseigneur has just arrived and the Princesses will not be long now. I shall go in after them. Courage!'

Just then a fanfare of trumpets somewhere in the recesses of the huge building announced the arrival of the Duke Philippe.

'Come,' said Garin briefly, holding out his hand.

The great hall presented such a dazzling spectacle that one hardly noticed the magnificent Arras tapestries, representing the twelve labours of Hercules, which Philippe had brought with him and which now covered the walls. Lords and ladies thronged together on the black and white marble floor which shone like a mirror, reflecting their sparkling figures.

Possibly because he stood out so starkly amid this bright-hued assembly Catherine saw none but the Duke as she entered the hall. He was as sombrely dressed as she was herself, still wearing the proud perpetual mourning that he had sworn to adopt over his murdered father's body as it lay in state in the chapel of the Chartreuse de Champnol. He stood on a dais raised several feet above the floor, on which three chairs had been placed for the three reigning Dukes, that of the Duke of Burgundy in the middle, that of the Englishman on the right and the Breton's on the left. The high backs of the chairs were embroidered with the arms of their occupants in gleaming silks, while the dais itself was covered with cloth of gold. Philippe stood out against this setting, a dark slender figure. A superb ruby necklace in a gold setting which hung over his breast lightened the starkness of his costume.

At Catherine's entry conversation stopped and a sudden silence fell throughout the hall, a silence so profound and unexpected that the musicians, in their gallery above the door, put down their instruments and leant forward to see better. Catherine hesitated for a second, nervously, but Garin's hand was steadying her and urging her forward all at once. She stepped forward, her eyes downcast so as not to intercept the looks she received, surprised and lustful from the men, and surprised and jealous from the women. The whispers that had started up were already quite embarrassing enough.

Ermengarde was right. Catherine's beauty that night *was* scandalous because no woman there could stand comparison with her. ... She felt as though she were walking forward between two threatening walls of eyes which would not forgive her the slightest false step. One slip and the walls would close in upon her to crush and reduce her to dust. She closed her eyes for a moment, taken by a spell of giddiness. Then she heard Garin's voice, cold, correct, and controlled.

'Your Grace, allow me to present my wife, Dame Catherine de Brazey, Your Grace's very humble and obedient servant...'

She opened her eyes and, looking straight before her, saw nothing but Philippe's long black legs and feet in their embroidered velvet shoes. The pressure of Garin's hand, which had led her to the dais, now communicated to her what she must do next. She bent one knee and bowed her head while her dress flowed out around her. Her curtsey was a marvel of slow and stately grace. As she stood up she looked up at the same time and saw that Philippe had descended from his throne, and was smiling at her as he took the hand which Garin had just relinquished.

'Venus alone, Madame, might have boasted of such charm and beauty. Our Court, which is already so rich in beauty, will be celebrated the world over now that it is graced by your presence,' said Philippe, loudly enough for all that concourse to hear. 'We thank your illustrious husband for introducing you to us. Our mother, we know, holds you in great esteem, and it pleases us to see that to such incomparable loveliness virtue and true modesty are allied.'

This produced a murmur in the crowd. The mention of the Dowager Duchess had had the effect on which Philippe had been counting. It raised a protective wall between Catherine and the jealousy and ill-will to which every ascending star gives birth. They would do all they could to destroy the Prince's future mistress, but if she were protected by the formidable Marguerite the task became more difficult.

Philippe's pale cheeks had flushed slightly, and his grey eyes glittered like ice in the sun as he studied Catherine's face with undisguised pleasure. His hands trembled slightly as they clasped the small fingers which had grown cold with nervousness. To her great astonishment, she saw a tear glisten for an instant in the Prince's eyes. Few men alive wept so freely as he. Any emotion, artistic, sentimental or otherwise would bring tears to his eyes, and when grief touched his heart they gushed forth in positive torrents. But Catherine knew nothing as yet about this curious trait of his.

Just then ten heralds, bearing long silver trumpets from which brilliant silken pennants fluttered, entered the hall. They stood in a line and raised their instruments to their lips. A silvery fanfare sounded, echoing and re-echoing against the high vaulted ceiling in wave after wave of joyful sound. Regretfully Philippe let fall Catherine's hand. The princely guests were arriving.

Three men crossed the threshold. John of Lancaster, Duke of Bedford, was at their head, followed by Jean de Bretagne. The Englishman, who was then thirty-four years old, red-headed and thin, had his fair share of the celebrated Lancastrian good looks, but there was something about his expression, a look of intense pride sharpened by a suggestion of innate cruelty, which made his features look hard and thus robbed them of any charm they might have had. He had a stony stare which masked a formidable intelligence and great administrative flair.

Beside him Jean de Bretagne, a square figure almost as broad as he was tall, looked like a peasant, despite his sumptuous ermine-lined costume and shrewd face. But the most interesting of the three men was undoubtedly the last. Also somewhat square, but athletically built and rather taller than the average, he might have been expressly designed to carry off a suit of armour. His cap of golden hair was close cut round a dreadfully damaged face, cross-hatched by recent scars and gashed across by one terrible deep wound. But his alert, deep-set eyes were as clear and blue as a child's, and when a smile played upon this ravaged countenance it acquired a strangely potent charm. Arthur of Brittany, Comte de Richemont, was no longer a handsome man despite his youth – he was only thirty years old. The history of that dread day at Agincourt was inscribed in every scar on his face. Only a month before he had languished in the dungeons of a London prison. But he was more than just a brave soldier. He was a kind and likeable man, and one in whom one instinctively sensed a true and loyal friend. Richemont was the Duke of Brittany's brother, and his reasons for accepting the Englishman as a brother-in-law were firstly that he had fallen in love with Marguerite de Guyenne, and secondly that this marriage would set the crown on his brother's political schemes, which were decidedly pro-Burgundy at that time.

Catherine caught herself examining the Breton Prince with considerable interest. He was one of those men whom one instantly wants as a friend, so true and staunch in their affections do they seem. She had felt little interest, however, in the English Duke and his numerous retinue. After a good deal of embracing the three Dukes took their seats on the dais and a troupe of dancers, dressed in fanciful red and gold costumes generally supposed to resemble those worn by the Saracens, bounded forward to perform a war-dance with much brandishing of scimitars and lances. At the same time servants carried round goblets of wine and crystallized fruits which would help stave off the guests' hunger until the time arrived for the banquet to begin.

Catherine was only half interested in the entertainment and in the other guests. She felt weary and her forehead ached dully where the black diamond hung upon it, as though the stone was digging into her flesh. She hoped she would be able to retire as soon as the Princesses arrived, which could not be long now. ... The Duke kept looking down at her from his throne as he talked to the Duke of Bedford, but this mark of interest annoyed instead of flattering her. She was embarrassed too by the many other stares and glances which came her way.

A new fanfare announced the arrival of the Princesses. They came in together, wearing identical silver gowns, their long trains carried by little pages in blue velvet and white satin. Behind them, scarlet-faced and beaming with satisfaction, came Dame Ermengarde. The Mistress of the Robes treated the assembled company to an Olympian stare. Then her glance lighted on Catherine and a conspiratorial smile flitted across her face, which Catherine returned. The item which gave Dame Ermengarde the keenest pleasure at these grand functions was the dinner, and Catherine guessed that she was already imaginatively savouring the repast to come, like some enormous cat.

As soon as the Duke had presented his sisters to their future husbands his steward stepped forward to begin marshalling the procession of guests towards the banqueting hall. As he was about to start, however, a herald suddenly appeared on the threshold, blew a great blast on his trumpet and proclaimed, in a voice which carried to the farthest corners of the room:

'An unknown knight, who will not give his name, demands an immediate audience of Your Grace.'

The buzz of conversation stopped. Once again silence fell on the glittering throng. Philippe le Bon's voice rang out:

'What does this knight want? And why does he seek me out here, in the midst of a banquet?'

'I know not, Monseigneur. But he insists that he must speak to you and that right here, in the midst of the feast. He gives his word of honour that he is of noble birth and worthy of Your Grace's attention. . . .'

The request was audacious to say the very least and it transgressed every rule of protocol, but the Duke was not averse to novelty. It made an unexpected interruption to the evening's festivities. . . . It would doubtless prove to be a witty ruse planned by one of his own high-ranking vassals to add to the excitement of the evening. And this refusal to reveal his identity was no doubt intended to make the surprise all the greater. Philippe raised his hand and commanded with a smile:

'Let this mysterious knight be brought before us with all haste. . . . We will wager this is some merry trick imagined by one of our loyal subjects and that we, and the ladies, may expect some joyous surprise to come of it. . . .'

A delighted murmur greeted this command. The arrival of the unknown knight had aroused a great deal of lively speculation. The guests waited expectantly for some magnificent figure to appear, sumptuously disguised perhaps as a Paladin of bygone days, and declaim some verses to his lady-love or pay the Duke some courtly compliment. . . . But when at last the mysterious knight appeared the cheerful hubbub in the hall instantly ceased.

He was dressed from head to foot in armour of sable black, and as he stood framed in the doorway of the hall he looked like an effigy of doom. Everything about him, from the crest of plumes which nodded with every movement of his helmet to the weapons he carried, which were unmistakably the weapons of war and not the courtesy ones normally worn by knights on festive occasions, was unrelievedly black. He stood for a moment with his visor down, a silent and sinister figure, gazing round at the glittering company. Then he handed the heavy sword he had been carrying in one hand to a guard and, amidst a stupefied silence, began slowly walking towards the throne where the Duke sat. In the hushed silence his armoured feet clanked across the flagged floor with the solemn rhythm of a death knell. The smile had vanished from Philippe's face and all present held their breath.

The black knight strode on, nearer and nearer the throne, and there was something about his heavy, measured stride which suggested the implacable approach of Fate itself. He stopped at the very foot of the throne. His next move was as shocking as it was unexpected. Tearing off his right gauntlet he flung it down at Philippe's feet. The Duke started back in surprise, his face all of a sudden ashen white. An angry mutter rose up in the crowd.

'How dare you? And who are you? Guards – unmask this man!' Philippe shouted, his face livid with anger.

'Wait!'

Slowly and deliberately the knight raised his hands to his helmet, and Catherine's heart suddenly started thumping wildly. An icy wave of horror swept over her and a cry escaped her lips before she could clap her hands over her mouth. The knight had removed his helmet. It was Arnaud de Montsalvy.

He stood at the foot of the throne, holding his helmet with its crest of black plumes under his left arm, a tall erect figure whose every line was eloquent of haughty contempt. His sombre gaze rose boldly to meet Philippe's own, and stayed there unflinching. Then he spoke.

'I, Arnaud de Montsalvy, Seigneur de la Châtaignerie and Captain in the service of King Charles VII, whom may God preserve, am come before you, Duke of Burgundy, to bring you my gage of battle. As traitor and felon I challenge you to single combat at whatever time and place you may choose and with the weapons of your choice. But I demand that it shall be a fight to the death. . . .'

A roar of anger and horror greeted this challenge which Arnaud's resonant voice had carried to the far corners of the hall. A menacing circle closed in behind the young man. Many

T—K

of the nobles present had drawn the slender daggers they wore and were brandishing them threateningly, oblivious of the fact that they would have proved quite ineffectual against a suit of armour. Catherine's heart was frozen in terror. Then Philippe imposed silence on his courtiers with a wave of his hand. The look of fury had gradually left his face and been replaced by one of intense curiosity. He sat down again, and leant forward on his throne.

'You are not wanting in audacity, Seigneur de Montsalvy. But why do you address me as a traitor and felon? Why this challenge to combat?'

Arnaud shrugged his shoulders, arrogant as a fighting cock.

'The answer to these questions is inscribed on the face of your guest of honour tonight, Philippe de Valois. Everywhere I look I see the red rose of Lancaster. You treat the Englishman as a brother and give him your sister in marriage. And yet you ask me to explain why you, a French prince who receives the enemy of France under his roof, are a traitor to your country.'

'I am not here to discuss politics with anyone who pleases.'

'Politics have nothing to do with it. This is a question of honour. You are a vassal of the King of France, as you well know. I have thrown down my gauntlet. Will you pick it up, or must I also consider you a coward?'

The young man was stooping down to pick up the gauntlet when the Duke stopped him with a curt gesture.

'Leave it . . . the gauntlet is thrown down and you no longer have the right to pick it up again.'

Arnaud's white teeth flashed for an instant in a wicked grin. But the Duke went on:

'Nevertheless, a ruling prince cannot engage in single combat against a mere knight. Our champion will take up the gauntlet.'

A burst of mocking laughter interrupted him. Catherine saw Philippe's hands tighten on the arms of his chair. He stood up.

'Has it occurred to you that I have only to say the word for my men to seize you and cast you into the nearest dungeon?'

'You could also send all your knights against me in the lists. But that would not be a knightly action either. On that bloody field at Agincourt, where the whole nobility, with the exception of your father and yourself, felt honour bound to fight till their lances shattered, more than one prince crossed swords with knights even humbler than myself.'

Philippe's voice, under pressure of uncontrollable fury, rose to a shrill pitch which few had ever heard in him before and which betrayed his rage more surely than his words.

'It is common knowledge that we bitterly regret not having been able to take part in that glorious and disastrous battle.'

'That is easily said some eight years after the event,' Arnaud replied sarcastically. 'I was there, my Lord Duke, and it is that, perhaps, which gives me the right to speak up so boldly here tonight. But be that as it may! If you prefer to drink, dance and fraternize with the enemy, carry on! Meanwhile I shall take up my gauntlet. . . .'

'I will take it up. . . .'

A giant of a knight, dressed in an outlandish costume chequered in red and blue which fitted closely round a body as massive as a bear's, stepped forward out of the crowd. He bent down with an agility unexpected in such a colossus and retrieved the gauntlet. Then he turned towards the black-clad knight.

'You wished to take up arms against a prince, Seigneur de la Châtaignerie. Content yourself instead with the blood of Saint Louis, even though 'tis crossed with the bar sinister. . . . I am Lionel de Bourbon, the Bastard of Vendôme, and I tell you that you are lying in your throat. . . .'

Catherine was on the verge of collapse. Feeling herself about to swoon she groped around instinctively for something to lean on. This she found in Dame Ermengarde's sturdy arm, the good lady having taken up a position near by. The Mistress of the Robes, eyes rolling and nostrils flaring, was snorting like a war-horse at the sound of the trumpet. Her attention was riveted by the scene which was taking place, and it was evident that she was enjoying it hugely. She gazed with shining eyes at the powerful black form of the Captain de Montsalvy, and her ample bosom swelled with emotion. The knight, meanwhile, stared with the utmost composure at his adversary's gigantic figure. The sight seemed to satisfy him, for he shrugged his broad, steel-clad shoulders and replied.

'All honour to the blood of good King Louis, though I am surprised to see it risked in such a sorry cause! I shall have the pleasure of slicing your ears off then, my Lord Bastard, instead of your master's. But mark this well; it is to the judgement of God that I have summoned you! You have chosen to defend the cause of Philippe of Burgundy as I have attacked it in my Royal Master's name. But this is not a question of politely measuring lances, in the ladies' honour. We shall be fighting to the death, till one of us is killed or cries for mercy!'

At this Catherine gave a soft moan which Garin overheard. He flashed a quick glance at his wife but refrained from comment. Dame Ermengarde also overheard. She shrugged.

'Don't take it to heart so, my dear! The judgement of God is a fine thing. And I am sure God will do justice to this young knight. 'Pon my word, he is a magnificent creature! What's his name? Montsalvy? An ancient name I believe, and worthily bestowed!'

These sympathetic words comforted Catherine a little. In the sea of hate which surrounded Arnaud, they were the only friendly ones to be heard. Then another voice spoke up for the young man. The Duke had just asked him dryly if he had a second for the combat.

'God's Death!' cried Arthur de Richemont. 'If he has not, I am ready to offer him my sword, for he is a brave comrade whom I fought beside at Agincourt. Do not see this as an insult to yourself though, brother Burgundy, but merely as a tribute to an old and valued brotherhood-at-arms.'

'You have *my* approval, milord,' said Marguerite, his fiancée, in a voice which shook with emotion. 'This knight is the younger brother of a squire I once had in my service in my Guyenne household, a gentle knight and a good friend who was cruelly wronged by the people of Paris during those dreadful days of the rule of Caboche. I begged for his life to be spared, but my father refused. If you take up arms on behalf of Arnaud de Montsalvy, my dear Lord, you will be wearing my colours twice over. For I cannot support my brother.'

Richemont, touched by these words, took his fair-haired fiancée's hand and kissed it tenderly.

'Sweet lady, in choosing you my heart chose wisely,' he said.

Meanwhile, however, Arnaud, after saluting the Breton nobleman, had haughtily pointed out a second knight, likewise fully accoutred, who had just appeared on the threshold.

'The Sire de Xaintrailles will second my cause, should the need arise.'

The new arrival, who was bareheaded, had a shock of carroty orange hair and a mocking smile on his lips. He too was tall and sturdily built. On hearing his name mentioned he took a few steps forward and bowed. Philippe of Burgundy, making a visible effort to control himself, stood up, but kept one hand resting on the arm of his chair.

'Messires,' he said, 'God willing, this encounter whose outcome He alone can foretell shall take place in my own town of Arras so that no blood may be spilt on the land of our Lord Bishop of Amiens. You have my word that you will be received there courteously and without danger to yourselves. And now, since this occasion is a festive one, let us forget the battle to come. I bid you number yourselves among my guests.'

Philippe's pride had come to his rescue at last. He had regained complete command over himself and no one could guess what savage and violent feelings might be raging within him as a result of Arnaud's public insult. He had an overweening sense of his own dignity and pre-eminence as a ruling prince. Besides, confident as he was of the huge strength of the Bastard of Vendôme, he could allow himself the luxury of behaving magnanimously and acquitting himself of the duties of a host even towards an avowed enemy.

But Arnaud de Montsalvy coolly replaced his helmet, raising the visor with a tap of the forefinger. Once more his black eyes met Philippe's cool grey stare.

'I thank you, Milord Duke. But as far as I am concerned my

enemies are enemies and foremost among them I place my King's enemies. I only drink with my friends. We shall meet again in three days . . . for the single combat. For the moment we return to Guise. Make way!'

With a curt nod of the head the knight spun round on his heel and moved slowly towards the door. But before he turned round his gaze had wavered momentarily and lighted for one brief instant on Catherine. The young woman, almost in tears, had seen a flash of recognition light up those black pupils. Without quite knowing what she was doing, she half raised her hands towards him in an imploring gesture. But by now Arnaud de Montsalvy was far across the room, and a moment later the great doors swung shut behind the two knights. When the black knight's figure vanished Catherine felt suddenly as if all the lights had been dimmed and the huge room had grown dark and cold.

Then the trumpets sounded to announce that the banquet was to begin.

CHAPTER ELEVEN

THE SINGLE COMBAT

THE BANQUET was like a long-drawn-out torture for Catherine. All she wanted was to be left alone in the peace and silence of her own room to think about the man who had so unexpectedly reappeared in her life. When she first caught sight of Arnaud that evening her heart had almost stopped beating, but after he left it had started beating all the faster and stronger and when his black-armoured figure vanished through the oak doors she had felt such an urge to run after him that it had needed all her self-control and common sense not to give way to it. She felt herself drawn towards him as though by a powerful magnet. She could not guess what *his* reaction would have been, but for the joy of speaking to him, touching him, feeling his fierce black gaze upon her – for these scant pleasures Catherine would have given everything she had. And for the ecstasy of one brief moment in his arms she would joyfully have sold her soul to the Devil.

Throughout that evening she talked, smiled, and graciously accepted the attentions and compliments which her beauty attracted. But her lips and eyes moved mechanically. In fact Catherine was miles away from the palace at Amiens. She was galloping alongside Montsalvy and Xaintrailles on the road to Guise, where King Charles's men were encamped. With a lover's unerring accuracy her mind's eye conjured up the black-armoured silhouette stooped over the horse's neck and his firm profile and set lips under the shadow of his visor. She could almost hear the dull thudding of the horses' hooves, the clinking of their weapons, even the beating of Arnaud's heart under his suit of armour. She was close to him, one with him, so much a part of him that she felt as if the knight were her own flesh, bones and blood. She paid no heed to Garin's curt tone when he suddenly said:

'Let us go home!'

Nothing mattered to her now that Arnaud had reappeared in her life. She had no thought for either Garin and his wealth or Philippe and his love. Not that the glance Arnaud cast her as he left the room had been particularly encouraging, except perhaps that somewhere in the anger and contempt she read there Catherine had seemed to detect something like a glimmer of admiration. And it was on this slender thread that she hung her hopes and dreams. He obviously detested her, and even more certainly despised her, but, as Abou-al-Khayr had pointed out, he desired her too. As the boat glided homewards along the green canal waters, Catherine, sitting at Garin's side, felt challenged by the prospect of a duel with Arnaud. It was an exhilarating experience in some ways to come face to face with one's destiny – a destiny which no longer seemed impossibly out of reach. The haughty Comte de Montsalvy might look down upon a cloth-merchant's niece, but the Dame de Brazey was his social equal. Catherine realized that her marriage had

placed her on almost the same footing as Arnaud. She was
absorbed into his world of pomp and splendour now whether
he liked it or not. And that evening she had had the opportunity
to try the power of her dazzling beauty. How often Philippe's
eyes had rested upon her that evening! . . . And other men's
too, all with that same hungry, eager expression in them! That
evening, for the first time, Catherine felt strong enough to
brush aside all the obstacles which stood between herself and
her love, such as Arnaud's hatred of the Legoix family for
instance. She promised herself she would soon cure him of that.
How could he possibly go on holding her responsible for his
brother's death once he learnt that she herself had all but died,
that her father had been hanged and her home destroyed as a
result ? Catherine knew that she wanted this man, who till now
had seemed such a remote figure, with every passionate fibre of
her body, and she would have neither rest nor respite until he
had made her finally and irrevocably his own.

Catherine returned home and went up to her room absorbed
in her secret thoughts. She was suddenly reminded of her
husband's existence when she noticed that he had followed her
into her apartments. He stood with one elbow propped on the
mantelpiece, staring at her curiously. Catherine could not guess
what thoughts lay behind that impassive countenance. She
gave him a vague smile as she relinquished her long black velvet
coat into Sara's waiting hands.

'Aren't you tired ?' she asked. 'I feel quite exhausted. All
those people, and the heat!'

As she spoke she moved towards her dressing-table. The
mirror reflected her dazzling beauty set off by the darkly
flashing diamond on her brow. Supposing Garin to have
followed her only in order to collect his precious jewel, she
hurriedly unfastened the gold chain and held it out to him.

'Here you are! Here is your beloved diamond back. I
imagine you must be longing to put it in a safe place. . . .'

Garin rejected the proffered jewel with an impatient gesture.
A disdainful smile curved his thin lips.

'Keep it!' he said. 'The diamond has nothing to do with my

presence here tonight. I came because I wanted to ask you a question. How long have you known Messire de Montsalvy?'

The question took Catherine by surprise, and she looked round anxiously for Sara. But the gipsy woman, sensing that her master wished to speak to his wife, had vanished from the room in her usual noiseless fashion and left them alone together. The young woman turned her head away from him, picked up an ivory comb and began carefully combing out her long hair.

'What makes you think I know him?' she asked.

'You gave yourself away with that show of emotion earlier this evening. The sight of a complete stranger would not have made you tremble so violently. Allow me to repeat my question. Where and when did you meet him?'

Garin's manner was perfectly courteous and his voice had not risen a note above its usual low timbre but Catherine was not deceived. He wanted an answer and he would wait till he got one. She decided that the wisest course would be to tell him the truth, or at least part of it, the part that he would understand. She briefly described the scene on the Tournai highway when she and Mathieu had found the wounded man, and how they had taken him to the inn and Abou-al-Khayr had subsequently taken care of him and nursed him back to health.

'As you see,' she said smiling, 'he is an old though distant acquaintance. But it was only to be expected that I should show some emotion when he reappeared so suddenly and surprisingly this evening, and in such tragic circumstances too.'

'Tragic is an apt word, my dear. It seems likely that you will soon be mourning your old acquaintance's untimely demise. The Bastard of Vendôme is a formidable foe who combines the cunning and agility of a serpent with the strength of a bull. . . . And it is a fight to the death. Perhaps you would rather not be present at the joust in view of your impressionable nature.'

'What an idea! Of course I shall see the combat. Has Monseigneur Philippe not invited us?'

'Yes, he has. Very well then, if you feel strong enough for

such an ordeal we will go. I wish you good night, Catherine.'

Catherine was tempted for a moment to detain him for a little while longer. His behaviour was puzzling and she would have liked to engage him in further conversation so as to gauge how far he believed her explanations. But her longing to be left to her thoughts of Arnaud was stronger. She allowed Garin to leave and even dismissed Sara when she returned to help her undress. She had no intention of confiding the hope which burgeoned within her as warmly and secretly as a child in the womb, and which she meant to nurture until the time came for her to reap her full harvest of happiness.

At the moment all her thoughts revolved around one word: Arras. She tried to forget that Arnaud would be risking his life there. All she could think of was that in two days' time the same city walls would encompass them both, under the same sky. Catherine told herself that this time she would not let Arnaud go without trying to win him back, whatever the consequences of that might be.

The Brazeys found it harder to get suitable lodgings in Arras than they had in Amiens. Philippe de Bourgogne was too solicitous of his good citizens of Arras to force them to make room for his guests in the cavalier fashion of the Bishop of Amiens. Catherine found herself obliged to share the two rooms which had been placed somewhat grudgingly at their disposal by a wool merchant in the centre of the town with Ermengarde de Châteauvilain, Marie de Vaugrigneuse and two other of the Princesses' ladies-in-waiting. Garin meanwhile joined Nicolas Rollin and Lambert de Saulx in an inn. This arrangement delighted Catherine, who regarded Garin's temporary separation from her as a good omen for the success of her plans.

The news that a single combat was to take place on the following day had filled the town to bursting point. People were streaming in from all the neighbouring castles and villages and even from quite distant towns. Tents were springing up like mushrooms right up to the city walls, so that Arras had somewhat the appearance of rising up out of a bed of enormous flowers. The joust was the only topic of conversation in the squares and at street corners, and many wagers were exchanged on the outcome of the fight. Catherine was furious to discover everywhere she went that the odds were heavily in favour of the Bastard of Vendôme. Nobody seemed prepared to get a high price on Arnaud de Montsalvy's skin, and the market-place seemed to be full of people loudly proclaiming that they would not like to be in his shoes. Catherine finally lost her temper.

'Since when has brute strength had the advantage over skill and courage?' she cried angrily as she helped Dame Ermengarde unpack her travelling chests and hang out the creases in her gowns in readiness for that evening's banquet and the joust on the following day. 'That Bastard is as strong as a bear, but that doesn't mean that he is certain to win.'

'A plague on't, my dear,' said Ermengarde, hastily snatching her precious Genoese velvet dress from Catherine, who was treating it somewhat roughly in her exasperation, 'this presumptuous young fellow seems to have found at least one ardent supporter! And yet it seems to me that your prayers should all be devoted to the Bastard, since it is he who will be fighting to defend our Duke's honour. Can it be that you are not quite the loyal Burgundian that you would like to appear?'

Catherine felt herself blushing under the stout Dame's sharp-eyed scrutiny and did not answer. She realized she had overstepped herself, but she would rather have had her tongue cut out than retract her last words. Ermengarde did not appear to be in the least offended, however. She gave a great roar of laughter and dealt her young friend such a hearty slap on the back that she almost sent her flying head first into the open coffer.

'Don't look at me like that, Dame Catherine!' she cried. 'Now that we are alone I don't mind admitting that I too have offered up a few prayers on behalf of this young upstart. Quite apart from the fact that I also consider King Charles to be our most legitimate sovereign, I have always liked handsome lads, especially when they are rash, headstrong and a little mad to boot. And, sacrebleu, he's a fine-looking fellow, that young stallion! If I were twenty years younger . . .'

'What would you do?' Catherine asked, with amusement.

'I don't know how I would set about it, but I can promise you that he wouldn't be able to get into bed at night without finding me waiting there! And, marry, it would need more than that great sword of his to get me out again! Unless I'm very much mistaken that lad not only has the looks of a real man but the mettlesome spirit of one. You can see it in his eyes! And I'm ready to swear he's a past-master when it comes to love-making. You can tell these things at a glance when you've had a bit of experience.'

Meanwhile Catherine made a great business of brushing the scarlet dress and spreading it out carefully across the immense bed which she was to share with the Mistress of the Robes. This, she hoped, would allow her to hide the blushes which Dame Ermengarde's frank and outspoken remarks had brought rushing to her face. But the Countess's eyes were uncommonly sharp.

'Leave that dress alone,' she cried gaily. 'Stop playing at prunes and prisms with me, miss, and don't try to hide your blushes so that I shall think I have shocked you. I have just told you what I would do if I were twenty years younger. . . . If I were you, for instance!'

'Oh!' cried Catherine, outraged.

'I've told you not to play the prude with me, Catherine de Brazey, and you mustn't take me for a fool either, my dear. I'm a silly old creature in some respects, but I know enough to recognize a love-sick face when I see it. It was as well for you that your husband could only see with one eye that other night at the ball. Your love for this man was written all over your face.'

Was Catherine's secret, then, which she had fondly supposed buried in her heart from prying eyes, so transparently visible in her face? In that case, who else had guessed it? How many other people at the betrothal banquet had fathomed the existence of a mysterious bond between the black knight and the lady with a black diamond on her brow? Garin, perhaps, which would account for his taciturn mood later that evening. The Duke possibly. And many of the women, no doubt, perpetually on the watch for weaknesses in their rivals which they could turn into deadly weapons against them. . . .

'Now don't torment yourself,' added Dame Ermengarde, from whom Catherine's expressive face clearly held no secrets. 'Your husband has only one eye. As for Monseigneur, he was far too taken up with your handsome knight at that point to notice you. And, at the risk of seeming impertinent, I must point out that while there's a handsome gallant like this Arnaud among them the women only have eyes for him and don't waste their time spying on each other. Each woman for herself! . . . Come now, don't distress yourself like this! Not many people have made such a study of people's faces as I have – and not everyone is as fond of you as I am. Don't worry. Your secret will be in safe hands.'

As she spoke the constriction in Catherine's throat gradually disappeared and her moment's panic yielded to a feeling of profound relief. It was reassuring and touching to discover such a loyal friend in the Dame. Ermengarde de Châteauvilain was famous for the frankness with which she voiced her feelings and opinions. She had never been known to stoop to deceit or pretence of any kind, even when her life might have depended on it. The consciousness of her high birth and rank was too strong and lively for that. But her noble birth did not prevent her being every bit as inquisitive as the next woman. She took Catherine's arm in such a way that to refuse would have been impossible, sat her down beside her on the immense bed and then turned a dazzling smile on her.

'Now that I have guessed half your secret, you must tell me the rest of it, my dear. Quite apart from the fact that I am longing to help you with this adventure, nothing delights me so much as a fine love story. . . .'

'I am afraid you will be disappointed,' Catherine sighed. 'There isn't much to tell.'

It was a long time since she had felt so secure. Sitting in the large low-ceilinged room with this staunch and dependable woman at her side, Catherine enjoyed a precious moment of respite and an atmosphere of mutual trust and confidence which helped her, as she recounted her story, to sound and chart the secrets of her own heart. Beyond these walls lay the bustle and confusion of the town and the motley crowd of human beings who, tomorrow, would throng to watch as two of their fellow creatures slaughtered each other. Catherine sensed dimly that a peaceful interval in her life was drawing to a close. She sensed too that the way which lay ahead of her would be harsh and difficult, and that her hands and knees would be torn by the cruel, jagged stones of a *via dolorosa* whose dim outlines she had just begun to perceive. What was that line which Abou-al-Khayr had quoted to her once? 'The path of true love is paved with flesh and blood. . . .' Well, she was ready to sacrifice her flesh, piece by piece, and her blood, drop by drop, among the thorns along the way if she could live but one hour of love. In that one hour she would compress a lifetime's living and feeling and loving, all the love which it was in her to give. Then a remark of Ermengarde's brought her sharply back to earth.

'And what if the Bastard of Vendôme should kill him tomorrow?' At once an icy spasm of terror swept through Catherine, painfully contracting her stomach and filling her mouth with bitterness and her eyes with tears. The thought that Arnaud might be killed had not even crossed her mind. There was something indestructible about him. He seemed life itself incarnate, and his body appeared to be constructed of a substance as solid as his steel armour. Catherine fought with all her might to blot out a picture of Arnaud lying in the sand of the arena with the blood slowly oozing out of his broken armour. He must not die! Death should not take him because he belonged to her, to Catherine! . . . But Ermengarde's words had found a chink in the stout walls of her confidence, and through it doubts and anxiety seeped in. She leapt to her feet and swiftly seized her cape and wrapped it round herself.

'Where are you going?' asked the astonished Dame Ermengarde.

'I'm going to see him. ... I must speak to him, and tell him. ...'

'What?'

'I don't know! That I love him! I can't let him be killed in the joust without knowing what he means to me. ...'

Half distracted she started across the room towards the door, but Ermengarde stopped her in mid-flight by grabbing one corner of her long cloak. Then she took her firmly by the shoulders and forced her to sit down on a chest.

'Are you mad? The King's men have pitched camp outside the town near the lists and the Bastard of Vendôme has raised his pavilion just opposite. The Duke's guards have surrounded both the camp and the lists, in complete accord for once with the King's Scots, who are under the command of John Stuart, Lord of Buchan and Constable of France. There is no way for you to get through the gates of the town unless you have yourself thrown over the walls at the end of a rope. And it would be quite impossible for you to reach the camp. And, finally, even if it *were* possible, I myself would stop you from going.'

'But why?' Catherine cried, almost in tears. Ermengarde's strong fingers were digging painfully into her shoulders. But she could not find it in herself to be angry with her because she knew that under the Dame's rough Burgundian manner there beat a warm and tender heart. Her broad red face suddenly took on a surprisingly majestic expression.

'Because a man who is going to fight for his life has no need of kisses. A woman's tears can only undermine his courage and weaken his resolve. Arnaud de Montsalvy believes you to be the Duke's mistress. That thought will only make him fight the better and harder. If he comes out alive there will be plenty of time to win him round then and beguile him with the sweet wiles of love.'

Catherine tore herself free and faced her friend wild-eyed.

'And what if he dies? What if he is killed tomorrow?'

'In that case,' Ermengarde shouted angrily, 'in that case it will be left to you to behave like a woman of spirit and show that, in spite of your bourgeois origins, you really are worthy of your present rank. You can choose suicide, if you are not afraid of God, or bury yourself alive in some nunnery with all the others whose broken hearts can never mend. All you can do for the man you love, Catherine de Brazey, is kneel down here beside me and pray, pray and pray again that My Lord Jesus and Milady the Virgin may stand guard over him and return him safely to you.'

The lists were situated outside the city walls on a large flat expanse of land bordered along one side, the longest, by the river Scarpe. Wooden stands for the spectators, built to imitate towers, had been erected facing the river. They consisted of two long galleries, one on either side of the large box where the Duke and his sisters and princely guests were to sit. Two large tents had been put up, one at each end of the long lists, around which crowds were already gathering. These were for the two contestants and were both under military guard. When Catherine reached the lists with Ermengarde she glanced quickly round, her gaze moving indifferently over the crimson silk pavilion above which the Bastard's banner with its device of a lion rampant crossed by the bar sinister of illegitimacy was fluttering. But her big violet eyes fastened eagerly on the other tent, round which the Constable's Scots in their silver armour and white heron's feathers were grouped, whereas the Bastard's tent was surrounded by the black and silver mail worn by Philippe's guards. Catherine had no need to consult the silver shield emblazoned with a black sparrow-hawk which hung above the entrance. Her loving heart divined Arnaud's presence behind those fragile silk walls, coloured the blue of France too surely to have need of coats-of-arms. Every atom of her body yearned towards him. The struggle inside her was all the more painful as she pictured the intense solitude which must be experienced by a man preparing himself to meet death. There was considerable coming and going outside the Vendôme pavilion, and knights and pages entered and left in a ceaseless, colourful, chattering stream. Arnaud's blue hangings, on the other hand, did not stir. The only person to enter his tent was a priest!

'If I didn't know the young hothead was in there,' said a modishly nasal voice from behind Catherine, 'I would have thought his tent was empty!'

Ermengarde de Châteauvilain, who had been making a great to-do of choosing a cushion upon which to repose her vast person, looked up at the same moment as Catherine, and they saw a young man standing there. He looked about twenty-seven or -eight years old. He was thin, fair-haired and elegant, but there was something about him which suggested that he was a bit of a ninny. He was undeniably handsome but to Catherine's way of thinking he seemed a little too conscious of this. Ermengarde found his remarks offensive and lost no time in acquainting him of the fact.

'You should keep your mischievous prattle to yourself, Saint-Rémy. That young Montsalvy certainly isn't the type to run away. . . .'

Jean de Saint-Rémy gave her a teasing smile, and then clambered unceremoniously over the back of the seat where the two ladies had installed themselves in order to place himself on their level.

'I know that as well if not better than you do, Dame Ermengarde. After all, I was at Agincourt and had ample opportunity to observe the prodigious feats of arms performed there by this young fellow, who could only have been fifteen or sixteen at the time. 'Od's death, what a lion-heart he is! He handled his curved sword in that carnage as easily and skilfully as a peasant scything wheat! Anyway, to tell the truth, my only reason for making that remark was to get into conversation with you. I want you to introduce me to this ravishing lady whom I have been admiring from a distance these last three days. The lady with the black diamond!'

The smile he bestowed upon Catherine was so dazzling that she completely forgave him his silliness. To be precise, she had already been on the point of forgiving him when she heard his warm praise of Arnaud. The young man seemed very much nicer all of a sudden, and less like someone who had stepped out of the pages of an illuminated missal in his magnificent green doublet, so densely striped with narrow gold ribbons that it looked like a wheatfield stirred by the wind.

His head was topped by a bizarre hat such as was not to be seen on any other man present at the lists that day – a sort of little toque crowned by a long and jaunty feather. Ermengarde started to laugh.

'Why didn't you say so in the first place, instead of beating about the bush like that! You see before you, my dear Catherine, Messire Jean Lefebre de Saint-Rémy, native of Abbeville, Privy Councillor to Monseigneur the Duke, a great expert on the subject of coats-of-arms, labels and armorial bearings of every sort, as well as the undisputed arbiter of elegance at the Court. As for you, my dear friend, you may now greet Dame Catherine de Brazey, wife of our Lord Treasurer and lady-in-waiting to the Dowager Duchess.'

Saint-Rémy bowed to Catherine with all the signs of keen admiration, while his knowing eye rapidly took in all the details of her gown and headdress.

'It is impossible to set eyes on madame without a positive frisson of pleasure,' he cried enthusiastically. 'What could be more elegant than the happy contrast of the studied simplicity of your gown and those superb amethysts! Since I arrived here today I have had eyes for you alone, madame, and if you will allow me to say so I am quite enraptured! Yes, that is the word, enraptured!'

That day Catherine was wearing the set of amethysts which Garin had given her on the day of their betrothal. With a view to concentrating attention on the magnificent jewels, her dress was plainly styled of white satin with mauve shadows in it. But it was a superb supple satin which moulded the contours of her body down to the hips as clingingly as if it had been soaking wet. Her headdress was of the same satin, but covered with a layer of delicate lace which floated cloudily round the young woman's bare shoulders. She had dressed herself for the occasion with unusual care and a sort of desperate urgency. She wanted to look more beautiful than ever when she came and watched Arnaud risk his life. She wanted him to be able to see her and pick her out from among all the other spectators.

She had arrived early with Ermengarde so as to find good seats in the stands reserved for the Princesses' Household. During the last few minutes the frail, colourful structure had been rapidly filling up with throngs of noble spectators. There were young girls and ladies, all brilliantly attired, young noblemen chattering excitedly among themselves, grave councillors of state and even a few elderly knights who had come to revive old memories by watching the feats of others. Catherine noticed Marie de Vaugrigneuse arriving and observed the young woman's pursed lips when she found that the Dame de Brazey was sitting in the front row. Meanwhile, Jean de Saint-Rémy had taken his seat beside them and chatted away incessantly, commenting good-humouredly on this or that outfit, and pointing out various of the new arrivals with a malicious but lively wit. Ermengarde, seated on Catherine's other side, replied to his sallies and the conversation between them helped to beguile Catherine's anxiety a little. But she could not resist asking:

'You say you have seen Messire de Montsalvy on the battlefield, Sire de Saint-Rémy? Are you also of the opinion, like so many here, that he has not got a chance against the Bastard of Vendôme?'

Ermengarde gave vent to a long sigh, at once understanding and exasperated. But Saint-Rémy stretched out his long legs and laughed cheerfully. Then he leant confidentially towards his neighbour:

'Don't repeat what I say to a soul or I shall find myself ostracized, but my own view is that the Bastard will be hard put to dispatch young Messire Arnaud. Lionel has the advantage of being as strong as a bull, but Montsalvy holds his ground, on the other hand, and he has the ugliest temper in the whole of France, so they say. He will take good care not to be killed unless he is absolutely driven to it. For no other reason but to annoy his adversary.'

He started to laugh, carelessly and a little fatuously, in such a way as to completely belie his true intelligence. Catherine, feeling suddenly enormously relieved and encouraged, joined in. She felt as if a great weight had been lifted off her chest, and her confidence seemed to be returning little by little. But to her great disappointment she was unable to pursue the conversation further because the Duke and the other princes were just entering their large box in the middle of the stands, which was entirely hung with crimson velvet fringed with gold. They were greeted by a long ovation. Philippe was dressed in his customary black with a large hood over his head, and a diamond necklace, each stone the size of a hazel-nut, around his neck. He was pale but impassive. Catherine noticed that he looked briefly in the direction of the lists where the ordinary people, penned up behind wooden barriers, were cheering enthusiastically. But he remained unsmiling. The two betrothed couples stood beside him: Bedford, wooden-faced and alarmingly English, solemnly led Anne forward by the hand, and then came Richemont and Marguerite, smiling and happily absorbed in each other. The Duke of Brittany took his place between the two couples, and the noble spectators then sat in the chairs worked with their own coats-of-arms which stood waiting for them. In the shadows, behind Philippe's chair, Catherine caught sight of her husband and Nicolas Rollin. The two men were arguing together and neither of them seemed to be looking at the lists.

As soon as he sat down Philippe made a brief sign. Twenty trumpeters lined up before the stands, raised their instruments to their lips and sounded a great blast which re-echoed towards the heavens, now mantled over with clouds. Catherine felt her hands go icy and her face tighten, while a cold shiver ran down her spine: it was the moment for the combat to begin! Beaumont, the Burgundian Herald-at-Arms, advanced with a white stick in one hand between the tight-stretched ropes which ran the length of the lists leaving only a narrow passage between. Behind him came six Herald Pursuivants in tunics emblazoned with their personal coats-of-arms. Jean de Saint-Rémy identified them in an undertone to Catherine. There were Fusil, Germoles, Montréal, Pélerin, Talant and Noyers. The young Councillor seemed extraordinarily excited.

'Monseigneur has promised me that when he creates the order of chivalry which he envisages as the crown of his achievements he will make me the King-at-Arms.'

'How marvellous!' Catherine said automatically, though she was secretly marvelling at his absurdity. Beaumont now claimed her entire attention. In the silence which had fallen after the trumpet fanfare he proclaimed the terms and clauses of the combat. Catherine knew them by heart. For the past twenty-four hours the heralds of both parties had been ranging the town, publishing them at the tops of their voices at every street corner. She mentally recited with Beaumont: 'The weapons chosen are the lance and battle-axe. Each of the combatants will break six lances. . . .' She heard the words but no longer thought what they meant. While the proclamation was going on Catherine was sending up a fervent prayer to the little Black Madonna of Dijon, Our Lady of Good Hope.

'Protect him,' she beseeched, 'protect him, sweet Mother of Christ. Don't let any harm befall him! Let him live, above all, let him live . . . even if it means that I must lose him for ever! At least let me have the comfort of knowing that he is alive somewhere, under the same sky. Keep him safe for me, Blessed Lady, please keep him safe. . . .'

Then, suddenly, her throat was dry. At the Herald's summons the Bastard of Vendôme, on horseback and fully accoutred, had trotted up and stationed himself before the Duke. Catherine gazed at the gigantic knight in alarm. His weapons of blue steel and his chestnut horse were almost hidden from sight under his silk tunic and crimson caparison. A rampart golden lion, his emblem, stood between two bull's horns on his helmet. He looked like a red and grey wall! He was nightmarish! Catherine could not tear her fascinated gaze from him. But then a cry of astonishment, issuing from thousands of throats, made her jump.

'Oh!' cried the admiring but scandalized Saint-Rémy, 'what audacity! . . . Or what a signal mark of esteem!'

For once Ermengarde was speechless. As for Catherine, she watched like one in a dream as Arnaud rode fully armed out of his pavilion. The gigantic Lionel de Vendôme watched him approach with an expression of unusual respect. The knight who now drew near was not the mere knight of the sparrow-hawk of the other evening. Thanks, no doubt, to some unusual mark of royal esteem, as Saint-Rémy said, Arnaud de Montsalvy wore the arms of the King of France!

He wore a tunic of blue silk embroidered with gold fleur-de-lys over his armour, matching the caparison which enveloped his horse down to its hooves. Also blue and gold was the leather mantling which hung down from his helmet and protected the back of his neck. The black sparrow-hawk and the Count's coronet on his helmet had been replaced by a tall gold fleur-de-lys which displayed a large flashing sapphire on each point. Only one thing indicated that this was not the King in person: the royal crown round the helmet had been replaced by a simple blue and gold fillet. As Arnaud rode up in the royal colours, he presented, with his visor raised showing his expressionless features, a magnificent image of chivalry and a striking feudal symbol which commanded respect.

'He is superb!' cried Ermengarde hoarsely at Catherine's side. 'He could be Michael the Archangel in person!'

But Saint-Rémy shook his head with a sceptical, uneasy expression on his face. 'I wish that he were!' he said. 'The fleur-de-lys must not bite the dust or the King is dishonoured! And see, Monseigneur has gone quite pale!'

This was indeed the case. Turning towards Philippe, Catherine saw that he had gone as white as a ghost. His face, between the black hood and doublet, was greyish-white tinged with green. He watched with clenched teeth as this magnificent and compelling image of the Sovereign he longed to repudiate rode towards him. His unblinking grey eyes were riveted chiefly on the fleur-de-lys on the helmet, an exact replica of the one which surmounted his own helmet when he wore armour. It was a bitter reproach to the Valois prince who had made the English welcome. But he had to keep command of himself.

With one accord the two knights, who were standing side by side with the ropes between, lowered their lances in the direction of the stands. Catherine was shaking in every limb. She clasped her hands so tightly together that she bruised them, a gesture habitual with her when she was deeply moved. A few places away from Philippe she saw a beautiful and magnificently gowned young woman bend forward and fasten a pink and gold embroidered scarf to the Bastard's lance, after first flashing a triumphant smile at the Duke. Jean de Rémy whispered:

'That is the Dame de Presles! Monseigneur's latest mistress! By giving his champion her colours to wear she indicates her hopes for her lover's cause. She has borne Philippe a son and already sees herself as the future Duchess!'

Catherine would have given everything in the world to fasten the floating mousseline veil she was carrying to Arnaud's lance. But now her attention was drawn to the royal box, where something seemed to be happening. Princess Marguerite had risen to her feet and stood looking at Richemont as she asked:

'Have I your permission, monseigneur?'

Her clear voice was heard by all present. Richemont nodded his head in assent with an amused smile which creased his scarred face. With tears in her eyes, for she remembered the Princess's tearful entreaties at the Hôtel de Saint-Pol, Catherine saw Marguerite lean forward and fasten her veil, which was of the same blue as the knight's caparisons, to his lance with a tender, troubled smile.

'May the Lord make you of good courage, Arnaud de Montsalvy. Your brother was my friend and your cause is a noble one! I shall pray for your success!'

Under his armour Arnaud inclined himself forward till he almost touched the horse's neck.

'I thank you, gracious lady! I will fight for love of you and the valiant captain who is to be your fortunate husband. I am proud of the honour and I will die rather than betray it! May God grant you a happiness as great as your own generous heart!'

Philippe of Burgundy's face twitched nervously. In one moment he seemed to have aged ten years. Marguerite returned to her seat without looking at her brother. The two adversaries turned their backs on each other and rode off to the far ends of the lists, where their squires were preparing their lances. The lances were of ash wood and iron with sharp points, not the usual light wood token lances. Catherine recognized de Xaintrailles' red poll close to Arnaud's squire. Later he would be trying a lance against the Sire de Rebecque, Vendôme's second. The trumpets sounded again. Then, in a loud voice, the Herald Beaumont cried:

'Cut the ropes and join battle when you will!'

The ropes fell to the ground severed by the Pursuivants' knives. The list was clear and the combat could now begin. With lances at the ready and shields held high the two combatants thundered towards each other.

Catherine closed her eyes for a second. She felt as though the heavy thudding of the horses' hooves, as they charged across the hard ground under their immense weight of armour, were thundering over her own heart. Everyone in the stands was holding his breath. Ermengarde placed her hand warningly over the girl's.

'Look! The sight is worthy of your attention. And a noblewoman must learn to look things in the face!' Then she added, in an undertone, 'Look now, for God's sake! Your husband is looking straight at you!' Catherine instantly opened her eyes.

There was a loud crash and a great cry went up from all present. The lances had struck the shields right in the centre. The shock was violent. Both knights were thrown forward in their saddles but without, in either case, being unseated. They trotted off once more down the list to get fresh lances from their squires.

'I think we shall see an excellent joust,' Saint-Rémy remarked in his affected voice. 'That was a splendid blow!'

Catherine glanced sidelong at him. Such sporting enthusiasm shocked her where men's lives were at stake. She decided to retaliate.

'How is it that you are not supporting the King of France, seeing that you were born in Abbeville?' she asked him, deliberately seeking to wound him. But he refused to be drawn.

'I did at one time,' he replied tranquilly. 'But Isabeau's Court is hopelessly corrupt and it is not certain anyway that the so-called Charles VII is the legitimate King of France. I prefer the Duke of Burgundy.'

'Yet you seem to support Arnaud de Montsalvy?'

'Because I like him very much. If he were Charles VII I should not have the pleasure of sitting here beside you. I should be with him.'

'The fact that he supports the King should be enough for you,' Catherine said severely. Ermengarde signed to her to be silent. The two knights were once more galloping headlong, and with renewed ardour, towards each other down the list. With too much ardour perhaps, because the blow misfired. The Bastard's horse wheeled aside just as it was about to pass Arnaud's charger. The lances missed their targets and the two combatants were carried some distance by the impetus of their charge before they could turn their horses round and return to their tents. On the way back to his pavilion Arnaud raised his visor to breath more freely. Catherine gazed at him as he passed in front of the stands at a slow trot, urgently willing him to look back at her. She saw a faint tremor pass over the young man's hard, handsome face and smiled at him with all the concentrated warmth of her love. Her face shone with such radiance that Arnaud started involuntarily. He bent over and made as if to secure the blue scarf he had knotted round his arm more tightly. He had paused for only a fraction of a second but the incident, slight as it was, inundated Catherine with joy. For the first time Arnaud's glance as it met hers had not been contemptuous or cold. It had disclosed a warmth of feeling such as Catherine had despaired of finding there again. But now the precious moment was over. The combat once more claimed the two knights.

The adversaries broke two more lances without much effect. Arnaud sometimes doubled up under the Bastard's mighty blows, but he always held firm in the saddle. At the fifth charge, however, Lionel's lance struck the young man's helmet on the left side just at the point where the visor was attached to it. Catherine thought his head must be knocked clean off. But both head and helmet stayed where they were, apart from the visor, which slipped to one side and disclosed Arnaud's face, now streaked with two trickles of blood.

'He is wounded!' Catherine cried, half rising out of her seat. 'Almighty God!'

She felt as though she were suffocating. A scream forced its way between lips now as white as her dress. Ermengarde had to literally hang on to her arm in order to force her back into her seat.

'You should not enter so wholeheartedly into the fray, child,' she cried warningly. 'Calm down, my dear, calm down at once! You are being watched!'

'It's nothing serious!' said Saint-Rémy, without looking at her. 'Just a scratch caused by the hinge as it broke.'

'But he was wounded in the head such a short time ago!' Catherine wailed in a voice so shaken by grief and anguish that her neighbour glanced at her curiously. Then he smiled.

'It seems as though I am not the only Burgundian supporter to entertain hopes for the success of King Charles's champion?' he remarked sweetly. 'I must remind you, as did the Countess Ermengarde, not to torment yourself unduly. The lad is solidly built. He has been through this sort of thing before. . . .'

Arnaud wrenched off the hanging visor with an impatient gesture. Then he seized a pitcher of water which de Xaintrailles held out to him and drank it thirstily, in great gulps. Catherine saw that the Bastard was doing likewise. In the same fraction of a second both men seized their sixth and last lance. If the two men were still in their saddles after this charge the combat would be continued on horseback but using battle-axes. Arnaud had the disadvantage of having no visor so that his face was exposed. As if to emphasize this Lionel closed his own with a triumphant click. The two chargers sped towards each other, sending the turf flying under their hooves. Catherine crossed herself hurriedly. The crash of splintering lances was thunderous. The Bastard had thrown all his formidable strength behind this last charge. Arnaud was struck on the shoulders, literally torn from the saddle. He was catapulted into the air and flung towards one of the barriers some five paces away from his horse, which fled snorting in terror. Meanwhile, however, the very violence of his charge had conspired to unseat Lionel, and the blow from Arnaud's lance, although it did not strike him squarely, did the rest. He sailed out of his stirrups, and crashed heavily to the ground with a clatter of metal.

'What an ungraceful fall!' Saint-Rémy began teasingly for Catherine's benefit. 'But at least it will equalize the struggle.'

Vendôme's fall was providential to his adversary. Arnaud sprang to his feet, lithe and agile as a cat despite the fifty pounds of metal on his back and a fresh wound in the shoulder which could be seen as the blood started spreading over his fleur-de-lys embroidered tunic. The long points of his steel shoes got in his way when he tried to walk and he hurriedly wrenched them off before seizing the battle-axe which stood ready near by. He was quite close to Catherine now, and she watched him creep up on his opponent with short little steps, his eyes dilated like a cat's, his buckler on his left forearm and his axe raised to strike. Meanwhile Lionel de Vendôme was struggling to his feet. On foot, and facing each other, the difference in height between the two knights was much more noticeable. Arnaud was close on six feet tall, but beside the Bastard's six foot six he seemed quite short. In Lionel's grasp the battle-axe looked as massive as a tree-trunk below its glittering deadly steel blade. Without giving the Bastard time to get his breath back Arnaud leapt upon him. He wanted to

win and win quickly. His wounds, as Catherine instinctively
realized, were losing blood too fast to leave him any alternative.
Merely to think of Arnaud's injuries, she found, caused her
actual physical pain. But his axe rebounded off Vendôme's
armour just as the giant himself let fly. Arnaud, with a nimble
movement, dodged aside to avoid the blow which would have
knocked him flying. Then he closed in rapidly, raised his axe
high and struck again. . . . The sound of steel on steel was like
the hollow clanging of a bell. Sparks flew. Then Arnaud dealt a
second blow which drew cheers and applause from the spectators. His axe smote the top of Lionel's helmet and struck off
the golden lion crest as cleanly as if it had been made of wax,
sending it tumbling in the dust. The Bastard's bellow of rage
was heard by all. He raised himself to his full height, and
seized his axe shaft with both hands, intending to pulverize
the insolent knave who had dared violate his crest. But his
iron-shod feet were clumsy. He stumbled and almost fell and
Arnaud had no difficulty in warding off the blow with his axe-
handle. Catherine guessed that Lionel was in the grip of a
blind fury. He wanted to kill, and kill quickly! He struck out
wildly in his rage. Blow followed blow in quick succession, but
they were aimed erratically and only succeeded in exhausting
him without achieving their real object. Arnaud, on the other
hand, seemed to grow cooler with every passing moment. He
was waiting for the right moment. Suddenly he struck several
rapid slicing blows at Lionel's visor, which cracked open,
revealing his foe's red and sweating face. The Bastard flung out
his hand to seize the young man's axe, but Arnaud had already
hurled it aside. Now he flung himself on the giant, the claws of
his steel gauntlets aimed straight for the other man's face. When
he felt the other knight's talons ploughing into his flesh Vendôme staggered back, slipped and fell heavily to the ground.
Arnaud fell with him and continued ferociously savaging his
opponent's face. The latter, suddenly drained of his strength
and half blinded, started bellowing like a panicky steer in the
slaughter-house. They heard him cry 'Mercy!'

Arnaud, who was kneeling on his enemy's throat, had been

on the point of seizing his dagger and plunging it into him when he heard the cry. He replaced it in its sheath, stood up, shaking the blood from his dripping gauntlets and then spoke contemptuously:

'God has judged!' he cried. 'Now stand up! The King of France's knight does not slaughter a man when he is down. You ask for "Mercy" and I give it to you . . . Duke of Burgundy!'

Without another word he turned on his heel, pursued by the enthusiastic cheers and 'vivats' of the crowd packed behind the barrier round the list. Catherine sensed him suddenly weaken as vividly as though it had been her own blood which trickled down into the ground. As he made his way back to his pavilion Arnaud staggered and reeled like a drunken man. His squire and Xaintrailles ran up just in time to catch him in their arms, before he completely lost consciousness and crashed to the ground.

'The lilies of France did not bite the dust after all,' said Saint-Rémy solemnly. 'I wonder if that is an omen.'

Catherine looked at him inquiringly, but his expression was inscrutable. It was impossible to tell whether the chevalier was pleased or dismayed by the result of the combat. Perhaps he dared not rejoice openly while the tears of anger still streamed down Philippe's stony countenance. The Duke stood there making little effort to conceal his rage and humiliation from the crowd. She shrugged contemptuously and stood up. Then she lifted up her trailing skirts and began moving towards the exit. Ermengarde stopped her.

'Where are you going?'

'You know very well where I'm going! And this time you can't stop me! No one can. Not even the Duke!'

'Why should you think I would stop you?' said the Countess with a shrug. 'Fly away, pretty butterfly, fly away and burn your wings. When you come back I'll see what I can do to help you put out the flames.'

But Catherine was already out of earshot.

CHAPTER TWELVE

UNDER A BLUE SILK ROOF

CATHERINE HAD some difficulty pushing her way through the excited throngs of people who had surged past the line of guards and were now crowding on to the list from all directions. However, most of them fell back in awe at the approach of this dazzling beauty in her magnificent gown. The great blue silk pavilion seemed to be beckoning to her above the heads of the crowd, and she caught herself smiling at it a little foolishly. When she finally reached the entrance to the tent the Scotsman who had been placed on guard there hesitated for a second before admitting her. But then the sight of her jewels and rich costume, all of which suggested the grand lady come a-visiting, reassured him, and he allowed her to enter. He stepped back with a polite bow, rolling his eyes admiringly above an impressively bushy red moustache, and even went so far as to gallantly hold back the blue silk flap which hung across the entrance so that she might go in. Then Catherine saw Arnaud. . . .

He was stretched out on a sort of low couch while his squire tended his injuries. As Catherine entered she only saw his black hair and the top of his head, which was propped up on a blue silk cushion. The armour which they had had to hastily divest him of lay strewn about the floor, with the exception of his helmet with its fleur-de-lys crest, and his bloody gauntlets, which had been placed on a chest. It was the first time that Catherine had ever been inside a knight's tent, and she was amazed by its size. Inside, the pavilion formed a spacious octagonal room entirely hung with tapestries and silk curtains. It was furnished with chairs, coffers, and wooden chests, on which stood pitchers and drinking vessels. There were weapons and armour everywhere, and the whole place was dreadfully untidy. The squire had opened a coffer near the bed which contained the knight's travelling medicine chest. The scent of some medicinal balm, at once sharp and sweet, arose from it. Catherine instantly recognized the scent as the one she had first come across in the Inn of the Grand Charlemagne while Abou-al-Khayr was tending Arnaud.

The latter meanwhile had shaken off his squire's hands and was sitting up looking at her with a mixture of astonishment and anger.

'You again!' he exclaimed ungallantly. 'Have you taken it into your head to rush to my bedside whenever I get a little bruise or cut ? If that's the case, my dear, you are going to have a busy time. . . .'

His voice was harsh and its inflection heavily sarcastic. But Catherine had vowed to herself that she would not lose her temper. She smiled at him with winning gentleness.

'I saw you lose consciousness, messire. And I was afraid that your old head wound might have re-opened. You seemed to be losing a great deal of blood.'

'I have just told you I don't require your sympathy, madame,' said Arnaud in his surliest manner. 'From what I hear you have a husband of your own, and if you have any compassion to spare I should reserve it all for your lover. The Duke Philippe needs it far more than I do!'

At this point Xaintrailles, whose sharp little brown eyes had been going from one to the other during this exchange, intervened.

'This cross-grained bear of an Auvergnat does not deserve your solicitude, madame. You should keep it for someone worthier. 'Pon my word, I have half a mind to let Rebecque deal me some hearty blows if by that I could expect to be ministered to by such gentle hands.'

Arnaud waved aside his friend and his squire. He was still clad in armour from the waist down. Above that he wore nothing but a white linen shirt, opened wide across the chest and showing the dressing which had been placed on his wound.

'I've nothing wrong with me except a few scratches!' he

said, getting painfully to his feet. 'Go and fight now! Rebecque is waiting for you. And let me remind you that if I am an Auvergnat bear, you are too!'

Xaintrailles flexed his knees two or three times to assure himself that his armour joints were in good condition. Then he slipped a silk tunic over his armour and took his helmet from the hands of a page. It was an impressive-looking thing surmounted by three towers and decorated with a coloured mantling.

'I go, I kill Rebecque and I return!' he announced cheerfully. 'For the love of God, madame, don't let this fellow's evil temper drive you out of the pavilion before my return, so that I may have the pleasure of contemplating you once more. Some people have more luck than they deserve! . . .'

Bowing once more he went out, taking up the song he had been singing when Catherine entered. 'Alas,' he sang, 'if you should refuse me your love . . .'

Arnaud and Catherine found themselves alone. The two squires and the page had gone out at Xaintrailles' heels to see the joust. They stood facing each other, with only the medicine chest between them. It stood on the ground, where the squire had left it.

But there was something else between them, something intangible, the strange antagonism which had sprung up in them and set them at loggerheads. Catherine found that she suddenly had no idea what to say. She had longed for this moment so much and yearned to find herself alone with him again so often that the realization of her dream left her weak and spent, like a swimmer who has battled against a storm and finally drags himself wearily ashore. . . . She stood gazing up at him, unaware that her lips were trembling and that her tear-wet eyes and entire body were like a supplication to him not to hurt her. He looked back at her, not angrily but with a sort of curiosity. Bending his head a little he studied the golden-skinned face which the lace headdress set off to perfection, the round, pink, delicious mouth, the short little nose and immense eyes whose outer corners slanted up slightly towards her temples.

'You have violet eyes,' he murmured softly, as though to himself, 'the biggest, loveliest eyes I have ever seen! Jean is right. You are wonderfully beautiful and wonderfully desirable! Worthy of a prince!' he added bitterly. At this his face hardened abruptly and his eyes became fierce once more. 'Now, tell me why you came here . . . and then go! I thought I had explained to you that we have nothing to say to each other.'

Catherine had regained her powers of speech and her courage. His smile and the few soft words he had spoken were all the encouragement she needed to make her attempt the impossible. She was no longer afraid of him or of anyone else. There was some unseen affinity between them which Arnaud himself might not be aware of, but which vibrated through every fibre of her being. Whatever Arnaud might say or do he could not prevent her being eternally wedded to him in the spirit as irrevocably as though he had possessed her in the flesh in the inn at the crossroads. Very softly, and without nervousness or hesitation, she said:

'I came to tell you that I love you.'

No sooner had she said the word than she felt wonderfully carefree. How easy and simple it had been! Arnaud had not protested, or insulted her as she had been afraid he might do! He had merely fallen back a step with a hand shading his eyes, as though protecting them from a bright light. A long moment later he whispered hoarsely:

'You mustn't! You are wasting your time and your love! I might have loved you once because you are beautiful and I desire you. But there are gulfs between us which cannot be bridged and which I could not cross without repugnance and shame even if I were to let my desire triumph for a moment over my will. Now go. . . .'

Instead of obeying him Catherine moved still closer till he was enveloped in the subtle, exquisite fragrance which Sara had so artfully concocted for her. The delicate perfume emanating from her clothes proved more potent than the smell of medicinal balm and blood which hitherto filled the tent. Then she took another step towards him, radiantly confident of herself and her power over him. She saw his hand tremble and he averted his face. How could he possibly escape her now?

'I love you,' she repeated, her voice lower and more passionate now. 'I have always loved you since the moment I first saw you. Remember that morning at dawn . . . when you found me by your bedside when you woke up. All you thought of then . . . was that I attracted you and you desired me. I let you make love to me. I was ready to surrender myself completely to you without a trace of shame or remorse. You see I no longer felt as though I belonged to myself. I had willed myself over to you from the bottom of my heart. Why do you turn away? Why don't you look at me? Are you afraid of me, Arnaud?'

It was the first time she had dared call him by name. He did not protest, instead he looked her directly in the eyes with a trace of bravado.

'Afraid? No, I'm not afraid of you, or your blandishments. Only of myself . . . and what I might do! What brings you here, talking of love? Do you really suppose you can fool me with your pretty speeches? They trip so smoothly off your lips, my pretty, that one would have to be a madman to believe in them!'

His courage seemed to return as he spoke, rekindling the wrath which was his surest line of defence.

'You don't believe I love you?' Catherine cried piteously. 'But why not?'

'I'll tell you! Because words used too often lose their meaning and force. Let's try and work out a little sum! We will assume that you have said the same words to your charming husband . . . and to the Duke Philippe, since he is your lover! And who else? Oh yes, that handsome young captain who chased after you to accompany you all the way back from Flanders. That makes it at least three, and then there are all the others I don't know.'

Despite her intention of keeping her temper Catherine found herself provoked beyond endurance. To have one's declaration of love treated in this flippant manner was intolerable! She flushed crimson and stamped her foot angrily.

'How dare you discuss things you know nothing about! I told you I loved you, and I say it again. . . . I love you! And, if you must know, I am still a maid – my husband has never touched me!'

'What proof do I have that you are speaking the truth?' Catherine's anger evaporated as quickly as it had appeared. She encompassed him with a radiant smile.

'Oh . . . my sweet Lord, I don't think that should prove too difficult!'

Before she could say another word he took a step towards her, irresistibly drawn to the candid face which glowed softly in the dim blue light of the tent. The look on his face as he stared at her was one of naked desire, the one she remembered from that morning in the inn at Tournai. He seemed oblivious of everything but the enchanting woman's body standing so close to him. . . . He was hers! Without taking her eyes from his she stepped over the medicine chest and slipped up close to him, twining her arms round his neck. Then she raised herself on tiptoe and tilted her face up towards him, waiting for his kiss. He stiffened. She felt his muscles grow tense all over as though his body were trying to fend her off, in a last effort to resist her. And a vain effort it proved to be! The supple rounded body clinging to him acted as powerfully on him as a love philtre. His self-control cracked and at almost the same moment Catherine yielded to the passion which was storming within her, rousing her senses to madness. Suddenly they were alone in the world. The blue silk walls of the tent, the time, place, even the uproar from the lists as three thousand throats roared and cheered lustily, sank into oblivion beside the greater reality of this moment.

Arnaud wrapped his arms round her, crushing her to him with savage urgency. The hunger which had been consuming him, unappeased for so many months, at last claimed its prey. His mouth swooped down on to hers, devouring the soft, rosy, inviting lips with greedy fierce kisses. He held her to him so tightly that Catherine, almost swooning with joy, could feel his heart beating wildly against her under her right breast. Their breathing merged into one and Catherine felt herself expiring under these hungry kisses which seemed to be sucking her very life away. . . .

As the passion within them fused and deepened their legs suddenly grew weak under them, and they stood locked together swaying like two solitary trees in a bare, storm-ravaged countryside. They did not hear Xaintrailles enter the tent, crimson and panting like a blacksmith, with one lip torn from the joust. He paused for a startled moment at the entrance, his battered helmet tucked under his arm, looking at them. Then a wide grin spread across his broad face. Without hurry and without once taking his eyes off the entwined lovers he crossed the tent and poured himself a generous ration of wine, which he drained at a gulp. Then he briskly signalled to the two squires to remain outside the tent, where they had been awaiting his orders, and began unhurriedly divesting himself of his different pieces of armour. He had got as far as the right armbrace when Arnaud raised his head a little and caught sight of him. He let go of Catherine so abruptly that she had to cling to his shoulder to stop herself falling.

'You might have said you were there!'

'I would have hated to disturb you,' Xaintrailles retorted. 'Don't pay any attention to me, please! I'm just going to finish peeling this armour off and then I'll be away.'

He went on removing the various parts of his armour as he spoke. He had now reached the thigh pieces, which was one stage further than the one his friend had reached. Arnaud was still wearing his. Catherine leant against Arnaud's shoulder and watched him with a smile. She felt not the slightest shame or embarrassment at having been surprised in the arms of the man she loved. She and Arnaud belonged to each other and it would have made no difference to her if Garin himself had walked in! He had encircled her with his arms once more, holding her close as though he were afraid she might run away, but he went on watching Xaintrailles as he undressed.

'What about Rebecque?' he asked. 'What's become of him?'

'He is going to have trouble sitting down for some time to

come, and he will have an enormous bump on his head, but apart from that he is all right.'

'You spared his life?'

'Forsooth, it's all the cowardly knave deserved! If you had seen him: he handled his axe as if it had been a church candle! 'Pon my word, it brought tears to my eyes!'

Xaintrailles had now removed all his armour. Clad only in his shirt and tight hose, he now proceeded to make a hurried toilet, starting by shaking half a bottle of perfume over his red hair. Then he took a short doublet of silver-embroidered green velvet out of a coffer and pulled on a pair of immensely elongated pointed shoes of the same cloth. This done, he addressed a deep, formal bow to Catherine.

'I kiss your feet, most fair lady! And I go somewhere else to bemoan my unlucky star . . . and your lack of taste! I shall at the same time renew my acquaintance with that good Beaune wine of yours. One thing to be said for these accursed Burgundians – they know how to make wine!'

And on this note he swaggered out, a majestic and arrogant figure, sighing like a furnace! Arnaud burst out laughing and Catherine with him. The immense happiness she felt just then made everything and everyone connected with her beloved dear to her. The red-headed Xaintrailles amused her. She felt she could easily have grown to love him . . . for Arnaud's sake.

Arnaud meanwhile had turned back to her. He made her sit down on the camp bed with him and cupped her lovely face gently in his hands to study it more closely. Then he bent towards her.

'How did you know I was crying out for you,' he murmured, 'that I needed you desperately? Back there, when death seemed a hair's-breadth away, I wanted to leap up into the stands and snatch a kiss from you so that I might at least leave this world with the taste of your lips on mine. . . .'

He began kissing her again and covered her face with soft little kisses. Catherine looked at him adoringly.

'Then you hadn't forgotten me?' she asked.

'Forgotten you? Never! I cursed you and hated you . . . or at least I tried to. But how could I forget you? What man having once held Beauty in his arms could ever forget her? You can never know how often I dreamed about you, dreamed I was holding you close to me, caressing you, making love to you. . . . But,' he added, sighing, 'it was always a dream and dreams must end.'

'It need not end now,' Catherine cried ardently. 'This time it is really me and not a dream that you are holding in your arms. You know that I am yours. . . .'

He did not answer, but smiled, and Catherine could not resist dropping a kiss on those smiling lips. No one else in the world smiled like that, so warmly and boyishly. His white teeth lit up his dark-skinned face like a flame. Arnaud stood up swiftly.

'Don't move,' he whispered to her.

One by one, with patient, skilful fingers he removed the pins which secured Catherine's headdress and placed the fragile confection of satin and lace next to his helmet. Then he loosened her hair, which cascaded like a silken, golden water-fall on to her shoulders and down her back.

'It's incredible!' he exclaimed rapturously, plunging his hands into the waves of living gold. 'No woman can ever have had a more glorious crown!'

He had come to her and now he took her into his arms again. His lips brushed her mouth, throat, shoulders. The heavy necklace of brilliant purple amethysts she was wearing irked him and so he took it off, throwing it on the ground like a worthless bauble. Then he began unfastening her gold belt with impatient fingers. But then, abruptly, Xaintrailles re-appeared. He was no longer smiling.

'Not you again!' cried Arnaud, furious at being disturbed. 'Now what do you want?'

'Forgive me, but I fear that this is not the moment for loving dalliance. There is something seriously wrong, Arnaud.'

'Wrong?'

'The Scots have all vanished. There is not one of our men to be seen round this tent, or indeed anywhere on the list.'

Arnaud sprang to his feet, disregarding Catherine's efforts to keep him beside her. The young woman's sharpened sensibilities in anything to do with her lover told her that something ominous and sinister had happened. Her love was threatened, and the presentiment smote her like a sharp physical pain.

'If this is your idea of a joke—' Arnaud began.

'Do I look as though I were joking?'

Xaintrailles was pale and his face betrayed his anxiety. But Arnaud scoffed at him, still trying to persuade him to leave them alone again.

'They must have gone drinking with the Burgundian soldiery. You surely can't suppose that they would have left without us?'

'I don't suppose anything. I am simply stating a fact. Our squires and pages have vanished too.'

Arnaud reluctantly crossed over to the entrance of the tent. Before he reached it the flap was thrown back by an arrogant featured individual, who remained standing on the threshold looking in. Catherine could just make out the gleaming weapons and breast-plates of a troop of soldiers behind him.

The newcomer was young, not more than thirty. He was sumptuously clad in armour damaskeened with gold and a red brocade tunic. But Catherine found herself disliking and mistrusting him. She remembered now having vaguely noticed him in the Duke's entourage. She disliked his thin lips, tightly folded above an aggressive chin. They remained closed when he smiled. He was smiling now, and it made him look cruel and gloating. His eyes, which were somewhat protuberant, were so cold that they seemed quite colourless. The ruthlessness and cruelty of Jean de Luxembourg, Commander-in-Chief of the Duke's armies, was common knowledge throughout Burgundy. He stood examining the two knights, looking rather like a cat about to devour some mice.

But, disquieting as his expression was, it seemed to have no effect on Arnaud or Jean de Xaintrailles. The latter hailed the Burgundian General in his bantering way.

'The Seigneur de Luxembourg, eh? To what do we owe the

honour?' Luxembourg dropped his casual attitude and stepped forward, followed by his men. They trooped in one after the other and posted themselves around the tent with their weapons at the ready, completely encircling the two men and the young woman, on whom the General's glance lingered thoughtfully.

'Methinks you have overstayed your welcome here, messires,' he remarked, with a heavy northern accent. 'Messire de Buchan and his men took off for Guise long since at full gallop.'

'That's a lie!' Arnaud retorted confidently. 'The Constable would never have abandoned us like that. . . .'

Luxembourg began to laugh, and the sound froze the blood in Catherine's veins.

'I will be quite frank with you . . . he is actually under the impression that you have ridden on ahead. We managed to make him believe that you had made haste to depart in order to rejoin some lady disconsolate with love for you. As for the men who were guarding your tent, we had no trouble with them.'

'May I ask what's behind all this?' Arnaud inquired haughtily.

'It means that you are my prisoners and that I intend teaching you the respect due from knights-at-arms to my Lord Duke. It would really be too absurd if just anyone could come and insult people in their own homes and then calmly ride off again.'

Enraged, Arnaud leapt for his sword and made as if to threaten the Burgundian leader with it. But before he could do so four men threw themselves upon him and overpowered him. Four others meanwhile closed in upon Xaintrailles. He allowed them to proceed with superb sang-froid.

'So this is how you respect the rules of chivalry and hospitality!' Arnaud shouted. 'So much for your master's word of honour and safe-conduct!'

'Let him be,' said Xaintrailles contemptuously. 'His master spends his time tearfully lamenting the fate of chivalry. He proclaims himself its most ardent supporter. Yet he marries his sister off to the Englishman! He is a Burgundian, that's all that needs to be said! We behaved like idiots in allowing ourselves to trust rabble like that. . . .'

Jean de Luxembourg went pale. He raised his hand and would have struck Xaintrailles if Catherine had not leapt between them.

'Messire,' she cried, 'do you know what you are doing?'

'I do indeed, madame. May I add that I am surprised to find you here with these people, you above all whom the Duke honours with his love. However, you need have no fear. I shall say nothing of your presence here. There is no need to distress the Duke unnecessarily. Besides, I owe you my thanks for having so effectively detained these gentlemen. . . .'

Arnaud's angry voice interrupted him.

'So that's it, is it? That's why you came here with your dewy eyes and soft words, you filthy little whore! 'Pon my word I came within an ace of believing you! You almost made me forget my murdered brother, my vow of vengeance and the hatred I have sworn to your entire family. . . .'

'It is not true! I swear it is not true!' Catherine cried despairingly, flinging herself upon the young man whom the archers held pinioned by the arms and shoulders. 'I beg of you don't believe a word of what he is saying! I am not Philippe's mistress, I didn't know they had laid a trap for you. . . . You won't believe me now, Arnaud, but I love you. . . .'

She tried to put her arms round the young man's neck but he stiffened and recoiled from her, raising his chin so that she could not touch his face. His eyes sought Jean de Luxembourg's over her head.

'Sire capitaine,' he said coldly. 'If you retain but a shadow of the respect you owe to your brother knights, either take us away at once or get rid of this slut, who may have found favour in your Prince's eyes but whose proper place to my mind is in the whorehouse. I must request that you remove her since I cannot do so myself.'

'Very well,' Luxembourg answered. 'You there, take the woman off and escort the prisoners to the castle.'

Two of the men-at-arms went up to Catherine, who was still

clinging desperately to Arnaud, tore her away from him and then threw her roughly on to the bed while Luxembourg stood by watching.

'The unfortunate Garin de Brazey really doesn't deserve the fate Monseigneur has reserved for him,' he observed. 'To be forced to take a common wench to wife is bad enough, but then to be cuckolded several times over seems a heavy cross to bear!'

Her body racked by convulsive sobs, Catherine watched in despair as the guards took Arnaud away. His face seemed to have turned to stone, and he left the tent without so much as a glance in her direction. Xaintrailles followed between his guards, as insouciant and cheerful as ever. He was singing the song she remembered from earlier:

'Oh fair one, what are you thinking?
Do you ever think of me?'

She was left alone in the blue silk tent, alone with the discarded weapons and all the masculine odds and ends which Jean de Luxembourg's soldiery would doubtless return to pillage sooner or later. But she was oblivious of everything just now. She lay huddled on the low bed, with her head buried in her arms, mourning her shattered hopes, and her love which had been so cruelly buffeted, spurned and vilified. . . . He had been so quick to reject her, so prompt to accuse her! He had accepted Luxembourg's calumnies unhesitatingly, for the sole reason that the general, though an avowed enemy, was a nobleman and a knight like himself. Arnaud de Montsalvy would never hesitate for a second between the word of a peer and the solemn promise of a humbly-born girl like herself, however passionately he loved her! How harshly and contemptuously he had cast her from him! The insults he had flung at her seared and scorched her heart like whip-lashes and her tears failed to soften the smarting pain. They soothed her nerves a little, perhaps, but the other wounds were still too recent!

She stayed there for some time, quite oblivious of time and place. She was prostrated by grief and despair. Nothing seemed to matter now that Arnaud had spurned her, now that he